GOVERNING IMMIGRATION THROUGH CRIME

GOVERNING IMMIGRATION

THROUGH CRIME

A Reader

EDITED BY

JULIE A. DOWLING

AND JONATHAN XAVIER INDA

STANFORD SOCIAL SCIENCES
An Imprint of Stanford University Press
Stanford, California

Stanford University Press
Stanford, California

Printed in the United States of America on acid-free, archival-quality paper

Library of Congress Cataloging-in-Publication Data
Governing immigration through crime : a reader / edited by Julie A. Dowling and Jonathan Xavier Inda.
    pages cm
 Includes bibliographical references and index.
 ISBN 978-0-8047-7880-0 (cloth : alk. paper)--ISBN 978-0-8047-7881-7 (pbk. : alk. paper)
 1. Illegal aliens--Government policy--United States. 2. Illegal aliens--United States. 3. United States--Emigration and immigration--Government policy. 4. Emigration and immigration law--United States.
 I. Dowling, Julie A., 1975- editor of compilation. II. Inda, Jonathan Xavier, editor of compilation.
 JV6483.G69 2013
 364.1'370973--dc23   2012043688

Typeset by Bruce Lundquist in 10/13.5 Minion

CONTENTS

ACKNOWLEDGMENTS

We owe special thanks to Leo Chavez and three anonymous reviewers for their helpful suggestions and wonderful insights. We are also deeply grateful to our editor at Stanford, Kate Wahl, for her enthusiastic support of this project. Finally, we thank our colleagues in the Department of Latina/Latino Studies at the University of Illinois, Urbana-Champaign, for their generosity and support.

In order to include as many essays as possible and produce a volume with broad coverage of how immigrants are governed through crime, we had to edit most of the pieces for length. In some cases, we simply cut down on bibliography and footnotes. In others, we also had to touch the main text. We thank the authors for understanding the need to excise portions of their well-crafted arguments. For the sake of readability, we have not used ellipses or other punctuation marks to indicate where we removed text. For readers wishing to consult the essays in their original form, we provide full bibliographic information with each essay.

INTRODUCTION

GOVERNING MIGRANT ILLEGALITY

Jonathan Xavier Inda and Julie A. Dowling

On May 12, 2008, U.S. Immigration and Customs Enforcement (ICE), in a massive action involving more than nine hundred agents, raided the Agriprocessors kosher meatpacking plant in Postville, Iowa (Rhodes 2008; Camayd-Freixas 2009). Three-hundred and eighty-nine suspected undocumented immigrants,[1] mainly of Guatemalan and Mexican origins, were taken into custody that day. Normally these workers would have "simply" faced deportation for being present in the United States without authorization. However, under the aggressive immigration enforcement regime of the George W. Bush administration, the vast majority—305 people—were detained on criminal charges (US ICE 2008a). They were accused of using fraudulent Social Security documents and false or stolen identities. Ultimately, most of these individuals pleaded guilty to Social Security fraud and were sentenced to five months in prison. Following their jail sentences, they were to be deported.

The arrestees were not the only ones affected by the raid. There was plenty of "collateral damage." The immigrants' families were particularly hard hit. Many lost their primary breadwinner. Husbands were separated from wives, parents from children, and siblings from each other. The community of Postville also suffered. In the immediate aftermath of

Jonathan Xavier Inda is associate professor of Latina/Latino Studies at the University of Illinois, Urbana-Champaign. Julie A. Dowling is assistant professor of Latina/Latino Studies at the University of Illinois, Urbana-Champaign.

1. Many terms can be used to describe those people who enter or reside in the United States without official authorization. In this chapter, we oscillate between two sets of terms: *illegal/illicit* and *undocumented/unauthorized*. The former terms are the more popular and politically charged. They are widely used in government and public discourses to draw a link between unauthorized immigrants and criminality—to highlight the conviction that crossing into or living in the United States without documents is a criminal act. The latter terms, *undocumented/unauthorized*, are commonly used in academic and progressive circles as less politically loaded alternatives. They signal that although certain people may not have official permission to enter or live in the United States, this does not necessarily make them criminals. Our general preference is to use the latter terms. However, because this book focuses on how immigrants are governed through crime, we deemed it necessary to use the terms *illegal* and *illicit* to indicate such criminalization. We thus move back and forth between *undocumented/unauthorized* and *illegal/illicit* to convey both our personal preferences and those of society at large. Also, because using the terms *undocumented* and *illegal* constantly to qualify the words *immigrant* and *migrant* can be rather cumbersome, we sometimes use only *immigrant* or *migrant* by itself. By doing this, we do not mean to reduce all immigration to undocumented immigration.

the raid, the town (pop. 2,273) lost about a third of its inhabitants. Not only were the arrestees gone, but many other immigrants also fled the area in fear. Some left to pursue life in other states; others undoubtedly returned to their home countries. As a consequence, businesses in Postville were virtually empty, schools were littered with unfilled seats, and those still in town were asking themselves, "What happened?" A whole community was in shambles. As one observer put it, "The humanitarian impact of this raid is obvious to anyone in Postville. The economic impact will soon be evident" (quoted in Camayd-Freixas 2009, 216).

The immigration enforcement action that took place in Postville is not unique.[2] It is actually emblematic of a broader practice of government that has aggressively criminalized unauthorized immigrants (see De Genova 2002; Miller 2003; Inda 2006a; Chacón 2009; Coutin 2010; Rosas 2012). Building on the work of Jonathan Simon (1997, 2007), we call this practice "governing immigration through crime." Basically, to govern immigration through crime is to make crime and punishment the institutional context in which efforts to guide the conduct of immigrants take place.[3] The objective is to shape the comportment of the undocumented in such a way as to incapacitate them and contain the "threat" they and their actions putatively pose to the security of the nation. The most notable form that this way of governing has assumed over the last twenty years or so is that of intensified law enforcement at the nation's borders (Andreas 2000; Nevins 2002; Inda 2006b; Heyman, this volume). The U.S. federal government has essentially determined that the best way to deal with the "problem" of undocumented immigration is by turning the United States into a fortified enclave of sorts. Since 9/11, however, political and other authorities have also placed a strong emphasis on the interior policing of the nation. For example, local and state law enforcement agencies have progressively become more involved in policing immigration matters; criminal prosecutions of immigration violations have increased; the number of undocumented immigrants incarcerated in county jails, federal prisons, and privately run immigration detention centers has surged; states have made it more difficult for unauthorized immigrants to obtain driver's licenses and other identity documents; and raids—of homes, worksites, and public spaces—have become rather prevalent (see Miller 2003; Chacón 2009; Coutin, this volume; Hernández, this volume; Stumpf, this volume). What we have witnessed, then, is the progressive criminalization of migrants and a significant expan-

2. Worksite raids have generally ceased under the Obama administration. However, this does not mean that ICE has stopped policing the nation's workplaces. Instead of raids, ICE now generally prefers to conduct workplace "audits" in order to "weed out" undocumented immigrants. These "silent raids" do not lead to deportation, but they do result in the firing of workers who cannot prove they have a legal right to work in the United States. See Bacon and Hing, this volume.

3. Following Michel Foucault (1991), we assigned the term *government* the rather broad meaning it enjoyed in the sixteenth century. It refers essentially to "the conduct of conduct"—that is, to all those more or less calculated and systematic ways of thinking and acting that aim to shape, regulate, or manage the comportment of others, whether these be workers in a factory, inmates in a prison, wards in a mental hospital, the inhabitants of a territory, or the members of a population. Understood this way, *government* designates not just the activities of the state and its institutions but, more broadly, any rational effort to influence or guide the conduct of human beings by acting on their hopes, desires, circumstances, or environment. The approach we take to analyzing modern political power is thus one that treats the state as only one element, albeit a rather important one, in a multiple network of actors, organizations, and entities involved in exercising authority over the conduct of individuals and populations. As will become clear, immigrants are governed through a host of state and nonstate actors.

sion in the space of policing. In the process, the boundaries of immigration enforcement have migrated inward, turning much of the interior of the United States into a border zone where governmental authorities endeavor to regulate putatively "dangerous" migrant illegalities.

In this book, we provide an interdisciplinary social science introduction to the governing of immigration through crime. Collectively, the various contributors—drawn from anthropology, sociology, law, ethnic studies, criminology, urban planning, communication, and political science—focus on how the main solution to the "problem" of undocumented immigration has been both to turn the United States into a fortified enclave as a way of discouraging illegal border incursions and to cast a wide net of control and surveillance across the country in order to police "troublesome" individuals already inside the nation. Furthermore, they draw attention to the tremendous and deleterious impact that such heavy policing has had on the immigrant community. For example, enhanced regulation of the physical border has made unauthorized crossing more difficult and dangerous, resulting in an upsurge of migrant deaths, while the policing of the interior has led to the deterioration of the already precarious living and working conditions of undocumented migrants. The contributors also suggest, however, that the United States is not simply a space of criminalization and policing. It is also a political site of struggle. Indeed, although the policing of immigrants has escalated, the undocumented have not simply accepted the new status quo. Rather, the effort to govern immigration through crime has been actively resisted by migrants and their allies. They have engaged in what we term *migrant counter-conducts* (see Inda 2011).[4] These are acts or forms of comportment that contest the criminalization and exclusion of undocumented migrants. The counter-conducts in which migrants have been engaged include labor and hunger strikes for justice, advocating for legalization and political rights, occupation of churches as a way of gaining sanctuary, public demonstrations, and fighting for legal redress for unpaid wages (McNevin 2009). Such counter-conducts ultimately speak to the political becoming of undocumented migrants and their enactments of citizenship.

In the rest of this introduction we broadly (but not exhaustively) map the governing of immigration through crime in the contemporary United States.[5] We begin by setting forth the broad neoliberal context in which the management of migrant illegality takes place. We then discuss, in separate sections, the construction of immigrants as illegal, the increased fortification of the U.S.-Mexico border, the push toward policing the interior of the country, the mass detention and deportation of immigrants, the negative consequences of the enhanced immigration enforcement climate, and the various ways that immigrants have actively resisted the punitive practices to which they have been subjected. We end the introduction with a brief overview of the book.

4. The term *counter-conducts* comes from Michel Foucault (2007; see also Gordon 1991). It is discussed later in the introduction.

5. Although our primary focus is on undocumented immigrants, we also touch on how legal residents have been important targets of current immigration enforcement efforts. Specifically, legal immigrants who have committed criminal offenses have been targeted for deportation.

NEOLIBERALISM AND ITS EXCLUSIONS

Since the 1970s, crime and punishment have become an increasingly central means by which political authorities in the United States seek to govern the conduct of individuals and populations. Jonathan Simon (1997, 2007) refers to such development as "governing through crime." This way of governing is intimately connected to the decline of the social and the rise of neoliberal rule (Rose 1999; Pratt 2005; Wacquant 2009). Put briefly, the ideal of the social-welfare state, dominant in some guise for much of the twentieth century in the United States, has generally yielded to that of the neoliberal state. This new ideal is such that the political apparatus no longer appears obligated to safeguard the well-being of the population by maintaining a sphere of collective security. Social insurance—as an ensemble of state mechanisms that sought to insure individuals against the insecurities of social life—has thus largely given way to the privatized and individualized government of risk. Individuals are now asked to take upon themselves the primary responsibility for managing their own security and that of their families. They are expected to adopt an entrepreneurial disposition toward life and insure themselves (using market mechanisms) against the vicissitudes of ill health, accidental loss, unemployment, and anything else that could potentially threaten their contentment.[6] Significantly, by placing such a strong emphasis on individual responsibility, neoliberal rule has tended to draw a rather marked distinction between the proper neoliberal citizen, who secures his or her own well-being through active self-promotion, and the deviant anti-citizen—the criminal, the poor person, the homeless person, the welfare recipient—who is deemed incapable of managing his or her own risks and thus lies outside the nexus of responsible activity. This is typically a racialized division: the subjects most often deemed irresponsible—mainly African Americans and Latinos—are those whose phenomenal and cultural characteristics serve to distinguish them from the dominant "white" population. Whereas the government of the "responsible" has largely taken place through the mechanisms of the market and outside the formal political apparatus, the regulation of the deviant anti-citizen has increasingly occurred through the widening reach of the repressive arms of the state. Indeed, law and order measures have become the preferred institutional contexts through which the government of marginal subjects is effected.

Governing through crime in the United States has come to be embodied in a number of specific practices. This facet of neoliberal rule is clearly visible, for instance, in the widespread popularity of tough-on-crime sentencing regimes of just desserts, deterrence, and

---

6. There is nothing patently wrong with expecting individuals to adopt an entrepreneurial disposition toward life. However, many of the problems that individuals encounter as they go about their daily lives are not individual problems but social ones. So, a major shortcoming of neoliberalism, as Wendy Brown (2006, 704) points out, is that it "converts every political and social problem into market terms, it converts them to individual problems with market solutions." Examples include the introduction of charter schools, private schools, and voucher systems as a way to deal with the crumbling quality of public education; boutique medicine as a reaction to the erosion of health care provision; and private security guards and gated communities as a response to the social insecurity produced by rising economic inequality. Thus, rather than providing collective solutions to socially and politically produced problems—whether improving public education, strengthening the health care system for everyone, or seeking to offset the destructive effects of economic cycles in order to ensure the collective welfare and reduce social inequality—neoliberalism leaves it to individuals to fend for themselves using the mechanism of the market. Individuals are quite often not in a position to deal with social problems all by themselves.

retribution. These regimes include such measures as quality-of-life campaigns and zero-tolerance policing, harsher penalties and the extensive utilization of imprisonment, three strikes and compulsory minimum sentencing policies, redress in juvenile court and the incarceration of minors, and extensive parole restrictions (Garland 2001, 12). Governing through crime is further visible in the common practice of securitizing private spaces as a way of dealing with crime risks and insecurities. The most notable manifestations of this practice are undoubtedly fortified enclaves (such as gated communities) (Blakely and Snyder 1997). These enclaves are segregated spatial enclosures designed to provide a safe, orderly, and secure environment for those who dwell within them. The rationale for governing through crime seems to be twofold (Rose 1999; Inda 2006a). First the thinking is that irresponsible individuals must be held accountable for their misdeeds, that they must be made to shoulder the burden of their lifestyle decisions. The calculus of punishment thus serves to press upon the offending (and potentially offending) agent the importance of being prudent and governing oneself responsibly. Second, there is the idea that responsible citizens must protect themselves and be protected from the "mass" of anti-citizens who threaten their security and quality of life. The containment of the few therefore becomes a prerequisite for the freedoms of the many.[7]

CONSTRUCTING IMMIGRANT ILLEGALITY

The neoliberal emphasis on governing through crime has had a significant impact on how undocumented migration is problematized (Inda 2006a; Miller 2008). In fact, in the contemporary United States, undocumented migration has come to be seen largely as a law and order issue.[8] Since the late 1970s, the nation has witnessed a rash of rather strong waves of anti-immigrant sentiment—a trend that has only intensified in the post-9/11 context (Chavez 2001; Inda 2006a). From social scientists, immigration officials, and policy analysts to immigration reform organizations and the public at large, it has been common for both individuals and groups to cast undocumented migrants—typically racialized as Mexican—as anti-citizens who threaten the overall well-being and security of the social body. The fundamental problem with the undocumented has been deemed to be their illegality. For

---

7. We should note that the neoliberal emphasis on governing through crime does not correspond to a transformation in the scale or nature of crime and delinquency. As Loïc Wacquant (2008) points out, it's not criminality itself that has changed but rather the attitude that society has toward the "criminal." Let's take the prison, for example. The prison has always been a highly punitive, confining, and exclusionary institution. For much of the twentieth century, however, it also had a rather strong rehabilitative mission. Its goal was not just to punish offenders but also to resocialize them—to turn them into law-abiding, if not productive, members of society. This rehabilitative ideal has generally gone by the wayside. The prison is nowadays by and large more narrowly concerned with simply neutralizing offenders. Its purpose is principally to incapacitate—to physically sequester lawbreakers as long as possible in order to prevent them from harming the public. It functions, in short, as a warehouse of sorts, a repository for people deemed dangerous (such as murderers and rapists) or simply troublesome (such as the mentally ill, drug addicts, and the poor). Thus, rather that seeing offenders as redeemable and seeking to reintegrate them into society, governmental and other authorities today generally construct such individuals as incorrigible and seek to keep them institutionalized.

8. There is no doubt that criminality has historically played a prominent role in the management of immigration. However, as a number of scholars have argued (Miller 2003; Chacón 2009; Stumpf, this volume), the extent to which crime and punishment now dominate how immigrants are governed is without precedent.

many people, "illegal" immigrants are inherently lawbreakers and necessarily criminals. The criminality of unauthorized migrants is generally attributed to their not having a legal right to be in the United States. Consider, for example, a basic government definition of unauthorized persons: "An illegal alien is a person who is in the United States in violation of U.S. immigration laws" (US GAO 1995, 1). Or consider the following statements drawn from policy and mass media documents:

> Illegal aliens are of concern to law enforcement officials, urban planners, and policymakers, first, because they are lawbreakers. (US GAO 1993, 10)

> The effect illegal immigration has on the economy is irrelevant. Whether illegal immigration stimulates or burdens economic growth is of no importance to the residual fact that the law is being broken. Illegal immigration is illegal. Period. (Olson 1994, Commentary 5)

> One of the most common and devastating crimes committed in America is committed by people who are not even American citizens. To many, it is not even considered a crime, even though its name, illegal immigration, makes it clear that it is. . . . People who enter or stay in this country illegally are criminals by definition. (Coleman 1994, B11)

In addition to being constructed as irresponsible lawbreakers, undocumented migrants have routinely been linked to a host of other problems. For example, they have been associated with such cultural, social, and economic maladies as overpopulation, deteriorating schools, urban crime and decay, energy shortages, and national disunity. Furthermore, they have been accused of displacing American workers, depressing wages, spreading diseases, and burdening public services. All of these "problems" are seen as compounding the fundamental problem of immigrant criminality.[9]

In the wake of 9/11, undocumented migrants continue to be constructed as criminal anti-citizens, but the threat they represent has been refigured in terms of homeland security (see Miller 2005; Chacón, this volume), forming what might be called the crime-security-migration nexus. "Homeland security" is a way of thinking and acting that developed in the wake of the September 11, 2001, "terrorist" attacks. It has been defined as "a concerted na-

9. Although undocumented immigrants may be constructed as a problem in popular and official discourse, the empirical evidence suggests quite the opposite: that this population is not generally troublesome and actually makes important contributions to American society (see Bauer 2009). For example, rather than taking jobs away from U.S. natives and shrinking their wages, unauthorized immigrants actually tend to complement these workers, raising their productivity and income. Furthermore, instead of being crime prone, undocumented immigrants are in fact much less likely to commit crimes than natives. Finally, it is too simplistic to cast undocumented immigrants as irresponsible lawbreakers just because they are in the United States without authorization. One needs to be mindful of why immigrants end up coming to the United States "illegally." A refrain often heard in debates over undocumented immigration is "Why don't they just get in line to become legal?" The reality is that there is no line for most immigrants to wait in. Although U.S. immigration law makes allowances for the legal importation of "highly skilled" workers, it generally does not do so for lower-skilled individuals, even though there is actually a great demand for them in the labor market. Furthermore, the reason that many people migrate in the first place is closely connected to neoliberal economic policies promoted by the U.S. government (Miller 2008). In Mexico, for example, neoliberal policies emphasizing free market capitalism, private ownership, free trade, and export-led growth have helped destroy certain sectors of the economy, creating pressure for Mexicans to cross into the United States in search of work. So immigrants are in effect forced to leave home because neoliberal economic policies have disrupted their livelihoods, and then are criminalized once they are in the United States, on account of the neoliberal emphasis on individual responsibility.

tional effort to prevent terrorist attacks within the United States, reduce America's vulnerability to terrorism, and minimize the damage and recover from attacks that do occur" (US OHS 2002, 2). Basically what has happened is that, subsequent to the 9/11 attacks, terrorism has generally come to be regarded as the greatest threat facing the nation. On the basis of the fact that the 9/11 hijackers were foreigners who somehow managed to get into the United States, the movement of people in and out of the country is now viewed as indissociable from this threat. It is thus commonly expressed in policy and public rhetoric that there is an ever-present possibility that foreigners might seek to enter the United States in order to commit acts of terrorism. Moreover, this discourse strongly articulates the need to protect the American people against the threat of terrorism and safeguard the homeland. Notably, the attitude of protecting the homeland has significantly influenced the governing of immigration: although migrants rarely have any connection to terrorism, they have generally come to be seen as threats to the security of the homeland. Protecting the nation thus involves not only preventing terrorist attacks, but also mitigating the "dangers" posed by "illegal" immigrants. Indeed, the undocumented have come to be seen as criminal threats to national security. On the basis of this reading, the homeland must be protected from these irresponsible "criminals."

STRATEGY OF DETERRENCE

Given that undocumented migrants have largely been constructed as criminal "illegal" immigrants who harm the well-being of American citizens and threaten the security of the nation, the measures employed to govern them have been extremely exclusionary and punitive.[10] Put otherwise, unauthorized migrants have come to be governed through crime. Governing immigration through crime has taken numerous forms in the United States. Undoubtedly the most notable form is that of enhanced border policing (Andreas 2000; Nevins 2002; Inda 2006b).[11] Since the early 1990s, the U.S. federal government has undertaken a major boundary-control offensive, one that aims to shape the conduct of "illegal" immigrants in such a way as to deter them from entering the United States. Federal authorities have basically concluded that expanding border enforcement operations is vital to the proper management of the undocumented immigrant "problem." The expansion of border policing as a way of governing "illegal" immigration has been most conspicuous along the U.S.-Mexico border. It is this border that has historically been seen as the primary source of migrant illegality (Nevins 2002). This expansion actually dates back to the late 1970s (Dunn 1996), but it really burgeoned in the early 1990s. That's when the Immigration

10. As legal scholar Gerald L. Neuman (2005, 1441) has noted, the linking of immigrant "illegality" to criminality has been taken to mean, at least in some circles, "that the alien's presence can give rise to no legal duties toward him because he should not be here in the first place. Like an illegal contract that creates no obligation, duties toward the alien are void or voidable. This notion reduces the alien to a non-person, an outlaw outside the protection of the legal system." Thus, the highly punitive treatment to which immigrants are subjected is seen as entirely legitimate.

11. The governing of immigration through crime is also highly visible in the realm of immigration law. Indeed, the criminalization of immigration has become highly entrenched in law, especially at the federal level. We do not deal with the question of law systematically in the introduction, but we cover it in Part I. See also Miller 2003; Chacón 2009.

and Naturalization Service (INS) put into effect a broad plan to gain control of the southwest border and reduce the flow of illicit immigration.[12] As articulated in the *Border Patrol Strategic Plan: 1994 and Beyond, National Strategy*, this comprehensive border control scheme was based on a strategy of "prevention through deterrence" (U.S. Border Patrol 1994, 6). The objective was to increase fencing, lighting, personnel, and surveillance equipment along the main gates of illegal entry—such as San Diego, California, and El Paso, Texas—in order to raise the probability of apprehension to such a high level that unauthorized "aliens" would be deterred from crossing the border. Programmatically, this strategy came to be embodied in such projects as Operation Gatekeeper and Operation Hold the Line, which respectively focused on fortifying the San Diego and El Paso border areas. In the end, the "prevention through deterrence" strategy resulted, during the course of the 1990s, in a significant amassing of law enforcement resources at the U.S.-Mexico border. For example, the number of Border Patrol agents assigned to police the southern border more than doubled during that decade, increasing from 3,555 in 1992 to 8,580 in 2000 (U.S. Border Patrol 2012a).

Now, in the post-9/11 context, the policing of the border as a way of managing unauthorized migration has only accelerated, as the fight against immigrant illegality has become conflated with the "war on terror." In November 2005, the Department of Homeland Security (DHS), the federal entity currently responsible for overseeing immigration matters, launched an updated scheme to manage the nation's borders. Dubbed the Secure Border Initiative (SBI), this scheme is a "comprehensive multi-year plan to secure America's borders and reduce illegal migration" (US DHS 2005). SBI generally amounts to a continuation and expansion of the policy of "prevention through deterrence." The idea is basically to use a mixture of "manpower," technology, and infrastructure to deter undocumented border crossings (US DHS 1999, 1). In terms of manpower, the number of Border Patrol agents stationed at the U.S.-Mexico border has continued to balloon, totaling 18,506 by 2011 (U.S. Border Patrol 2012a).[13] Technological enhancements have included the now defunct SBI*net*, an effort to build a virtual fence of electronic surveillance. The goal was to augment the Border Patrol's capacity to deter illicit entries by using a combination of unmanned aerial vehicles, remotely operated cameras, tower-mounted radars, and unattended ground sensors to monitor remote areas of the border (US GAO 2009). Due to problems with cost

12. The Immigration and Naturalization Service (INS) was a federal agency within the United States Department of Justice that was responsible for dealing with immigration-related issues. On March 1, 2003, it was disbanded and its functions were transferred to the Department of Homeland Security (DHS). These functions included providing services and benefits such as naturalization and work authorization, now the purview of U.S. Citizenship and Immigration Services (USCIS); investigating breaches of and enforcing federal immigration, customs, and air security laws, now the task of United States Immigration and Customs Enforcement (ICE); and border security, now the domain of U.S. Customs and Border Protection (CBP). Within CBP, the Border Patrol is responsible for policing the border between official ports of entry.

13. Besides the Border Patrol, the military (National Guard) and civilians have also been involved in policing the U.S.-Mexico border. From 2006 to 2008, as part of Operation Jump Start, President Bush deployed six thousand troops to the Southwest border (National Immigration Forum 2010). President Obama has likewise sent the National Guard to help CBP with border security. It should also be noted that military involvement in border enforcement is not new but predates 9/11 (see Dunn 1996). In terms of civilians, a number of groups, including the Minuteman Project, concerned with the federal government's putative inability to stop "illegal" immigrants from entering the United States, have taken it upon themselves to police the Southwest border (see Chavez, this volume).

overruns and ineffectiveness, the DHS terminated the SBI*net* program in January 2011 (Preston 2011). Infrastructure has involved installing more stadium-style lights along the border, building access roads to enable Border Patrol agents to respond quickly to illegal crossings, and most important, increasing physical barriers to entry (US DHS 2005). In 2006, through the Secure Fence Act, Congress mandated the construction of 670 miles of pedestrian and vehicle fencing across the Southwest border. As of February 10, 2012, 651 miles of this border wall had been completed (US CBP 2012).

Beyond these upgrades in manpower, technology, and infrastructure, the Department of Homeland Security has enhanced its deterrence strategy by making tactical changes in how it handles people caught entering the United States without proper documentation. With respect to apprehended Mexican nationals, the norm in the recent past has been to ask them to sign voluntary departure forms and then to quickly send them back across the border to Mexico without formal removal proceedings (Kohli and Varma 2011). This means that apprehendees were neither asked to plead guilty to any infractions nor placed in detention centers. For non-Mexicans, voluntary return has not been an option (Smith 2010). Such migrants cannot simply be shipped across the border but must be repatriated to their home countries, a more complicated, expensive, and time-consuming process. The standard practice, known as "catch and release," has thus been to release non-Mexicans into the United States on their own recognizance and to ask them to show up at a removal hearing at a later date.[14] Quite often these unauthorized migrants have failed to appear at their hearings. The DHS has rethought the use of both "catch and release" and voluntary departure. Concerning the former, the DHS officially announced on August 23, 2006, that it was ending the practice (US CBP 2006). Rather than catching and releasing non-Mexican nationals, U.S. Customs and Border Protection (CBP), the agency overall responsible for border security and parent of the Border Patrol, now generally detains them until their "removal" (the official term for deportation) from the United States. Importantly, putting an end to "catch and release" has involved expanding a procedure known as "expedited removal" (US DHS 2006a; Ewing 2010). This procedure basically allows DHS agents to detain unauthorized border crossers from countries other than Mexico and place them in expedited deportation proceedings without the conventional opportunity of a hearing or appeal before an immigration judge.[15] The rationale for expedited removal is that it makes the deportation process more efficient, permitting DHS agents to return undocumented immigrants quickly to their countries of origin. Initially, the procedure was applied only to individuals arriving at official ports of entry. Currently, it covers undocumented immigrants apprehended within one hundred miles of any U.S. border (land or coastal) who cannot demonstrate that they have been in the country for more than fourteen days (US DHS 2006a). As

---

14. Although the term *catch and release* appears benign, it actually serves to dehumanize immigrants. The term comes from sport fishing, where it refers to the practice of catching fish and then throwing them back into the water. Using such a term in the context of immigration policing essentially reduces the apprehension and incarceration of human beings to a sport.

15. Prior to the institution of expedited removal, immigrants were generally guaranteed the fundamentals of due process: the right to a hearing in front of an immigration judge and the right to have a removal decision reviewed on appeal. Expedited removal is also applied to Canadians and Mexicans with histories of criminal conduct or immigration infractions. See Siskin and Wasem 2008.

regards voluntary departure, the procedure is still widely used to deal with undocumented Mexican border crossers. However, through an initiative known as Operation Streamline, the DHS has also started criminally prosecuting immigrants (regardless of nationality but Mexicans are the most affected) for illegal entry (US CBP 2005; National Immigration Forum 2010). This castigatory practice started in the Del Rio, Texas border area in December 2005 and has now spread to much of the Southwest border. The DHS's premise is that routing immigrants through the federal criminal justice system and into prison, rather than simply removing them, serves to increase deterrence. First-time border crossers are generally charged with misdemeanors punishable by up to six months in jail, while those who enter after being deported can be charged with felonies carrying a maximum penalty of twenty years in prison.

The post-9/11 policing of the border, then, involves deterring undocumented migration by simultaneously making it more difficult to cross clandestinely into the United States and punishing migrants who dare to trespass. A primary solution to the illegal immigration "problem" has thus been to install a rigid apparatus of control and surveillance across the Southwest border in order to prevent illegal incursions and thus keep putatively "threatening" individuals out of the body politic. It has been to build walls and barriers and turn the United States into a veritable fortified enclave. As with the government of crime more generally, the rationale for managing undocumented migrants through police and punitive measures is that the public must be protected from the would-be criminals or "dangerous people" who threaten their security and contentment (US CBP 2009a, 13).

THE BORDER AS A MOBILE TECHNOLOGY

Along with the continued expansion of border enforcement, the federal government has recently (since the early 2000s) intensified its policing of the nation's interior.[16] Indeed, interior policing, led by ICE, has become a central component of the border fight against "terror" and "illegal" immigration. Basically, the border, as a regime of security and immigration control (Cunningham 2009), has been deterritorialized and projected into the nation's interior (Euskirchen, Lebuhn, and Ray 2009). Put otherwise, there has been a "disaggregation of border functions"—basically the policing and control of mobility—away from the physical border (Walters 2006, 193). As part of this border disaggregation, certain spaces of everyday life—workplaces, homes, neighborhoods, and a variety of public spaces—have been identified as strategic sites and become subject to intensified policing. Numerous locales across the interior of the United States have thus been turned into border zones of enforcement. The border, then, is no longer simply (if it ever really was) a location at the nation's edge where the regulation of movement takes place; it is also a mobile technology: a portable, diffused, and decentered control apparatus interwoven throughout the nation.[17] Indeed, we are in the presence of the border at any time when and in any space where immigration policing and control take place.

---

16. Interior policing is, of course, not new. However, it has intensified in the post-9/11 context. See Coleman 2007.

17. For a discussion of neoliberalism as a mobile technology, see Ong 2007.

This turn to interior enforcement, or what could be called the bordering of the interior, is part of a new explicit border security doctrine developed by the DHS. The thinking is that only by developing a "continuum of border security," treating the territorial boundaries and the interior of the United States as a seamless security space, will it be possible to buttress the physical border and deter the flow of illicit immigration (US DHS 2006b, 7).[18] The increased preoccupation with policing the interior of the nation was notably signaled with the DHS's publication of *Endgame: Office of Detention and Removal Strategic Plan, 2003–2012* (US DHS 2003). *Endgame* essentially lays out the DHS's vision for a secure homeland. The stated goal is to develop "the capacity and capability to remove all removable aliens," focusing on those with criminal records or outstanding orders of deportation or both (US DHS 2003, 1.2). The rationale here is that striving for 100 percent removal allows ICE to provide the level of immigration enforcement necessary to "thwart and deter continued growth in the illegal alien population" (ibid., 4.4) and thus "to keep America secure" (ibid., 2.9). Without such interior enforcement, "apprehensions made by other DHS programs (such as the Border Patrol, Inspections, and Investigations) will not provide the deterrent or the enforcement tool necessary to secure America's borders" (ibid.). This prioritization of interior policing and removing "aliens" from the country was reiterated in the DHS's blueprint for the Secure Border Initiative, the *Secure Border Strategic Plan* (US DHS 2006b). The text places a strong emphasis on enhancing "interior enforcement and compliance with immigration and customs law" as a way to stop the illicit flow of people into the United States (ibid., 6). In line with *Endgame*, one of the goals articulated in the *Strategic Plan* is the need "to identify, apprehend, and expeditiously remove the criminal alien and fugitive population" (ibid.). However, this text goes further and also highlights the importance of investigating and punishing "employers who systematically employ or exploit aliens unauthorized to work" (ibid.). ICE's interior targets would thus be not just individual aliens but also places of work.

One important mechanism that ICE has employed to carry out its interior policing mission is the raid. A raid is a practice whereby immigration authorities, sometimes with the help of other policing agencies, descend *en masse* on homes, places of work, and other spaces with the express purpose of apprehending individuals believed to be in the country illegally. Like border policing, the raid is a practice that seeks to securitize the nation through the abjection and exclusion of individuals and populations deemed threatening to the social body. ICE's initial targets, under a strategy called the National Fugitive Operations Program (NFOP), were what the agency calls fugitives. A fugitive is "an alien who has failed to leave the United States based upon a final order of removal, deportation or exclusion, or who has failed to report to ICE after receiving notice to do so" (US ICE 2011a). Some of these fugitives are people with criminal histories; others have no criminal record at all. According to ICE, the NFOP gives "top priority to cases involving aliens who pose a threat to national

---

18. The DHS expands on the idea of the border continuum as follows: "Achievement of our long-term goals requires a new approach, which includes addressing the continuum of the land and maritime borders, the interior, and threats and risks that originate beyond the borders" (US DHS 2006b, 10). So the border continuum, or new spatiality of the border, actually involves not just projecting the border inward but also pushing it outward. Here we do not deal with the extension of border policing beyond the boundaries of the United States, but see Coleman 2007. On border security in the United Kingdom as a continuum, see Vaughan-Williams 2010.

security and community safety, including members of transnational street gangs, child sex offenders and 'aliens' with prior convictions for violent crimes" (ibid.). This program, which was launched in 2003, typically works through dispatching Fugitive Operation Teams (FOTs) across the nation to apprehend fugitives. Using databases such as the Deportable Alien Control System, these teams first identify the addresses of "aliens" of interest (Mendelson, Strom, and Wishnie 2009). Then, often early in the morning, they descend on the identified addresses in search of their targets. Once there, the FOTs may arrest not only their initial targets, but also anyone else present in the home whom they believe to be in the country illegally. From 2003 to 2009, such home raids resulted in the apprehension of more than 131,000 undocumented migrants (US ICE 2008b, 2011b). But despite the avowed goal of targeting dangerous fugitives, about three-quarters of FOT arrestees from 2003 through February 2008 had no criminal history (Mendelson, Strom, and Wishnie 2009, 11). And in 2006 and 2007, nonfugitives—immigrants who did not have orders of deportation but were thought to be in the country without authorization—constituted about 35 and 40 percent, respectively, of total FOT arrests (ibid.). The arrest of a nonfugitive is sometimes referred to as a "collateral arrest."

Soon after ICE began raiding homes, the agency also started to focus on worksite enforcement. Indeed, during the latter half of the 2000s, ICE pursued an aggressive program of policing the nation's workplaces using raids. Between 2006 and 2008, the agency apprehended about 14,000 undocumented migrants through worksite raids (US ICE 2008c). This compares to only about 2,700 arrests between 2002 and 2005 (ibid.). Although raids have decreased in more recent years as ICE has shifted to workplace audits (see Bacon and Hing, this volume), they nevertheless continue to be a part of ICE's arsenal. Worksite enforcement is a priority, according to ICE, because "employment is a primary driving force behind illegal immigration. By working with employers to ensure a legal workforce, ICE is able to stem the tide of those who cross our borders illegally or unlawfully remain in our country to work" (US ICE 2009b). ICE deems the hiring of undocumented immigrants a problem for several reasons. First, the agency suggests that "illegal aliens often turn to criminal activity: including document fraud, Social Security fraud or identity theft, in order to get jobs" (ibid.) Such crimes are seen to impact negatively the lives of the U.S. citizens and legal immigrants whose identities are stolen. Second, the need of undocumented migrants for fraudulent documents is said to create thriving criminal markets. Third, there is a perception that for every job taken by an undocumented immigrant there is one less job for a lawful U.S. resident. Fourth, employers are believed to exploit "illegal" workers by ignoring wage laws and safety standards. Finally, undocumented migrants are seen "as easy targets for criminals who want to use them to gain access to sensitive facilities or to move illegal products" (ibid.). Worksite enforcement, then, is deemed necessary in order to stem the tide of illegality purportedly produced by undocumented migrants. The conviction seems to be that "illegal" immigration generally erodes respect for authority—that the toleration of lawlessness undermines consideration for law and order. For not only do the undocumented supposedly fail to conduct themselves responsibly, they also compel others to follow suit. Unauthorized immigrants are thus seen to represent a danger to the social body. Their disregard for the rule of law is understood to pose a threat to the general welfare of the population.

Another strategy that ICE has employed in policing the interior is to partner with local and state police forces, sometimes using them as proxy immigration officers.[19] The idea behind these partnerships, and the devolution of immigration authority from federal powers to nonfederal law enforcement agencies, is that they serve as a "force multiplier" for the DHS, significantly expanding the reach of immigration policing authority (US ICE 2009a). ICE has placed its partnering initiatives under an umbrella program called ICE ACCESS (Agreements of Cooperation in Communities to Enhance Safety and Security) (US ICE 2008d). The most well known ICE ACCESS initiatives are probably the Criminal Alien Program (CAP), Secure Communities, and Delegation of Immigration Authority Section 287(g) (Gardner II and Kohli 2009; Keaney and Friedland 2009; Kohli and Varma 2011). CAP focuses on identifying "criminal aliens" detained in federal, state, and local jails and prisons in the United States. Under this program, ICE agents screen inmates for immigration status either in person, by phone, or by video teleconference, and then, after positive identification, work to secure a final order of removal prior to the end of an individual's sentence so that she or he will be deported and not released back into the general public. Secure Communities is essentially a technologically driven version of CAP. Through this program, local and state police are able to run the fingerprints of anyone they arrest, regardless of guilt or eventual prosecution, through DHS immigration and other databases. If there is a "hit," the system automatically alerts ICE, which then interviews the individual and decides whether or not to seek his or her removal. The 287(g) program permits state and local law enforcement agencies, on the basis of a memorandum of agreement (MOA) with ICE, to function as immigration agents. By entering into such agreements, ICE can authorize local police officers to carry out certain immigration enforcement functions, ranging from arresting people for immigration violations and screening local jails for "criminal aliens" to working with ICE on immigration investigations. In theory, ICE ACCESS programs are supposed to prioritize targeting immigrants "who pose a danger to national security or risk to public safety" (Morton 2010). However, ICE tends to cast a very wide net. The majority of those apprehended are not immigrants convicted of serious criminal offenses—for example, murder, kidnapping, or rape (Barry 2009). Rather, they tend to be individuals who have committed minor transgressions such as speeding, driving without a license, and jaywalking. Also, in many cases, ICE programs ensnare immigrants who are never convicted of any crime but merely arrested or stopped by police officers.

Importantly, interior immigration policing at the local level is taking place not just under the auspices of the federal government. Driven by the belief that federal authorities are not doing enough to secure the border and stop the flow of "illegal" immigrants, states and localities have independently taken it upon themselves to become involved in governing

19. In U.S. law, the federal government has, in recent history, had sole authority to regulate immigration. As legal scholar Juliet Stumpf (2008, 1558–1559) has noted, "More than 100 years ago, the Supreme Court sidelined state and local government from any major role in the arena of immigration law. In a series of cases beginning in 1875, the Supreme Court declared that the entry of noncitizens into the United States and the conditions under which they may remain were matters of foreign policy over which the federal government had exclusive power." Today, however, states and localities are increasingly becoming involved in the regulation of noncitizens. The trend began more or less in the mid-1990s in California with the passage of Proposition 187 (a voter initiative that sought to deny public services to undocumented immigrants) and has accelerated since 9/11.

immigration. At the state level, Utah, Alabama, Georgia, and Arizona, to name only a few, have all recently passed tough immigration laws, while a number of other states have considered or are considering punitive legislation (Lacayo 2011). The best-known case is that of Arizona. On April 23, 2010, Governor Jan Brewer signed into law SB 1070, widely regarded as a highly punitive anti-immigrant measure (Sáenz, Menjívar, and García, this volume; Cisneros 2012). This legislation requires police officers to determine a person's immigration status during the course of a "lawful stop, detention, or arrest" when there is "reasonable suspicion that the person is an alien and is unlawfully present in the United States" (State of Arizona Senate 2010).[20] Legal status is generally verified via a phone call to DHS authorities, and if a person is deemed deportable, the expectation is that he or she will be transferred to the custody of ICE or CBP. At the local level, since 2006, hundreds of cities and towns across the nation—from Escondido, California, and Farmers Branch, Texas, to Hazleton, Pennsylvania, and Prince William County, Virginia—have passed ordinances or strategically deployed existing laws to manage the presence of undocumented immigrants in their localities (Gilbert, this volume). Some of these ordinances are explicitly meant to regulate immigration. In Hazleton, for example, the city council approved a law to penalize landlords for renting to unauthorized residents and employers for hiring them. Other ordinances are used to police immigrants "through the back door" (Varsanyi 2008). These ordinances are not outwardly focused on immigration, but they are used tactically to constrain the life prospects and conduct of undocumented immigrants. In Escondido, for example, city officials have targeted Latino immigrants, who tend to live in poorer neighborhoods, through a crackdown on dilapidated homes, illegal garage conversions, graffiti, abandoned vehicles, and other violations of city regulations (Johnson 2009). And the local police department has set its sights on this population through traffic checkpoints designed to catch unlicensed drivers. Because undocumented immigrants are ineligible for driver's licenses in California (as in many other states), they are disproportionately affected.

DETAIN AND DEPORT

Ultimately, today's stepped-up immigration enforcement climate, both at the border and in the interior, has resulted in the massive detention, incarceration, and deportation of immigrants (see Boehm, this volume; Coutin, this volume; Hernández, this volume). As we noted earlier, the goal that the DHS established in *Endgame* was to deport all removable "aliens" (US DHS 2003). Although this objective is highly unrealistic, because ICE simply cannot arrest and remove all 10.8 million undocumented migrants estimated to be residing in the United States (Hoefer, Rytina, and Baker 2010, 1), the number of removals—that is, official deportations—has gone up significantly in the post-9/11 period, part of a steep

---

20. In addition to the "show me your papers" requirement, three other major provisions were originally contained in SB 1070. One provision required all immigrants to carry alien registration documents, another made it a misdemeanor criminal offense for an undocumented migrant to seek work or hold a job, and the third allowed state officers to arrest, without a warrant, individuals who they suspected had committed a crime that rendered them deportable. However, on June 25, 2012, the Supreme Court struck down these provisions as unconstitutional, noting that they are preempted by federal law (National Immigration Forum 2012a).

upward trend that began in the 1990s.[21] In fiscal year 2011, ICE removed 391,953 non-citizens from the United States (US DHS 2012a, 4). This compares to 189,026 in 2001 and only 50,924 in 1995 (US DHS 2010, 95). Basically, the number of removals has doubled in the post-9/11 era, and increased more than sevenfold since the mid-1990s. The populations most affected by the current deportation drive are Mexicans and Central Americans. Over the past decade, nationals from Mexico, Guatemala, Honduras, and El Salvador have consistently been at the top of the deportation charts (ibid., 97–105). In 2011, for example, these nations accounted for 93 percent of all removals, with Mexico constituting the largest share at 75 percent (US DHS 2012a, 4–5). Also important to point out is that 188,382 removals (about 48 percent) in 2011 were of "criminal aliens," individuals who had a criminal conviction (ibid., 6). This means that the majority of those deported that year, as in other recent years, actually had no criminal record but were simply ordinary unauthorized migrants. Even the "criminal alien" designation is rather misleading. In 1996, Congress passed two laws, the Antiterrorism and Effective Death Penalty Act and the Illegal Immigration Reform and Immigrant Responsibility Act, which significantly increased the number of offenses, known as "aggravated felonies" in the context of immigration law, for which a noncitizen (whether an undocumented immigrant or a legal resident) could be formally removed (Johnson 2001; Coleman 2007; Chacón, this volume).[22] Whereas prior to these laws noncitizens had to be given a sentence of at least five years in order for their misdeeds to count as aggravated felonies, now any crime carrying a sentence of a year or more, including misdemeanors, can render someone an aggravated felon (Johnson 2001). Included in the list of offenses currently classified as aggravated felonies for immigration purposes are bribery, car theft, counterfeiting, drug possession, drug addiction, forgery, perjury, petty theft, prostitution, shoplifting, simple battery, tax evasion, and undocumented entry following deportation (Coleman 2007, 58). Noncitizens currently being deported as "criminal aliens" are thus not necessarily what one would call hardened criminals who represent a threat to the public's safety, but more often than not are low-level, nonviolent offenders (Human Rights Watch 2009).[23]

21. The DHS distinguishes between removal and return. *Removal* is the "compulsory and confirmed movement of an inadmissible or deportable alien out of the United States based on an order of removal" (US DHS 2012a, 2), or in other words, the official deportation of an individual from the country. Importantly, an individual who is removed may face administrative or criminal consequences on subsequent reentry by virtue of having been removed. *Return* is defined as the "confirmed movement of an inadmissible or deportable alien out of the United States not based on an order of removal" (ibid.). This means that individuals are returned to their home countries without being placed in immigration proceedings, that is, they are not officially deported. This procedure is common with noncitizens without criminal records who are apprehended at the border. Our focus here is on removal.

22. Legal immigrants who had committed criminal acts were the main targets of these laws.

23. We should also note that many migrants subject to deportation are denied the opportunity of a hearing or appeal before an immigration judge. For example, of the 391,953 people removed in fiscal year 2011, 123,180 were expedited removals (US DHS 2012a, 5). As discussed earlier, expedited removal is a procedure that allows for certain "aliens"—generally those apprehended within one hundred miles of any U.S. border who cannot demonstrate that they have been in the country for more than fourteen days—to be removed without a hearing before an immigration court (US DHS 2006a; Ewing 2010). Such "aliens" are simply not legally entitled to have their cases reviewed (unless they express intent to apply for asylum). Importantly, there are also noncitizens who are eligible to go before an immigration judge to contest their deportations—long-term residents, for example—but are coerced into giving up their right do so. According to the National Immigrant Justice Center (2007, 81), "ICE routinely pressures detainees to waive their rights by signing 'stipulated orders of removal,' which are documents in

To facilitate the current deportation drive, the DHS has developed, over the past decade and a half or so, a vast complex of carceral spaces in which to detain immigrants pending their removal from the United States. The growth of the carceral complex has been such that ICE's Enforcement and Removal Operations (ERO) directorate now runs the largest detention operation in the nation (Schriro 2009). In 2011, ICE detained 429,247 foreign nationals, more than five times the number of people held in 1994 (81,707) and about a 105 percent increase from 2001 (209,000) (US DHS 2012a, 4; Taylor 1995, 1107; Kerwin and Lin 2009, 7). Meanwhile, the number of INS/ICE detainees per day has risen from 6,785 in 1994 to 20,429 in 2001, and all the way up to 33,384 in 2011 (Kerwin and Lin 2009, 6; US ICE 2012). The average length of stay for immigrants in ICE custody is twenty-nine days (US ICE 2012). However, there is considerable variation between individual cases. Many of those detained are released within one day of admission, but it is not uncommon for some to be held for a year or longer (Schriro 2009, 6). Generally, detainees who agree to voluntary removal have shorter stays than those who challenge their deportation or file an asylum claim. ICE houses its detainee population in a variety of facilities. These include six ICE-owned Service Processing Centers (SPCs), seven private prisons known as Contract Detention Facilities (CDFs), and more than two hundred forty Intergovernmental Service Agreement facilities—basically local and county jails (both public and private) that contract with ICE to hold immigrant detainees (National Immigration Forum 2012b; US ICE 2012).[24] Notably, for-profit prison corporations play a huge role in managing the immigrant detention complex. They not only own and operate the seven CDFs, but also manage all but one of ICE's SPCs and most of the largest local and county jails with which ICE contracts (Kerwin 2009). Given the control that private entities have gained over immigration detention facilities, Judy Greene and Sunita Patel (2007, 48) suggest that "immigrants are fast becoming the modern day cash crop of the prison industry." Indeed, with ICE paying its contractees an estimated average of one hundred twenty-two dollars per day for each immigrant detained, there is a lot of money to be made in the immigration detention business (National Immigration Forum 2012b, 2).Ultimately, the delegation of immigrant confinement to organizations whose main purpose is to generate profits inevitably produces pressure to increase detentions: the more immigrants confined, the higher the profits. Immigrant bodies have thus become valuable commodities whose worth lies in being placed and kept behind bars.[25]

The immigrant population in ICE custody is only part of the immigration confinement story. The DHS has also ramped up its criminal prosecution of immigration-related conduct, resulting in a marked increase in the number of immigrants incarcerated in federal

---

which an immigrant admits to his or her own deportability. When an immigrant signs a stipulated order, he or she can be deported without seeing a judge, without consulting an immigration lawyer, without understanding their legal rights, and without hearing a basic presentation on how to navigate the legal system alone." What generally happens is that noncitizens are given the "choice" of accepting a stipulated removal order (and thus agreeing to being deported) or staying in immigration detention (for an indeterminate amount of time) to fight their cases.

24. It should also be noted that about 50 percent of the detainee population is held in facilities focused principally on immigrant detention, while the other half is scattered among spaces generally used to detain local criminal defendants and prisoners (Schriro 2009, 6).

25. For an exploration of the link between privatization and immigration enforcement, see Koulish 2010.

prisons (Chacón 2009). Such immigrants are not simply being detained pending the resolution of their immigration cases but are actually serving criminal sentences.[26] One kind of immigration-related conduct that the DHS has criminalized, and for a time aggressively prosecuted, is the use of false documents to gain employment. Because undocumented immigrants cannot work legally in the United States, some end up buying false or, generally unbeknownst to them, stolen identity documents and Social Security numbers in order to work. Until a 2009 Supreme Court decision rendered the practice unconstitutional (see discussion of this decision in "Migrant Counter-Conducts" section later in this chapter), migrants were sometimes charged with aggravated identity theft and Social Security fraud when they used an identity belonging to another person. In 2008, more than 960 migrants were charged with such criminal offenses, including many of the people apprehended in the Agriprocessors meatpacking raid discussed earlier (US ICE 2008c, 3). A second, and perhaps more important, type of immigration-related conduct that the DHS has criminalized is entry without inspection. Due to the aforementioned Operation Streamline, what used to be generally treated as an administrative infraction that simply rendered someone deportable is now being handled as a federal crime punishable with time in prison. The campaign to punish entry without inspection is such that "illegal entry" (a misdemeanor for first-time offenders) and "illegal reentry" (a felony for repeat violators) were the most commonly recorded lead charges brought by federal prosecutors during the first half of fiscal year 2011 (October 1, 2010–March 30, 2011) (TRAC Immigration 2011). Illegal reentry alone accounted for 23 percent of overall criminal prosecutions and 47 percent of all immigration-related actions. Such penalizing treatment of immigrants represents a remarkable change from only a decade and a half ago: illegal entry as a lead charge shot up from 557 in 1994 to 43,688 in 2010, while that of illegal reentry went from 2,695 to 35,836 during the same period (ibid.). A major result of the criminal prosecution of immigration-related conduct is that Latinos now make up close to half of all individuals sentenced for federal felony crimes (Associated Press 2011). According to an Associated Press analysis of United States Sentencing Commission data, about 87 percent of the rise in the number of Latinos incarcerated in federal prisons over the past decade is due to sentences for felony immigration crimes, including illegal reentry (ibid.). The end result, then, is that the DHS is not just increasingly placing immigrants, particularly Latinos, in detention. The agency's practices are also leading to more and more noncitizens being warehoused in federal prisons.

The current push to detain, incarcerate, and deport noncitizens is very much part of the DHS's general policy of prevention through deterrence. As ICE puts it, "Strengthening the nation's capacity to detain and remove criminal and other deportable aliens is a key component of ICE's comprehensive strategy to deter illegal immigration and protect public safety" (US ICE 2010a). Speaking specifically in reference to Operation Streamline, former Homeland Security Secretary Michael Chertoff notes, "This has an unbelievable deterrent effect. When people who cross the border illegally are brought to face the reality

26. Detention pending removal is not in a legal sense a punitive measure and thus not considered incarceration. For immigrants, however, the distinction between detention and incarceration is simply a semantic one (Wilder 2007). The facilities that ICE uses to detain noncitizens were generally built, and are run, as jails and prisons (Schriro 2009, 4).

that they were committing a crime, even if it's just a misdemeanor, that has a huge impact on their willingness to try again" (Root 2008). The general idea is to use the criminalization and incarceration of noncitizens to send a message to would-be border crossers that the risk of seeking to enter the United States without proper authorization more than offsets any potential rewards (Barry 2008). The function of detention and deportation is thus not simply to expel putatively dangerous individuals from the social body but also to deter future migrants (Martin 2012). Thus the United States has been turned not only into a fortified enclave in its zeal to police immigration, but also into a carceral space. Indeed, a criminal dragnet has been cast over the United States in order to manage the "dangers" of migrant illegality.[27]

IMMIGRATION ENFORCEMENT AS A FORM OF RACIAL GOVERNANCE

Crucially, the heavy policing of migrant illegality has had a profound and highly negative impact on immigrants and their communities, with Latinos bearing the major brunt. In many ways, immigration enforcement functions as a form of racial governance, that is, as a mechanism for managing the conduct of somatically different, and putatively "unruly," populations (see Hing 2009; Provine and Doty 2011). Indeed, it is quiet evident that the targets of immigration policing are not just any bodies, but physically and culturally distinct ones. It is thus racialized migrants, Latinos in particular, who disproportionately suffer the consequences of immigration policing. We can illustrate the impact of immigration enforcement as a form of racial governance using as examples the blockading of the U.S.-Mexico border, workplace raids, and local police involvement in immigration matters.

At the U.S.-Mexico border it "appears" that the amassing of personnel, technology, and infrastructure has had the desired effect of reducing the flow of undocumented immigrants into the United States. We can get a sense of this reduction from the number of people apprehended while attempting to cross the Southwest border without authorization. From a high of 1,643,679 in 2000, the number decreased to 327,577 in 2011 (U.S. Border Patrol 2012b). This is certainly a precipitous drop. However, it is not clear that this reduction can actually be attributed to increased enforcement. The recession that began in 2007 (and arguably continues into 2013) has no doubt been the most significant factor affecting the flow of undocumented immigrants (Aguilera 2011). With the decline in employment opportunities, many would-be migrants have simply decided to stay home, at least for the time being. According to immigration scholar Wayne Cornelius, for most potential border crossers, the act of migrating is merely being postponed until the U.S. economy recovers

---

27. On August 18, 2011, the Obama administration declared plans to review all three hundred thousand–plus pending deportation cases and halt the removal of people deemed low-priority—those with no criminal record and with strong ties to the United States (Carroll 2011). Then, on June 15, 2012, Secretary of Homeland Security Janet Napolitano announced that "effective immediately, certain young people who were brought to the United States as young children, do not present a risk to national security or public safety, and meet several key criteria will be considered for relief from removal from the country or from entering into removal proceedings" (US DHS 2012b). These actions appear to be part of a strategy to transform the way immigration enforcement works and to focus the DHS's resources on "high-risk offenders": repeat immigration violators, recent illegal entrants, and individuals who pose a threat to public safety and national security (Preston 2012). It remains to be seen how this strategy is carried out and whether it will affect the overall policing of undocumented immigrants.

(Mac 2010). But if it is the case that enhanced border policing has had an impact on stemming the flow of illicit bodies, this success has come with a rather high price: that of undocumented immigrant life.

In some ways, the U.S.-Mexico border has always been a place of danger for those trying to cross it illegally (Nevins 2002). Immigrants have had to traverse the Rio Grande and other fast-moving waterways under the cover of darkness, to travel in sealed and inadequately ventilated freight compartments of trains or trucks, to trek through the desert terrain of the American Southwest, and to climb fences and other steel barriers erected by the U.S. government to secure the border (Eschbach et al. 1999). Given such danger, clandestine border crossings have sometimes had tragic consequences. Over the years, more than a few migrants—it is hard to say exactly how many—have lost their lives trying to reach the United States. Today, crossing the border has become considerably more difficult and dangerous (Nevins 2002; Inda 2006b; Doty, this volume). As the Border Patrol has closed off traditional illicit routes into the United States—namely urban locations such as San Diego and El Paso—the migrant traffic has been channeled through remote and less policed mountain and desert locations. These out-of-the-way places through which most unauthorized immigrants are currently crossing the border—the deserts of Arizona, for example—are less than ideal entry points. First, the fact that they are apt to be far removed from urban centers means that the undocumented now have to walk long distances, often for days, before reaching areas where they can be picked up and transported elsewhere. Second, there is the rugged terrain of the new crossing places. Because they tend to be barren deserts or mountains, anyone entering through them potentially has to contend with freezing temperatures at night and torrid weather during the day. What having to walk long distances though hostile landscape means, basically, is a rather perilous border crossing experience. The peril is so great that border-crossing-related deaths have become routine events. In 1994, prior to the full implementation of the Border Patrol's strategy of prevention through deterrence, there were only 24 recorded migrant deaths (Jimenez 2009, 17). By contrast, in 2007, the peak year for migrant fatalities, an estimated 827 border crossers lost their lives (ibid.). The American Civil Liberties Union calculates that, altogether, between 1994 and 2008 an estimated 5,607 migrants, mainly Mexicans, died attempting to enter the United States without authorization—that's an average of about 374 migrant deaths per year (ibid.). All indications are, then, that enhanced boundary policing has made illicit border crossing a more hazardous venture. Indeed, there is little doubt that as the traffic of illicit bodies has moved from urban areas to rural locations, the risk of death has become greater and the border has become an exhibit of death.

Significantly, the fact that large numbers of border-crossers are dying has not escaped the Border Patrol's attention. The agency actually seems quite concerned about this development. In 1998, for example, it created the Border Patrol Search, Trauma, and Rescue Unit (BORSTAR) to focus on the search and rescue of migrants in distress (US CBP 2009b). However, although the Border Patrol may have acknowledged that immigrants are dying and taken some steps to remedy the situation, the agency has not conceded that its operations brought about the problem in the first place. Indeed, the agency has failed to take any responsibility for the rise in migrant deaths. As one Border Patrol officer put it, "Death on the border is unfortunate, but it's nothing new. It's not caused by the Border Patrol. It's not caused by [Operation] Gatekeeper" (Ellingwood 1999, A28). The logic behind this refusal to accept any blame is rather straightforward. The Border Patrol contends that it is simply doing its duty of safeguarding the nation's borders when it closes off busy urban crossing points. If immigrants consequently choose to cross through rural terrains, the responsibility for any unfortunate incidents that may occur is deemed to lie not with the Border Patrol but with the immigrants themselves and the smugglers who guide them. The reality is, however, that as long as urban crossing points stay virtually closed and immigrants are steered to seek passage through risky mountain and desert locations, border crossers will continue to die. So, although the Border Patrol may not, strictly speaking, be liable for the fatalities at the border, it does bear a certain amount of responsibility for them because these deaths are an effect of the strict policing of the border. Indeed, immigrants are dying, and they are dying as a consequence of a stringent policy that propels them to cross the border through dangerous terrain.

Shifting to the effects of interior policing, we find that workplace raids have also had a severely negative impact on immigrants and their communities. The most palpable impact of such raids has been their effect on the families, particularly the children, of the individuals who have been apprehended and deported. In 2007, the Urban Institute released a report titled *Paying the Price: The Impact of Immigration Raids on America's Children* (Capps et al. 2007). The report focused on the aftermath of large-scale ICE raids in three communities: Greeley, Colorado; Grand Island, Nebraska; and New Bedford, Massachusetts. Greeley and Grand Island were two sites hit as part of a larger raid on Swift & Company meat-processing facilities in six states (Colorado, Nebraska, Texas, Utah, Iowa, and Minnesota). New Bedford was the location of a raid on Michael Bianco, Inc., a textile product company. The authors detail how the children and families of apprehended immigrants, who were mainly Latinos, experienced significant hardship, "including difficulty coping with the economic and psychological stress caused by the arrest and the uncertainty of not knowing when or if the arrested parent would be released" (ibid., 3). Moreover, they note that

> hardship increased over time, as families' meager savings and funds from previous paychecks were spent. Privately funded assistance generally lasted for two to three months, but many parents were detained for up to five or six months, and others were released but waited for several months for a final appearance before an immigration judge—during which time they could not work. Hardship also increased among extended families and nonfamily networks over time, as they took on more and more responsibility for taking care of children with arrested parents.
>
> After the arrest or disappearance of their parents, children experienced feelings of abandonment and showed symptoms of emotional trauma, psychological duress, and mental health problems. Many lacked stability in child care and supervision. Families continued hiding and feared arrest if they ventured outside, increasing social isolation over time. Immigrant communities faced the fear of future raids, backlash from nonimmigrants, and the stigma of being labeled "illegal." The combination of fear, isolation, and economic hardship induced mental health problems such as depression, separation anxiety disorder, post-traumatic stress disorder, and suicidal thoughts. However, due to cul-

tural reasons, fear of possible consequences in asking for assistance, and barriers to accessing services, few affected immigrants sought mental health care for themselves or their children. (ibid., 3–4)

By removing a parent and breadwinner from the home, then, worksite operations have significant consequences for families and children. Not only does the removal of a breadwinner reduce a family's income and increase its material hardship, it also creates a rather unstable home environment. Moreover, the fear and stigma produced by a raid can lead to the social isolation of immigrant families and have an adverse psychological effect on children.

Worksite raids have also helped to erode the rights of immigrant workers. In a number of cases, ICE has conducted raids on workplaces that were in the middle of labor disputes or being investigated by other government agencies (such as the Department of Labor) for violation of workers' rights (Smith, Avendaño, and Martínez Ortega 2009). The Postville raid is particularly illustrative here. When the raid at Agriprocessors took place, at least three state and federal labor agencies were investigating the meatpacking plant for long-standing safety and workplace violations. Moreover, since 2006, the United Food and Commercial Workers (UFCW) International Union had been waging a campaign to organize workers at the plant. ICE was very well aware of this situation. On May 2, 2008, a week before the raid, the UFCW had sent a letter to the ICE special agent in charge of carrying out operations in Iowa, saying that the union was in the middle of an organizing campaign, that various local and federal labor agencies were investigating the plant, and that any immigration enforcement action would have a detrimental impact on labor rights. In the past, unions had achieved positive results with such letters, which alerted immigration officials to ongoing organizing efforts so that they would not interfere and undermine the enforcement of labor standards. The practice of sending letters was based on an internal ICE policy (put in place in 1996 by the INS) that cautioned agents about getting involved in labor disputes. The policy, initially known as Operating Instruction 287.3(a) and now redesignated 33.14(h) of the Special Agent Field Manual, specifies that

> when information is received concerning the employment of undocumented or unauthorized aliens, consideration should be given to whether the information is being provided to interfere with the rights of employees to form, join or assist labor organizations or to exercise their rights not to do so; to be paid minimum wages and overtime; to have safe work places; to receive compensation for work related injuries; to be free from discrimination based on race, gender, age, national origin, religion, handicap; or to retaliate against employees for seeking to vindicate these rights. (US INS 1996)

In the case of Agriprocessors, ICE appears to have completely disregarded the policy, arresting hundreds of undocumented workers and in effect undermining the UFCW's organizing campaign. It also appears that ICE carried out the raid without consulting the various agencies investigating safety and other violations at the plant, thus undermining their work as well (Smith, Avendaño, and Martínez Ortega 2009).

Although workplace raids have had a significant impact on immigrant populations, ICE's ACCESS programs have undoubtedly had an even more profound effect. This is partly a matter of sheer numbers: more deportations have resulted from initiatives such as 287(g) than from raids.[28] Just as important, however, is that ICE ACCESS programs have generally helped to disrupt the everyday lives of immigrants and produce a heightened sense of insecurity. As we have indicated, ICE's law enforcement partners are supposed to target dangerous "criminal aliens," but most immigrants who get caught are actually low-level offenders or people who simply crossed paths with local police. Clearly, what is happening, at least in some locations, is that police officers are engaging in the heavy racial profiling of Latinos, making pretextual stops and arrests of people believed to be immigrants just so that their information (such as fingerprints) can be checked against DHS databases.[29] In Irving, Texas, for example, the number of Latinos arrested for minor offenses increased twofold following the expansion of the CAP program (Gardner II and Kohli 2009). A typical police tactic is to set up sobriety checkpoints or other traffic operations in or near immigrant neighborhoods. Once caught in these traps, immigrants without authorization to be in the United States are routinely arrested, often for driving without a license. More generally, it has become common for police to pull over "immigrant-appearing" drivers for no obvious reason or for minor traffic violations such as cracked windshields, broken taillights, improperly tinted windows, and so forth. Not surprisingly, this targeted policing has produced a deep distrust of local police authorities among Latinos in communities where ICE ACCESS programs operate. The distrust is such that Latinos, particularly those without documents, are scared to have any kind of interaction with local police for fear that they will be punished or end up in deportation proceedings. In fact, it appears that some immigrants have been prompted to change their behavior patterns in order to dodge contact with police officers or other authorities. Studies have reported that immigrants are, for example, failing to report crimes against them, visiting local businesses with less frequency, curtailing interaction with schools and other institutions, altering their driving habits, venturing into public spaces less often, and in some cases leaving particular communities altogether (Capps et al. 2011, 43). ICE ACCESS programs, then, have basically hampered the ability of immigrants to go about their daily lives, making them afraid to go out in public and have contact with any kind of authorities or institutions, and forcing some to look for a better life in more welcoming communities.

Altogether, there is no doubt that the effect of current immigration policing practices has generally been to unsettle immigrant communities in the United States, Latinos in particular. A survey conducted by the Pew Hispanic Center in 2008 paints a rather grim picture of the psychological state of U.S. Latinos—legal residents, citizens, and undocumented immigrants alike (Lopez and Minushkin 2008). Latinos generally reported feeling anxious and discriminated against amid public immigrant bashing and enhanced immigration enforcement. Among the survey's general findings were the following: within the year prior to the taking of the survey, one in ten Latinos, both citizens and noncitizens, reported being stopped by

28. From January 2006 through October 2010, for example, the number of noncitizens identified for removal through the 287(g) program was more that 185,000 (US ICE 2010b). By contrast, as we have seen, only about 14,000 undocumented migrants were apprehended through worksite raids between 2006 and 2008 (US ICE 2008c).

29. The racial profiling of Latinos, and the general impact of ICE ACCESS programs on this community, has been well documented in a number of recent reports. See American Civil Liberties Union of Georgia 2010; Waslin 2010; Capps et al. 2011. On racial profiling, see also Romero 2011.

the police or other authorities and asked about their immigration status; one in seven said they had trouble finding or keeping a job because they are Latino; and one in ten reported difficulties finding or keeping housing. Significantly, the survey also found that a majority of Latinos worry about deportation. Approximately 40 percent reported being worried "a lot" that they, a family member, or a close friend would be deported, while 17 percent said they worried "some." Not surprisingly, immigrants are particularly concerned about deportation, with 72 percent reporting being worried either "a lot" or "some." In effect, then, the immigration enforcement climate has helped to create a sense of unease among Latinos, immigrants in particular. It has helped to produce an increased feeling of insecurity.

Ultimately, it is clear that the governing of migrant illegality today is not just about deterrence. It is also about incapacitation and attrition (Gilbert, this volume). Indeed, the creation of insecurity among immigrants—by depriving them of the ability to participate meaningfully in quotidian life—appears to be a willful production designed to isolate this population from society and render them utterly powerless.[30] It is a tactic that seeks to incapacitate immigrants, Latinos in particular, in order to wear down their will to work and live in the United States. Immigration policing, particularly in the interior, thus amounts to what has been called a policy of "attrition through enforcement" (Krikorian 2006). The goal is not so much to actually expel all unauthorized immigrants as it is to "persuade" a large share of this population to self-deport.[31] As Mark Krikorian, executive director of the anti-immigrant Center for Immigration Studies, puts it, the idea is to "prevent illegals from being able to embed themselves in our society. That would involve denying them access to jobs, identification, housing, and in general making it as difficult as possible for an illegal immigrant to live a normal life here, so as to persuade a large number of them to give up and self-deport" (ibid.). Attrition through enforcement is not an official government policy, but it does appear to be the de facto way that undocumented immigration is being governed (Doty 2009). Current immigration policing practices are undoubtedly making it more difficult for undocumented immigrants to live normal lives. Such practices serve to dehumanize immigrants, undermine workers' rights, break families apart, and generally deny immigrants human dignity and peace of mind.

MIGRANT COUNTER-CONDUCTS

Given the preceding discussion, there is no doubt that the governing of immigration through crime has had a negative impact on the conduct of undocumented migrants. Indeed, it is clear that one of the effects of immigration policing has been to incapacitate

30. As Nicholas De Genova (this volume) argues, the vulnerability of undocumented immigrants is connected to their "palpable sense of deportability"—to the ever-present possibility that they may be removed from the territory of the U.S. nation-state. The current policing climate serves to exacerbate the sense of vulnerability and insecurity of the undocumented.

31. De Genova (this volume) makes the argument that the goal of immigration enforcement is not necessarily to deport immigrants. He suggests that instead the goal is to produce a population of migrants who, due to their deportability (that is, the ever-present possibility that they may be deported), are highly susceptible to workplace exploitation and hence to being treated as disposable labor. In other words, immigration enforcement is about the disciplining and regulation of the labor force.

undocumented migrants—through expulsion, the induction of fear, and so forth. However, the United States cannot be reduced to a mere space of policing. It is also most certainly a site of political struggle. Migrants have not stood idly by and accepted the highly punitive treatment to which they have been subjected. Rather, they and their allies have actively sought to challenge the anti-immigrant climate and the governing of immigration through crime. In his Collège de France lectures on security, territory, and population, Michel Foucault (2007, 201) suggests that there is a strategic reversibility to power relations such that any governmental effort to shape the conduct of individuals and populations is interwoven with dissenting counter-conducts, that is, with "struggle[s] against the processes implemented for conducting others." This is precisely the case with respect to the government of immigration through crime. This way of governing immigrants has elicited dissenting counter-conducts, or what we have called migrant counter-conducts (Inda 2011). These struggles against the punitive practices employed to direct the conduct of migrants range from street protests, advocacy for political rights, and sanctuary politics to legislative interventions, court challenges, labor organizing, and so forth.[32] Here we highlight public marches and protests, legal challenges to the criminalization of migrants, and border activism. Such counter-conducts seek to call into question the criminalization and marginalization of unauthorized migrants.

One of the most visible counter-conducts in which undocumented migrants and their allies have engaged is public protesting. Across the country, unions, religious institutions, immigrant rights groups, Latino organizations, and the general public have banded together in varying assemblages to publically protest immigration policing and its drastic effects on migrants and their communities. Undocumented migrants themselves have played an active role in these acts of protest. The best known pro-immigrant public actions occurred in the spring of 2006 (see Wang and Winn 2006; Chavez 2008; Hondagneu-Sotelo and Salas 2008; Cisneros, this volume). The previous December, the U.S. House of Representatives had passed HR 4437, the Border Protection, Antiterrorism, and Illegal Immigration Control Act of 2005. Among other provisions, the law would have made it a felony to be in the United States illegally, and for anyone to provide aid or assistance, including transportation, to undocumented immigrants. Prompted by the bill's harsh nature, Latino and immigrant communities across the country mobilized to defeat the legislation (it was still being considered in the Senate), calling for just immigration reform that included a path to citizenship for undocumented immigrants. Over the course of the spring, principally from March through May 2006, millions of people—including many who were undocumented—took to the streets in cities around the country in support of immigrant rights. On March 25,

32. Undocumented immigrants also engage in what could be called everyday counter-conducts. These are the less spectacular, more mundane acts of resistance that immigrants employ in their struggle for everyday survival in a context of intensified policing. For example, rather than avoid driving altogether, with its risks of police roadblocks and traffic stops, immigrants have developed a number of strategies to evade such obstacles. These include not driving at night or on weekends (when checkpoints are more common), biking or using taxis when practical, relying on U.S.-born children to drive, texting information to others regarding the location of roadblocks, and staying away from areas known for high police activity. Such strategies amount to counter-conducts in the sense that they contest, albeit subtly, the punitive practices employed to govern the undocumented. That is, they are conducts that make it possible for undocumented immigrants to continue living in the United States in defiance of governmental and other authorities. On avoiding police roadblocks, see Capps et. al. 2011, 43–44.

for example, five hundred thousand protesters—many carrying American flags to signify belonging in American society—filled the streets of downtown Los Angeles (Chavez 2008, 156). On April 10, a day organizers called "A National Day of Action for Immigrant Justice," marches and rallies took place in more than sixty cities—from Phoenix, Houston, and Omaha to Boston, Atlanta, and Washington D.C. (Chavez 2008, 164; Hondagneu-Sotelo and Salas 2008, 221). On May 1, more than one million people heeded the call to demonstrate in support of "A Day Without an Immigrant" (Hondagneu-Sotelo and Salas 2008, 221). The idea was for immigrants to stay home from work in order to show their importance to the U.S. economy. In a number of cities, including Los Angeles, the loss of workers who attended the marches and rallies or simply stayed home greatly affected businesses such as restaurants, markets, trucking, and other service-related enterprises. In the end, although the immigration reform that the spring marchers called for did not materialize, HR 4437 did fail to make it through the Senate.

In addition to the megamarches of 2006, numerous small-scale protests focused on local immigration policing actions have taken place throughout the country. Recall, for example, the case of Postville, Iowa, site of the raid on the Agriprocessors kosher meatpacking plant. A couple of months after the raid, on Sunday, July 27, 2008, more than one thousand people marched down the streets of Postville to protest against ICE's actions. The protestors were mainly Latino migrants, local citizens, immigrant rights advocates, and members of the Jewish, Catholic, and Lutheran communities (Agence France-Presse 2008; Fair Immigration Reform Movement 2008). They marched in Postville not only to speak out against the raid, which tore apart the local community and devastated migrant families, but also to call for the just treatment of workers and, like the marchers in the spring of 2006, for comprehensive immigration reform legislation that would include the right to legal status for unauthorized migrants (Bobo 2008). They marched carrying signs that said, "An injury to one is an injury to all. Immigrant Rights Now!" "Born in the USA. Why are you taking our families away?" and "Stop destroying families." They chanted, "No more raids!" "No justice, no peace!" and "Yo no soy terrorista, ni criminal. Y ningun ser humano es illegal. Basta, basta!"— "I'm neither a terrorist nor a criminal. And no human being is illegal. Enough, enough!" Significantly, among the marchers were forty-three women who had been apprehended during the raid but released on humanitarian grounds to take care of their children (Agence France-Presse 2008). Still under house arrest, these women wore electronic monitoring bracelets around their ankles. Two of them spoke at a rally. Maria L. Gomez bore witness to the post-raid suffering of her family: of her sister's detention and of the painful trips to visit her in prison. Cruz Rodriguez asked everyone to "stand together for our families, be a voice for those who cannot speak, who are detained. . . . Remain with us through this process" (Cullen 2009, 1).

Beyond public protests, migrants have been engaged in legal challenges to the criminalization of the undocumented. We can take as an example the case of Ignacio Flores, an undocumented migrant from Mexico (Liptak and Preston 2009). In 2000, he used a false name, birth date, Social Security number, and alien registration card to secure employment at a steel plant in Illinois. Neither the Social Security number nor the alien card belonged to real people. A few years later, however, in 2006, Flores informed his employer that he wanted to use his real name and provided a new Social Security number and alien registration card. When the employer reported this change-of-name request to ICE, the agency discovered that Flores's new documents actually belonged to other people. The U.S. government consequently indicted Flores with, among other things, aggravated identity theft. Flores was charged under federal statute 18 USC §1028A (a)(1), which imposes a mandatory two-year prison term on any person convicted of certain predicate crimes if during or in relation to the commission of those other crimes the offender "*knowingly . . . uses, without lawful authority, a means of identification of another person*" (Fernandez 2009). The law was meant to stop credit card thieves and would-be "terrorists," but the Bush administration interpreted it broadly and used it to criminally charge migrants caught using a Social Security number or identity belonging to someone else. They were charged regardless of whether they intended to defraud another individual. Rather than accept the identity theft charge, Flores fought to be acquitted. He argued that the U.S. government needed to prove that he knew the numbers on his documents belonged to other people. Flores was initially convicted of the identity theft charge, but he appealed his case all the way to the U.S. Supreme Court. The Court determined that it was not OK to eliminate the element of intent in the law. In other words, it was not enough simply to catch a person with a stolen identity or Social Security number. The government also had to show that migrants were knowingly (and with the intent to defraud) using someone else's identity. As a consequence, Flores was acquitted of the aggravated identity theft charge, and because most migrants who use false Social Security numbers are simply looking to procure a job and are not out to defraud others, ICE is no longer able to charge undocumented migrants with identity theft indiscriminately.

Finally, the U.S.-Mexico border has also been an important site of political struggle. One tactic used by immigration rights advocates has been to stage actions critiquing the militarization of the border. From November 5 to 11, 2007, for example, youth from the United States, Mexico, and other countries staged a "No Borders" camp along the Southwest border in the cities of Calexico, California, and Mexicali, Mexico (Burridge 2010). The action, which was modeled on the setting up of No Borders camps in Australia and the European Union, involved youth congregating on both sides of the fence separating the cities and setting up a camp underneath the watchful eyes of the U.S. Border Patrol and other law enforcement entities. The idea was to call attention to the arbitrary nature of national boundaries and the horrific consequences of enhanced border policing in the lives of immigrants. From their base camp, the youth also organized a number of other activities: a "die-in" at the port of entry in downtown Mexicali; a protest at the El Centro Detention Facility, which on average held between five hundred and six hundred detainees a day; the operation of a pirate radio station; and a memorial at a cemetery where about four hundred unidentified migrants were buried. Another tactic among pro-immigrant activists has been to engage in activities to "humanize the border environment" (Walsh, this volume). Two such activities are the mobilization of citizen-organized foot patrols to locate and assist border crossers in distress, and the construction of water stations in the desert. Notably, faith-based organizations have been centrally involved in these endeavors. For example, Humane Borders, a faith-based humanitarian group committed to "taking death out of the immigration equation" (Hoover 2008) has been building water stations in the Arizona desert since 2001 (Walsh, this volume). These stations—each stocked with food, clothing, first-aid kits, and a hundred-gallon water tank—are meant to serve as lifelines for migrants crossing through the treacherous desert terrain. The placement of the stations is determined with the help of geographic information systems (GIS) and other locational technologies. Humane Borders uses such technologies to map desert-crossing routes and the spatial distribution of migrant deaths, and then strategically locates the stations in areas with high rates of fatalities. Another faith-based group, No More Deaths, is dedicated to providing humanitarian aid directly to border crossers. This group sends out volunteer patrols into the Sonoran desert of Arizona to find migrants in need of medical and humanitarian aid. If necessary, the patrols transfer migrants to a local medical facility or hand them over to a Border Patrol search and rescue unit. No More Deaths conceives of its activities as a *civil initiative*, a form of nonviolent protest against the unjust consequences of border policing, a protest that is grounded in the "conviction that people of conscience must work openly and in community to uphold . . . human rights" (ibid.).

The counter-conducts in which migrants and their allies have engaged, particularly as they have involved the participation of the undocumented, are significant in various respects. First, they speak to the political becoming of undocumented migrants. As Peter Nyers (2006) has pointed out, refugees and the undocumented are expected to be docile. Their lives tend to be represented in popular and legal discourse as the inverted image of political life. Whereas the citizen is expected to speak and act politically, the unauthorized migrant is supposed to remain silent. But in the context of contemporary policing, undocumented migrants have refused to be quiet. They have spoken out against the dehumanizing effects of such policing, and they have demanded dignity and recognition, asking to be seen not as criminals who harm the larger society but as human beings who contribute to it (Beltrán 2009). That undocumented migrants are standing up and speaking is an important act of symbolic resistance. They are speaking out in a context that does not recognize migrants—in particular undocumented migrants—as legitimate speaking subjects. Second, migrant counter-conducts amount to noncitizen "acts of citizenship" or what we call *unauthorized citizenship*.[33] Unauthorized migrants are not simply speaking out, they are actually claiming and exercising rights. A main message of the anti-raid public protests, as well as of the legal challenges to the criminalization of migrants, is that undocumented migrants are legitimate members of U.S. society and deserve the right to work, to raise families, and to be free from the fear of persecution. In other words, they are asking to be recognized as legitimate political subjects with social, civil, and political rights. In making such claims, unauthorized migrants are in effect enacting citizenship. Indeed, through their engagement in a variety of democratic processes, from collective protesting and campaigning for rights to court battles, the undocumented are basically acting as citizens. In the process, citizenship is transformed from a strictly juridical condition to a practice one can engage in regardless of legal status.

33. On acts of citizenship generally, see Nyers 2003; Isin 2008.

THE ORGANIZATION OF THE BOOK

Such is the contemporary landscape of governing immigration through crime. Our basic suggestion is that, to the extent that undocumented migrants have been constructed as subjects who harm the well-being of American citizens, the measures employed to govern them have become extremely exclusionary and punitive. Thus, much like the government of the poor and of other anti-citizens, unauthorized migrants have increasingly been regulated through crime and police measures. Indeed, crime and punishment have become the preferred means for governing the undocumented. In short, unauthorized migrants have effectively been criminalized and treated as delinquent subjects—with rather unfortunate (if not downright horrific) consequences for many migrant families and communities. The picture is not all bleak, however. Migrants and their allies have forcefully pushed back against the expanded boundaries of enforcement. For one, they have gone to court and filed lawsuits to end such practices as the charging of undocumented workers with identity theft. Furthermore, undocumented migrants themselves have taken to the streets and marched to claim rights and to voice their rejection of the dehumanizing effects of immigration policing. Although the enforcement climate has been stepped up and the border respatialized, migrants and their allies have kept hope alive and mounted political campaigns bent on gaining rights and recognition for the undocumented. Thus, as a border zone of governing immigration through crime, the United States is also a site where exclusionary and castigatory techniques of control are subject to resistance and contestation.

The aim of this book, as noted earlier, is to provide an interdisciplinary introduction to this terrain of governing immigration through crime. The articles gathered here are a selection of the best recent social science work on the topic. We have organized this rich material into five thematic parts, each of which carries a short introduction of its own, along with suggestions for further reading. Part I, "Law and Criminalization," sets forth the legal context underpinning the criminalization of immigrants and the governing of migrant illegality. Part II, "Managing Borders," is concerned with the intensified policing of the U.S.-Mexico border. Part III, "Policing the Interior," focuses on the respatialization of immigration enforcement—its radical expansion into the interior of the United States. Part IV, "Detention and Deportation," deals with how the stepped-up policing environment has resulted in the mass detention and deportation of immigrants. Part V, "Immigrant Contestations," explores how migrants and their allies have sought to resist and challenge the punitive governance of immigration and its dehumanizing effects.

As a final point, we would like to call attention to some of the realities that have shaped the construction of this book. The literature on immigration policing is rather large and rapidly growing. We would have liked to capture all of the key aspects of this exciting literature. Unfortunately, the limitations on space and the realities of budgets necessarily made such a task impossible. The book therefore contains a number of important gaps (some of which we attempt to fill through the list of suggested readings at the end of the part introductions). There is no intellectual justification for these exclusions other than the need to erect artificial limits. Let us point to some of the most obvious of these gaps. First, a number of important immigration policing practices are absent from the chapters or dealt with only briefly. These include ICE raids, the Secure Communities program, Operation Stream-line, the denial of driver's licenses to immigrants, sanctuary cities, immigrant labor orga-nizing, the privatization of immigration enforcement, the detention of families and children, California's Proposition 187, the policing of the U.S.-Canada border—and the list goes on. Second, although the governing of immigration through crime has a long history, the chapters generally pay the most attention to contemporary, post-9/11 policing prac-tices. Third, although some of the chapters incorporate analysis of gender, we would like to have included more on this topic. Finally, although the stepped-up enforcement climate affects all immigrants, the articles by and large concentrate on Latinos. This population has without a doubt been the main target of immigration policing. Such are the omissions of this book, or at least some of them. There are certainly others. We hope the reader will forgive us for these exclusions and gain from the material that *is* included here.

WORKS CITED

Agence France-Presse. 2008. "Hundreds Protest Immigration Raid in Small-Town America." *Agence France-Presse*, July 27. http://afp.google.com/article/ALeqM5j9I_ty9Pc3E6nBPTJC9cbtQtfyqg.

Aguilera, Elizabeth. 2011. "Illegal Immigration from Mexico Continues to Decline." *San Diego Union-Tribune*, July 7. http://www.utsandiego.com/news/2011/jul/07/illegal-immigration-mexico-continues-decline.

American Civil Liberties Union (ACLU) of Georgia. 2010. *The Persistence of Racial Profiling in Gwinnett: Time for Accountability, Transparency, and an End to 287(g)*. Atlanta: ACLU of Georgia.

Andreas, Peter. 2000. *Border Games: Policing the U.S.-Mexico Divide*. Ithaca, NY: Cornell University Press.

Associated Press. 2011. "More Hispanics Go to Federal Prison." *USA Today*, June 4. http://www.usatoday.com/news/nation/2011-06-04-immigration-hispanic-offenders-federal-prison_n.htm.

Barry, Tom. 2008. "The Deterrence Strategy of Homeland Security." June 2. http://www.detentionwatchnetwork.org/node/1207.

———. 2009. *Immigrant Crackdown Joins Failed Crime and Drug Wars*. Washington, DC: Center for International Policy.

Bauer, Mary. 2009. *Under Siege: Life for Low-Income Latinos in the South*. Montgomery, AL: Southern Poverty Law Center.

Beltrán, Cristina. 2009. "Going Public: Hannah Arendt, Immigrant Action, and the Space of Appear-ance." *Political Theory* 37 (5): 595–622.

Blakely, Edward J., and Mary Gail Snyder. 1997. *Fortress America: Gated Communities in the United States*. Washington, DC: Brookings Institute Press.

Bobo, Kim. 2008. "Religious Leaders Protest Postville Raid." *Religious Dispatches*, August 8. http://www.alternet.org/story/94429/religious_leaders_protest_postville_raid.

Brown, Wendy. 2006. "American Nightmare: Neoliberalism, Neoconvervatism, and De-Democrati-zation." *Political Theory* 34 (2): 690–714.

Burridge, Andrew. 2010. "Youth on the Line and the *No Borders* Movement." *Children's Geography* 8 (4): 401–411.

Camayd-Freixas, Erik. 2009. "Interpreting After the Largest ICE Raid in U.S. History: A Personal Account." *Latino Studies* 7 (1): 123–139.

Capps, Randy, Rosa Maria Castañeda, Ajay Chaudry, and Robert Santos. 2007. *Paying the Price: The Impact of Immigration Raids on America's Children.* Washington, DC: Urban Institute and National Council of La Raza.

Capps, Randy, Marc R. Rosenblum, Cristina Rodriguez, and Muzaffar Chishti. 2011. *Delegation and Divergence: A Study of 287(g) State and Local Immigration Enforcement.* Washington, DC: Migration Policy Institute.

Carroll, Susan. 2011. "As Feds Review Cases, 'Low-Priority' May Avoid Deportation." *Houston Chronicle*, August 18. http://www.chron.com/news/article/As-feds-review-cases-low-priority -may-avoid-2132768.php.

Chacón, Jennifer M. 2009. "Managing Migration Through Crime." *Columbia Law Review Sidebar* 109: 135–148.

Chavez, Leo R. 2001. *Covering Immigration: Popular Images and the Politics of the Nation.* Berkeley: University of California Press.

———. 2008. *The Latino Threat: Constructing Immigrants, Citizens, and the Nation.* Stanford, CA: Stanford University Press.

Cisneros, Josue David. 2012. "Looking 'Illegal': Affect, Rhetoric, and Performativity in Arizona's Senate Bill 1070." In *Border Rhetorics: Charting Enactments of Citizenship and Identity on the U.S.-Mexico Frontier*, edited by D. Robert DeChaine, 133–150. Tuscaloosa: University of Alabama Press.

Coleman, James. 1994. "Illegal Immigrants Are, by Definition, Criminals." *Los Angeles Times*, September 12, B11.

Coleman, Mathew. 2007. "Immigration Geopolitics Beyond the U.S.-Mexico Border." *Antipode* 39 (1): 54–76.

Coutin, Susan Bibler. 2010. "Confined Within: National Territories as Zones of Confinement." *Political Geography* 29 (4): 200–208.

Cullen, William. 2009. "Postville Rally Is Display of Ecumenism." *The Witness*, August 10. http:// www.arch.pvt.k12.ia.us/PostvilleRelief/pdf/PostvilleRally7_27_08.pdf.

Cunningham, Hilary. 2009. "Mobilities and Enclosures After Seattle: Politicizing Borders in a 'Borderless' World." *Dialectical Anthropology* 33 (2): 143–156.

De Genova, Nicholas P. 2002. "Migrant 'Illegality' and Deportability in Everyday Life." *Annual Review of Anthropology* 31: 419–437.

Doty, Roxanne Lynn. 2009. *The Law into Their Own Hands: Immigration and the Politics of Exceptionalism.* Tucson: University of Arizona Press.

Dunn, Timothy J. 1996. *The Militarization of the U.S.-Mexico Border, 1978–1992: Low-Intensity Conflict Doctrine Comes Home.* Austin, TX: CMAS Books.

Ellingwood, Ken. 1999. "Border Policy Violates Rights, Groups Charge." *Los Angeles Times*, February 11, A3, A28.

Eschbach, Karl, Jacqueline Hagan, Nestor Rodriguez, Ruben Hernandez-Leon, and Stanley Bailey. 1999. "Death at the Border." *International Migration Review* 33 (2): 431–454.

Euskirchen, Markus, Henrick Lebuhn, and Gene Ray. 2009. "Big Trouble in Borderland: Immigration Rights and No-Border Struggles in Europe." *MUTE: Culture and Politics After the Net*, February 11. http://www.metamute.org/community/your-posts/big-trouble-borderland-immigration -rights-and-no-border-struggles-europe.

Ewing, Walter. 2010. *Looking for a Quick Fix: The Rise and Fall of the Secure Border Initiative's High-Tech Solution to Unauthorized Immigration.* Washington, DC: Immigration Policy Center.

Fair Immigration Reform Movement. 2008. "1,000 March to Protest Postville Raid." July 28. http://www.fairimmigration.org/2008/07/28/1000-march-to-protest-postville-raid.

Fernandez, Henry. 2009. "Supreme Court Rules That Immigrants Have Rights, Too," May 5. http://www.americanprogress.org/issues/2009/05/supreme_court_immigration.html/print.html.

Foucault, Michel. 1991. "Governmentality." In *The Foucault Effect: Studies in Governmentality*, edited by Graham Burchell, Colin Gordon, and Peter Miller, 87–104. Chicago: University of Chicago Press.

———. 2007. *Security, Territory, Population: Lectures at the Collège de France, 1977–1978*. New York: Palgrave Macmillan.

Gardner II, Trevor, and Aarti Kohli. 2009. *The C.A.P. Effect: Racial Profiling in the ICE Criminal Alien Program*. Berkeley: Warren Institute on Race, Ethnicity, and Diversity, University of California, Berkeley Law School.

Garland, David. 2001. *The Culture of Control: Crime and Social Order in Contemporary Society*. Chicago: University of Chicago Press.

Gordon, Colin. 1991. "Governmental Rationality: An Introduction." In *The Foucault Effect: Studies in Governmentality*, edited by Graham Burchell, Colin Gordon, and Peter Miller, 1–51. Chicago: University of Chicago Press.

Greene, Judy, and Sunita Patel. 2007. "The Immigrant Gold Rush: The Profit Motive Behind Immigrant Detention." In *Briefing Materials Submitted to the United Nations Special Rapporteur on the Human Rights of Migrants*, edited by Detention and Deportation Working Group, 44–51. Washington, DC: Lutheran Immigration and Refugee Service and Detention Watch Network.

Hing, Bill Ong. 2009. "Institutional Racism, ICE Raids, and Immigration Reform." *University of San Francisco Law Review* 44: 1–49.

Hoefer, Michael, Nancy Rytina, and Bryan C. Baker. 2010. *Estimates of the Unauthorized Immigrant Population Residing in the United States: January 2009*. Washington, DC: Department of Homeland Security, Office of Immigration Statistics.

Hondagneu-Sotelo, Pierrette, and Angelica Salas. 2008. "What Explains the Immigrant Rights Marches of 2006? Xenophobia and Organizing with Democratic Technology." In *Immigrant Rights in the Shadows of Citizenship*, edited by Rachel Ida Buff, 209–225. New York: New York University Press.

Hoover, Robin. 2008. "The Story of Humane Borders." Originally published in *A Promised Land, A Perilous Journey: Theological Perspectives on Migration*, edited by Daniel G. Groody and Gioacchino Campese. Notre Dame, IN: University of Notre Dame Press. http://robinhoover.com/uploads/THE_STORY_OF_HUMANE_BORDERS_2008.pdf

Human Rights Watch. 2009. *Forced Apart (by the Numbers): Non-Citizens Deported Mostly for Nonviolent Offenses*. New York: Human Rights Watch.

Inda, Jonathan Xavier. 2006a. *Targeting Immigrants: Government, Technology, and Ethics*. Malden, MA: Wiley-Blackwell.

———. 2006b. "Border Prophylaxis: Technology, Illegality, and the Government of Immigration." *Cultural Dynamics* 18 (2): 115–138.

———. 2011. "Borderzones of Enforcement: Criminalization, Workplace Raids, and Migrant Counterconducts. In *The Contested Politics of Mobility: Borderzones and Irregularity*, edited by Vicki Squire, 74–90. London: Routledge.

Isin, Egin F. 2008. "Theorizing Acts of Citizenship." In *Acts of Citizenship*, edited by Egin F. Isin and Greg M. Nielsen, 15–43. London: Zed Books.

Jimenez, Maria. 2009. *Humanitarian Crisis: Migrant Deaths at the U.S.-Mexico Border.* San Diego, CA: American Civil Liberties Union of San Diego and Imperial Counties and Mexico's National Commission on Human Rights.

Johnson, Dawn Marie. 2001. "The AEDPA and the IIRIRA: Treating Misdemeanors as Felonies for Immigration Purposes." *Journal of Legislation* 27: 477–491.

Johnson, Kevin R. 2009. "The Intersection of Race and Class in U.S. Immigration Law and Enforcement." *Law and Contemporary Problems* 72: 1–35.

Keaney, Melissa, and Joan Friedland. 2009. *Overview of the Key ICE ACCESS Programs: 287(g), the Criminal Alien Program, and Secure Communities.* Los Angeles: National Immigration Law Center.

Kerwin, Donald. 2009. "Testimony of Donald Kerwin, Vice President for Programs, Migration Policy Institute." In *Moving Toward More Effective Immigration Detention Management.* Hearing before the Committee on Homeland Security, Subcommittee on Border, Maritime, and Global Counterterrorism, U.S. House of Representatives. http://hsc-democrats.house.gov/SiteDocuments/2009 1210105631-76330.PDF.

Kerwin, Donald, and Serena Yi-Ying Lin. 2009. *Immigrant Detention: Can ICE Meet Its Legal Imperatives and Case Management Responsibilities?* Washington, DC: Migration Policy Institute.

Kohli, Aarti, and Deepa Varma. 2011. *Borders, Jails, and Jobsites: An Overview of Federal Immigration Enforcement Programs in the U.S.* Berkeley: Warren Institute on Race, Ethnicity & Diversity, University of California, Berkeley Law School.

Koulish, Robert. 2010. *Immigration and American Democracy: Subverting the Rule of Law.* New York: Routledge.

Krikorian, Mark. 2006. "A Third Way." *Palm Beach Post*, May 7. http://www.cis.org/node/419.

Lacayo, A. Elena. 2011. *One Year Later: A Look at SB 1070 and Copycat Legislation.* Washington, DC: National Council of La Raza.

Liptak, Adam, and Julia Preston. 2009. "Justices Limit Use of Identity Theft Law in Immigration Cases." *New York Times*, May 5. http://www.nytimes.com/2009/05/05/us/05immig.html?_r=1& pagewanted=print.

Lopez, Mark Hugo, and Susan Minushkin. 2008. *2008 National Survey of Latinos: Hispanics See Their Situation in U.S. Deteriorating; Oppose Key Immigration Enforcement Measures.* Washington, DC: Pew Hispanic Center.

Mac, Ryan. 2010. "Researcher: Securing State's Borders Costly, Ineffective." *Bay Citizen*, October 1. http://www.baycitizen.org/immigration/story/researcher-securing-states-borders.

Martin, Lauren L. 2012. "'Catch and Remove': Detention, Deterrence, and Discipline in U.S. Noncitizen Family Detention Practice." *Geopolitics* 17 (2): 312–334.

McNevin, Anne. 2009. "Doing What Citizens Do: Migrant Struggles at the Edges of Political Belonging." *Local-Global: Identity, Security, Community* 6: 67–77.

Mendelson, Margot, Shayna Strom, and Michael Wishnie. 2009. *Collateral Damage: An Examination of ICE's Fugitive Operations Program.* Washington, DC: Migration Policy Institute.

Miller, Teresa A. 2003. "Citizenship and Severity: Recent Immigration Reforms and the New Penology." *Georgetown Immigration Law Journal* 17: 611–666.

———. 2005. "Blurring the Boundaries Between Immigration and Crime Control After September 11th." *Boston College Third World Law Journal* 25: 81–124.

———. 2008. "A New Look at Neo-Liberal Economic Policies and the Criminalization of Undocumented Migration." *Southern Methodist University Law Review* 61: 171–188.

Morton, John. 2010. "Memorandum for All ICE Employees: Civil Immigration Enforcement." June 30. http://www.ice.gov/doclib/news/releases/2011/110302washingtondc.pdf.

National Immigrant Justice Center. 2007. "Access to Counsel and Due Process for Detained Immigrants." In *Briefing Materials Submitted to the United Nations Special Rapporteur on the Human Rights of Migrants*, edited by Detention and Deportation Working Group, 75–82. Washington, DC: Lutheran Immigration and Refugee Service and Detention Watch Network.

National Immigration Forum. 2010. "Southwest Border Security Operations." *Backgrounder*. December. http://www.immigrationforum.org/images/uploads/SouthwestBorderSecurityOperations.pdf.

———. 2012a. "Arizona SB 1070 in the Supreme Court." June 25. http://www.immigrationforum.org/legislation/arizona-sb-1070-in-the-supreme-court.

———. 2012b. *The Math of Immigration Detention: Runaway Costs for Immigration Detention Do Not Add Up to Sensible Policies*. August. http://www.immigrationforum.org/images/uploads/MathofImmigrationDetention.pdf.

Neuman, Gerald. 2005. "Aliens as Outlaws: Government Services, Proposition 187, and the Structure of the Equal Protection Doctrine." *UCLA Law Review* 42: 1425–1452.

Nevins, Joseph. 2002. *Operation Gatekeeper: The Rise of the "Illegal Alien" and the Making of the U.S.-Mexico Boundary*. New York: Routledge.

Nyers, Peter. 2003. "Abject Cosmopolitanism: The Politics of Protection in the Anti-deportation Movement." *Third World Quarterly* 24 (6): 1069–1093.

———. 2006. "Taking Rights, Mediating Wrongs: Disagreements over the Political Agency of Nonstatus Refugees." In *The Politics of Protection: Sites of Insecurity and Political Agency*, edited by Jef Huysmans, Andrew Dobson, and Raia Prokhovnik, 48–67. New York: Routledge.

Olson, W. 1994. "Letter to the Editor: Hardworking or Not, Illegals Are a Burden to Social-Service Programs." *Orange County Register*, May 8, Commentary 5.

Ong, Aihwa. 2007. "Neoliberalism as a Mobile Technology." *Transactions of the Institute of British Geographers* 32 (1): 3–8.

Pratt, Anna. 2005. *Securing Borders: Detention and Deportation in Canada*. Vancouver: University of British Columbia Press.

Preston, Julia. 2011. "Homeland Security Cancels 'Virtual Fence' After $1 Billion Is Spent." *New York Times*, January 14. http://www.nytimes.com/2011/01/15/us/politics/15fence.html.

———. 2012. "Agents' Union Stalls Training on Deportation Rules." *New York Times*, January 7. http://www.nytimes.com/2012/01/08/us/illegal-immigrants-who-commit-crimes-focus-of-deportation.html.

Provine, Doris Marie, and Roxanne Lynn Doty. 2011. "The Criminalization of Immigrants as a Racial Project." *Journal of Contemporary Criminal Justice* 27 (3): 261–277.

Rhodes, Deborah J. 2008. "Statement of Deborah J. Rhodes, Senior Associate Deputy Attorney General, United States Department of Justice." In *Immigration Raids: Postville and Beyond*. Hearing Before the Subcommittee on Immigration, Citizenship, Refugees, Border Security, and International Law of the Committee on the Judiciary, House of Representatives. 110 Cong. 2d Sess. http://judiciary.house.gov/hearings/printers/110th/43682.PDF.

Romero, Mary. 2011. "Keeping Citizenship Rights White: Arizona's Racial Profiling Practices in Immigration Law Enforcement." *Law Journal for Social Justice* 1 (1): 97–113.

Root, Jay. 2008. "Jail Growth Explodes as Feds Crack Down on Illegal Immigrants." *McClatchy Wash-*

ington Bureau, May 26. http://www.mcclatchydc.com/2008/05/26/v-print/38555/jail-growth -explodes-as-feds-crack.html.

Rosas, Gilberto. 2012. *Barrio Libre: Criminalizing States and Delinquent Refusals of the New Frontier.* Durham, NC: Duke University Press.

Rose, Nikolas. 1999. *Powers of Freedom: Reframing Political Thought.* Cambridge, UK: Cambridge University Press.

Schriro, Dora. 2009. *Immigration Detention: Overview and Recommendations.* Washington, DC: U.S. Immigration and Customs Enforcement.

Simon, Jonathan. 1997. "Governing Through Crime." In *The Crime Conundrum: Essays on Criminal Justice,* edited by Lawrence M. Friedman and George Fisher, 171–189. Boulder, CO: Westview Press.

———. 2007. *Governing Through Crime: How the War on Crime Transformed American Democracy and Created a Culture of Fear.* Oxford, UK: Oxford University Press.

Siskin, Alison, and Ruth Ellen Wasem. 2008. *Immigration Policy on Expedited Removal of Aliens.* Washington, DC: Congressional Research Service.

Smith, Dennis. 2010. "Program Streamlining Immigration Enforcement." *Frontline: U.S. Customs and Border Protection* Fall: 24–27.

Smith, Rebecca, Ana Avendaño, and Julie Martínez Ortega. 2009. *ICED OUT: How Immigration Enforcement Has Interfered with Workers' Rights.* New York and Washington, DC: AFL-CIO, American Rights at Work Education Fund, and National Employment Law Project.

State of Arizona Senate. 2010. Senate Bill 1070. http://www.azleg.gov/legtext/49leg/2r/bills/sb1070s .pdf.

Stumpf, Juliet P. 2008. "States of Confusion: The Rise of State and Local Power over Immigration." *North Carolina Law Review* 89: 1557–1618.

Taylor, Margaret H. 1995. "Detained Aliens Challenging Conditions of Confinement and the Porous Border of the Plenary Power Doctrine." *Hastings Constitutional Law Quarterly* 22: 1087–1158.

TRAC Immigration. 2011. "Illegal Reentry Becomes Top Criminal Charge." June 10. http://trac.syr .edu/immigration/reports/251.

U.S. Border Patrol. 1994. *Border Patrol Strategic Plan: 1994 and Beyond—National Strategy.* Washington, DC: U.S. Border Patrol.

———. 2012a. "Border Patrol Agent Staffing by Fiscal Year." Accessed September 22. http://www .cbp.gov/linkhandler/cgov/border_security/border_patrol/usbp_statistics/staffing_92_10.ctt/ staffing_92_11.pdf.

———. 2012b. "Total Illegal Alien Apprehensions by Fiscal Year." Accessed September 22. http:// www.cbp.gov/linkhandler/cgov/border_security/border_patrol/usbp_statistics/99_10_fy_stats .ctt/99_11_fy_stats.pdf.

U.S. Customs and Border Protection (US CBP). 2005. "DHS Launches 'Operation Streamline II': Enforcement Effort Focusing on Prosecuting and Removing Illegal Aliens in Del Rio, Texas." News release. December 16. http://www.cbp.gov/xp/cgov/newsroom/news_releases/archives/ 2005_press_releases/122005/12162005.xml.

———. 2006. "DHS Secretary Announces End to 'Catch and Release' on Southern Border." News release. August 23. http://www.cbp.gov/xp/cgov/admin/c1_archive/messages/end_catch_release.xml.

———. 2009a. *Secure Borders, Safe Travel, Legal Trade.* Washington, DC: U.S. Customs and Border Protection.

———. 2009b. "Fact Sheet: Border Patrol Search, Trauma, and Rescue (BORSTAR)." May. http://

www.cbp.gov/linkhandler/cgov/newsroom/fact_sheets/border/border_patrol/borstar.ctt/borstar
.pdf.

———. 2012. "Southwest Border Fence Construction Progress." Accessed April 25. http://www.cbp
.gov/xp/cgov/border_security/ti/ti_news/sbi_fence.

U.S. Department of Homeland Security (US DHS). 1999. *Progress in Addressing Secure Border Initiative Operational Requirements and Constructing the Southwest Border Fence.* Washington, DC: Office of the Inspector General.

———. 2003. *Endgame: Office of Detention and Removal Strategic Plan, 2003–2012.* Washington, DC: U.S. Department of Homeland Security, Bureau of Immigration and Customs Enforcement.

———. 2005. "Fact Sheet: Secure Border Initiative." News release. November 2. https://www.hsdl.org/
?view&did=440470.

———. 2006a. "Department of Homeland Security Streamlines Removal Process Along Entire U.S.
Border." News release. January 30. http://www.hsdl.org/?view&did=476965.

———. 2006b. *Secure Border Strategic Plan.* Washington, DC: U.S. Department of Homeland Security.
http://www.hlswatch.com/sitedocs/sbiplan.pdf.

———. 2010. *Yearbook of Immigration Statistics: 2009.* Washington, DC: U.S. Department of Homeland Security, Office of Immigration Statistics.

———. 2012a. *Immigration Enforcement Actions: 2011.* September. http://www.dhs.gov/sites/default/
files/publications/immigration-statistics/enforcement_ar_2011.pdf.

———. 2012b. "Secretary Napolitano Announces Deferred Action Process for Young People Who
Are Low Enforcement Priorities." News release. June 15. http://www.dhs.gov/ynews/
releases/20120612-napolitano-announces-deferred-action-process-for-young-people.shtm.

U.S. General Accounting Office (US GAO). 1993. *Illegal Aliens: Despite Data Limitations, Current
Methods Provide Better Population Estimates.* Washington, DC: GAO.

———. 1995. *Illegal Aliens: National Net Cost Estimates Vary Widely.* Washington, DC: GAO.

U.S. Government Accountability Office (US GAO). 2009. *Briefing on U.S. Customs and Border Protection's Secure Border Initiative Fiscal Year 2009 Expenditure Plan.* Washington, DC: GAO.

U.S. Immigration and Customs Enforcement (US ICE). 2008a. "297 Convicted and Sentenced Following ICE Worksite Operation in Iowa." News release. May 15. http://www.ice.gov/news/
releases/0805/080515waterloo.htm.

———. 2008b. "Fact Sheet: ICE Fugitive Operations." November 19. http://www.ice.gov/doclib/pi/
news/factsheets/NFOP_FS.pdf (no longer available).

———. 2008c. "Worksite Enforcement Overview." November 25. http://www.ice.gov/doclib/pi/news/
factsheets/worksite.pdf (no longer available).

———. 2008d. "Fact Sheet: ICE Agreements of Cooperation in Communities to Enhance Safety and
Security." June. http://www.ice.gov/doclib/news/library/factsheets/pdf/access.pdf.

———. 2009a. "Secretary Napolitano and ICE Assistant Secretary Morton Announce That the Secure
Communities Initiative Identified More Than 111,000 Aliens Charged with or Convicted of Crimes
in Its First Year." News release. November 12. http://www.ice.gov/news/releases/0911/091112
washington.htm.

———. 2009b. "Worksite Enforcement Overview." April 30. http://www.aila.org/content/default.asp
x?bc=1016|6715|12053|26286|31038|28771.

———. 2010a. "ICE Acquires New Facility Near Phoenix to Hold Detainees Before Flights to Central
America." News release. March 25. http://www.ice.gov/news/releases/1003/100325phoenix.htm.

———. 2010b. "287(g)-Identified Aliens for Removal." October 31. http://www.ice.gov/doclib/foia/reports/287g-masterstats2010oct31.pdf.

———. 2011a "Fact Sheet: ICE Fugitive Operations Program." November 7. http://www.ice.gov/news/library/factsheets/fugops.htm.

———. 2011b. "Fugitive Operations." Accessed March 30. http://www.ice.gov/fugitive-operations.

———. 2012. "Fact Sheet: A Day in the Life of ICE Enforcement and Removal Operations." Accessed September 22. http://www.ice.gov/doclib/news/library/factsheets/pdf/day-in-life-ero.pdf.

U.S. Immigration and Naturalization Service (US INS). 1996. "Memorandum to Management Team: Revised Operations Instruction 287.3a." December 20. http://www.scribd.com/doc/22636334/INS-Operations-Instruction-287-3a.

U.S. Office of Homeland Security (US OHS). 2002. *National Strategy for Homeland Security*. Washington, DC: Office of Homeland Security. http://www.ncs.gov/library/policy_docs/nat_strat_hls.pdf.

Varsanyi, Monica. 2008. "Immigration Policing Through the Backdoor: City Ordinances, the 'Right to the City,' and the Exclusion of Undocumented Day Laborers." *Urban Geography* 29 (1): 29–52.

Vaughan-Williams, Nick. 2010. "The UK Border Security Continuum: Virtual Biopolitics and the Simulation of the Sovereign Ban." *Environment and Planning D: Society and Space* 28 (6): 1071–1083.

Wacquant, Loïc. 2008. "Ordering Insecurity: Social Polarization and the Punitive Upsurge." *Radical Philosophy Review* 11 (1): 9–27.

———. 2009. *Punishing the Poor: The Neoliberal Government of Social Security*. Durham, NC: Duke University Press.

Walters, William. 2006. "Border/Control." *European Journal of Social Theory* 9 (2): 187–203.

Wang, Ted, and Robert C. Winn. 2006. *Groundswell Meets Groundwork: Preliminary Recommendations for Building on Immigrant Mobilizations*. New York: Four Freedoms Fund and Grantmakers Concerned with Immigrants and Refugees.

Waslin, Michele. 2010. *The Secure Communities Program: Unanswered Questions and Continuing Concerns*. Washington, DC: Immigration Policy Center.

Wilder, Forrest. 2007. "Detention Archipelago: Jailing Immigrants for Profit." *NACLA Report on the Americas* 40 (3): 19–24, 41.

I   LAW AND CRIMINALIZATION

The chapters in Part I of this book focus on the crucial role of federal law in the governing of immigration through crime. Law is crucial in the sense that it provides the general foundation for immigration-related enforcement. There are at least two important dimensions to the law's involvement in the criminalization of immigrants. First, U.S. immigration laws enacted since 1965 have generally served to restrict the legal flow of immigrants, especially from Latin America. This has resulted in the illegalization of various migrant streams—that of Mexicans, for instance—and the formation of a large population of undocumented persons. Second, as the unauthorized population in the United States has grown, federal authorities have developed a series of largely punitive laws designed to control the immigrant "threat." This effort began with the Immigration Reform and Control Act of 1986, which significantly increased resources for border enforcement and made it illegal for employers to hire undocumented workers. Since then, major immigration reforms during the mid-1990s and contemporary post-9/11 "war on terror" initiatives have criminalized an increasing range of immigration-related conduct, including filing an immigration application without a reasonable basis, falsely claiming citizenship in order to obtain a benefit or employment, voting in a federal election as a noncitizen, and entry without inspection. Not only has the law produced "illegal" immigrants, it has also progressively criminalized their existence.

The chapters in this section explore these two dimensions of the law's criminalization of immigrants. Chapter 1, by Nicholas De Genova, focuses on the legal production of Mexican migrant illegality. Specifically, he looks at how practically all major changes in U.S. immigration law since 1965 have served to place ever greater restrictions on the legal movement of people from Mexico into the United States. Given that Mexicans continue to migrate, a chief consequence of such restrictions has been the creation of a legally vulnerable population of undocumented workers. The vulnerability of these migrants, De Genova suggests, is connected to their "palpable sense of deportability"—to the ever-present possibility that they may be removed from the territory of the U.S. nation-state. What deportability in effect does is produce a population of migrants who, due to the fear of being deported, is highly susceptible to workplace exploitation and hence to being treated as disposable labor. Ultimately, De Genova argues that Mexican illegality cannot be treated as a natural fact of social life, but has to be seen as a willful legal production designed to render immigrant workers vulnerable and disposable.

Chapter 2, by Juliet P. Stumpf, shifts the focus to the nature of the laws designed to manage the "threat" of immigrants. In particular, Stumpf looks at how the growing merger of immigration and criminal law has created a highly punitive stance toward immigrants. This merger, which Stumpf refers to as "crimmigration law," has taken place on three fronts. First, the substance of immigration law and criminal law increasingly intersect. For example, since the 1980s, there has been a marked proliferation in the scope of criminal grounds for excluding and deporting noncitizens. Second, immigration enforcement has come to significantly resemble criminal law enforcement. The idea here is that the activities of immigration enforcement agencies nowadays resemble fundamentally those of any other police force. Third, the procedural features of prosecuting immigration infractions have assumed many of the characteristics of criminal procedures. For instance, the practice of detention, a sanction increasingly used in immigration matters, has a clear parallel in the criminal penalty of incarceration. Stumpf's conclusion is that the crimmigration merger has helped to create a society in which noncitizens, often identifiable by race and class, are physically, politically, and socially cast out of the mainstream community.

Chapter 3, by Jennifer M. Chacón, focuses on the reconfiguration of immigration law in the post-9/11 context. Specifically, she examines how "national security" has come to provide the primary justification for immigration lawmaking and enforcement. Essentially, subsequent to the 9/11 attacks, terrorism has generally come to be regarded as the greatest threat facing the nation. On the basis of the fact that the 9/11 hijackers were foreigners who somehow managed to get into the United States, the movement of people in and out of the country has been seen as indissociable from this threat. It is thus commonly expressed in both policy and public rhetoric that there is an ever-present possibility that foreigners might seek to enter the United States in order to commit acts of terrorism. Moreover, this discourse strongly articulates the need to safeguard the homeland against the threat of terrorism. Notably, the attitude of protecting the homeland has significantly influenced the governing of immigration: although migrants rarely have any connection to terrorism, they have generally come to be seen as threats to the security of the nation. National security thus involves not only preventing terrorist attacks, but also mitigating the dangers posed by "illegal" and other immigrants. In the contemporary context, then, the powerful rhetoric of security has come to overlay the merger of criminal and immigration law.

SUGGESTIONS FOR FURTHER READING

Chacón, Jennifer M. 2009. "Managing Migration Through Crime." *Columbia Law Review Sidebar* 109: 135–148.

Coleman, Mathew. 2008. "Between Public Policy and Foreign Policy: U.S. Immigration Law Reform and the Undocumented Migrant." *Urban Geography* 29 (1): 4–28.

Eagly, Ingrid V. 2010. "Prosecuting Immigration." *Northwestern University Law Review* 104 (4): 1281–1359.

Hines, Barbara. 2006. "An Overview of U.S. Immigration Law and Policy Since 9/11." *Texas Hispanic Journal of Law and Policy* 12 (1): 9–28.

Hing, Bill Ong. 2004. *Defining American Through Immigration Policy*. Philadelphia: Temple University Press.

Johnson, Kevin R. 2009. "The Intersection of Race and Class in U.S. Immigration Law and Enforcement." *Law and Contemporary Problems* 72: 1–35.

Kanstroom, Daniel. 2004. "Criminalizing the Undocumented: Ironic Boundaries of Post-September 11th 'Pale of Law.'" *North Carolina Journal of International Law and Commercial Regulation* 29: 639–670.

Legomsky, Stephen H. 2007. "The New Path of Immigration Law: Asymmetric Incorporation of Criminal Justice Norms." *Washington and Lee Law Review* 64: 469–528.

Miller, Teresa A. 2003. "Citizenship and Severity: Recent Immigration Reforms and the New Penology." *Georgetown Immigration Law Journal* 17: 611–666.

———. 2005. "Blurring the Boundaries Between Immigration and Crime Control After September 11th." *Boston College Third World Law Journal* 25: 81–123.

Stumpf, Juliet. 2009. "Fitting Punishment." *Washington and Lee Law Review* 66: 1683–1741.

Welch, Michael. 2003. "Ironies of Social Control and the Criminalization of Immigrants." *Crime, Law and Social Change* 39: 319–337.

1 THE LEGAL PRODUCTION OF MEXICAN/MIGRANT "ILLEGALITY"

Nicholas De Genova

Mexican migration to the United States is distinguished by a seeming paradox that is seldom examined: while no other country has supplied nearly as many migrants to the US as has Mexico since 1965, virtually all major changes in US immigration law during this period have created ever more severe restrictions on the conditions of "legal" migration from Mexico. Indeed, this seeming paradox presents itself in a double sense: on the one hand, apparently liberalizing immigration laws have in fact concealed significantly restrictive features, especially for Mexicans; on the other hand, ostensibly restrictive immigration laws purportedly intended to deter migration have nonetheless been instrumental in sustaining Mexican migration, but only by significantly restructuring its legal status as undocumented. Beginning in the 1960s, precisely when Mexican migration escalated dramatically—and ever since—persistent revisions in the law have effectively foreclosed the viable possibilities for the great majority who would migrate from Mexico to do so in accord with the law, and thus have played an instrumental role in the production of a legally vulnerable undocumented workforce of "illegal aliens."

This study elaborates on the historical specificity of contemporary Mexican migration to the US as it has come to be located in the legal (political) economy of the US nation-state, and thereby constituted as an object of the law, especially since 1965. More precisely, this chapter interrogates the history of changes in US immigration law through the specific lens of how these revisions have had a distinct impact upon Mexicans in particular. Only in light of this sociolegal history does it become possible to sustain a critical perspective that is not complicit in the naturalization of Mexican migrants' "illegality" as a mere fact of life, the presumably transparent consequence of unauthorized border crossing or some other violation of immigration law.[1] Indeed, in order to sustain an emphatic concern to de-naturalize

Nicholas De Genova is senior lecturer in anthropology at Goldsmiths, University of London.

Reprinted with permission of Palgrave MacMillan, from "The Legal Production of Mexican/Migrant 'Illegality,'" *Latino Studies* 2: 160–185 by Nicholas De Genova. Copyright © 2004 by Palgrave MacMillan.

1. The category "migrant" should not be confused with the more precise term "migratory"; rather, "migrant" is intended here to serve as a category of analysis that disrupts the implicit teleology of the more conventional term "immigrant," which is posited always from the standpoint of the "immigrant-receiving" US nation-state (cf. De Genova, 2005).

the reification of this distinction, I deploy quotes throughout this chapter, wherever the terms "legal" or "illegal" modify migration or migrants.

In addition to simply designating a juridical status in relation to the US nation-state and its laws of immigration, naturalization, and citizenship, migrant "illegality" signals a specifically *spatialized* sociopolitical condition. "Illegality" is lived through a palpable sense of deportability—the possibility of deportation, which is to say, the possibility of being removed from the space of the US nation-state. The legal production of "illegality" provides an apparatus for sustaining Mexican migrants' vulnerability and tractability—as workers—whose labor-power, inasmuch as it is deportable, becomes an eminently disposable commodity. Deportability is decisive in the legal production of Mexican/migrant "illegality" and the militarized policing of the US-Mexico border, however, only insofar as some are deported in order that most may ultimately remain (*un*deported)—as workers, whose particular migrant status has been rendered "illegal." Thus, in the everyday life of Mexican migrants in innumerable places throughout the US, "illegality" reproduces the practical repercussions of the physical border between the US and Mexico across which undocumented migration is constituted. In this important sense, migrant "illegality" is a spatialized social condition that is inseparable from the particular ways that Mexican migrants are likewise racialized as "illegal aliens"—invasive violators of the law, incorrigible "foreigners," subverting the integrity of "the nation" and its sovereignty from *within* the space of the US nation-state. Thus, as a simultaneously spatialized and racialized social condition, migrant "illegality" is also a central feature of the ways that "Mexican"-ness is thereby reconfigured in *racialized* relation to the hegemonic "national" identity of "American"-ness (De Genova, 2005). Although it is beyond the scope of this chapter, it is nevertheless crucial to locate these conjunctures of race, space, and "illegality" in terms of an earlier history of the intersections of race and citizenship. That history is chiefly distinguished, on the one hand, by the broader historical formulation of white supremacy in relation to "immigration" and, on the other, by the more specific legacy of warfare and conquest in what would come to be called "the American Southwest," culminating in the Treaty of Guadalupe Hidalgo of 1848, which occasioned the first historical deliberations in the US over questions concerning the citizenship and nationality of Mexicans.

THE "REVOLVING DOOR" AND THE
MAKING OF A TRANSNATIONAL HISTORY

Originating in the shared, albeit unequal, history of invasion and war by which roughly half of Mexico's territory came to be conquered and colonized by the US nation-state, the newly established border long went virtually unregulated and movement across it went largely unhindered. During the latter decades of the 19th century, as a regional political economy took shape in what was now the US Southwest, mining, railroads, ranching, and agriculture relied extensively upon the active recruitment of Mexican labor (Acuña, 1981). There was widespread acknowledgment that Mexicans were encouraged to move freely across the border and, in effect, come to work without any official authorization or documents (Samora, 1971; García, 1980).

After decades of enthusiastically recruiting Chinese migrant labor, among the very first actual US immigration laws was the Chinese Exclusion Act of 1882. So began an era of immigration regulation that sought to exclude whole groups even from entry into the country, solely on the basis of race or nationality. Eventually, with the passage of the Immigration Act of 1917, an "All-Asia Barred Zone" was instituted, prohibiting migration from all of Asia (Hing, 1993). In the wake of repeated restrictions against "Asiatics," Mexican migrant labor became an indispensable necessity for capital accumulation in the region. During and after the years of the Mexican Revolution and World War I, from 1910 to 1930, approximately one-tenth of Mexico's total population relocated north of the border, partly owing to social disruptions and dislocations within Mexico during this period of political upheaval, but principally driven and often directly orchestrated by labor demand in new industries and agriculture in the US (cf. Cardoso, 1980).

During this same era, a dramatically restrictive system of national-origins immigration quotas was formulated for European migration and put in place through the passage of the Quota Law of 1921, and then further amplified by the Immigration Act of 1924 (also known as the Johnson-Reed Act). The 1924 law's national-origins system limited migration based on a convoluted formula that made unequal numerical allotments for immigrant visas, on a country-by-country basis. In effect, this regulatory apparatus had confined migration from the entire Eastern Hemisphere to approximately 150,000 annually; within that ceiling, it had guaranteed that roughly 85% of the allotments were reserved for migrants from northwestern European origins (Reimers, 1985 [1992]). Drawing upon 42 volumes (published in 1910 and 1911 by the US Immigration Commission) that compiled "findings" concerning the "racial" composition and "quality" of the US population, the 1924 Immigration Act codified the gamut of popular prejudices about greater and lesser inherent degrees of "assimilability" among variously racialized and nationally stigmatized migrant groups. The *Congressional Record* bears ample testimony to the avowed preoccupation with maintaining the "white"/"Caucasian" racial purity of "American" national identity—"an unmistakable declaration of white immigration policy" (Hutchinson, 1981, 167). Remarkably, in spite of the vociferous objections of some of the most vitriolic nativists and, more importantly, as a testament to the utter dependency of employers upon Mexican/migrant labor, particularly in the Southwest, migration from the countries of the Western Hemisphere— Mexico foremost among them—was left absolutely unrestricted by any numerical quotas.

It is revealing that the US Border Patrol, from 1924—when it was first created—until 1940, operated under the auspices of the Department of Labor. By the late 1920s, the Border Patrol had very quickly assumed its distinctive role as a special police force for the repression of Mexican workers in the US (Ngai, 2004). Selective enforcement of the law—coordinated with seasonal labor demand by US employers—instituted a "revolving door" policy, whereby mass deportations would be concurrent with an overall, large-scale importation of Mexican migrant labor (Cockcroft, 1986). Although there were no *quantitative* restrictions (numerical quotas) on "legal" Mexican migration until 1965, Mexican migrants could nonetheless be conveniently denied entry into the US, or deported from it, on the basis of a selective enforcement of *qualitative* features of immigration law, beginning at least as early as the 1920s.

During this era, the regulatory and disciplinary role of deportation operated against Mexican migrants on the basis of rules and regulations governing *who* would be allowed to migrate, with *what* characteristics, *how* they did so, as well as *how* they conducted themselves once they had already entered the country. Thus, attempted entry could be refused on the grounds of a variety of infractions: a failure upon entry to pay a required immigrant head tax and a fee for the visa itself, or perceived "illiteracy," or a presumed liability to become a "public charge" (due to having no prearranged employment), or on the other hand, violation of prohibitions against contracted labor (due to having pre-arranged employment through labor recruitment). Likewise, Mexican workers could be subsequently deported if they could not verify that they held valid work visas or could otherwise be found to have evaded inspection, or if they could be found to have become "public charges" (retroactively enabling the judgment of a prior condition of "liability"), or to have violated US laws, or to have engaged in acts that could be construed as "anarchist" or "seditionist." All of these violations of the qualitative features of the law rendered deportation a crucial mechanism of labor discipline and subjugation, not only coordinated with the vicissitudes of the labor market but also for the purposes of counteracting union organizing among Mexican/migrant workers (cf. Acuña, 1981; Gómez-Quiñones, 1994).

With the advent of the Great Depression of the 1930s, however, the more plainly racist character of Mexican illegalization and deportability became abundantly manifest. Mexican migrants and US-born Mexican citizens alike were systematically excluded from employment and economic relief, which were declared the exclusive preserve of "Americans," who were presumed to be more "deserving." These abuses culminated in the forcible mass-deportation of at least 415,000 Mexican migrants, as well as many of their US-citizen children, and the "voluntary" repatriation of 85,000 more (Hoffman, 1974). Notably, Mexicans were expelled with no regard to legal residence or US citizenship or even birth in the US—simply for being "Mexicans."

In the face of the renewed labor shortages caused by US involvement in World War II, however, the United States federal government, in a dramatic reversal of the mass deportations of the 1930s, initiated the mass importation that came to be known as the Bracero Program, as an administrative measure to institutionalize and regiment the supply of Mexican/migrant labor for US capitalism (principally for agriculture, but also for the railroads). The Bracero accords were effected unceremoniously by a Special Committee on Importation of Mexican Labor (formed by the US Immigration Service, the War Manpower Commission, and the Departments of State, Labor, and Agriculture) through a bilateral agreement with Mexico. Predictably, the US Department of Agriculture was granted primary authority over the program. Ostensibly an emergency wartime measure at its inception in 1942 (Public Law 45), the program was repeatedly renewed and dramatically expanded until its termination in 1964. This legalized importation of Mexican labor meant that migrant workers, once contracted, essentially became a captive workforce under the jurisdiction of the US federal government, and thus a guarantee to US employers of unlimited "cheap" labor. In addition to this protracted contract-labor migration, however, the Bracero Program facilitated undocumented migration at levels that far surpassed the numbers of "legal" braceros—both through the development of a migration infrastructure and through employers' encouragement of braceros to overstay the limited tenure of their contracts. Preferring the undocumented workers, employers could evade the bond and contracting fees, minimum employment periods, fixed wages, and other safeguards required in employing braceros (Galarza, 1964). Indeed, as early as 1949, US employers and labor recruiters were assisted with instantaneous legalization procedures for undocumented workers, known as "drying out wetbacks" (Calavita, 1992). Some have estimated that four undocumented migrants entered the US from Mexico for every documented bracero.[2] Early in 1954, in an affront to the Mexican government's negotiators' pleas for a fixed minimum wage for braceros, the US Congress authorized the Department of Labor to unilaterally recruit Mexican workers, and the Border Patrol itself opened the border and actively recruited undocumented migrants (Galarza, 1964; Cockcroft, 1986). This period of official "open border" soon culminated, predictably in accord with the "revolving door" strategy, in the 1954–1955 expulsion of at least 2.9 million "illegal" Mexican/migrant workers under the militarized dragnet and nativist hysteria of "Operation Wetback" (García, 1980). Thus, the Bracero years were distinguished not only by expanded legal migration through contract labor, but also by the federal facilitation of undocumented migration and the provision of ample opportunities for legalization, simultaneously coupled with considerable repression and mass deportations.

LEGISLATING MEXICAN "ILLEGALITY"

Prior to 1965, as already suggested, there were absolutely no *quantitative* restrictions on "legal" migration from Mexico imposed at the level of statute, and none had ever existed. There had literally never before been any *numerical* quota legislated to limit migration from Mexico. This was true for all of the countries of the Western Hemisphere (excluding colonies), and so has implications for nearly all Latino groups (with Puerto Ricans as the very important exception), but none of these countries has ever had numbers of migrants at all comparable to those originating from Mexico. Furthermore, the reformulation of the legal specificities of "illegality" in 1965 and thereafter, it bears repeating, transpired in the midst of an enthusiastic and virtually unrelenting *im*portation of Mexican/migrant labor (increasingly impervious even to the ebbs and flows of unemployment rates). The end of the Bracero Program in 1964 was an immediate and decisive prelude to the landmark reconfiguration of US immigration law in 1965. Indeed, anticipating unemployment pressures due to the end of the Bracero Program, the Mexican government simultaneously introduced its Border Industrialization Program, enabling US-owned, labor-intensive assembly plants (maquiladoras) to operate in a virtual free-trade zone along the US border. As a result, migration within Mexico to the border region accelerated. By 1974, one-third of the population of Mexico's border states was comprised of people who had already migrated from elsewhere, and a mere 3% of them were employed in the maquiladoras (Cockcroft,

2. Approximately 4.8 million contracts were issued to Mexican workers for employment as braceros over the course of the program's 22 years, and during that same period there were more than 5 million apprehensions of undocumented Mexican migrants (Samora, 1971). Both figures include redundancies and thus are not indicative of absolute numbers, but they reveal nonetheless a more general complementarity between contracted and undocumented flows.

1986, 109). Thus, a long established, well organized, deeply entrenched, increasingly diversified, and continuously rising stream of Mexican migration to the US had already been accelerating prior to 1965, and circumstances in the region that might induce subsequent migration to the US simply continued to intensify. As a consequence of the successive changes in US immigration law since 1965, however, previously unknown *quantitative* restrictions—and specifically, the apparently uniform application of numerical quotas to historically distinct and substantially incommensurable migrations—became central to an unprecedented, expanded, and protracted production of a more rigid, categorical "illegality," for Mexican/migrant workers in particular, than had ever existed previously.

An ever-growing, already significant, and potentially indispensable segment of the working class within the space of the US nation-state (both in agriculture and in numerous metropolitan areas), Mexican/migrant labor is ubiquitously stigmatized as "illegal," subjected to excessive and extraordinary forms of policing, denied fundamental human rights, and thus is consigned to an always uncertain social predicament, often with little or no recourse to any semblance of protection from the law. Since the 1960s, Mexico has furnished 7.5–8.4 million ("legal" as well as undocumented) migrants who currently reside in the United States (in addition to unnumbered seasonal and short-term migrants). Approximately half of them (49.3%) are estimated to have arrived only during the decade of the 1990s (Logan, 2002). By May 2002, based on estimates calculated from the 2000 Census, researchers have suggested that 4.7 million of the Mexican/migrant total were undocumented, of whom as many as 85% had arrived in the US only during the 1990s (Passel, 2002). No other country has supplied even comparable numbers; indeed, by 2000, Mexican migrants alone constituted nearly 28% of the total "foreign-born" population in the US. It may seem paradoxical, then, that virtually all major changes in the quantitative features of US immigration law during this period have created ever more severe restrictions on the conditions of possibility for "legal" migration from Mexico. Indeed, precisely because no other country has supplied comparable numbers of migrants to the US during this time period, all of the repercussions of the uniform numerical restrictions introduced by these legislative revisions have weighed disproportionately upon Mexican migration in particular. This legal history, therefore, constitutes a defining aspect of the historical specificity— indeed, the effective singularity—of contemporary Mexican migration to the US.

To a great extent, the seeming enigma derives from the fact that the very character of migrant "illegality" for Mexicans (as well as other migrations within the Western Hemisphere) was reconfigured by what was, in many respects, genuinely a watershed "liberalization" of immigration policy in 1965. The Hart-Celler Act of 1965, which entailed amendments to the Immigration and Nationality Act (INA) of 1952, comprised an ostensibly egalitarian legislation. The monumental overhaul of US immigration law in 1965 dismantled the US nation-state's openly racist formulation of immigration control. The reform of immigration law in 1965 dramatically reversed the explicitly racist exclusion against Asian migrations, which had been in effect and only minimally mitigated since 1917 (or, in the case of the Chinese, since 1882). Likewise, the 1965 amendments abolished the draconian system of national-origins quotas for the countries of Europe, first enacted in 1921 and amplified in 1924.

With the end of the national-origins quota system, predictably, the 1965 amendments have been typically celebrated as a liberal reform, and US immigration policy suddenly appeared to be chiefly distinguished by a broad inclusiveness, but with respect to Mexico, the outcome was distinctly and unequivocally restrictive. These same "liberal" revisions (taking effect in 1968) established for the first time in US history an annual numerical quota to restrict "legal" migration from the Western Hemisphere. Indeed, the new cap imposed for the Western Hemisphere came about as a compromise with those who sought to maintain the national-origins quota system, whom Aristide Zolberg (1990, 321) has described as "traditional restrictionists, who sought to deter immigration of blacks from the West Indies and 'browns' from south of the border more generally." However, David Reimers (1985 [1992, 79]) notes that few expressed blatantly racist attitudes, and the restriction for the Americas was notably defended in a more apparently liberal idiom, out of a concern with "fairness" for "our traditional friends and allies in Western Europe" (quoted on p. 77). Although hundreds of thousands already migrated from Mexico annually, and the number of apprehensions by the Immigration and Naturalization Service (INS) of "deportable alien" Mexicans was itself already 151,000 during the year prior to the enactment of the new quota, now no more than 120,000 "legal" migrants (excluding quota exemptions) would be permitted from the entirety of the Western Hemisphere. Notably, the Eastern Hemisphere quota—170,000— was higher than the 120,000 cap set for the Western Hemisphere, but the individual countries of the Eastern Hemisphere were each limited to a maximum of 20,000, whereas the quota for the Western Hemisphere was available to any of the countries of the Americas on a first-come, first-served basis, subject to certification by the Department of Labor. Nevertheless, although no other country in the world was sending numbers of migrants at all comparable to the level of Mexican migration—and this has remained true, consistently, ever since—the numerical quota for "legal" migrants within the entire Western Hemisphere (i.e., the maximum quota within which Mexicans would have to operate) was now restricted to a level far below actual and already known numbers for migration from Mexico.

The 1965 amendments have also been characterized as expansively liberal in their provisions for migrant family reunification. For both Hemispheres, some family members would be considered "exempt" from the quota restrictions, and thus could migrate without being counted against the quotas. These "quota exemptions" for family reunification were restricted to the spouses, unmarried minor children, and parents of adult US *citizens* (usually migrants, but only those who had already been naturalized). Counted within the Western Hemisphere quota (i.e., non-exempt), notably, the spouses, unmarried minor children, and parents of *permanent residents*, as well as preference for professionals and skilled non-professionals with labor certifications from the Department of Labor, were variously privileged through a system of ranked preferences. The respective systems of preferences within the two quotas, however, were markedly different. For the Eastern Hemisphere, in addition to the explicit ranked preferences included under the Western Hemisphere quota for the relatives of *permanent residents*, there were also provisions for the unmarried *adult* children, married children (adult or minor), and also brothers and sisters (adult or minor) of US *citizens*. Here again, the specifications for "legal" migration from the Eastern Hemisphere were clearly different and, one might say, more liberal. Furthermore, they could be interpreted to have provided additional advantages (hence, greater incentives) for naturalized US citizenship, while those for the Western Hemisphere were considerably more circumscribed and provided no such exceptional benefits for naturalization. Thus, the unequal provisions for family reunification under the two distinct hemispheric quotas imposed generally disadvantageous limitations for Western Hemisphere migrations, and in fact did so disproportionately to Mexican migration in particular. Likewise, although the provisions for quota-exempt family reunification were equal for both Hemispheres, these exemptions privileged the kin of US citizens (usually naturalized migrants), and so also disadvantaged Mexico because of the pronounced disinclination of most Mexican migrants, historically, to naturalize as US citizens (Sánchez, 1993). In short, the consequences of the new numerical restrictions would weigh disproportionately, almost singularly, on migration from Mexico—above all because of Mexico's overwhelming numerical preponderance among *all* migrations—and furthermore, even the new law's more expansive and apparently liberal provisions for family unification were likewise structured in a manner that made them less easily applicable to or accessible by Mexicans.

There is still another feature of the 1965 legislation that had an exceptionally important consequence for undocumented Mexican migrants. A preference category for legal migration within the annual quota was established for migrants from the Western Hemisphere, but not the Eastern Hemisphere, who were the parents of US-citizen *minors*. In other words, a kind of legalization procedure was available to undocumented Western Hemisphere migrants who were the parents of children born in the US (hence, US citizens). In effect, a baby born in the US to an undocumented Mexican migrant served to provide the parents with a virtual apprenticeship for eventual legal residency. Thus, in a manner analogous to earlier "drying-out" procedures, Mexican migrants would be required to serve a term as undocumented workers but then could eventually be "legalized," contingent upon bearing a child in the US.[3]

Especially following more than twenty years of enthusiastic legal contract-labor importation from Mexico, orchestrated by the US federal government through the Bracero Program, an already established influx of Mexican migrants to the US was accelerating prior to 1965. With elaborate migration networks and extensive historical ties already well established, Mexicans continued to migrate, but given the severe restrictions legislated in 1965 (implemented in 1968), ever-greater numbers of Mexicans who were already migrating increasingly had no alternative than to come as undocumented workers, relegated to an indefinite condition of "illegality." From 1968 onward, INS apprehensions of "deportable" Mexican nationals skyrocketed annually, leaping 40% in the first year. Although these apprehension statistics are never reliable indicators of the actual numbers of undocumented migrants, they clearly reveal a pattern of policing that was critical for the perpetuation of the "revolving door" policy: the disproportionate majority of INS apprehensions were directed at surreptitious entries along the Mexican border, and this was increasingly so. In 1973, for instance, the INS reported that Mexicans literally comprised 99% of all "deportable aliens" who had entered surreptitiously and were apprehended (cf. Cárdenas, 1975, 86).

3. This particular "drying-out" procedure was ultimately available to the undocumented parents of babies born in the US between July 1, 1968, and December 31, 1976, due to the elimination of this clause by the 1976 amendments to the INA.

While the total number of apprehensions for all other nationalities from the rest of the world (combined) remained consistently *below* 100,000 annually, the apprehensions of Mexicans rose steadily from 151,000 in 1968 to 781,000 in 1976, when migration was, once again, still more severely restricted. These persistent enforcement practices, and the statistics they produce, have made an extraordinary contribution to the pervasive fallacy that Mexicans account for virtually all "illegal aliens." This effective equation of "illegal immigration" with unauthorized border-crossing, furthermore, has served to continuously re-stage the US–Mexico border in particular as the theater of an enforcement "crisis," and thus constantly re-renders "Mexican" as the distinctive national name for migrant "illegality" (see Chavez, this volume).

Immigration law, of course, was not the only thing that was changing in 1965. It has been widely recognized that the sweeping 1965 revisions of immigration policy originated from a generalized crisis of Cold War-era liberalism, in which US imperialism's own most cherished "democratic" conceits were perpetually challenged. Taking shape in a context of Cold War international relations imperatives, confronted not only with monumental popular struggles over racial oppression at home but also with decolonization and national liberation movements abroad, US immigration policy was redesigned in 1965 explicitly to rescind the most glaringly discriminatory features of existing law. This crisis was exacerbated by the rising combativeness, in particular, of the black struggle for "civil rights," which is to say, the mass movement of African Americans to demand their rights of *citizenship*. The Civil Rights struggle was increasingly articulated as a militant repudiation of the "second-class" (ostensible) citizenship conferred upon African Americans since the adoption of the Fourteenth Amendment following the Civil War. This intransigent movement forcefully exposed and articulately denounced the treacherous fact of racially subordinated citizenship. Furthermore, the end of the Bracero Program had been principally accomplished through the restrictionist efforts of organized labor, especially on the part of the predominantly Chicano and Filipino farmworkers movement. Thus, the specific historical conjuncture from which the 1965 amendments emerged was deeply characterized by political crises that manifested themselves as both domestic and international insurgencies of racialized and colonized working peoples. So began a new production of an altogether new kind of "illegality" for migrations within the Western Hemisphere, with inordinately severe consequences for transnationalized Mexican labor migrants in particular—a kind of transnational fix for political crises of labor subordination (cf. De Genova, 2005).

It is particularly revealing to note here that the explicit topic of "illegal immigration" had been almost entirely absent from the legislative debate leading to the 1965 law. David Reimers calls attention to the irony that the US Congress "paid little attention to undocumented immigrants while reforming immigration policy in 1965," but "as early as 1969"—that is, the first year after the 1965 law had taken effect!—"Congress began to investigate the increase in illegal immigration along the Mexican border" (1985 [1992, 207–08]). By 1976, however, legislative debate and further revisions in the law had succeeded to produce "illegal immigration" as a whole new object within the economy of legal meanings in the US Immigration regime—the explicit "problem" toward which most of the major subsequent changes in immigration policy have been at least partly directed.

In 1976, new amendments to the INA were enacted (Public Law 94–571; 90 Stat. 2703), this time within days of the national elections in the US. The 1976 revisions summarily eliminated the legalization provision described above, by extending to the Western Hemisphere a system of statutory preferences for legal migration that more closely resembled that which had previously been established for the Eastern Hemisphere. More importantly, the 1976 statutes imposed a fixed national quota for every individual country in the Western Hemisphere for the first time, now establishing a maximum number (excluding quota exemptions) of 20,000 legal migrants a year, for every country in the world—again, with an incomparably dramatic, singularly disproportionate impact on Mexico in particular. Once again (and also in the liberal idiom of "fairness"), immigration law was still more dramatically revised, restricting "legal" (non-exempt) migration from Mexico to a meager 20,000 a year.[4] Then again, after legislation in 1978 (Public Law 95–412; 92 Stat. 907) abolished the separate hemispheric quotas, and established a unified worldwide maximum annual immigration quota of 290,000, the Refugee Act of 1980 further reduced that maximum global quota to 270,000, and thereby diminished the national quotas of 20,000 per country to an even smaller annual maximum of 18,200 "legal" migrants (excluding quota exemptions). In the space of less than 12 years, therefore, from July 1, 1968 (when the 1965 amendments went into effect), until the 1980 amendments became operative, US immigration law had been radically reconfigured for Mexicans. Beginning with almost unlimited possibilities for "legal" migration from Mexico (literally no numerical restrictions, tempered only by qualitative preconditions that, in practice, had often been overlooked altogether), the law had now severely restricted Mexico to an annual quota of 18,200 non-exempt "legal" migrants (as well as a strict system of qualitative preferences among quota exemptions, with weighted allocations for each preference). At a time when there were (conservatively) well over a million Mexican migrants coming to work in the US each year, the overwhelming majority would have no option but to do so "illegally."

There is nothing matter-of-fact, therefore, about the "illegality" of undocumented migrants. "Illegality" (in its contemporary configuration) is the product of U.S. immigration law—not merely in the abstract sense that without the law nothing could be construed to be outside of the law, nor simply in the generic sense that immigration law constructs, differentiates, and ranks various categories of "aliens," but in the more profound sense that the history of deliberate interventions beginning in 1965 that have revised and reformulated the law has entailed an active process of inclusion through illegalization (cf. Calavita, 1982, 13; Hagan, 1994, 82; Coutin, 2000). Indeed, the legal production of "illegality" has made an object of Mexican migration in particular, in ways both historically unprecedented and disproportionately deleterious.

A new kind of landmark in the history of US immigration law was achieved with the passage in 1986 of the Immigration Reform and Control Act (IRCA) because its principal explicit preoccupation was undocumented immigration. IRCA was finally adopted as the culmination of years of recommendations (first by the Select Commission on Immigration and Refugee Policy established by Congress in 1978 and then by a presidential cabinet-level

---

4. Mexico was immediately backlogged, with 60,000 applicants for 20,000 slots, and the backlog became more severe every year thereafter.

task force in 1981) and repeated efforts over four years by the two houses of Congress to pass a variety of bills aimed at revisions in immigration policy. The 1986 amendments provided for a selective "amnesty" and adjustment of the immigration status of some undocumented migrants.[5] Once again, the law instituted a legalization procedure for those undocumented workers who had reliably (and without evident interruption) served their apprenticeships in "illegality," while intensifying the legal vulnerability of others. Indeed, IRCA foreclosed almost all options of legalization for those who did not qualify, and for all who would arrive thereafter. Furthermore, INS decisions concerning the implementation of IRCA legalization procedures contributed to the pervasive equation of "illegal alien" with "Mexican." The INS persistently battled in the courts to reserve the amnesty for those whose undocumented status began with having "entered without inspection" (i.e., surreptitious border-crossers), rather than those who had overstayed their visas. In short, the INS seemed intent to exclude from the amnesty those applicants who did not match the profile of "illegality" most typical of undocumented Mexican migrants (González Baker, 1997, 11–12). As a predictable result, whereas pre-implementation estimates had figured Mexicans to be roughly half of the total number of undocumented migrants, Mexican migrants accounted for 70% of the total pool of legalization applicants, and even higher proportions in California, Illinois, and Texas, the areas of highest Mexican/migrant concentration (ibid., 13).

The Immigration Reform and Control Act of 1986 also established for the first time federal sanctions against employers who knowingly hired undocumented workers (see Bacon and Hing, this volume). Nevertheless, the law established an "affirmative defense" for all employers who could demonstrate that they had complied with the verification procedure. Simply by having filled out and kept on file a routine form attesting to the document check, without any requirement that they determine the legitimacy of documents presented in that verification process, employers would be immune from any penalty. What this meant in practice is that the employer sanctions provisions generated a flourishing industry in fraudulent documents, which merely imposed further expenses and greater legal liabilities upon the migrant workers themselves, while supplying an almost universal protection for employers (cf. Chávez, 1992, 169–71; Mahler, 1995, 159–87; Coutin, 2000, 49–77). Likewise, in light of the immensely profitable character of exploiting the legally vulnerable (hence, "cheap") labor of undocumented workers, the schedule of financial penalties imposed by IRCA simply amounted to a rather negligible operating cost for an employer found to be in violation of the law. Given that the employer sanctions would require a heightening of INS raids on workplaces, inspectors were required to give employers a three-day warning prior to inspections of their hiring records, in order to make it "pragmatically easy" for employers to comply with the letter of the law (Calavita, 1992, 169). Furthermore, in order to avoid fines associated with these sanctions, employers would typically fire or temporarily discharge workers known to be undocumented prior to a raid.

---

5. Undocumented agricultural workers could adjust their status to temporary resident simply by proving that they had worked in perishable agriculture for at least 90 days during that prior year alone, and could apply for permanent resident status after a year or two, depending on how long they had been employed in agriculture. Otherwise, those who could establish that they had resided continuously in the US since before January 1, 1982, were eligible for temporary resident status, and after a period of 18 months, would be eligible to apply for permanent resident status.

Thus, these provisions primarily served to introduce greater instability into the labor-market experiences of undocumented migrants, and thereby instituted an internal "revolving door." What were ostensibly "employer sanctions," then, actually functioned to aggravate the migrants' conditions of vulnerability and imposed new penalties upon the undocumented workers themselves.

The Immigration Act of 1990 was not primarily directed at undocumented migration, but it did nonetheless introduce new regulations that increased the stakes of "illegality." Specifically, this legislation expanded the grounds for the deportation of undocumented migrants, introduced new punitive sanctions, and curtailed due-process rights in deportation proceedings. Among other stipulations,[6] the 1990 legislation also created a special visa program which sought, in the name of "diversity," to encourage more migration from countries that had been sending relatively low numbers of migrants (clearly not Mexico!). In addition, the 1990 legislation restricted jurisdiction over the naturalization of migrants petitioning to become US citizens, rescinding a practice that had been in place since 1795 permitting the courts to award citizenship, and now confining this authority exclusively to the federal office of the Attorney General.

The Illegal Immigration Reform and Immigrant Responsibility Act of 1996 was, quite simply, the most punitive legislation to date concerning undocumented migration in particular (cf. Fragomen, 1997, 438; see also Stumpf, this volume; Chacón, this volume). It included extensive provisions for criminalizing, apprehending, detaining, fining, deporting, and also imprisoning migrants for a wide array of "infractions" and significantly broadened and elaborated the *qualitative* scope of the law's production of "illegality" for undocumented migrants and others associated with them. It also barred undocumented migrants from receiving a variety of social security benefits and federal student financial aid. In fact, this so-called immigration reform (signed September 30, 1996) was heralded by extensive anti-immigrant stipulations in the Antiterrorism and Effective Death Penalty Act—AEDPA (signed into law on April 24, 1996), as well as in the so-called Welfare Reform Act, passed as the Personal Responsibility and Work Opportunity Reconciliation Act (signed August 22, 1996). The AEDPA entailed an "unprecedented restriction of the constitutional rights and judicial resources traditionally afforded to legal resident aliens" (Solbakken, 1997, 1382). The Welfare Reform Act enacted dramatically more stringent and prolonged restrictions on the eligibility of the great majority of "legal" immigrants for virtually all benefits available under federal law, and also authorized states to similarly restrict benefits programs. Without belaboring the extensive details of these acts, which did not otherwise introduce new *quantitative* restrictions, it will suffice to say that their expansive provisions (concerned primarily with enforcement and penalties for undocumented presence) were truly unprecedented in the severity with which they broadened the purview and intensified the ramifications of the legal production of migrant "illegality." By penalizing access to public services and social welfare benefits, these legislations especially targeted undocumented migrant women (and their children), who had come to be equated with Mexican/Latino long-term settlement, families, reproduction, and thus the dramatic growth of a "minority group" (Coutin and

6. The 1990 law increased the global annual quota for non-exempt migration and also significantly restructured the preference system.

Chock, 1995). Given the already well-entrenched practices that focus enforcement against undocumented migration disproportionately upon Mexican migrants in particular, there can be little doubt that these acts, at least prior to September 11, 2001, nonetheless weighed inordinately upon Mexicans as a group. Indeed, the language of the 1996 legislation, with regard to enforcement, was replete with references to "the" border, a telltale signal that could only portend a further disciplining of Mexican migration in particular.

THE BORDER SPECTACLE

Mexican migration in particular has been rendered synonymous with the US nation-state's purported "loss of control" of its borders, and has supplied the preeminent pretext for what has in fact been a continuous intensification of increasingly militarized control (Andreas, 2000; Nevins, 2002; see also Chavez, this volume). And it is precisely "the Border" that provides the exemplary theater for staging the spectacle of "the illegal alien" that the law produces. Indeed, "illegality" looks most like a positive transgression—and can thereby be equated with the behavior of Mexican migrants rather than the instrumental action of immigration law—precisely when it is subjected to policing at the US–Mexico border. The elusiveness of the law, and its relative invisibility in producing "illegality," requires this spectacle of "enforcement" at the border, precisely because it renders a racialized Mexican/migrant "illegality" visible, and lends it the commonsensical air of a "natural" fact.

The operation of the "revolving door" at the border that is necessary to sustain the "illegality" effect always combines an increasingly militarized spectacle of apprehensions, detentions, and deportations—as well as increasingly perilous and sometimes deadly circumstances required to evade detection (see Doty, this volume)—with the banality of a virtually permanent importation of undocumented migrant labor. This seeming paradox is commonly evoked in many Mexican (especially male) migrants' border-crossing narratives, in which stories of great hardship are often followed by accounts of quite easy passage (Chávez, 1992; De Genova, 2005). Indeed, US immigration enforcement efforts throughout the 20th century consistently targeted the US–Mexico border disproportionately, sustaining a zone of relatively high tolerance within the interior (Chávez, 1992). The legal production of Mexican/migrant "illegality" requires the spectacle of enforcement at the US–Mexico border in order for the spatialized difference between the nation-states of the US and Mexico to be enduringly inscribed upon Mexican migrants in their spatialized (and racialized) status as "illegal aliens." The vectors of race and space, likewise, are both crucial in the constitution of the class specificity of Mexican labor migration (see Heyman, this volume). It is not at all uncommon, therefore, for Mexican migrants to conclude their border-crossing narratives, tellingly, with remarks about low wages. These narratives of the adventures, mishaps, as well as genuine calamities of border crossing seem to be almost inevitably punctuated with accounts of life in the US that are singularly distinguished by arduous travail and abundant exploitation (De Genova, 2005; cf. Mahler, 1995).

The "enforcement" spectacle at the border, however, is not the only way that Mexican/migrant "illegality" generates and sustains a kind of border spectacle in everyday life. The "illegality" effect of protracted vulnerability has to be recreated more often than simply on the occasion of crossing the border. Indeed, the 1986 legislation that included the institution (at the federal level) of "employer sanctions" was tantamount to an extension of the "revolving door" to the internal labor market of each workplace where undocumented migrant workers were employed. The policing of public spaces outside of the workplace, likewise, serves to discipline Mexican/migrant workers by surveilling their "illegality," and exacerbating their sense of ever-present vulnerability (Chávez, 1992; Heyman, 1998; De Genova, 2005). The "illegalities" of everyday life are often, literally, instantiated by the lack of various forms of state-issued documentation that sanction one's place within or outside of the strictures of the law (Hagan, 1994; Mahler, 1995; Coutin, 2000; see also Sáenz et al., this volume). The lack of a driver's license, for instance, has typically been presumed by police in much of the US, at least through the 1990s, to automatically indicate a Latino's more generally *undocumented* condition (cf. Mahler, 1995). Indeed, without driver's licenses or automobile insurance cards, undocumented migrants can be readily compelled to pay hundreds of dollars in bribes as a consequence of pervasive and casual police corruption and abuse, on the basis of the cynical presumption that those who are legally vulnerable are therefore easily exploitable. In effect, there is virtually no way for undocumented migrants to not be always already culpable of some kind of legal infraction. This condition ultimately intensifies their subjection to quotidian forms of intimidation and harassment. And it is precisely such forms of everyday "illegality" that confront many undocumented Latino migrants with quite everyday forms of surveillance and repression. There are also those "illegalities," furthermore, that more generally pertain to the heightened policing directed at the bodies, movements, and spaces of the poor, and especially those racialized as nonwhite. Inasmuch as any confrontation with the scrutiny of legal authorities is already tempered by the discipline imposed by their susceptibility for deportation, such mundane forms of harassment likewise serve to relentlessly reinforce Mexican and other Latino undocumented migrants' characteristic vulnerability as a highly exploitable workforce.

Yet the disciplinary operation of an apparatus for the everyday production of migrant "illegality" is never simply reducible to a presumed quest to achieve the putative goal of deportation. It is *deportability*, and not deportation *per se*, that has historically rendered Mexican labor as a distinctly disposable commodity. Here I am emphasizing what have been the real *effects* of this history of revisions in US immigration law. Without engaging in the unwitting apologetics of presumptively characterizing the law's consequences as "unintended" or "unanticipated," and without busying ourselves with conspiratorial guessing games about good or bad "intentions," the challenge of critical inquiry and meaningful social analysis commands that one ask: What indeed do these policies *produce*? Although their argument is insufficiently concerned with the instrumental role of the law in the production of "illegality," Douglas Massey and his research associates have understandably nominated the post-1965 period as "the era of undocumented migration" and even characterize the effective operation of US immigration policy toward Mexico as "a de facto guestworker program" (2002, 41, 45). There of course has never been sufficient funding for US immigration authorities to evacuate the country of undocumented migrants by means of deportations, nor even for the Border Patrol to "hold the line." The Border Patrol has never been equipped to actually keep the undocumented out. At least until the events of September 11, 2001, the very existence of the enforcement branches of the now-defunct INS (and the Border Patrol, in particular) were always premised upon the persistence of undocumented migration and a continued presence of migrants whose undocumented legal status has long been equated with the disposable (deportable), ultimately "temporary" character of the commodity that is their labor-power. In its real effects, then, and regardless of competing political agendas or stated aims, the true social role of much of US immigration law enforcement (and the Border Patrol, in particular) has historically been to maintain and superintend the operation of the border as a "revolving door," simultaneously implicated in importation as much as (in fact, far more than) deportation (Cockcroft, 1986). Sustaining the border's viability as a filter for the unequal transfer of value (Kearney, 1998), such enforcement rituals also perform the spectacle that fetishizes migrant "illegality" as a seemingly objective "thing in itself."

With the advent of the antiterrorism state, the politics of immigration and border enforcement in the US have been profoundly reconfigured under the aegis of a remarkably parochial US nationalism and an unbridled nativism, above all manifest in the complete absorption of the INS into the new Department of Homeland Security (as of March 1, 2003). Nevertheless, this same sociopolitical moment within the US has been distinguished by a deadly eruption of genuinely global imperialist ambition. Thus, it should hardly come as a surprise that, on January 7, 2004, the Bush administration proposed a new scheme for the expressly temporary regularization of undocumented migrant workers' "illegal" status and for the expansion of a bracero-style migrant labor contracting system orchestrated directly by the US state. Such a "legalization" plan aspires only for a more congenial formula by which to sustain the permanent availability of disposable (and still deportable) migrant labor, but under conditions of dramatically enhanced ("legal") regimentation and control (see De Genova 2009). Like all previous forms of migrant "legalization," and indeed, in accord with the larger history of the law's productions and revisions of "illegality" itself, such an immigration "reform" can be forged only through an array of political struggles that are truly transnational in scale, and ultimately have as their stakes the subordination—and insubordination—of labor.

WORKS CITED

Acuña, Rodolfo. 1981. *Occupied America: A History of Chicanos.* Second Edition New York: Harper & Row.

Andreas, Peter. 2000. *Border Games: Policing the U.S.-Mexico Divide.* Ithaca, NY: Cornell University Press.

Calavita, Kitty. 1982. *California's "Employer Sanctions": The Case of the Disappearing Law.* Research Report Series, Number 39. San Diego: Center for U.S.-Mexican Studies, University of California.

Calavita, Kitty. 1992. *Inside the State: The Bracero Program, Immigration, and the I.N.S.* New York: Routledge.

Cárdenas, Gilberto. 1975. United States Immigration Policy Toward Mexico: An Historical Perspective. *Chicano Law Review* 2: 66–89.

Cardoso, Lawrence. 1980. *Mexican Emigration to the United States, 1897–1931.* Tucson: University of Arizona Press.

Chávez, Leo R. 1992. *Shadowed Lives: Undocumented Immigrants in American Society*. Ft. Worth, TX: Harcourt Brace Jovanovich.

Cockcroft, James D. 1986. *Outlaws in the Promised Land: Mexican Immigrant Workers and America's Future*. New York: Grove Press.

Coutin, Susan Bibler. 2000. *Legalizing Moves: Salvadoran Immigrants' Struggle for U.S. Residency*. Ann Arbor: University of Michigan Press.

Coutin, Susan Bibler, and Phyllis Pease Chock. 1995. "Your Friend, the Illegal": Definition and Paradox in Newspaper Accounts of U.S. Immigration Reform. *Identities* 2(1–2): 123–148.

De Genova, Nicholas. 2005. *Working the Boundaries: Race, Space, and "Illegality" in Mexican Chicago*. Durham, NC: Duke University Press.

De Genova, Nicholas. 2009. Conflicts of Mobility, and the Mobility of Conflict: Rightlessness, Presence, Subjectivity, Freedom. *Subjectivity* 29: 445–466.

Fragomen Jr., Austin T. 1997. The Illegal Immigration Reform and Immigrant Responsibility Act of 1996: An Overview. *International Migration Review* 31(2): 438–460.

Galarza, Ernesto. 1964. *Merchants of Labor: The Mexican Bracero Story*. Santa Barbara, CA: McNally and Loftin.

García, Juan Ramon. 1980. *Operation Wetback: The Mass Deportation of Mexican Undocumented Workers in 1954*. Westport, CN: Greenwood Press.

Gómez-Quiñones, Juan. 1994. *Mexican American Labor, 1790–1990*. Albuquerque: University of New Mexico Press.

González Baker, Susan. 1997. The "Amnesty" Aftermath: Current Policy Issues Stemming from the Legalization Programs of the 1986 Immigration Reform and Control Act. *International Migration Review* 31(1): 5–27.

Hagan, Jacqueline Maria. 1994. *Deciding to Be Legal: A Maya Community in Houston*. Philadelphia: Temple University Press.

Heyman, Josiah McC. 1998. State Effects on Labor: The INS and Undocumented Immigrants at the Mexico–United States Border. *Critique of Anthropology* 18(2): 157–180.

Hing, Bill Ong. 1993. *Making and Remaking Asian America Through Immigration Policy, 1850–1990*. Stanford, CA: Stanford University Press.

Hoffman, Abraham. 1974. *Unwanted Mexican Americans in the Great Depression: Repatriation Pressures 1926–1939*. Tucson: University of Arizona Press.

Hutchinson, Edward P. 1981. *Legislative History of American Immigration Policy, 1798–1965*. Philadelphia: University of Pennsylvania Press.

Kearney, Michael. 1998. Peasants in the Fields of Value: Revisiting Rural Class Differentiation in Transnational Perspective. Unpublished manuscript. Department of Anthropology, University of California at Riverside.

Logan, John R. 2002. Hispanic Populations and Their Residential Patterns in the Metropolis. Press Conference Advisory. Lewis Mumford Center for Comparative Urban and Regional Research at the State University of New York at Albany.

Mahler, Sarah J. 1995. *American Dreaming: Immigrant Life on the Margins*. Princeton, NJ: Princeton University Press.

Massey, Douglas S., Jorge Durand, and Noland J. Malone. 2002. *Smoke and Mirrors: Mexican Immigration in an Era of Economic Integration*. New York: Russell Sage Foundation.

Nevins, Joseph. 2002. *Operation Gatekeeper: The Rise of the "Illegal Alien" and the Making of the U.S.–Mexico Boundary*. New York: Routledge.

Ngai, Mae M. 2004. *Impossible Subjects: Illegal Aliens and the Making of Modern America.* Princeton, NJ: Princeton University Press.

Passel, Jeffrey S. 2002. New Estimates of the Undocumented Population in the United States. *Migration Information Source.* Washington, DC: Migration Policy Institute.

Reimers, David M. 1985 [1992]. *Still the Golden Door: The Third World Comes to America.* 2nd Edition. New York: Columbia University Press.

Samora, Julian. 1971. *Los Mojados: The Wetback Story.* Notre Dame, IN: University of Notre Dame Press.

Sánchez, George J. 1993. *Becoming Mexican American: Ethnicity, Culture, and Identity in Chicano Los Angeles 1900–1945.* New York: Oxford University Press.

Solbakken, Lisa C. 1997. The Anti-Terrorism and Effective Death Penalty Act: Anti-Immigration Legislation Veiled in Anti-Terrorism Pretext. *Brooklyn Law Review* 63: 1381–1410.

Zolberg, Aristide R. 1990. Reforming the Back Door: The Immigration Reform and Control Act of 1986 in Historical Perspective. In *Immigration Reconsidered: History, Sociology, Politics*, ed. Virginia Yans-McLaughlin, pp 315–339. New York: Oxford University Press.

2   THE CRIMMIGRATION CRISIS

IMMIGRANTS, CRIME, AND SOVEREIGN POWER

Juliet P. Stumpf

INTRODUCTION

Immigration law today is clothed with so many attributes of criminal law that the line between them has grown indistinct. Scholars have labeled this the "criminalization of immigration law."[1] The merger of the two areas in both substance and procedure has created parallel systems in which immigration law and the criminal justice system are merely nominally separate.

The criminalization of immigration law, or "crimmigration law," has generated intense interest from legislators, immigrants, the media, and the public. In 2006, the specter of legislation that would have criminalized all immigrants present in the country without authorization ignited nationwide marches and protests (see Cisneros, this volume). The intersection of criminal and immigration law has captured the attention of immigration and criminal law scholars alike. Scholarship to date has detailed the existence of this merger, described the parallels between deportation and criminal punishment, and outlined the constitutional consequences of criminalizing immigration law.[2] Yet, little has been written about why this merger has occurred, and what are its theoretical underpinnings.

This chapter begins to fill that void. It unearths the roots of the confluence of criminal and immigration law and maps the theoretical impulses that motivate the merger. It offers a unifying theory for this crimmigration crisis intended to illuminate how and why these two areas of law have converged, and why that convergence may be troubling. I propose here that membership theory, which limits individual rights and privileges to the members of a

Juliet P. Stumpf is professor of law at Lewis & Clark Law School.

Reprinted with permission of the *American University Law Review*, from "The Crimmigration Crisis: Immigrants, Crime, and Sovereign Power," *American University Law Review* 56 (2): 367–419, by Juliet P. Stumpf. Copyright © 2006 by the *American University Law Review*.

1. Teresa Miller, *Citizenship & Severity: Recent Immigration Reforms and the New Penology*, 17 GEO. IMMIGR. L.J. 611, 616 (2003) [hereinafter *Citizenship & Severity*].

2. *See generally Citizenship & Severity, supra* note 1; Daniel Kanstroom, *Deportation, Social Control, and Punishment: Some Thoughts About Why Hard Laws Make Bad Cases*, 113 HARV. L. REV. 1889, 1893–94 (2000).

social contract between the government and the people,[3] is at work in the convergence of criminal and immigration law. Membership theory has the potential to include individuals in the social contract or exclude them from it. It marks out the boundaries of who is an accepted member of society. It operates in this new area to define an ever-expanding group of immigrants and ex-offenders who are denied badges of membership in society such as voting rights or the right to remain in the United States. Membership theory manifests in this new area through two tools of the sovereign state: the power to punish and the power to express moral condemnation.

The application of membership theory places the law on the edge of a crimmigration crisis. This convergence of immigration and criminal law brings to bear only the harshest elements of each area of law, and the apparatus of the state is used to expel from society those deemed criminally alien. The undesirable result is an ever-expanding population of the excluded and alienated. Excluding and alienating a population with strong ties to family, communities, and business interests in the United States fractures our society in ways that extend well beyond the immediate deportation or state-imposed criminal penalty.

The chapter is divided into two parts. The first part describes the many ways in which criminal law and immigration law have come to intersect. Many criminal offenses, including misdemeanors, now result in mandatory deportation. Immigration violations previously handled as civil matters are increasingly addressed as criminal offenses. The procedures for determining whether civil immigration laws are violated have come to resemble the criminal process. I argue that the trend toward criminalizing immigration law has set us on a path toward establishing irrevocably intertwined systems: immigration and criminal law as doppelgangers.

The second part analyzes the motivation for this development. I theorize that the merger of immigration and criminal law is rooted in notions of membership in U.S. society that emphasize distinctions between insiders and outsiders. Membership theory plays similar roles in both areas, and both areas employ similar tools to draw lines of belonging and exclusion. Both immigration and criminal law marshal the sovereign power of the state to punish and to express societal condemnation for the individual offender. The use of that powerful tool in this new area of crimmigration law is troubling precisely because of the use of membership theory. Because membership theory is inherently flexible, the viewpoint of the decision maker as to whether an individual is part of the community often determines whether constitutional and other rights apply at all.

This part raises several questions. Does connecting immigration and criminal law result in better decisions about who to include as members of the U.S. community? Or, does it re-cast the membership lines drawn around citizenship, or guilt, or both, in unintended and undesirable ways?

---

3. *See generally* ALEXANDER M. BICKEL, THE MORALITY OF CONSENT 34 (1975); Sarah H. Cleveland, *Powers Inherent in Sovereignty: Indians, Aliens, Territories, and the Nineteenth Century Origins of Plenary Power over Foreign Affairs*, 81 TEX. L. REV. 1, 20 (2002).

IMMIGRATION AND CRIMINAL LAW CONVERGENCE

The merger of criminal and immigration law is both odd and oddly unremarkable. It is odd because criminal law seems a distant cousin to immigration law. Criminal law seeks to prevent and address harm to individuals and society from violence or fraud or evil motive. Immigration law determines who may cross the border and reside here, and who must leave. Historically, courts have drawn closer connections between immigration law and foreign policy than between immigration and the criminal justice system.

Yet, criminal law and immigration law are similar in the way that they differ from other areas of the law. Most areas of law center on resolving conflicts and regulating the relationships of individuals and businesses. Torts, contracts, property, family law, and business-related law primarily address disputes or regulate the creation, maintenance, and dissolution of personal and business relationships. Criminal law and immigration law, in contrast, primarily regulate the relationship between the state and the individual.

Both criminal and immigration law are, at their core, systems of inclusion and exclusion. They are similarly designed to determine whether and how to include individuals as members of society or exclude them from it. Both create insiders and outsiders. Both are designed to create distinct categories of people—innocent versus guilty, admitted versus excluded or, as some say, "legal" versus "illegal." Viewed in that light, perhaps it is not surprising that these two areas of law have become entwined. When policymakers seek to raise the barriers for noncitizens to attain membership in this society, it is unremarkable that they would turn to an area of the law that similarly functions to exclude.

Crimes committed by immigrants have influenced the direction of immigration law since its inception. The first federal statutes restricting immigration barred the entry of foreigners with criminal convictions, among others. Since then, the relationship between immigration and criminal law has evolved from merely excluding foreigners who had committed past crimes to the present when many immigration violations are themselves defined as criminal offenses and many crimes result in deportation (see Chacón, this volume).

This increasing overlap between criminal and immigration law highlights choices about who is a member of U.S. society. Criminal and immigration law primarily serve to separate the individual from the rest of U.S. society through physical exclusion and the creation of rules that establish lesser levels of citizenship. Moreover, the law often imposes both immigration and criminal sanctions for the same offense.[4] Whether a noncitizen violates immigration law that has been defined as criminal, or a crime that is a deportable offense, both incarceration and deportation may result.

The crimmigration merger has taken place on three fronts: (1) the substance of immigration law and criminal law increasingly overlaps, (2) immigration enforcement has come to resemble criminal law enforcement, and (3) the procedural aspects of prosecuting immigration violations have taken on many of the earmarks of criminal procedure. Some distinctions between immigration and criminal law persist and shed light on the choices our system has made about when and how individuals may be excluded from the community.

4. *See Citizenship & Severity, supra* note 1, at 618 (explaining that in addition to deportation, immigrants who have unlawfully entered often face harsh criminal penalties, including incarceration, fines, or the forfeiture of property).

Overlap in the Substance of the Law

Immigration law has evolved from a primarily administrative civil process to the present day system that is intertwined with criminal law. In the beginning, immigration law intersected with criminal law only in denying entry to those with a criminal history. Entering without authorization was not punished, and those who committed crimes after entering the country were not deportable. Once immigrants had crossed the border, with or without government sanction, the federal government did little to expel them. Only in 1917 did the government begin to deport convicted noncitizens.

Over time, immigration law became infused with the substance of criminal law itself. First, there has been "unprecedented growth in the scope of criminal grounds for the exclusion and deportation of foreign-born non-U.S. citizens."[5] Second, violations of immigration law are now criminal when they were previously civil, or carry greater criminal consequences than ever before. Third, recent changes in immigration law have focused on detaining and deporting those deemed likely to commit crimes that pose a threat to national security (see Chacón, this volume).

Since the late 1980s, grounds for excluding and deporting aliens convicted of crimes have proliferated. Until then, deportation of aliens with criminal backgrounds was mostly confined to past convictions for crimes of moral turpitude, drug trafficking, and some weapons offenses. Deportation of permanent residents, including those who had committed crimes, was relatively rare. Detention of aliens with criminal backgrounds was less common than now, and relief from detention more readily available based on a range of circumstantial considerations. Criminal sanctions for purely immigration-related violations were far more limited in comparison to the present day.

In 1988, Congress vastly expanded the range of crimes leading to deportation by creating a category of "aggravated felonies" that included murder, drug trafficking, and firearms trafficking.[6] Almost every immigration statute passed since then has expanded the list of crimes leading to exclusion and deportation. The Immigration Act of 1990 defined an aggravated felony as any crime of violence for which the sentence was at least five years, regardless of how the statute under which the alien was actually convicted defined the crime. In the mid-1990s, Congress added a plethora of offenses to the list of aggravated felonies, many of which do not involve violence. The Antiterrorism and Effective Death Penalty Act of 1996 made a single crime of "moral turpitude" a deportable offense. Congress soon broadened the definition of an aggravated felony still further by reducing to one year the sentence length required to constitute a "crime of violence" or a deportable theft offense.[7]

The convergence of immigration and criminal law has been a two-way street. Not only has there been an increase in the number and type of crimes that resulted in deportation, but actions by immigrants that were previously civil violations have crossed the boundary

5. *Id.* at 619.

6. The Anti-Drug Abuse Act of 1988 (Drug Kingpin Act), Pub. L. No. 100–690, § 7342, 102 Stat. 4181, 4469 (1988).

7. Illegal Immigration Reform and Immigrant Responsibility Act of 1996 ("IIRIRA"), Pub. L. No. 104–208, Div. C., § 321, 110 Stat. 3009–546, 3009–627 (1996) (codified as amended at 8 U.S.C. § 1101(a)(43)(F)-(G) (2000)).

to become criminal offenses, or have come to carry harsher criminal penalties with heightened enforcement levels.

Until 1929, violations of immigration laws were essentially civil matters. In 1929, unlawful entry became a misdemeanor, and unlawful re-entry a felony. In recent decades, the number and types of immigration-related acts that carry criminal consequences have proliferated. In 1986, Congress passed legislation that for the first time sanctioned employers for knowingly hiring undocumented workers and provided for imprisonment and criminal fines for a pattern or practice of such hiring (see De Genova, this volume; Bacon and Hing, this volume).[8] Since 1990, marrying to evade immigration laws, voting in a federal election as a noncitizen, and falsely claiming citizenship to obtain a benefit or employment have become criminal violations leading to both incarceration and deportation.[9] The criminal penalty for unlawfully re-entering the United States after deportation or exclusion increased from two years to a maximum of ten or twenty years,[10] and enforcement of these violations has increased dramatically.

The national focus on terrorism has also had the effect of connecting criminal and immigration law (see Chacón, this volume). After the events of September 11, anti-terrorism efforts employed both immigration control and criminal law to reduce terrorist threats. As an example, the Department of Homeland Security (DHS) enters civil immigration warrant information into national law enforcement databases accessible to state and local police, which has in effect imposed on state and local police a role in enforcing civil immigration law. Also, Operation Tarmac prosecutes and deports unauthorized airport screeners working with forged employment documents.

The association between immigration and criminal law has become so strong that in some arenas immigration law has usurped the traditional role of criminal law. Immigration law is now often used in lieu of criminal law to detain or deport those alleged to be involved in terrorism. Because of the lesser substantive and procedural barriers to deportation compared to a criminal conviction, federal officials have been able to undertake initiatives based on citizenship status and ethnicity that are not possible within the criminal justice system.

As examples, soon after September 11, 2001, the Department of Justice initiated the National Security Entry-Exit Registration System (NSEERS) that required noncitizen men from certain Muslim and Arab countries to register with the Immigration and Naturalization Service (INS). The DHS Absconder Apprehension Initiative targeted for detention and deportation noncitizen men of Muslim faith and Arab ethnicity who had criminal convictions or immigration violations, regardless of whether the crimes or violations related to terrorism. The USA PATRIOT Act of 2001 has resulted in detentions of noncitizens without charge for an undefined "reasonable period of time" under extraordinary

---

8. Immigration Reform and Control Act of 1986, Pub. L. No. 99–603, 100 Stat. 3359 (1986) (codified at 8 U.S.C. § 1324a).

9. See IIRIRA, supra note 7; Immigration Marriage Fraud Amendments of 1986, Pub. L. No. 99–639, 100 Stat. 3537 (codified as amended in scattered sections of 8 U.S.C.).

10. See Violent Crime Control and Law Enforcement Act of 1994, Pub. L. No. 103–322, § 13001, 108 Stat. 1796, 2023 (codified at 8 U.S.C. § 1326 (1994)); Anti-Drug Abuse Act of 1988, Pub. L. No. 100–690, § 7345, 102 Stat. 4181, 4471.

circumstances.[11] All of these examples permit the government to employ immigration rules to detain or deport noncitizens suspected of terrorist tendencies without resort to the criminal justice system.

As a result of this interlacing of criminal and immigration law, the number of deportations has risen dramatically. Between 1908 and 1980, there were approximately 56,000 immigrants deported based on criminal convictions.[12] In 2004 alone, there were more than 88,000 such deportations.[13]

Similarities in Enforcement

Immigration enforcement has come to parallel criminal law enforcement. The authority of federal agencies to regulate immigration as a law enforcement matter, however, has not always been clear. In 1930, members of the House Committee on Immigration and Naturalization expressed concern that the Border Patrol was overreaching its authority when they discovered that the agency operated as far as 100 miles inside the border and considered itself authorized to make arrests without a warrant. Because the Border Patrol was not a criminal law enforcement agency, Congress was uneasy about the agency's lack of statutory authority to make warrantless arrests and its claim to jurisdiction well within the nation's edge.

The contrast between the doubts expressed by that earlier Congress and the current authority of the immigration agency could not be more marked. Between 1875, when Congress passed the first federal immigration exclusion law, and 1917, when it appropriated funds for deporting those unlawfully in the country, there was no federal mechanism for enforcing the deportation sanction (see Chacón, this volume; De Genova, this volume). Yet, today the appearance and powers of the two immigration enforcement agencies—U.S. Immigration and Customs Enforcement and U.S. Customs and Border Protection—are almost indistinguishable from those of a criminal law enforcement organization. Representative of the shift from a civil administrative agency to law enforcement is the transfer of responsibility for immigration control from the Department of Commerce and Labor to the Department of Justice in 1940 and ultimately to the DHS in 2002.

The Border Patrol is perhaps the most apparent example of the way immigration enforcement has evolved to parallel criminal law enforcement. The Border Patrol has transformed from its original embodiment as a collection of 450 ranchers, military men, railway mail clerks, and local marshals and sheriffs to a trained and uniformed enforcement body whose activities resemble those of any police force. Border Patrol agents are empowered to conduct surveillance, pursue suspected undocumented aliens, make stops, and effectuate arrests. In 1986, Congress legislated the first of a series of significant increases in appropriations for the Border Patrol.[14] Today, the immigration enforcement arms of DHS constitute

---

11. 8 C.F.R. § 287.3(d) (2006).

12. 2004 YEARBOOK OF IMMIGRATION STATISTICS tbl.45, *available at* http://www.uscis.gov/graphics/shared/statistics/yearbook/2004/Table45.xls (last visited Oct. 1, 2006).

13. 2004 DHS ANN. REP. 1, *available at* http://www.uscis.gov/graphics/shared/statistics/publications/Annual ReportEnforcement2004.pdf (last visited Oct. 1, 2006).

14. Immigration Reform and Control Act of 1986, Pub. L. No. 99–603, § 111(b), 100 Stat. 3359, 3381 (1986) (codified at 8 U.S.C. § 1101(b) (2000)).

the largest armed federal law enforcement body. For the first time, immigration prosecutions outnumber all other types of federal criminal prosecutions, including prosecutions for drugs and weapons violations.

Procedural Parallels

The parallels between criminal procedure and the rules governing immigration law and proceedings are legion. The two areas have vastly different constitutional procedural protections. Criminal process rights are embodied in the Fourth, Fifth, and Sixth Amendments,[15] while immigration proceedings are generally governed by the Fifth Amendment's Due Process Clause.[16] Nevertheless, immigration proceedings have come to bear a striking resemblance to criminal processes. As in criminal law, an immigration judge's decision in an exclusion or deportation case concerns the physical liberty of the individual. Immigration law enforcement officers execute warrants, make arrests, and detain suspected violators. The violation is adjudicated in a hearing where the individual has the opportunity to present evidence and examine witnesses. The functions of prosecutor and adjudicator are generally separated, and the immigrant has a right to counsel, though not at government expense.

Hand in hand with the greater overlap between criminal and immigration law and the creation of a police-like enforcement agency has been the increased use of an immigration sanction—detention—that parallels the criminal sanction of incarceration (see Hernández, this volume). Congress has recently narrowed the circumstances under which noncitizens convicted of crimes can avoid administrative detention after completing their criminal sentences. DHS has expanded the categories of immigrants subject to detention that it had formerly released and now detains permanent residents, women, and children. The USA PATRIOT Act of 2001 authorized the Attorney General to detain noncitizens for seven days without criminal charges. Much longer detentions became prevalent, however, based on expanded administrative rules that permitted detention without charge for a "reasonable period of time" under extraordinary circumstances.[17] In April 2003, citing national security concerns, the Attorney General expanded the grounds for detention of asylum-seekers from Haiti based on his belief that "Pakistanis, Palestinians, etc." might use Haiti as a "staging point" for terrorism.[18]

Distinctions Between Immigration and Criminal Law

Convergence of the immigration and criminal justice systems appears inevitable. Yet, significant distinctions remain. First, the constitutional rights of noncitizens in immigration

15. *See* U.S. CONST. amend. IV (affording suspected criminals the right to be free from unreasonable searches and seizures of their persons or property); *id.* amend. V (providing the procedural protections of grand jury hearings and the double jeopardy shield, as well as the right to protect against self-incrimination); *id.* amend. VI (granting defendants the rights to speedy and neutral trials, during which the defendant may confront witnesses against him, call witnesses to support him, and be ensured the assistance of counsel).

16. *See* Yamataya v. Fisher, 189 U.S. 86, 100–02 (1902) (declaring that deported aliens are protected only by the Fifth Amendment's constitutional guarantee of due process); *see also* Galvan v. Press, 347 U.S. 522, 530–31 (1954) (holding that deportation of noncitizens is not criminal punishment, but rather a civil penalty, and therefore, procedural protections of criminal trial do not attach to deportation proceedings).

17. 8 C.F.R. § 287.3(d) (2006).

18. *In re* D-J, 23 I. & N. Dec. 572, 579 (2003).

proceedings are far more limited than those of criminal defendants, whose Fourth, Fifth, Sixth, and Fourteenth Amendment rights lattice the structure of the criminal trial.

Courts have offered two justifications for this distinction. Unlike criminal law, courts have historically connected immigration law with foreign policy (see Chacón, this volume). Immigration law is governed primarily by the plenary power doctrine, which grants vast power to Congress and the President over foreign policy, including immigration, and limits the reach of the Constitution and the scope of judicial review. The second justification is that courts have historically treated immigration-related exclusion, deportation, and detention as civil remedies, not as punishment comparable to criminal sanctions.

As a result, only the Due Process Clause protects noncitizens in deportation proceedings, and those seeking to enter the country have essentially no constitutional protections at all. Fifth and Sixth Amendment rights, prominent features of criminal trials, do not apply in deportation proceedings except to the limited extent that "fundamental fairness" requires them. The Fourth Amendment's exclusionary rule does not apply in removal cases. Noncitizens in immigration proceedings do not enjoy the protections of the Eighth Amendment against cruel and unusual punishment. They generally do not have the right to appointed counsel at government expense or the protection of the privilege against self-incrimination. Nor does the Ex Post Facto Clause prohibit retroactive application of laws to immigrants in the deportation context.

Second, the circumstances under which noncitizens may find themselves detained are much broader than in the criminal context. In the criminal justice system, detention occurs primarily in three situations: (1) pre-conviction, when a criminal defendant is detained prior to and during trial; (2) post-conviction, in connection with a sentence mandating incarceration; or (3) when a material witness is detained to ensure his presence at trial.

In contrast, government power to detain noncitizens in the immigration context is vast. Noncitizens are detained if they are not clearly entitled to entry, are awaiting removal proceedings, or have a final order of removal. Those who have committed aggravated felonies and have served their prison terms are detained pending the conclusion of deportation proceedings. DHS regulations permit detention of a noncitizen pending a decision to file immigration charges for a "reasonable" period of time "in the event of an emergency or other extraordinary circumstance."[19] DHS has also singled out for detention asylum seekers from thirty-three designated countries which are primarily Muslim or Arab (see Chacón, this volume).

Third, race and national origin are relevant in different ways in criminal and immigration law. This is most easily seen in the context of the Fourth Amendment, which the Supreme Court has interpreted to permit an immigration agent to rely on national origin and ethnicity as a factor in making a stop.[20] The exclusionary rule, which prohibits the use in criminal trials of evidence seized in violation of the Fourth Amendment, does not apply in deportation proceedings. Nor does it apply to a noncitizen in a domestic criminal trial when the seizure took place abroad.

19. *See supra* note 17.

20. *See* United States v. Brignoni, 422 U.S. 873, 886–87 (1975) (acknowledging that Mexican appearance can be a relevant factor when stopping a car).

One final distinction between the criminal and immigration contexts deserves mention. Societal perceptions of immigrants and criminal defendants differ. Public perceptions of immigrants have tended to be more positive than perceptions of criminal offenders. Scholars describe the archetype of the undocumented immigrant as a hard-working individual drawn to enter the United States clandestinely with the hope of rising economic prospects and a better life for herself and her family.[21]

This vision, however, is in transition. Undocumented immigrants are increasingly perceived as criminals, likely to commit future criminal acts because of their history of entering the country unlawfully. More recently, immigrants have been identified with terrorism, perceived as either complicit in the acts precipitating September 11 or prone to such acts in the future. It is membership theory that is driving this change.

MEMBERSHIP THEORY AND CRIMMIGRATION

Why has this merger of criminal and immigration law taken place? Using criminal law to enforce immigration law seems to take the long way around. It tends to address the problem ex post and on an individual basis, after unauthorized immigration has occurred or a foreigner has committed an offense. Using exclusion or deportation to punish criminal offenses and prevent recidivism may be efficient, but it circumvents criminal constitutional protections and fails to account for serious costs to the noncitizen, family members, employers, and the community.

The Role of Membership Theory in Criminal and Immigration Law

The answer to this puzzle may lie in the core function that both immigration and criminal law play in our society. Both systems act as gatekeepers of membership in our society, determining whether an individual should be included in or excluded from our society. True, the outcomes of the two systems differ. A decision to exclude in criminal law results in segregation within our society through incarceration, while exclusion in immigration law results in separation from our society through expulsion from the national territory. Yet, at bottom, both criminal and immigration law embody choices about who should be members of society: individuals whose characteristics or actions make them worthy of inclusion in the national community.

Membership theory influences immigration and criminal law in similar ways. Membership theory is based in the idea that positive rights arise from a social contract between the government and the people.[22] Those who are not parties to that agreement and yet are subject to government action have no claim to such positive rights, or rights equivalent to those held by members. "Only members and beneficiaries of the social contract are able to make claims against the government and are entitled to the contract's protections, and the government may act outside of the contract's constraints against individuals who are non-members."[23]

---

21. Bill Ong Hing, *The Immigrant as Criminal: Punishing Dreamers*, 9 HASTINGS WOMEN'S L.J. 79, 79–80, 85–87 (1998).

22. Bickel, *supra* note 3, at 34; Cleveland, *supra* note 3, at 20.

23. Cleveland, *supra* note 3, at 20.

When membership theory is at play in legal decision making, whole categories of constitutional rights depend on the decision maker's vision of who belongs. Membership theory is thus extraordinarily flexible. Expansive notions of membership may broaden the scope of constitutional rights; stingier membership criteria restrict rights and privileges. In *Plyler v. Doe*, the Court's reasoning that undocumented schoolchildren are potential members of the United States citizenry led to a ruling that Texas could not deny those children equal access to a public school education. More often, membership theory has been used to narrow constitutional coverage by defining the scope of "the People" to exclude noncitizens at the perimeter of society.[24]

Introducing membership theory into criminal law, and especially into the uncharted territory of crimmigration law, undermines the strength of constitutional protections for those considered excludable. A decision maker's perspective on who is excludable can also affect the willingness to extend statutory rights and benefits, or interpret legal and other norms in ways that advantage ex-offenders and immigrants. It becomes critical, therefore, to trace how membership theory plays out in both immigration and criminal law.

Immigration law defines membership in this society explicitly, by establishing a ladder of accession to permanent residence and then formal U.S. citizenship, and a set of criteria to determine whether an individual meets the requirements for these various levels of membership. These criteria often reflect acceptance and invitation by established members of the nation, such as spouses, other family members, or employers.[25] However, when the immigrant violates prescribed rules, primarily criminal laws, immigration law requires deportation of the offender and often bars re-entry, effectively revoking the membership of the noncitizen.

Criminal law defines membership implicitly, by stripping critical elements of citizenship from individuals who commit relatively serious offenses. First, through incarceration, offenders lose the ability to associate with the rest of society. They are then often stripped of the basic political rights that are the earmarks of citizenship in the United States. In many states, the commission of a felony results in loss of the right to vote, serve in public office, or serve on a jury. Many offenders also lose social and welfare rights and benefits open to other citizens, including access to government assistance and certain employment opportunities. Like noncitizens, offenders are often required to register with a government agency. The resulting status of an ex-felon strikingly resembles that of an alien. Through incarceration and collateral sanctions, criminal offenders are—literally—alienated.

Immigration and criminal law approach the acquisition and loss of membership from two different directions. Criminal law presumes that the defendant has full membership in our society and places the burden on the government to prove otherwise. This pro-membership perspective is reflected in the comparatively stronger constitutional protections that criminal defendants possess: the presumption of innocence embodied in the burden of proof, and

---

24. *See* United States v. Verdugo-Urquidez, 494 U.S. 259, 260 (1990) (denying constitutional protection to a noncitizen because he had no voluntary connection to the United States that might place him among "the People").

25. *See* Immigration and Nationality Act ("INA"), 8 U.S.C. § 1153(a)-(b) (2000) (mandating that immigration visas be extended on a preferred basis to children, spouses, and family members of United States citizens and for people who demonstrate exceptional ability in a particular field, or who are skilled in a field for which there is a shortage of qualified workers in the United States).

entitlement to constitutional rights under the Fourth, Fifth, and Sixth Amendments.[26] When the government seeks to exercise its power to punish, these rights provide protection to all those within the constitutional community against exclusion from society without a substantial justification.

Immigration law assumes non-membership. In contrast to the presumption of innocence, arriving aliens are presumed inadmissible unless they show they are "clearly and beyond a doubt entitled to be admitted."[27] The government's burden of proof in deportation cases is also lighter than in a criminal case—"clear and convincing evidence"[28] rather than "beyond a reasonable doubt."[29]

Levels of constitutional protection in immigration law depend in large part upon the individual's connection or potential for connection with the national community. Citizens have the highest level of constitutional protection. Lawful permanent residents are next, due to their ties in this country. Lawful permanent residence acts as a sort of probationary membership. Once admitted to the country and given permission to remain, the permanent resident has approximately five years of probation, after which, assuming she has complied with the criminal laws and shown herself to be of good moral fiber and likely to contribute to society, she has the opportunity to become a full member through naturalization.

Unlike citizens, lawful permanent residents cannot vote or hold certain public offices. They are subject to deportation, and the Supreme Court has deferred to the political branches' power over the substance of deportation grounds that affect legal permanent residents. Nevertheless, legal permanent residents' rights to enter into contracts and own property are equivalent to those of citizens, and the courts have consistently upheld procedural due process protection for permanent residents.

Lawfully present nonresidents have weaker, though still cognizable constitutional claims, while undocumented immigrants, regardless of the strength of their actual ties here, have more ephemeral constitutional claims. At the bottom, those seeking entry for the first time without a prior stake in this country have essentially no constitutional protections, and courts have almost no power to review decisions barring their entry.

As such, government plays the role of a bouncer in the crimmigration context. Upon discovering that an individual either is not a member or has broken the membership's rules, the government has enormous discretion to use persuasion or force to remove the individual from the premises.

Sovereign Power and Penology in Criminal and Immigration Law

Delineating the major role that membership theory plays in the merger of criminal and immigration law only partially addresses the question of how this new crimmigration area developed. This section describes how membership theory has channeled the evolution of criminal and immigration law in ways that have brought the two areas closer together.

26. *See supra* note 15.

27. INA, 8 U.S.C. § 1225(b)(2)(A) (2000).

28. *Id.* § 1229a(c)(3)(A) (2000).

29. *Winship*, 397 U.S. at 363.

Two developments inform the discussion. First, the rapid importation of criminal grounds into immigration law is consistent with a shift in criminal penology from rehabilitation to harsher motivations: retribution, deterrence, incapacitation, and the expressive power of the state. Second, criminal penology began to embrace sovereign power as a basis for policy making, a tool that immigration law has relied on since its inception. This cross-pollination of legal tools and theories bridged the distant relationship between immigration and criminal law. It led the way to more exclusionary definitions of who was a member of the U.S. community and to an expansion of the consequences of loss of membership to include mass deportation of noncitizens and loss of the privileges of citizenship for ex-offenders.

From the 1950s through the 1970s, both criminal and immigration sanctions reflected a rehabilitation model.[30] Criminal penology favored indeterminate sentences that could be shortened for good behavior, alternatives to incarceration, individualized treatment, and re-education. This philosophy was consistent with the idea that the criminal act was separable from the individual actor, and that the actor could be rehabilitated, integrated into society, and given a second chance. It was grounded in a social ideology that sought to redeem offenders and restore "full social citizenship with equal rights and equal opportunities."[31]

The rehabilitation model fell into disfavor after the 1970s, and criminal penology turned to retribution, incapacitation, and deterrence as motivating ideologies.[32] One consequence was higher incidences of incarceration for lesser crimes and for longer periods, the purpose being to punish, incapacitate the offender from further crimes, and deter the offender and others from similar conduct.

Government also began to rely heavily on sanctions that reached beyond the post-trial sentence. The federal and state governments began to remove certain hallmarks of citizenship as a consequence of a criminal conviction. These hallmarks included loss of voting rights, exclusion from public office and jury service, ineligibility for public benefits, public housing, government support for education, and exclusion from professional license eligibility. The increasing use of these "collateral consequences"[33] for crimes made clear that retribution rather than rehabilitation was driving the modern criminal justice system.

The most logical motivation for the accumulation of these collateral consequences is that they constitute decisions about the membership status of the convicted individual. Collateral consequences diminish the societal membership status of the individual convicted. The lost privileges often bear no relation to the context of the crime. Nor do they appear to be an attempt to prevent future criminal conduct in the areas declared off-limits to the convicted. For example, loss of voting rights is not tied to the commission of political crimes, nor is loss of government benefits limited to those convicted of defrauding the government or crimes related to public housing, education, or welfare.

30. See DAVID GARLAND, THE CULTURE OF CONTROL: CRIME AND SOCIAL ORDER IN CONTEMPORARY SOCIETY 34–35 (U. Chicago Press 2001); Douglas A. Berman, *Distinguishing Offense Conduct and Offender Characteristics in Modern Sentencing Reforms*, 58 STAN. L. REV. 277, 278 (2005).

31. GARLAND, *supra* note 30, at 46.

32. *See* GARLAND, *supra* note 30, at 54; Berman, *supra* note 30, at 279–81.

33. Nora V. Demleitner, *Preventing Internal Exile: The Need for Restrictions on Collateral Sentencing Consequences*, 11 STAN. L. & POL'Y REV. 153, 154 (1999).

Several of these collateral consequences eliminate the incidents of citizenship. Voting rights are often seen as the hallmark of citizenship, perhaps because the right to vote is one of the most familiar and fundamental divisions between citizens and noncitizens. In the same category are the opportunities to seek public office and serve as a juror. Excluding the convicted individual from these activities translates into exclusion from full participation in the social and political structure of society. The loss of these markings of citizenship demotes the convicted individual to the status of a noncitizen, constitutionally incapable of voting in a federal election, serving on a jury, or seeking high public office.

Loss of access to public goods such as welfare benefits, public housing, or educational grants suggests a different kind of membership decision. These limited public goods require the government to make choices about how to distribute them equitably. Generally, the criteria for obtaining these public goods are based on the individual's need for the particular social resource, usually financial need. Exclusion from eligibility for these public goods based on noncitizenship status or status as an ex-felon, on the other hand, is unrelated to need. Instead, the basis for exclusion seems to be desert: those who have lost the social status of a full citizen through a criminal conviction, or never gained citizenship in the first place, must not deserve to share in the limited pie of public benefits. The safety net of public benefits is only available to those who enjoy full citizenship.

Immigration law seems to have followed the same path toward more exclusive membership.[34] In immigration law prior to the 1980s, most crimes did not trigger immigration sanctions for permanent residents. Only the most serious crimes or crimes involving "moral turpitude" that presumably revealed an inherent moral flaw in the individual resulted in the ultimate sanction of deportation. Otherwise, criminal conduct was handled as a domestic affair through the criminal justice system, not as an immigration matter. In both areas of the law, this approach affirms the individual's claim to membership in the society. Members obtain the club's benefits, but are also bound by the club's rules and are subject to its processes and sanctions for breaking those rules.

The emphasis on retribution, deterrence, and incapacitation in immigration law is apparent from the expanded use of deportation as a sanction for violating either immigration or criminal laws. With few exceptions, immigration sanctions including deportation now result from a wide variety of even minor crimes, regardless of the noncitizen's ties to the United States (see Boehm, this volume; Coutin, this volume). Permanent residents are as easily deported for crimes defined as "aggravated felonies" as is a noncitizen without any connection to the United States or without permission to be in the country.

This scheme might be characterized as merely a way of removing those who have broken the rules conditioning their presence in this country. However, the ascendance of these harsher rules concurrently with the shift in criminal penology suggests a different premise—that more exclusionary notions of membership in both areas resulted in reliance on harsher ideologies of punishment. Government could thus achieve both punishment and deterrence of crimes through imposition of any lawful retributive means available, including immigration sanctions. Removing the individual from the country incapacitates her from commit-

34. *See* Kanstroom, *supra* note 2, at 1894.

ting future crimes in the United States, and is often imposed with the intent to punish. Using removal as a sanction also makes a statement about membership: that the permanent resident belongs more readily to her country of origin, regardless of length of residency or connections to the U.S. community.

In sum, the criminalization of immigration law has resulted in a more exclusionary membership. Just as important as defining the role of membership theory, however, is describing the means by which these notions of membership define who is excluded. In this new area of crimmigration law, specific powers of the sovereign state are the primary means of inclusion and exclusion.

In moving toward retribution and away from rehabilitation and integration into society, the criminal justice system turned to a model that immigration law has relied on for centuries.[35] Criminal law embraced certain powers of the sovereign state as the primary response to crime: the power to exact extreme sanctions and the power to express society's moral condemnation.

Decisions about membership are at play in the use of both powers. The state as sovereign has the authority to control the territory within its boundaries and protect it from external and internal enemies. In immigration law, sovereign power is the authority that enables the government to exercise enormous discretion to decide who may be excluded from the territory and from membership in the society (see Chacón, this volume).

In criminal law, the sovereign state strategy relies on the state as the main player in controlling crime. As David Garland has observed, "[l]ike the decision to wage war, the decision to inflict harsh punishment or extend police powers exemplifies the sovereign mode of state action."[36] Garland theorizes that disillusionment with the rehabilitation model combined with persistently high crime rates led to ratcheting up punitive measures such as longer sentences and fewer opportunities for parole. These changes paralleled the increase in the use of deportation in immigration law as a punitive measure.

The expressive function of the state, in which the state's power to punish becomes a channel for society's moral condemnation of crime rather than a means of exacting retribution or enabling rehabilitation, is also a manifestation of state sovereignty in criminal law. The expressive dimension of punishment matches the harshness of a criminal penalty with the level of society's moral condemnation of the crime. For example, when the state imposes a harsher punishment for a racially motivated murder than for a mother who kills a child abuser, it expresses different levels of condemnation for each crime. By imposing lesser punishment on the mother who kills her child's abuser than on the racially motivated murderer, the state expresses a moral distinction between them and a greater degree of exclusion from society for the racist based on that moral condemnation.

This turn to a sovereign state model as the central response to crime control mirrors the substantial role that federal sovereignty plays in immigration law. The power of the federal government as a sovereign state is at its apex in immigration law. The exercise of sovereign

35. *See* GARLAND, *supra* note 30, at 134–35; *see also* Cleveland, *supra* note 3, at 81–163.
36. *Id.* at 135.

power is intricately connected to the power to define membership within a political community, as Justice White emphasized in *Cabell v. Chavez-Salido*:

> The exclusion of aliens from basic governmental processes is not a deficiency . . . but a necessary consequence of the community's process of political self-definition. Self-government, whether direct or through representatives, begins by defining the scope of the community of the governed and thus of the governors as well: Aliens are by definition those outside of this community.[37]

The state's expressive role is the same in immigration law as in criminal law. By imposing the sanction of deportation for crimes and by criminalizing immigration violations, the state expresses moral condemnation both for the crime through criminal punishment and for the individual's status as a noncitizen offender. As such, the sovereign state strategy expresses the insider or outsider status of the offender. The expressive dimension of punishment in this context communicates exclusion. Unlike the rehabilitative model, which sought to protect the public by reintegrating the offender into a community, the use of sovereign power has the effect of excluding the offender and the immigrant from society. Under the sovereign state model, ex-offenders and immigrants become the "outsiders" from whom citizens need protection.

One theory that has been offered for this turn to the state's expressive powers and the emphasis on harsh punishment is that persistently high rates of crime and unauthorized immigration have led to distrust of the state's ability to control both crime and immigration.[38] It is politically infeasible to acknowledge that the state's ability to control crime is limited. Politicians, therefore, employ the sovereign power of the state more heavily to reassure the public of their commitment to controlling crime. As a result, the sovereign state power is used in ways that are divorced from effective control of either crime or unauthorized immigration. Imposing increasingly harsh sentences and using deportation as a means of expressing moral outrage is attractive from a political standpoint, regardless of its efficacy in controlling crime or unauthorized immigration.

Consequences of Narrowing the Scope of Membership

The result of the application of membership theory has been to create a population, often identifiable by race and class, that is excluded physically, politically, and socially from the mainstream community.[39] This consequence raises a curious question: what is in it for the members? What is the advantage to U.S. society of creating and policing these membership lines?

In the case of a limited pie such as public benefits, it seems at least facially logical to exclude those with weaker claims to membership as a way of ensuring an adequate slice for

---

37. T. Alexander Aleinikoff, *The Tightening Circle of Membership*, 22 HASTINGS CONST. L.Q. 915, 923 (1995).

38. *See* GARLAND, *supra* note 30, at 110.

39. Cf. Linda S. Bosniak, *Membership, Equality, & the Difference That Alienage Makes*, 69 N.Y.U. L. REV. 1047, 1073–75 (1994).

those with stronger membership claims. Withholding the bundle of rights and privileges that includes voting, holding public office, and serving on a jury has a less tangible benefit for U.S. society. The purpose here is not to protect a scarce resource. Barring ex-offenders and noncitizens from these activities seems to have more value to the membership as an expressive statement. It enhances the apparent value of those rights and privileges to the members by making them privileges over which the membership has control, rather than inalienable rights belonging to the individual. Because those rights and privileges are susceptible to loss, they become more precious to the individual who holds them. Since members decide how those rights may be lost and who loses them, the rights become more valuable to the members.

Thus, the value to the members is twofold: excluding ex-offenders and noncitizens from the activities of voting, holding public office, and jury service creates a palpable distinction between member and non-member, solidifying the line between those who deserve to be included and those who have either shown themselves to be deserving of exclusion or have not yet shown themselves worthy of inclusion. In this light, withholding these privileges conceivably improves the quality of the membership by excluding those less deserving of membership. Perhaps withholding these privileges is meant to enhance the public trust in the integrity of the voting process and of public officeholders, and in the outcome of jury trials. If the public perceives ex-offenders and noncitizens to be unworthy of the public trust, one could argue that excluding them from these fora of public participation increases confidence in the products of voting, public officeholding, and jury deliberations.

All this begs the question, of course, whether the membership should have the power to create a class of outsiders without access to these rights or privileges. Excluding individuals who have a stake in public affairs and the fairness of the judicial process, such as ex-offenders and noncitizens who pay taxes or raise children, seems contrary to the democratic ideal that those governed have a say in the composition of the government. Moreover, excluding ex-offenders and noncitizens from public benefits and public participation seems to conflict with the need to integrate these groups into society, especially if lack of resources and exclusion from participation results in alienation and contributes to the commission of further crimes.

These significant costs seem to outweigh the uncertain benefits outlined above. The costs become greater upon examining who is most often excluded. Both immigration and criminal law tend to exclude certain people of color and members of lower socioeconomic classes.

Immigration law does this explicitly. Immigration law takes socioeconomic status into account when it excludes a noncitizen likely to become a public charge because of lack of financial resources, and by prioritizing entry of certain professionals, managers, executives, and investors.[40] The prevalence of sovereign power in immigration law has its roots in excluding racial and cultural groups, beginning with the Chinese and other Asian Americans in the late 1880s, and including the deportation of U.S. citizens of Mexican origin in the 1930s (see Chacón, this volume; De Genova, this volume). Today, the rules governing entry tend to favor citizens from European countries. The diversity visa (also known as "the Lot-

---

40. *See supra* note 25.

tery") grants up to 55,000 applications for permanent resident status to applicants from specific countries using a random selection process, and results in disproportionate advantages to European applicants.[41] The visa waiver program allows citizens from primarily European countries to enter for ninety days without a visa.

Inside the borders, immigration enforcement is unabashedly race- and ethnicity-based. A prime example is NSEERS's focus on deporting noncitizen men from Muslim and Arab countries. The DHS's enforcement priorities have also targeted particular ethnic groups. The Supreme Court has sanctioned the use of race and ethnicity as a factor in making Fourth Amendment stops relating to suspected immigration law violations.[42]

Unlike immigration law, criminal law's disparate treatment of members of certain minorities and income levels is not explicit. Instead, criminal law has a disparate impact: the rules of the criminal justice system are neutral on their face, but their effect on racial and ethnic minorities is notoriously disproportionate to the number in the general population.[43]

The movement toward retributive justice in criminal law, the turn to the sovereign state as the answer to public fears about crime, and the disproportionate representation of minorities and low-income classes in the offender population contribute to the perception of criminal offenders as noncitizens. Rather than viewing rehabilitation as a way of creating a more integrated citizenry, the view of the offender is as a profoundly antisocial being whose interests are fundamentally opposed to those of the rest of society.

Within this framework, the criminal becomes "the alien other," an underclass with a separate culture and way of life that is "both alien and threatening."[44] The result has been a tendency toward publicly marking out the offender through community notification schemes, sex offender registers, distinctive uniforms, and the proliferation of sanctions such as deprivation of the franchise and the ability to otherwise participate in public life. This new penology has transformed offenders from members of the public in need of realignment with society to deviant outsiders "deprived of their citizenship status and the rights that accompany it."[45]

CONCLUSION

The role of membership theory in shaping the convergence of immigration and criminal law seems likely to lead to a downward spiral of protections for non-members and a significant constriction of the definition of who is a member. A significant overlap between criminal law and immigration law inevitably will affect the way that decision makers view the consequences of exclusion from membership in each area. As criminal sanctions for immigration-related conduct and criminal grounds for removal from the United States

41. *See* Jonathan H. Wardle, Note, *The Strategic Use of Mexico to Restrict South American Access to the Diversity Visa Lottery*, 58 VAND. L. REV. 1963, 1984–90 (2005).

42. *See supra* note 20.

43. *See* Kasey Corbit, Note, *Inadequate and Inappropriate Mental Health Treatment and Minority Overrepresentation in the Juvenile Justice System*, 3 HASTINGS RACE & POVERTY L.J. 75, 75–77 (2005) (collecting statistics on disproportionate representation of African Americans, Latinos, and Native Americans in the criminal justice system).

44. *See* GARLAND, *supra* note 30, at 135–36.

45. *Internal Exile*, *supra* note 33, at 181.

continue to expand, aliens become synonymous with criminals. As collateral sanctions for criminal violations continue to target the hallmarks of citizenship and community membership, ex-offenders become synonymous with aliens.

When noncitizens are classified as criminals, expulsion presents itself as the natural solution. The individual's stake in the U.S. community, such as family ties, employment, contribution to the community, and whether the noncitizen has spent a majority of his lifetime in the United States, becomes secondary to the perceived need to protect the community. Similarly, when criminals become aliens, the sovereign state becomes indispensable to police the nation against this internal enemy. In combating an internal invasion of criminal outsiders, containing them through collateral sanctions such as registration and removal from public participation appears critical.

Although criminal law and immigration law begin with opposite assumptions about the membership status of the individuals that they regulate, once the individual is deemed unworthy of membership, the consequences are very similar in both realms. The state treats the individual—literally or figuratively—as an alien, shorn of the rights and privileges of membership. This creates an ever-expanding population of outsiders with a stake in the U.S. community that may be at least as strong as those of incumbent members. The result is a society increasingly stratified by flexible conceptions of membership in which non-members are cast out of the community by means of borders, walls, rules, and public condemnation.

3 THE SECURITY MYTH

PUNISHING IMMIGRANTS IN THE NAME OF NATIONAL SECURITY

Jennifer M. Chacón

In times of national crisis, the U.S. government has a consistent history of responding by incarcerating, and in many cases removing, large numbers of foreign nationals or groups that are seen as "foreign" based on their national, racial, ethnic, or religious background. The U.S. government's actions after the attacks on the Pentagon and World Trade Center on September 11, 2001, presented another example of the classic response to crisis in the United States. Many potential "suspects" were identified primarily on the basis of racial and ethnic profiling. As in the past, these suspects were detained on immigration-related charges on lower standards of proof than that which would have been required for criminal investigations. Their confinement was subject to far fewer procedural constraints than would have been required for criminal detention, and many were removed from the country without public hearings.

While post-September 11 detentions and removals of noncitizens resembled many other historical moments of crisis in the United States, the "emergency" response to September 11 is not entirely of a piece with past responses. This is because the post-September 11 era of immigration enforcement has been not only a crisis response but also the continuation of an expansive trend in immigration enforcement that has been emerging for more than a decade. Prior to 2001, most lawmakers and their constituents viewed the expansion of immigration restrictions and immigration law enforcement primarily as a matter of crime control. While some U.S. lawmakers began to view immigration laws as an important vehicle for anti-terrorism efforts in the early 1990s, a national security rationale for immigration reform did not dominate legislative or national discussions in the pre-September 11 era. Since September 11, however, the rationale of "national security" has provided the primary justification for more vigorous immigration law enforcement.

Jennifer M. Chacón is professor of law at the University of California, Irvine.

Reprinted with permission of the University of Pittsburgh Press, from "The Security Myth: Punishing Immigrants in the Name of National Security," by Jennifer M. Chacón in *Immigration, Integration, and Security: America and Europe in Comparative Perspective,* edited by Ariane Chebel d'Appollonia and Simon Reich. Copyright © 2008 by the University of Pittsburgh Press.

Al Qaeda's successful infliction of massive damage on U.S. soil on September 11, 2001, revealed the shortcomings of the U.S. government's intelligence capabilities. Because the violent acts of September 11 were perpetrated by noncitizens, it is not surprising that immigration laws and the immigration enforcement bureaucracy came under scrutiny in the period that followed. At that point, an appropriate crisis response would have been to demand genuine changes in immigration enforcement, as well as other areas of law enforcement. Responsive reforms to the immigration bureaucracy could have included the implementation of uniform, comprehensive registration programs for noncitizens admitted or already present in the country. Another reform option would have been to ensure appropriate information sharing between immigration enforcement agencies and other law enforcement bodies. Similarly, the government might have systematically increased the investigation of immigration crimes that provide the foundation for terrorist activity, such as alien smuggling and document fraud.

Instead of rethinking immigration enforcement priorities, the U.S. government reorganized many of the immigration administrative institutions and consolidated them under the umbrella of the Department of Homeland Security. The rhetoric of "national security" was then used to justify the ongoing expansion of the immigration enforcement apparatus and the implementation of harsh new immigration regulations that increasingly criminalized immigrants. Post-September 11 immigration "reform" has done little to enhance U.S. security, but national security rhetoric increasingly insulates the immigration enforcement apparatus from many of the constitutional constraints that apply to the criminal justice system.

In this chapter, I discuss the origins and implications of the growing mismatch between the legal doctrines governing immigration enforcement and the realities of the post-September 11 immigration enforcement bureaucracy in the United States. I explain the historical evolution of the doctrinal link between national security and immigration enforcement in U.S. constitutional law. I also explore the legislative changes that have converted many aspects of immigration enforcement into an adjunct of domestic crime control—changes that call into question the historical constitutional understanding of immigration enforcement. I then describe the post-September 11 security responses effectuated through immigration enforcement and explain how these responses illustrate the wide-ranging powers of the contemporary immigration enforcement bureaucracy. Finally, I discuss the threat to individual rights posed by the growth of a relatively unchecked immigration bureaucracy that conflates crime control with national security. In a "nation of immigrants," where 11.5 percent of the population is foreign born, the increasing reliance on the immigration bureaucracy to serve the ends of the criminal justice system has the potential to transform the general administration of criminal justice in the United States in fundamentally illiberal ways.[1] These changes suggest increasing challenges to conventional civil liberties protections.

---

1. On the percentage of foreign-born citizens, see Thomas Alexander Aleinikoff, David A. Martin, and Hiroshi Motomura, *Immigration and Citizenship: Process and Policy*, 5th ed. (St. Paul, MN: Thomson/West, 2003), 266.

IMMIGRATION AND THE PLENARY POWERS DOCTRINE

The link between security and immigration finds its roots in the earliest doctrines authorizing Congress to control immigration policy at the federal level. This is true even though the vast majority of the practices of immigration enforcement are not actually concerned with national security, at least as that notion has been traditionally conceived. According to Gerald L. Neuman, "the vast bulk of immigration enforcement involves such routine matters as poverty, crime, regulatory violations, and protection of the domestic labor market. These restrictions do not rely on sensitive foreign policy choices for their justification."[2]

Early in American history, the source and scope of federal congressional power over immigration law and policy were unimportant issues; Congress made no effort to regulate immigration through federal statute until 1875. The only significant exceptions were the Alien Friends Act of 1798, which was never enforced and expired after two years, and the Enemy Alien Act of 1798, which has remained a part of the law through the present day. The Enemy Alien Act authorizes the president to detain, expel, or otherwise restrict the freedom of any citizen of a country upon which the United States has declared war. It was almost a century before this wartime provision was joined by other, more general federal immigration legislation.

The rise of federal immigration restrictions, and the legal challenges mounted against these restrictions, required the courts to answer the question of whether the U.S. Congress actually had the power to regulate immigration. The Constitution of the United States contains no express provision granting the federal legislature the power to regulate immigration. Courts variously have discussed the possibility of finding this power implicit in the Commerce Clause, the Migration or Importation Clause, the Naturalization Clause, and the War Clause. But none of these sources is entirely satisfactory as a basis for congressional power over immigration. Thus, in granting the U.S. Congress tremendously broad authority to regulate immigration, the Supreme Court of the United States relied heavily upon the notion that immigration regulation was an inherent power of a sovereign nation. The Court rationalized that the power to regulate immigration was a necessary part of the power of a sovereign state to defend itself.

In 1882, Congress enacted the first general, federal immigration provision—the Immigration Act of 1882—which permitted the deportation of people who entered the United States without authorization and created the Office of Immigration within the Department of the Treasury. The law imposed a head tax of fifty cents per immigrant and excluded "idiots, lunatics, convicts, and persons likely to become a public charge."[3] The Congress also enacted the Chinese Exclusion Act of 1882, suspending all future immigration of Chinese laborers. In the so-called Chinese Exclusion Case of 1889, the Supreme Court first upheld Congress's authority to pass laws excluding "foreigners" as "an incident of sovereignty belonging to the government of the United States."[4]

---

2. Gerald L. Neuman, *Strangers to the Constitution: Immigrants, Borders, and Fundamental Law* (Princeton, NJ: Princeton University Press, 1996), 137 (quote).

3. "An Act to Regulate Immigration," (Immigration Act of 1882), Aug. 3, 1882, 22 Stat. ch. 376.

4. *Chae Chan Ping v. United States* (Chinese Exclusion Act Case), 130 U.S. 609 (1889).

Cases decided shortly after the Chinese Exclusion Case made clear that this "sovereign" power was not simply the broad power to exclude noncitizens from entering the United States but also the power to deport noncitizens from within the United States. In 1893, in *Fong Yue Ting v. United States*, the Court extended the holding of the Chinese Exclusion Case, taking a deferential stance toward congressional decisions to deport noncitizens residing in the United States without authorization. Specifically, the Court upheld a law that required a noncitizen seeking to avoid deportation to produce a "credible white witness" to vouch for their physical presence in the United States prior to a certain time.[5] "The right of a nation to expel or deport foreigners who have not been naturalized, or taken any steps towards becoming citizens of the country, rests upon the same grounds, and is as absolute and unqualified, as the right to prohibit and prevent their entrance into the country."[6]

The Court continued to justify the political branch's plenary power over immigration. This plenary power included the authority to deport noncitizens physically present in the United States, by characterizing such power as "an inherent and inalienable right of every sovereign and independent nation, essential to its safety, its independence, and its welfare."[7] The rationale is that immigration is inextricably tied up with foreign policy. The protection of the national interest in such areas is "so exclusively entrusted to the political branches of government as to be largely immune from judicial inquiry or interference."[8] The view of immigration administration as a function of sovereignty, and as inextricably tied to the nation-state's foreign powers and right of self-defense, has immunized immigration law from a great deal of the judicial scrutiny that usually applies when state actions affect individual rights. This is true despite almost universal scholarly condemnation of the plenary powers doctrine.[9]

The vision of immigration control articulated in these early rulings also resulted in the legal treatment of deportation as distinct from—and requiring less procedural protections than—criminal punishment. The legal distinction between removal and "punishment" has its roots in very early immigration cases. For example, in the *Fong Yue Ting* case, even as the Court recognized Congress's seemingly unlimited authority to deport noncitizens in the name of sovereignty and security, the dicta of the 1893 *Fong Yue Ting* decision also distinguished the deportation of noncitizens from "transportation." In contrast to transportation or banishment, the Court found that "[t]he order of deportation is not a punishment for crime." Instead deportation was "a method of enforcing the return to his own country of an alien who has not complied with . . . conditions" for residence in the United States.[10] In this circumscribed context, the Court recognized Congress's broad power to deport noncitizens and constructed deportation not as punishment but as an administration of the sovereign immigration function.

5. *Fong Yue Ting v. United States*, 149 U.S. 732 (1893).

6. Ibid., 707.

7. Ibid., 711.

8. *Harisiades v. Shaughnessy*, 342 U.S. 580, 589 (1952).

9. See, e.g., Neuman, *Strangers to the Constitution*.

10. *Fong Yue Ting v. United States*, 149 U.S. 730 (1893).

The deliberate distinction between deportation and criminal punishment was again a theme in the 1896 case of *Wong Wing v. United States*. In that case the Court upheld the deportation of a noncitizen and also held that his detention pursuant to his deportation was constitutional and did not constitute punishment. But the Court struck down the portion of the law that authorized that a deportable noncitizen could be subject to up to a year of hard labor, which could be imposed as a part of the order of deportation. The Court considered imprisonment at hard labor as the imposition of punishment, requiring a jury trial. The Court held that "[i]t is not consistent with the theory of our government that the legislature should, after having defined an offense as an infamous crime, find the fact of guilt and adjudge the punishment by one of its own agents."[11]

At the time the Court decided *Wong Wing*, deportation by and large looked to be a measure meant to cure inadvertent failures in admission and exclusion policies. It was not linked to offenses committed after entry. It was a backward-looking remedy. In this context, the distinction between deportation and punishment had some basis in reality. Over time, the distinction between deportation when used to expel those who never should have entered and deportation when used as punishment for post-entry conduct has faded.

IMMIGRATION CONTROL MEASURES
BECOME A MEANS OF CRIME CONTROL

The line between administrative policy and criminal punishment has blurred since the deportation of Wong Wing. Over the course of the past one hundred years, immigration detention and removal increasingly have become tools for achieving domestic crime control ends. However, the Court has continued to maintain that immigration control is a security function and that deportation is not criminal punishment but an administrative means to achieve national security through border control. A look at the evolution of immigration law in the United States over the past century reveals that these legal doctrines are increasingly out of step with the realities of immigration enforcement. Even though certain immigration enforcement measures legitimately and necessarily serve the ends of security, the security rationale has come to justify a host of immigration laws and enforcement measures that are properly characterized as criminal law enforcement and that are, as such, clearly distinct from security concerns.

The shift in immigration enforcement began as long ago as 1903. The immigration law of 1903 barred entry to "anarchists, or persons who believe in or advocate the overthrow of the Government of the United States or of all government or of all forms of law."[12] The consequence of this provision was that foreign nationals could be excluded from entry on the basis of speech or actions that were protected by the First Amendment when undertaken by a citizen in the United States. More significant shifts followed. In 1917, Congress extended the exclusion provisions to those who advocated the unlawful destruction of property, disbelieved or were opposed to organized government, or were members of

11. *Wong Wing v. United States*, 163 U.S. 228 (1896).
12. *Immigration Act of 1903*, ch. 1012, § 2, 32 Stat. 1213, 1214 (1903).

organizations espousing such ideas.[13] A year later, Congress added a new category of immigrant subject to exclusion: subversives. The Anarchist Act of 1918 provided for the exclusion of "subversive" aliens and also authorized their expulsion without time limits. At this point, deportation began its shift from a purely corrective administrative tool to one sometimes used to complement the criminal law in sanctioning certain post-entry conduct. The shift to the use of immigration law as a means of punishing the deviant noncitizen was doubly masked—it was constructed as a security issue and its remedy was constructed as an issue of immigration control. Since deportation of the "subversive" was not legally understood as criminal punishment, the deportation provisions had an advantage over criminal law: Congress could subject noncitizens engaged in certain conduct to deportation even when that conduct was constitutionally protected from criminal punishment. And by that time, it was already becoming apparent that the flexible notions of due process that governed deportation proceedings did not carry the same degree of procedural protections guaranteed in criminal proceedings. Thus, the Immigration Act of 1917 and the Anarchist Act provided a quick and effective means to detain thousands of noncitizens and to deport hundreds of them in a series of raids—the Palmer Raids—carried out in 1919 and 1920 in response to a series of violent domestic attacks, even when no evidence existed to link most of these people to the crimes.[14]

A few short years after the raids, the Immigration Act of May 26, 1924, changed the face of U.S. immigration forever. Before 1920, very few people had been deported from the United States.[15] This changed with the enactment of strict racial quotas that were included in the 1924 law. The 1924 immigration law eliminated the statute of limitations on deportation for nearly all forms of unlawful entry and entry without a valid visa. It also created a land Border Patrol, the principal function of which was to police the southern border. In 1929, the act of illegal entry itself was criminalized for the first time. Congress enacted a law making entry at a point not designated by the U.S. government, or by means of fraud or misrepresentation, a misdemeanor.[16] A previously deported "alien" who reentered the country could be convicted of a felony.[17] In other words, the act of immigration itself, when performed outside of legal channels, became a violation of criminal law.

The change in law was followed by a change in the discourse around undocumented migrants. Until the 1930s, immigrants were categorized descriptively as either "legitimate" immigrants on the one hand or "illegitimate" or "ineligible" immigrants on the other. But the changes in the immigration laws that Congress enacted in the 1920s created the "illegal alien" (see De Genova, this volume). Over time, would-be Mexican immigrants greatly out-

13. *Immigration Act of Feb. 5, 1917*, ch. 29, § 19, 39 Stat. 874 (1917).

14. See David Cole, *Enemy Aliens: Double Standards and Constitutional Freedoms* (New York: Free Press, 2003), 117–23.

15. "Between 1892 and 1907 the Immigration Service deported only a few hundred aliens a year and between 1908 and 1920 an average of two or three thousand a year—mostly aliens removed from asylums, hospitals or jails" (Mai M. Ngai, *Impossible Subjects: Illegal Aliens and the Making of Modern America* [Princeton, NJ: Princeton University Press, 2004], 59–60).

16. Act of Mar. 4, 1929, 45 Stat. 1551 (1929).

17. According to U.S. immigration law, "any person not a citizen or national of the United States" is an "alien" (8 U.S.C.A. § 1101[a][3] [2000]).

numbered lawfully available immigrant visas. Those who entered without visas violated the new immigration laws. According to Mae Ngai, "[p]ositive law thus constituted undocumented immigrants as criminals both fulfilling and fueling nativist discourse."[18] By the 1950s, the phrases "illegal immigrant" and "illegal aliens" had become staples of the popular lexicon. Today, the phrases "illegal alien" and "illegal immigrant" are still commonly used in the press and by politicians when describing unauthorized migrants in the United States. One result is that the linkage between alien status and illegal status is cemented in the public mind. With their entry and eventually their labor criminalized, certain groups of people—most commonly Mexicans—have increasingly been constructed as "illegal aliens," whether or not that label applies to them (see De Genova, this volume).

The labeling of certain groups of immigrants so as to convey their "illegality" has left these groups particularly vulnerable to deportation, which can be seen as a natural and appropriate means of dealing with the transgressions of perceived outsiders. Thus, it is perhaps unsurprising that as the illegality of certain immigrants was constructed by legal definition and cemented by popular discourse, Congress expanded deportation grounds based on post-entry conduct. The list of deportable offenses came to include a laundry list of mundane post-entry criminal or quasi-criminal actions. Immigration law became an effective tool not only for barring the admission of undesired "aliens" but also for punishing through deportation many noncitizens (either lawfully admitted or illegally present). The law was simple to use because there was no need to adhere to the due process norms of criminal procedure institutionalized in a series of Supreme Court rulings during the civil rights revolution of the 1960s.

Two 1996 laws—the Antiterrorism and Effective Death Penalty Act (AEDPA) and the Illegal Immigration Reform and Immigrant Responsibility Act (IIRIRA)—resulted in a significant expansion of grounds for removal under criminal law. These laws altered prior national policies by increasing penalties for violations of immigration laws, expanding the class of noncitizens subject to removal for the commission of crimes, and imposing a system of tough penalties that favor removal even in cases involving relatively minor infractions or very old crimes. The changes applied retroactively, so even if an offense would not have rendered a noncitizen removable at the time of its commission, the noncitizen was subject to removal if the offense was a removable offense under the new law.

Following the enactment of these laws, noncitizens can be removed and permanently barred from reentry for the commission of an "aggravated felony." This category, as Nancy Morawetz has explained, has an "Alice-in Wonderland"-like quality in that such offenses need be neither aggravated nor a felony.[19] These include not only things like "murder, rape, or sexual abuse of a minor" but also a crime of violence or a theft offense "for which the term of imprisonment is at least a year."[20] The limits of the law are still being tested. For example, hundreds of noncitizens—many legal residents, many long-term residents—were deported for driving under the influence before the Supreme Court found that such an act

18. Ngai, *Impossible Subjects*, 61.

19. Nancy Morawetz, "Understanding the Impact of the 1996 Deportation Laws and the Limited Scope of Proposed Reforms," *Harvard Law Review* 113 (2000): 1936, 1951.

20. 8 U.S.C.A. § 1101(a)(43)(A) (2000); 8 U.S.C.A. § 1101(a)(43)(F)&(G) (2000).

did not qualify as an "aggravated felony."[21] Aggravated felons are statutorily barred from seeking virtually any form of relief from removal. There is no statute of limitations on these provisions, so noncitizens can be removed for "aggravated felonies" committed years ago. The more than 156,000 "aggravated felons" who have been removed from the United States since 1997 had been in the country an average of fifteen years prior to being put into removal proceedings; 25 percent had been in the United States more than twenty years.[22]

Nor do the penalties stop with noncitizens convicted of "aggravated felonies." The 1996 laws, operating in conjunction with a host of immigration restrictions that have evolved over the past century, create harsh immigration consequences for many other crimes as well. The commission of two or more "crimes involving moral turpitude" at any time after entry subjects a noncitizen to deportation, no matter how long that person has been present in the United States.[23] After 1996, relief from removal is not available for anyone falling into this category who has not been a lawful permanent resident for at least five years. Before 1996, a single crime involving moral turpitude within five years of entry was not a ground of deportability for lawful permanent residents unless the individual was actually sentenced to at least one year of incarceration. However, after 1996, removal turned not on whether the sentence was for one year but on whether a sentence of a year or more was possible. In New York, for example, a person could receive mandatory deportation for such offenses as jumping a turnstile or the unauthorized use of cable television service.

At the same time that the 1996 laws massively expanded the number of removable offenses, they also greatly decreased the power of judges to exercise discretion in cases involving the deportation of noncitizens who had committed certain crimes. For example, during the period between 1989 and 1995, immigration judges and the Board of Immigration Appeals had collectively waived deportation in about 51 percent of the cases in which a noncitizen had committed a deportable offense. To do so, they relied on the discretionary waiver of deportation permitted by Section 212(c) of the Immigration and Nationality Act (INA). But the 1996 law eliminated relief under the former Section 212(c). In its place, the 1996 law provided for much more limited "cancellation of removal" under Section 240A of the INA. Explicit in the Congressional Record is the fact that section 240A(a) relief is intended only for "highly unusual cases involving outstanding aliens."[24] Among its many limitations, cancellation of removal is not available to anyone who commits any offense that falls under the expansive "aggravated felony" umbrella. Finally, in a twist that rendered the immigration law quite detrimental to the liberty interests of noncitizens, the law vastly expanded the number of instances in which a noncitizen would be subject to mandatory detention during the course of removal proceedings.

As a practical matter, these changes in law and policy mean that tens of thousands of noncitizens in the United States are now vulnerable to removal based on post-entry crimi-

21. *Leocal v. Ashcroft*, 543 U.S. 1 (2004).

22. TRAC Immigration, "How Often Is the Aggravated Felony Statute Used?" http://trac.syr.edu/immigration/reports/158 (accessed July 22, 2006).

23. 8 U.S.C.A. § 1227(a)(2)(A)(ii) (2000).

24. Julie K. Rannik, "Comment, 'The Anti-Terrorism and Effective Death Penalty Act of 1996': A Death Sentence for the 212(c) Waiver," 28 *University of Miami Inter-American Law Review* 28 (1996): 139.

nal conduct. They are also vulnerable to lengthy detention, pending the outcome of their immigration proceedings (see Hernández, this volume). In enacting these provisions, members of Congress clearly viewed the measures as a means of punishing the criminal conduct of noncitizens. Nevertheless, the Supreme Court has not revisited its generic nineteenth-century pronouncement that deportation is not punishment. Consequently, widespread detention and removal for post-entry criminal conduct is carried out through administrative bodies of the executive branch and is subject to relatively few procedural constraints and limited judicial review. The government's response to the attacks of September 11, 2001, illustrates the absence of procedural protections available to noncitizens subject to punitive immigration detentions and removals in times of national crisis.

In light of the legal and political developments of the 1990s, September 11, 2001, cannot accurately be labeled a watershed for U.S. immigration policy. Most of the expansive removal provisions had already been enacted into law prior to that time. The spike in American immigration enforcement began in the 1990s, not after 2001. But the response to September 11 that was carried out through immigration policy is still worth examining. It demonstrates the degree to which the criminalization of immigration, which reached its legal zenith with the 1996 laws, blurred easily into the "securitization" of immigration policy that took place after September 11. The post-September 11 response illustrates the degree to which the long-standing rhetoric of security in the area of immigration law enforcement has created a startling degree of insularity for the immigration bureaucracy. This insularity is not limited to "national security" issues but comfortably extends just as readily to basic crime control functions carried out by the immigration enforcement bureaucracy.

POST–9/11 CHANGES TO THE SUBSTANTIVE LAW

In response to the September 11 attacks, the U.S. Congress enacted a wide range of legislation, including the USA PATRIOT Act in 2001, the Homeland Security Act (HSA) and the Enhanced Border Security and Visa Entry Reform Act (EBSVERA) in 2002, the Intelligence Reform and Terrorism Prevention Act in 2004, and the REAL ID Act in 2005.

Many of the post-September 11 laws are aimed primarily at increasing the ease with which the government can monitor noncitizens. EBSVERA mandated the creation of an integrated entry and exit data system and specified the technological standards for such a system, including the use of biometric identifiers. It also mandated the creation of a detailed database for monitoring noncitizens present on student visas.[25] Both of these programs are being integrated into a single comprehensive database called the U.S. Visitor and Immigrant Status Indicator Technology Program (US VISIT).

The HSA rolled all of the functions of the Immigration and Naturalization Service (INS) into a newly created Department of Homeland Security. The DHS is responsible not only for immigration enforcement and oversight but also for the oversight of disaster response agencies such as the Federal Emergency Management Agency (FEMA), which is charged with responding to disasters, including hurricanes, floods, and tornadoes. As with most of

---

25. This is known as the Student and Exchange Visitor Information System, or SEVIS.

the other post-September 11 legislation, the Homeland Security Act focused on consolidating governmental immigration functions with other security-related functions.

Congress also enacted several notable changes to the law of removal. First, both the PATRIOT Act and later the REAL ID Act expanded the definition of "terrorist aliens" who would be subject to removal as security threats. The PATRIOT Act retroactively amended the INA, expanding the reach of the terrorism definition to subject to removal aliens who provided "material support" to terrorism. This includes support to organizations that are not designated as terrorist organizations in the INA or through publication in the Federal Register but were deemed to have engaged in "terrorist activity." That category includes actions involving the use of any "dangerous device" (not just explosives and firearms) for anything other than "mere personal monetary gain."[26] The REAL ID Act greatly expanded the definition of "terrorist organization" to include "a group of two or more people, whether organized or not, which engages in or has a subgroup which engages in any form of terrorist activity."[27] It thus further expanded the grounds for inadmissibility based on support of terrorism as well as being a member of a terrorist organization. Although these provisions are purportedly security related, their impact on security is dubious. The definitions sweep so broadly that they can clearly encompass not just "terrorism" but general criminal acts as well. The expanded provisions thus imbue immigration enforcement agencies with tremendous discretion but do not provide a more effective tool for identifying and removing people who engage in acts of terrorism. Indeed, the expansive provisions have had a demonstrably negative effect on U.S. asylum policy. The United States is excluding thousands of refugees who are victims of terrorism because many refugees flee after being forced to give food, shelter, or other support to armed or terrorist groups or authoritarian regimes that qualify as "terrorist organizations" under the law. Ironically, the law bars them from admission for precisely the same reason that they are seeking refugee status.

One additional post-September 11 legal provision was aimed directly at facilitating the arrest and removal of noncitizens who purportedly posed security risks. Section 412 of the PATRIOT Act added a section to the INA that would allow the Attorney General to "certify" noncitizens when there are "reasonable grounds to believe" that the person is inadmissible or deportable on certain national security grounds.[28] The provision mandates detention for anyone so certified, and the government has up to seven days to initiate removal proceedings against any individual detained under this provision. These detentions may be indefinite, so long as the case is reviewed every six months. In contrast to the procedures permitted under Section 412, standard immigration and criminal procedures generally limit detention to two days prior to the commencement of proceedings. This legal change sounds significant, if not drastic. In reality, however, Section 412 has never been invoked. Immigration enforcement officials do not need Section 412 because the vast power of the executive branch in the area of immigration law enforcement has allowed the federal government to arrest and detain noncitizens for lengthy periods even without invoking section 412. Indeed, by the time the provision was enacted, the Immigration and Naturalization

26. USA PATRIOT Act § 411 (codified as amended at 8 U.S.C.A. § 1226a[a][3][2001]).
27. REAL ID Act, § 103.
28. 8 U.S.C.A. §1226a.

Service had already amended its own regulations to allow for the possibility of extended detention of noncitizens beyond the standard two-day period for a "reasonable period of time" in the event of an "emergency or other extraordinary circumstances."[29]

The post-9/11 legislative changes with the most practical significance have taken place not in substantive immigration law but in appropriations bills, in which Congress has steadily increased the budget of Immigration and Customs Enforcement (ICE) to an all-time high. Large increases in the immigration enforcement budget began before September 11 but accelerated in the wake of the events of that day. From fiscal year (FY) 1993 to FY 2005, the Border Patrol budget quadrupled from $362 million to $1.4 billion, with the largest annual increase taking place after the events of September 11, 2001.[30] Since the creation of ICE in 2003, the budget for that agency has grown each year. In FY 2006, that budget totaled $3.9 billion in direct appropriations and fees for ICE—an increase of more than $216 million or 6.3 percent above FY 2005.[31] The resulting enforcement bureaucracy touches millions of lives, including the lives of thousands of noncitizens who pose no security threat of any kind.

CHANGES IN IMMIGRATION ENFORCEMENT

After 9/11, Attorney General John Ashcroft made this pronouncement: "Let the terrorists among us be warned: If you overstay your visa by even one day we will arrest you. If you violate local law, you will be put in jail and kept in custody as long as possible."[32] The surveillance of certain noncitizens and the enforcement of immigration laws continue to expand. The entire immigration bureaucracy has been reorganized through the prism of security concerns. Despite these changes, neither legislation nor executive enforcement efforts have been efficiently tailored toward the elimination of security threats. Furthermore, changes in immigration enforcement have increased racial and ethnic profiling in newly expanded immigration enforcement efforts and flooded an overburdened administrative and judicial system with detainees and cases that are unrelated to security concerns. The most troubling aspects of the U.S. government's response to September 11 in the area of immigration were not the result of new legislation. Instead they were the result of changes in administrative rules governing immigration enforcement and of exercises of prosecutorial power that sometimes seemed contrary to existing law.

"Security" and Prosecutorial Discretion

Ashcroft's warning to the "terrorists among us" summarizes the Justice Department's clear policy of using the immigration enforcement bureaucracy as a means of preventatively

29. See Muzzaffar A. Chishti et. al., *America's Challenge: Domestic Security, Civil Liberties, and National Unity After September 11* (Washington, DC: Migration Policy Institute, 2003), 52–53.

30. Walter Ewing, *Border Insecurity: U.S. Border-Enforcement Policies and National Security*, Immigration Policy Center Report, Washington, DC, Spring 2006.

31. U.S. Immigration and Customs Enforcement, Public Information, "ICE Budget Gains 6.3 Percent in FY 06 DHS Spending Bill," *Inside ICE* 2, no. 23 (2005), http://immigrantsolidarity.org/Documents/ICE/ICENewsletter 111505.pdf.

32. Attorney General John Ashcroft, quoted in U.S. Department of Justice, *The September 11 Detainees* (Washington, DC: U.S. Office of the Inspector General, April 2003), 12, http://www.justice.gov/oig/special/0306/full.pdf.

detaining any perceived "terrorists." Immigration law already provided an effective tool for widespread detention and removal of noncitizens. Therefore, simple changes in immigration enforcement practices, rather than changes to law or regulation, truly account for the bulk of the most troubling post-September 11 changes to the immigration landscape.

For example, on November 9, 2001, Attorney General Ashcroft called on thousands of noncitizens from countries suspected of harboring terrorists to participate in "voluntary" interviews. Those in violation of the immigration laws could be subjected to jail without bond. A second wave of such interviews was carried out in March 2002. No change in law was needed to enable this discriminatory application of immigration laws. Nor were changes in the law needed to enact the so-called "Operation TIPS" (Terrorism Information and Prevention System), which encouraged U.S. citizens to report "suspicious" activity.

Young male Arabs and Muslims were prioritized in immigration investigations on the basis of their race, ethnicity, and national origin. On October 31, 2001, Ashcroft announced the creation of a Foreign Terrorist Tracking Task Force (FTTTF) aimed at detaining potential terrorists on the grounds of alleged immigration violations. The task force targeted Arab and Muslim immigrant communities. One important tool for accomplishing the stated goal was the initiation of the National Security Entry-Exit Registration System (NSEERS). The Department of Justice initiated the NSEERS program in September 2002. The program required noncitizen men from certain—predominantly Arab and Muslim— countries to register with the INS.[33] Many who registered were detained on the basis of immigration violations. Those who failed to register could also be detained for that failure. It is difficult to estimate how many noncitizens were detained under these programs aimed at alleged immigration violators meeting certain profiles. David Cole writes that "a conservative estimate would . . . place the number of domestic detentions in the war on terrorism as of May 2003 at over 5,000."[34]

U.S. law enforcement agencies thus arrested and interviewed thousands of noncitizens in the wake of September 11. Immigration detention became the central tool of this enforcement effort. When the FBI suspected that their detainees had violated immigration law, those individuals were transferred into INS custody. In the eleven months following September 11, 2001, the INS detained 738 such individuals.[35] To justify their detention on immigration charges, the FBI sent routine, boilerplate memoranda to the Executive Office for Immigration Review stating that "the FBI has been unable to rule out the possibility that the respondent is somehow linked to, or possesses knowledge of, the terrorist attacks."[36] Detention in many cases continued while the investigation of the person in detention proceeded under a controversial "hold until cleared by the FBI" policy.[37] When the Office of Inspector General later conducted an investigation of post-September 11

33. Designated countries included Afghanistan, Algeria, Bahrain, Eritrea, Iran, Iraq, Lebanon, Morocco, North Korea, Oman, Pakistan, Qatar, Somalia, Saudi Arabia, Syria, Tunisia, United Arab Emirates, and Yemen.

34. Cole, *Enemy Aliens*, 25.

35. U.S. Department of Justice, *The September 11 Detainees*, 12.

36. American Immigration Lawyers Association (AILA), "Boiling the Frog Slowly: Executive Branch Actions Since September 11, 2001," *Bender's Immigration Bulletin* 7 (Oct. 15, 2002): 1236.

37. U.S. Department of Justice, *The September 11 Detainees*, 37–43.

detention policy, it found problems with the length of detention and the INS's automatic opposition to bond. It also found significant problems in the treatment of the detainees. These problems included physical and verbal abuse by some correctional officers, twenty-four-hour lighting in certain cells, and the imposition of a "communications blackout" that deprived detainees of the opportunity to make their confinement known to family members or counsel.[38]

The obvious problem with the strategy of pursuing national security through expansive immigration enforcement techniques is that it ensures that many innocent people will be detained, mistreated, and pressed into removing themselves from the country. The federal government is currently in the process of trying to address some of the wrongs committed in the frenzy of post-September 11 activity. In February 2006, the federal government reached its first settlement in a lawsuit arising out of its treatment of noncitizens in the days following September 11. The government agreed to pay $300,000 to settle a lawsuit brought by an Egyptian citizen, Ehab Elmaghraby, who was among dozens of Muslim men swept up and detained in the New York area.[39] Elmaghraby and a co-plaintiff, Javaid Iqbal of Pakistan, faced tremendous barriers to filing their lawsuits since they had already been sent back to their home countries. Unfortunately, for this and other reasons, many noncitizens will never receive compensation for their unjust detentions and their coerced "voluntary" departures from the United States.

Administrative Rulemaking

In addition to changes in practice, the government also changed some of the implementing regulations that governed the enforcement of immigration laws. Sometimes these changes were of questionable legality.

One example can be found in ICE's detention policies. Prior to 2001, if an immigration judge found that a noncitizen was entitled to release on bond pending immigration proceedings, that person was generally freed unless the INS made a strong case to the contrary. After September 11, Attorney General Ashcroft oversaw a change in administrative regulations requiring that an individual be detained through the appeal of the decision to the Board of Immigration Appeals, even after an immigration judge ordered a noncitizen's release from detention. Additionally, as previously noted, the regulations were amended to allow for protracted pre-hearing detention in cases of emergency.

A second example of an expansive administrative rule change is the alteration of the Department of Justice's regulation on racial profiling. Attorney General Ashcroft strengthened the power of the administrative bodies responsible for immigration enforcement. He did so through the issuance of regulations expressly authorizing executive officials to engage in certain forms of racial profiling in immigration enforcement, even though such profiling was formally prohibited in other federal law enforcement endeavors. Even before those regulatory changes, racial profiling had become an important component of the law enforcement response to September 11. However, in June 2003, with the passage of new guide-

---

38. Ibid., ch. 7.
39. Nina Bernstein, "U.S. Is Settling Detainee's Suit in 9/11 Sweep," *New York Times*, Feb. 28, 2006, A1.

lines on racial profiling, the Justice Department formally sanctioned the use of race in the context of "national security" investigations. It simultaneously continued an earlier ban on racial profiling in traditional domestic criminal investigations.[40]

Unfortunately, this rule provides few real limitations on the use of profiling. The problem extends well beyond the selective (and overly aggressive) enforcement of immigration laws against Arabs and Muslims. As domestic crimes and national security concerns are conflated, other ethnic groups are becoming a target for aggressive crime control measures undertaken through immigration laws.

Generally, the legislative and administrative changes enacted after September 11, 2001, reflect the sort of crisis response that has been deployed against noncitizens in the United States at various points in history. As such, although these examples are deeply troubling, they are not surprising. More surprising is the degree to which this security response subsequently has become blurred and been altered into a more general mechanism for effectuating domestic crime control.

THE RHETORIC AND REALITY OF IMMIGRATION POLICY AND NATIONAL SECURITY

The perceived link between immigration and security is driving a massive effort to deport noncitizens, but there does not appear to be any systematic effort to apply these efforts to the most serious offenders or the most dangerous security threats. As "national security" is defined with increasing breadth, virtually all noncitizens can be targeted based on national, ethnic, and racial profiling. Such profiling generally tends to affect the rights of citizens as well. The resulting frenzy of activity to deport or prosecute immigration violators usurps resources—prosecutorial, bureaucratic, and judicial—which might be better spent on identifying and incapacitating those who pose genuine threats to security. Rather than increasing security, the current approach seems more likely to undermine due process protections and individual rights.

As previously noted, the security and terrorism grounds for removal were expanded with the passage of the 1996 laws and further expanded after September 11. The breadth of the resulting provisions raises serious questions as to whether the law is tailored to address an appropriately narrow class of security threats. Paradoxically, despite the significant expansion of these categories, the number of immigrants removed on security and terrorism grounds has contracted, not expanded, over the course of the past decade. In the early 1990s, removals on security and terrorism grounds numbered approximately fifty each year. After the 1996 enactment of AEDPA and IIRIRA, these numbers dropped drastically; by 1999, there were only ten.[41] Given the rhetorical linkage of immigration enforcement and national security in the wake of September 11, 2001, one would anticipate a spike in security-related removals after that date. Yet there is no such spike.

40. U.S. Department of Justice, Civil Rights Division, "Guidance Regarding the Use of Race by Federal Law Enforcement Agencies" (June 2003), 1–2, http://www.justice.gov/crt/about/spl/documents/guidance_on_race.pdf.

41. U.S. Department of Homeland Security, Office of Immigration Statistics, *2003 Yearbook of Immigration Statistics* (Sept. 2004).

At the same time, however, the number of people processed through the immigration enforcement bureaucracy is large and growing. On any given day in the United States, there are more than four million foreign nationals authorized to be present in the U.S. for a temporary period of time, usually on "nonimmigrant visas."[42] Additionally, in 2005 alone, more than one million people became legal permanent residents of the United States.[43] The average number of lawful permanent residents admitted each year for the past ten years is approximately eight hundred thousand.[44] Given that the average time between obtaining legal permanent residency and citizenship is about eight years, this means that there are more than ten million noncitizens lawfully present at any given time in the United States, in addition to an estimated twelve million people who are in the country without legal authorization.[45] The administrative bodies charged with immigration enforcement have potential jurisdiction over all of these noncitizens.

Large numbers of people are processed through administrative immigration enforcement mechanisms in the United States. In 2004, Immigration and Customs Enforcement completed 202,842 removals of noncitizens from the United States. Of those removed, 88,897 were classified as "criminal aliens."[46] The Department of Homeland Security detained a total of 1,241,089 foreign nationals during 2004, although many of them "voluntarily departed" without further proceedings.[47] That year is not anomalous; it simply continues a significant upward trend that began in 1997 and accelerated after 2001 (see Coutin, this volume).

Furthermore, the detention of noncitizens is the most rapidly expanding segment of the prison system in the United States (see Hernández, this volume). As of March 2004, on an average day, 22,812 individuals were in the custody of the Department of Homeland Security.[48] That number fell slightly to 21,919 in 2004. These averages—although significant in and of themselves—mask the scope of immigration detentions in the United States. The

42. Elizabeth M. Grieco, Report of the Department of Homeland Security Office of Immigration Statistics, *Estimates of the Nonimmigrant Population in the United States: 2004* (June 2006), 1, http://www.dhs.gov/xlibrary/assets/statistics/publications/NIM_2004.pdf.

43. Kelly Jeffreys and Nancy Rytina, Report of the Department of Homeland Security Office of Immigration Statistics, *U.S. Legal Permanent Residents: 2005* (June 2006), http://www.dhs.gov/xlibrary/assets/statistics/publications/USLegalPermEst_5.pdf.

44. See U.S. Department of Homeland Security, Office of Immigration Statistics, *Yearbook of Immigration Statistics: 2005* (2006), table 3, Legal Permanent Resident Flow by Region and Country of Birth, Fiscal Year 2003, http://www.dhs.gov/xlibrary/assets/statistics/yearbook/2005/OIS_2005_Yearbook.pdf.

45. John Symanska and Nancy Rytina, Report of the Department of Homeland Security Office of Immigration Statistics, *Naturalizations in the United States: 2005* (June 2006), 3, http://www.dhs.gov/xlibrary/assets/statistics/publications/2005NatzFlowRpt.pdf; Jeffrey S. Passel, "Size and Characteristics of the Unauthorized Migrant Population in the U.S.," Pew Hispanic Center Report, Mar. 7, 2006, http://pewhispanic.org/reports/report.php?ReportID=61.

46. Mary Dougherty, Denise Wilson, and Amy Wu, U.S. DHS Management Directorate, Office of Immigration Statistics, *Immigration Enforcement Actions: 2004* (Nov. 2005), 1, http://www.dhs.gov/xlibrary/assets/statistics/publications/AnnualReportEnforcement2004.pdf.

47. Dougherty, Wilson, and Wu, *Immigration Enforcement Actions*, 1. In the process of "voluntary departure," a noncitizen agrees that his or her entry was illegal, waives his or her right to a hearing, and remains in custody until he or she is removed under supervision. Many, but not all, of these voluntary departures occur shortly after entry.

48. Allison Siskin, *Immigration Related Detention: Current Legislative Issues*, CRS Report for Congress (Apr. 28, 2004), ii, www.fas.org/irp/crs/RL32369.pdf.

Department of Homeland Security estimates that it detained 235,247 noncitizens in 2004.[49] The boom in immigration detention has spurred an accompanying boom in the private industries responsible for building and managing immigration detention facilities in the United States.

In addition to the removals and detentions effectuated through administrative channels, there has also been a significant increase in the criminal prosecution of immigration violations (see Stumpf, this volume). In 2004, federal prosecutors filed charges in 37,854 cases on the basis of criminal immigration law violations. This is a 300 percent increase since 2000; immigration violations now surpass even drug prosecutions, constituting the single largest category of federal crimes.[50] Although noncitizens in criminal proceedings are entitled to many of the same procedural rights as citizens in criminal proceedings, their conviction exposes them to removal under the less protective administrative system, since many of those convicted of crimes become eligible for removal as "criminal aliens."

If security removals are on the decline and represent a small portion of ever-expanding immigration enforcement efforts, why does the rhetoric of security dominate the U.S. justifications for its immigration policy? The simple answer seems to be that general crime control measures achieved through immigration enforcement are now depicted and understood as national security matters. As previously noted, in the wake of the September 11 attacks, the U.S. government detained and removed large numbers of people on immigration violations under the pretext of national security concerns. This was done even where a national security threat had not been, and perhaps could not be, substantiated. Moreover, as the events of September 11 recede, the government has been able to continue to use the language of security to justify immigration detentions and removals on security grounds. This was possible not only because of the apparently endless character of the "war on terror" but also because, in the context of immigration enforcement, the boundaries between national and personal security have become blurred.

After September 11, 2001, crime control efforts through immigration have increasingly been discussed as "security measures"—suggesting that national security is at stake—when in fact the policies are aimed at basic crime control. ICE's strategic plans reflect the complete conflation of its security and crime control agenda.[51] This conflation is echoed in the halls of Congress. For example, the immigration bills debated in Congress during the 2006 session were almost universally referred to as "security" measures, even though they contain numerous anti-crime measures, including further proposed expansions to the definition of the "aggravated felony" category. The media has accepted and emulates these characterizations of expanded alien removal provisions and proposals to militarize the border region

49. Dougherty, Wilson, and Wu, *Immigration Enforcement Actions*, 5.

50. Transactional Records Access Clearinghouse, Syracuse University, TRAC Report, "Timely New Justice Department Data Show Prosecutions Climb During Bush Years: Immigration and Weapons Enforcement Up, White Collar and Drug Prosecutions Slide" (2005), http://trac.syr.edu/tracreports/crim/136 (accessed July 22, 2006).

51. In 2006 ICE unveiled a "comprehensive immigration enforcement strategy for the nation's interior." The report states that one goal is to "[t]arget and remove aliens that pose criminal/national security threats" (U.S. Department of Homeland Security, "Department of Homeland Security Unveils Comprehensive Immigration Enforcement Strategy for the Nation's Interior" [press release], Apr. 20, 2006, http://www.freerepublic.com/focus/f-news/1618358/posts.

and reported them as efforts to "protect the border."[52] The consequence is that immigration enforcement has become a powerful adjunct to the criminal justice system, but one that lacks comparable judicial oversight, and operates to facilitate arbitrary and excessive forms of punishment.

In the post-September 11 era, the powerful rhetoric of security masks the degree to which contemporary immigration enforcement improperly blurs the boundaries between external security measures and internal crime control in the United States. Historically, contingent notions of who is really a "citizen" and who is an "alien" ensure that many Latinos, Asian Americans, Arabs, and Muslims—citizens, legal permanent residents, authorized noncitizens and the undocumented—have been and will continue to be subjected to crime control measures achieved through the highly punitive and insufficiently protective immigration enforcement bureaucracy. Although the result is a developing two-tier system of criminal justice administration, U.S. courts have generally ignored the problem by relying on age-old notions that immigration policy and security policy are one and the same. The changing nature of crime and security demands a new approach.

52. See Rachel L. Swarns, "Hastert Hints at Compromise," *New York Times*, Mar. 30, 2006, A22, http://www .nytimes.com/2006/03/30/politics/30immig.html.

II   MANAGING BORDERS

Beyond the law, the most notable form that the governing of immigration through crime has assumed over the last few decades is that of intensified border policing. Since the early 1990s, the U.S. federal government has undertaken a major boundary-control offensive, one that aims to increase fencing, lighting, personnel, and surveillance equipment along the main gates of "illegal" entry in order to deter unauthorized immigrants from crossing the border. Federal authorities have essentially determined that one of the best ways to deal with the "problem" of "illegal" immigration is by expanding its border enforcement operations. The expansion of border policing as a way of governing "illegal" immigration has been most conspicuous along the U.S.-Mexico border. It is this border that has historically been seen as the primary source of the undocumented immigrant "problem." A primary solution to unauthorized migration has thus been to install a rigid apparatus of control and surveillance across the Southwest border in order to prevent illegal incursions and thus keep "troublesome" individuals out of the body politic. It has been to build walls and barriers and turn the United States into a veritable fortified enclave.

The chapters in this section deal with various facets of enhanced border policing. Chapter 4, by Josiah McC. Heyman, focuses broadly on efforts to fortify and blockade the U.S.-Mexico border. Specifically, he examines how U.S. border-control policy has entailed erecting not only a physical wall (that is, hundreds of miles of fencing), but also a virtual one. *Virtual* has two meanings here. Narrowly, it refers to the utilization of advanced surveillance and computer technologies in border law enforcement. Such technologies include unmanned aerial vehicles, remotely operated cameras, tower-mounted radars, and unattended ground sensors to monitor remote areas of the border. More broadly, the virtual wall points to the amassing of police forces, including military and intelligence agencies, in the border area in order to create a dense web of barriers to the northward flow of people and goods deemed "illegal." Heyman's basic argument is that the walling of the United States is driven by the widespread belief that social and economic insecurity in the country is the result of bad forces coming in from the outside and that America would be safe if the border were to be properly sealed. He suggests, however, that the threats to the American dream of prosperity and security "will not go away because of a wall on the border, for these threats are both more global and more internal than anything a boundary can control."

Chapter 5, by Leo R. Chavez, draws attention to how the management of the border involves not only agents of the state, but nonstate actors as well. Concerned with the federal government's putative inability to stop "illegal" immigrants from entering the United States, a number of civilian groups have taken it upon themselves to police the Southwest border. Chavez focuses on one such group: the Minuteman Project. This organization brought together volunteers—some would say vigilantes—to surveil the Arizona-Mexico desert in order to locate and deter unauthorized border crossers. Chavez argues that although the Minuteman Project did not have much of a deterrent effect on illicit crossings, it did have other important ramifications. Most significantly, by drawing national attention to the "out of control" nature of the U.S.-Mexico border, the Minuteman Project helped to turn the public debate on immigration reform decidedly in favor of increased border enforcement and away from legalization and guest-worker programs. Furthermore, it helped to spawn copycat projects along the border in California, New Mexico, and Texas. Finally, the spectacle of the Minutemen tracking "illegal" immigrants functioned as an important symbolic performance that helped shore up U.S. national identity, defining who properly belongs and who does not belong (unauthorized immigrants) to the nation.

Chapter 6, by Roxanne Lynn Doty, deals with one of the major consequences of enhanced border enforcement: the endangerment of migrant life. Today, crossing the border has become a rather difficult and dangerous affair. Essentially, as the Border Patrol has fortified traditional illicit routes into the United States—namely urban locations such as San Diego and El Paso—the traffic of migrants has been channeled through remote and less policed mountain and desert locations. These out-of-the-way places where most unauthorized immigrants are currently crossing the border—the deserts of Arizona, for example—are less than ideal entry points. The fact that they are apt to be far removed from urban centers means that the undocumented now have to walk long distances, often for days, before reaching areas where they can be picked up and transported elsewhere. Also, because these places tend to be barren deserts or mountains, anyone entering through them potentially has to contend with freezing temperatures at night and torrid weather during the day. What having to walk long distances though hostile landscape basically means is a rather perilous border crossing experience. The peril is so great that border-crossing-related deaths have become routine events. Doty's central contention is that current border policy renders unauthorized migrants "bare life"—individuals whose deaths are deemed of little consequence.

SUGGESTIONS FOR FURTHER READING

Andreas, Peter. 2009. *Border Games: Policing the U.S.-Mexico Divide.* 2nd ed. Ithaca, NY: Cornell University Press.

Burridge, Andrew. 2009. "Differential Criminalization Under Operation Streamline: Challenges to Freedom of Movement and Humanitarian Aid Provision in the Mexico-U.S. Borderlands." *Refuge* 26 (2): 78–91.

Chávez, Sergio. 2011. "Navigating the U.S.-Mexico Border: The Crossing Strategies of Undocumented Workers in Tijuana, Mexico." *Ethnic and Racial Studies* 34 (8): 1320–1337.

Coleman, Mathew. 2005. "U.S. Statecraft and the U.S.-Mexico Border as Security/Economy Nexus." *Political Geography* 24 (2): 185–209.

Cornelius, Wayne A. 2001. "Death at the Border: Efficacy and Unintended Consequences of U.S. Immigration Control Policy." *Population and Development Review* 27 (4): 661–685.

Doty, Roxanne Lynn. 2009. *The Law into Their Own Hands: Immigration and the Politics of Exceptionalism.* Tucson: University of Arizona Press.

Inda, Jonathan Xavier. 2006. *Targeting Immigrants: Government, Technology, and Ethics.* Malden, MA: Wiley-Blackwell.

Kil, Sang Hea, and Cecilia Menjívar. 2006. "The 'War on the Border': Criminalizing Immigrants and Militarizing the U.S.-Mexico Border." In *Immigration and Crime: Race, Ethnicity, and Violence,* edited by Ramiro Martinez Jr. and Abel Valenzuela Jr., 164–188. New York: New York University Press.

Koskela, Hille. 2010. "Did You Spot an Alien? Voluntary Vigilance, Borderwork, and the Texas Virtual Border Watch Program." *Space and Polity* 14 (2): 103–121.

Martin, Lauren. 2011. "Constructing the Border Wall—The Social and Environmental Impacts of Border: Mexico-U.S. Border Policy." In *Engineering Earth: The Impacts of Megaengineering Projects,* edited by Stanley D. Brunn, 1701–1722. Dordrecht, The Netherlands: Springer Science+Business Media.

Nevins, Joseph. 2012. *Operation Gatekeeper and Beyond: The War on "Illegals" and the Remaking of the U.S.-Mexico Boundary.* New York: Routledge.

Walsh, James. 2008. "Community, Surveillance, and Border Control: The Case of the Minuteman Project." *Sociology of Crime, Law, and Deviance* 10: 11–34.

4 CONSTRUCTING A VIRTUAL WALL

RACE AND CITIZENSHIP IN U.S.–MEXICO BORDER POLICING

Josiah McC. Heyman

The U.S.-Mexico border wall is not just physical—it is also virtual. *Virtual* in this instance has two meanings, one narrower and one broader. More narrowly, the virtual wall involves applying advanced surveillance and computer technologies to border law enforcement. Ground-level radar can be used to detect movement; information processed through a computer model indicates if it is, say, a cow or a person, and if the latter, the direction the person is likely to move, given the terrain. More broadly, the virtual wall points to the massing of police forces, including military and intelligence agencies, in the border region, which presents a web of obstacles to northward movement of illegalized people and goods, obstacles that usually are overcome, but at great risk and cost. Physical walls and fences and the technological "wall" are parts of this wider development, and should be understood in these terms.

The physical walls and fences present visible symbols of the coercive side of U.S. immigration policy (enforcement against undocumented migration; of course, there is also extensive legal immigration). They are crudely imposed between twinned border communities with long-standing ties, and they insult Mexico by treating it as a threat rather than a partner. Thus, U.S. governmental and policy circles hope that a technological system will pose an invisible wall with the same enforcement effects but without the negative attention.

We do not, however, have to accept the "technological solution" discourse at face value. Jason Ackleson (2003, 2005) has demonstrated that border-control technology claims are overstated and that they face significant limitations in implementation. My goal here is to widen this critique by asking how and why the broad pattern—the construction of physical, technological, and mass law-enforcement walls—has occurred, and what are its contradictions and limitations.

Josiah McC. Heyman is professor of anthropology and chair of the Sociology and Anthropology Department at the University of Texas, El Paso.

Reprinted with permission of the *Journal of the Southwest*, from "Constructing a Virtual Wall: Race and Citizenship in U.S.-Mexico Border Policing," *Journal of the Southwest* 50 (3): 305–334 by Josiah McC. Heyman. Copyright © 2008 by the *Journal of the Southwest*.

I begin this chapter by delineating how the border-enforcement "wall" operates at the tactical level, and following that I explore the fundamental assumptions behind those tactics. Doing so helps take these technologies and tactics out of the realm of the normal and natural, to examine them as an overall system. I then state what these operations ideally should accomplish, from their immediate law-enforcement goals to the wider social goals that they are supposed to address. In turn, I consider the evidence on whether the border-enforcement wall has been effective or not. If it has been ineffective, why is the border wall being raised even higher? To answer this question, I explore some circumstances of the United States at the present moment, and some of the history through which we arrived at this point. This includes insecure prosperity and clinging to order in a world of vast inequalities of lifestyle, class, and power, and how such concerns are expressed in two ways: citizenship differences between deserving insiders and serving (but not deserving) outsiders, and racism against Latinos, especially Mexicans and Central Americans.[1] A serious limitation of our current border policy is that it attempts to solve with one rigid and coercive mechanism a wide variety of issues in the societies on both sides of the boundary (Canada, the United States, Mexico, and Central America). I close by agreeing that citizenship, openness, security, and prosperity are important values, but argue that we err in displacing the challenges involved in obtaining them onto a single, illusory answer: a virtual border wall that has little effectiveness and causes much suffering.

THE VIRTUAL WALL IN PRACTICE

Enforcement occurs in three broad places along the Mexican border: at the ports of entry from Mexico into the United States, at or near the boundary between the ports, and in the buildings, streets, and roads of the borderlands extending north from the boundary. At ports, literally millions of commercial vehicles, noncommercial vehicles, and pedestrians seek to enter the country. The bulk of this flow is legitimate, including international commerce and manufacturing, cross-border shopping and tourism, legal commuting across the boundary to work, and visits to friends and family living in the adjacent nation. Various laws and regulations are applied by Customs and Border Protection to this flow, such as declarations of imported goods.

Amid this vast array of legitimate entries, the U.S. government attempts to detect law violations. These include the smuggling of a number of restricted or prohibited goods, including drugs. They also include people entering the United States by hiding in vehicles, by falsely claiming U.S. citizenship, by presenting counterfeit documents, or by presenting real documents that have been altered to falsify identity. Likewise, they include detecting people

---

1. In the original version of this chapter, the author points to the introduction of national security frames for the drug and immigration debates—a process called "securitization"—as also being central to explaining the impulse behind creating ever-higher walls. The death threat of international terrorism to the U.S. homeland after 9/11—that is, the idea that foreigners are seeking to come to the United States to do harm—provided a powerful rationale for expanding the security frame to cover flows across the U.S.-Mexico border, even though this border had nothing to do with 9/11. On the link between security and immigration, see also Chacón, this volume. Eds.

who enter with legitimate documents, such as Border Crossing Cards and nonimmigrant visas, but who violate the terms by working or residing in the United States.[2]

The ports of entry face an inherent contradiction in that they cannot function purely as a wall. They must serve as a filter that differentiates among entrants. Legitimate traffic must be cleared through the port in order for economic and social ties between the United States and Mexico to thrive, given that Mexico is the United States' second largest trading partner and its largest source of foreign-born residents. At the same time, the openness to entry and exit inherent in their filtering role represents a substantial gap in the outward security of the nation. Probably the bulk of illegal drugs enters through commercial shipments at land, air, and sea ports, while the 9/11 hijackers entered through airports (notably, not through the U.S.–Mexico ports). The ideal port would have an efficient, rapid detection process that sorted out law-violating from non-law-violating entries, that registered entries, and that assigned them regulations and tariffs as appropriate. Ports are far from this ideal, but their operations and technologies have strengthened in the last decade.

First, the documentation needed to enter the United States has become more rigorous. The Border Crossing Card is now hard to counterfeit, has a good-quality photograph, and has biometric identification (fingerprints) loaded on a computer-readable strip. Misuse of legitimate cards to reside and work in the United States continues, however, because few card-bearers are pulled aside for thorough questioning about their activities in the United States. As for false claims to citizenship, these have become much harder to make since 2008, as land border entrants need to have a passport (possibly a less-expensive border identification card may also be issued). Border inspectors vary in how carefully they examine documents and ask questions, however, and they often do not or cannot enter computer-readable documents into databases, meaning that watch lists are not checked and entry registration does not occur.

Second, ports are being equipped with advanced detection technologies. Radiation detection devices, chemical signature "sniffers," and activated neutron scanners can potentially detect both terrorist materials and (infinitely more frequently) smuggled drugs. Such devices are, however, inconsistently deployed and most commercial cargoes are not inspected with advanced detection technologies. The volume of border commerce is simply too great and the time required for inspection, even with such devices, too long for each and every shipment to be examined without bringing cross-border trade to a halt.

Another development is separate ports for privileged border crossers (both commercial shippers and noncommercial vehicles). To be predesignated as trusted, the border crosser registers with the U.S. and Mexican governments, pays substantial fees, passes a background check, and in the case of shippers, follows security procedures in documentation, warehousing, loading, and trucking. In turn, the trusted entrant can go through special lanes with faster transit times, while the U.S. government can dedicate less effort to examining such entrants, shifting resources to scrutinize nontrusted entrants.

---

2. A Border Crossing Card (sometimes called a local passport or laser visa) allows a Mexican border city resident with local ties such as a job and a house to enter up to twenty-five miles into the United States for up to seventy-two hours to visit and shop, but does not allow U.S. employment or residence. A nonimmigrant visa (sometimes called a *permiso*) allows the bearer to visit the United States beyond the twenty-five-mile border zone, for a period of up to six months, but again not to work or reside in the United States.

Most non-borderlanders think of the border as those segments that are fenced or otherwise closed off, however, and not as open places of interchange. It is illegal to cross the border outside the ports of entry, and the Border Patrol works to detect and interdict such entries, including unauthorized migrants and drugs. The Border Patrol can either deter crossings by making the entrance too risky, or apprehend law violators, seizing contraband and returning or deporting migrants. The land border between ports can be roughly divided into two tactical zones: in or near densely populated areas and away from such areas. In the former, such as the boundary in San Diego County from the Pacific Ocean to Otay Mountain; at and near Nogales and Douglas, Arizona; and so forth, the government has already implanted walls of solid iron plates or razor wire–topped chain-link fence, accompanied by high-intensity outdoor lighting and constant air surveillance. Since late 1993, in these locales the Border Patrol has stationed units in close proximity to the boundary and in tight spacing relative to one another, which has had the effect of discouraging most unauthorized crossers from entering there. This has not, however, stopped or slowed the flow of undocumented migrants, but rather has displaced that flow along the border to more remote desert and mountain crossing areas. The concomitant rise in injuries, deaths, and smuggling costs will be discussed shortly (see also Doty, this volume).

The remote border areas have long been prime locations for drug smuggling, although most drugs probably pass through commercial corridors. After the change in migration policing tactics in late 1993, undocumented human crossing also rose dramatically in those areas. The government raced to catch up by deploying large numbers of patrol officers and extensive surveillance systems into the expanses of rural border. Such areas are too large for massed policing, however; urban deterrence strategies do not work in rural areas. Rather, people cross the boundary in these areas and move northward, while the Border Patrol attempts to detect their movement at or shortly after entrance, cut off southward escape routes, trap them, and effect arrests and seizures. This takes place over wide swaths of small settlements, farms, and deserts (including badlands and mountains), usually shot through with roads and trails. Walls and fences may be constructed but are constantly being cut, climbed over, or otherwise bypassed, and cannot in themselves constitute meaningful barriers without the activity of Border Patrol officers.

It is to this situation that the high-technology, virtual wall responds for the most part.[3] For decades, the Border Patrol has used fixed-wing aircraft and helicopters to monitor border areas from the air (as well as for other needs, such as emergency evacuation). Likewise, since the Vietnam War era the Border Patrol has used electronic motion detectors. Beginning in the late 1980s, heavily instrumented balloons and airplanes monitored the airspace over the border. The virtual wall, in part, involves increasing the density of and upgrading these existing technologies—to take just one example, by deploying unmanned aerial vehicles ("drones") to carry surveillance cameras over the boundary. The application of new detection technologies forms a parallel development. They widen the ranges of electromag-

3. In 2007, the Department of Homeland Security announced that it would spend $1.2 billion for 700 miles of border "wall," 370 miles of it to be double-layered fencing, mainly in urban areas, and the remaining 330 miles to use cameras, sensors, radar, and so forth. This is on top of the 107 miles of walls and fencing already along the border.

netic radiation used in surveillance, deploy near-ground radar, place high-resolution visual cameras on high towers, and possibly use the satellites of the military or the National Security Agency. Another important development is computer integration of information from these detection systems, using landscape and movement models with multiple data inputs to guide Border Patrol units on the ground to arrest unauthorized entrants. But it does still take ground units—no matter how much data is gathered, no matter how effective the models—to handle encounters in the field, to arrest people, to deal with emergencies, to transport people and contraband back to be processed, and to do the processing for seizure, voluntary departure, or deportation.

Some contraband and some undocumented immigrants remain in the borderlands, but mostly they move northward, precisely because these flows are embedded in U.S. society. This movement north requires transiting the roads of the border region, waiting in safe houses, and being transported through interior checkpoints by car, truck, and airplane. There is thus enforcement not only at or near the boundary, but in a heavily policed zone in the entire borderlands, including large cities, many small cities and towns, and farm districts. Almost all of these areas count majority Latino populaces. Houses are watched, streets cruised, and strip malls and swap meets monitored. Transportation points, such as bus stations, are checked often, and main airports always have officers watching passengers. Roughly twenty-five to fifty miles into the interior, fixed Border Patrol checkpoints halt traffic on all major highways, constituting a second line of questioning and identification before vehicles enter the rest of the nation. The whole border zone virtually becomes a wall.

People arrested for immigration violations are subject to criminal charges for illegal entry. But almost all such people are instead expelled through one of two administrative law processes: (1) deportation, a formal process of removal from the country, conveying a legal record and various consequent penalties (barriers to subsequent legal immigration, criminal penalties for reentry after deportation); and (2) voluntary departure, in which the migrant and the government waive the deportation process for quick (in the Mexican case, near-immediate) removal to the home country. For Mexicans, this option allows for repeated attempts at entry until the person finally makes it through the border, meaning that all the efforts at enforcement are for naught. This practice of voluntary departure crucially allows for the steady influx of undocumented workers into U.S. society in spite of apparently massive efforts at border enforcement.

Since 2005, the U.S. government has held for formal deportation larger numbers of undocumented migrants, especially Central Americans but also many Mexicans. The government's motivation is more effective deterrence, an effect that has not been demonstrated. It certainly is more legally punitive and involves time in prison (euphemistically known as a detention center). Small-scale smugglers rarely face significant penalties, unless they are abusive or defiant, simply being deported, or given minor criminal charges (misdemeanor illegal entry, for example) because of the burden that border enforcement places on federal prosecutors, courts, and prisons in this region. In general, the high volume of arrests at the border imposes significant logistical barriers to full use of legal penalties as tools of deterrence or punishment.

The border has been partially militarized since the late 1970s, even though U.S. relations with Mexico are quite peaceable (see also Chavez, this volume). National Guard units recently have been deployed to the border, as other military units have been in years past. One component of their work is logistical (such as construction and maintenance) and another is rear-echelon assistance in training in and using surveillance technologies. But often military units are assigned to frontal listening post/operation post positions, where they conduct observations (but not arrests) and their visible, armed presence presumably acts as a deterrent. Joint Task Force North, operating out of Fort Bliss, Texas, coordinates military support to border law enforcement, especially in the areas of intelligence and surveillance. A web of civilian and military intelligence units also operates out of this location. In addition to literal military involvement in law enforcement, the border police organizations themselves have adopted approaches and tactics drawing on or related to military low-intensity conflict doctrine, bringing about the militarization of responses to civilian policy issues such as migration.

Immigration law enforcement is disproportionately concentrated along the border, although interior enforcement has modestly increased in the last three years (see Coleman 2007). The overall unauthorized immigration process—which we can think of as involving not only entry but transportation, employment, residence, consumption, and community life—extends far from the boundary and involves not only illegal entrants but also employers, landlords, stores, churches, and so forth. However, more than 90 percent of immigration arrests are made within twenty-five miles of the border. Also, these arrests are almost entirely of migrants, who are the most powerless people in the process, and to a very small extent, of petty smugglers. Employers and other interior participants in the migratory process are rarely touched by law enforcement, and if affected at all, they are usually inconvenienced (temporary loss of employees) or fined; criminal prosecutions occur but are exceedingly rare (see Bacon and Hing, this volume). The geography of drug law enforcement is more complex (there is more interior enforcement), but has a comparable overemphasis on the border. Likewise, migrant- and drug-producing processes occur far from the border in the interiors of the United States, Mexico, and the rest of Latin America and the Caribbean. These observations pose an important question. If these processes span such a wide range of locales and could be regulated or reshaped at those locales, why does law enforcement focus so disproportionately on one boundary? That puts into question the very essence of the "wall." Furthermore, because of the disproportionate enforcement focus on illegal entry at the border, Mexicans and Central Americans who enter without documents (about 60 percent of unauthorized migrants) are greatly overrepresented (well more than 90 percent of arrestees), while people who violate the terms of their nonimmigrant visas by staying past the expiration dates and working without authorization (about 40 percent of the unauthorized migrant population) are underrepresented in enforcement actions. Visa violators are more diverse by national origin and, it is worth mentioning, included most of the 9/11 terrorists (some of whom were still within the legal terms of their visas).

Control of terrorism includes identification of small numbers of people by intelligence operations; their interdiction at airports, seaports, and the northern and southern land borders; and long-term law-enforcement operations against them within the nation. It is thus very different from the current U.S.–Mexican border obsession. The post-9/11 persistence and growth of unselective, non-intelligence-based, and non-investigative mass enforcement along the southern land border thus represents a policy choice to deemphasize protection from terrorist threats to civilian lives in favor of the regulation of Mexican and Central American service, construction, farm, and manufacturing workers. It uses the tools and rhetoric of national security for policy concerns about the class, ethnic, and citizenship composition of the nation.

This review of U.S. operations and tactics may prove a bit overwhelming. It is therefore worth highlighting its basic assumptions. Illegal activities, including unauthorized migration and drug smuggling, are to be kept out of the country at the place of entry, the border zone, rather than addressed within society. Such police action rests on the fundamental idea that the people involved in these activities can be deterred in two ways: being turned away by the visible presence of a border enforcement "wall," or being discouraged by effective detection, arrest, seizure, and expulsion from the country. In turn, deterrence is enabled by information about movement through the border area, that is, by comprehensive intelligence, surveillance, and assignment of police resources to prevention and interdiction. At the same time, the virtual wall must apply only to illegal flows, and must not misidentify or impede legal flows. This means that the virtual wall must also include an effective means of identifying and selecting those people and goods to be trusted as they cross the border or move near the border, versus those to be distrusted and targeted for law-enforcement operations. Again, deterrence is key: legitimate movers are not to be deterred, and illegitimate ones are.

THE IDEAL OF A VIRTUAL WALL

The ideal virtual wall would be *smart* and *secure* in several senses. Through advanced technology and tactics, the government would have the ability to sense and respond to almost all unauthorized incursions. The border would thus function as a hermetic seal against "bad forces" coming into the home space. Also, ports would intelligently and efficiently distinguish among people, vehicles, and shipments to sort out the lawbreakers, or at least those meriting close scrutiny, from trustworthy entrants. In other words, the border would be smart enough to deliver security to the United States while at the same time not impeding the cross-border flows crucial to Mexico's serving as a low-wage export platform for U.S., Asian, and European corporations. The home space would thus be open to "good," or at least profitable, outside forces. The ideal border would be a powerful and intelligent filter.

An underlying ideal of the smart and secure border sharpens the distinction between legal and illegal. The ideal situation is that people with legal and trusted status would be able to move about near or cross the border without inappropriate stops, detention, and arrest, because of highly effective systems of surveillance and identification. U.S. citizens and legal immigrants would have nothing to fear, as is stated so often in the current immigration debate, because they would not have broken the law. Privileged cross-border commuters and commercial shippers would actually move faster and with less scrutiny and inconvenience because of their high value, command of resources (ability to pay the costs of the program), and trusted status with the government. Only lawbreakers would have reason to fear surveillance, detention, interrogation, and arrest by the border-enforcement apparatus.

With respect to illegality, the smart and secure border would largely resolve three major societal problems: terrorism, psychotropic drug use, and unauthorized migration. This assumption posits that such problems come from outside the national territory. Hence, they would decline or disappear if they were prevented from entering the home space. Unauthorized migrants, for example, would be so discouraged by the difficulty of crossing the boundary that they would quit coming in meaningful numbers. The United States would be saved from the illegal immigrant "problem." The assumption states that the United States itself is not involved in the creation and perpetuation of these three issues—for example, that the U.S. domestic economy is not really involved in the employment, housing, and so forth of undocumented immigrants, and that the North American economy does not mobilize them from their homes in Mexico and Central America. Rather, bad actors from outside who penetrate an insecure boundary are entirely to blame, and the solution is to have a comprehensively smart and secure border.

The border thus separates rightness, orderliness, and self from badness, disorderliness, and others. This conceptual boundary has been at terrible risk, but an ideal wall will reassert clarity and order. The virtual wall will reduce the ambiance of illegality and disorder, and renew the sense of protection and control. This will reassure a nation that no longer has unquestioned primacy in international relations, is stuck in intractable wars, has enemies that are difficult to discern, receives confusing global headlines from the mass media, and has an economy deeply penetrated by global forces, including both U.S. corporations moving outward and foreign corporations competitively pushing in. The United States also faces disorderly internal trends, including widening income inequalities and rapid inflation of health care costs, for which a perfect wall against lawbreaking outsiders offers a satisfying magic solution. We would all be safe and secure.

To an important domestic constituency, the ideal border would reverse the tide of social and cultural change that followed from the post-1965 Latin American, Caribbean, and Asian "new" immigration. Specifically, it would stem the so-called brown tide that has "invaded" the United States (Chavez 2001; Santa Ana 2002), the rapid growth in Latinos, especially people of Mexican origin, that is no longer just in long-standing Mexican-immigrant settlement areas but throughout the entire nation. It would stabilize socially, culturally, and economically an imagined America of the 1950s, after the cessation of mass European immigration and before both the new immigration and the long decline of many regional economies that began in the 1970s. It would also reverse the forces of sprawl, expense, and degradation in the Sunbelt, restoring the perfect California, Arizona, Colorado, and so forth of the era when just internal U.S. migrants moved there, not these new international migrants. Of course, this vision confuses immigration of all kinds, including millions of legal immigrants, with the specific phenomenon of illegal entry, which a perfect border would prevent; it also neglects unauthorized migration via legal visa overstays. I discuss later the nuances of race, citizenship, and legality in the politics of borders and immigration.

However, multiple and contradictory visions of a perfect border complicate the ideal. To one set of interests and perspectives, the virtual wall would be the first step toward a managed, imported labor force, a new Bracero Program made up of people who would labor hard, be glad (as it were) to receive a modest wage, and return home when no longer needed or when being too demanding and assertive. Unauthorized migration would cease but well-controlled legal migration—permanent and temporary—would then grow. This is a vision in line with the border seen as a perfect filter of trade, as discussed. An ideal border would thus be open to capital investment, property ownership, commodity trade, information transmittal, and business trips and tourist breaks for the prosperous and well connected, but would tightly control working people—not completely closed to them, but always monitoring them, knowing when they entered and exited, and how they comported themselves while in the United States. Sometimes allied with but also sometimes bitterly opposed to proponents of this approach are the holders of a nationalist-isolationist vision of a restored past and a stable social, cultural, and economic present within the clearly delimited territory of the sacred nation.

IDEAL AND REALITY:
HOW WELL HAS THE VIRTUAL WALL WORKED SO FAR?

The answer to this question is, not very well. The buildup of immigration enforcement and the tactical shift toward walls and intensive frontal policing in heavily traveled corridors began in late 1993. The Border Patrol, for example, grew from approximately 4,000 to 14,000 officers from 1994 to 2007, and projected having 20,000 officers by 2009. What might appear to be powerful additions to law enforcement may actually prove ineffective, however, if the entries simply shift elsewhere or the undocumented migrants repeat their efforts at entry until they are successful—that is, if the deterrence assumption does not work. Surveying likely undocumented migrants in Mexico, for example, Fuentes et al. (2007) found that (1) information about U.S. border law enforcement did not deter them, (2) the rate at which past undocumented entrants reported being apprehended *fell* during the period of massive Border Patrol buildup, and (3) the rate of use and cost of smugglers rose dramatically during this period (see also Cornelius 2006 for an overview of evidence about success versus failure).

What do these findings suggest about the likely effect of a virtual wall along the border? Human smugglers have apparently kept ahead of the government, despite the post-1993 tactical shifts, the added technology, and the buildup of forces. Likewise, unauthorized migrant flows have shifted to more remote sections of the border rather than being altogether deterred.

The migrants' "success" comes at a cost, sadly. Migrants now pay more money to smugglers, borrow more and thus are deeper in debt, and have higher levels of obligation to moneylenders, labor contractors, and so forth. They have been driven deeper into life outside the law, while smuggling organizations have become richer and better organized. Also, deaths and injuries at the border have risen dramatically because of the displacement of migration out of relatively safe urban corridors into mountain and desert areas (see Doty, this volume). Conservatively, around four hundred people die each year crossing this border (Cornelius 2001; Eshbach et al. 1999; Eshbach, Hagen, and Rodríguez 2003).

A similar story can be told about illegal drugs, although street price data (a proxy for supply levels) are collected for the United States as a whole and not disaggregated for supplies specifically smuggled across the Mexican border. Drug law enforcement along the border started its recent intensification in the late 1980s, somewhat before the immigration enforcement surge. Michael Grossman, Frank J. Chaloupka, and Kyumin Shim (2002) found, however, that prices of heroin and cocaine fell substantially during the 1981–2000 period, and marijuana (more of which is domestically produced) rose in price but then fell again. As the authors point out, there are complex factors affecting illegal drug prices and diverse ways to assess law enforcement effectiveness, but drug prices offer no evidence that the virtual border wall has worked.

No publicly available evidence indicates that terrorists or terrorist materials have entered the United States through the Mexican border (Leiken and Brook 2006). It is possible that such activities have been deterred by border enforcement, and it is reasonable to argue that border inspectors should be trained and equipped for such an eventuality. But as we have seen, the high degree of attention to the southern land border is a partial distraction from other risk locations, including seaports, airports, the northern land border, and internal terrorist actors. It is also arguable that the strengthening of smuggling organizations in response to immigration law enforcement makes the task of terrorism interdiction potentially harder.

The technology involved in the virtual wall, so far, is more promise than reality. Jason Ackleson (2003, 2005) and Rey Koslowski (2006) have identified the main limitations. Technologies often are not yet proven to be operational and durable, and their usefulness for ground officers has not been demonstrated thus far. Detection technologies and computer database linkages have been deployed only in a limited number of places, and officers often do not use them regularly. Elaborate, integrated surveillance and targeting systems, in particular, are more in the realm of technological imagination than rugged, field-tested reality. The pilot project in Arizona for the virtual wall was an operational failure and will be redone from scratch, though with some lessons learned (Rotstein 2008, United States Government Accountability Office 2008). Without dismissing the new border technologies, we need to be skeptical about the grandiose rhetoric of corporations and government upper management, and likewise cautious about the U.S. cultural theme of "technology as miraculous solution."

At the same time, we cannot assume that the virtual border wall will continue to be a porous failure. Annual border undocumented migrant arrests are down from 2006 to 2007, reports abound of shortages of undocumented workers in U.S. labor markets, and field observations suggest that immigrant communities are more scared than in the past. It is conceivable that crossing the border has become sufficiently difficult and expensive that either undocumented immigrants or drug smugglers, or both, will be deterred. We do not know, however, what to make of short-term fluctuations, and likewise do not yet have convincing evidence of a long-term change.

In the rhetoric of border buildup, the idea prevails that weak and flawed efforts were made in the past, that the border is in a state of crisis, and that only adding more and more enforcement can address a situation that is out of control (see Chavez, this volume). These propositions are clearly wrong. The level of border-control effort has been both large and growing, whether measured in personnel or funding. So why continue to escalate border law enforcement? Shouldn't failure lead to reconsidering this approach? And why does the gap between the ideal of the walled border and the reality of continued flows not lead to rethinking these imagined ideals and their relationship to the realities of the United States, Mexico, and Central America?

Analysis suggests several possible replies to these questions. For example, many advocates of border escalation hold that not enough has been done, and that it has not been done well enough. But what drives this impulse to do the same thing, over and over again, in the face of failure? Another reading is that border law enforcement has grown and is reasonably competent, but simply cannot succeed in the face of wider social forces, such as underdevelopment in Mexico and demand for immigrant labor in the United States. This may explain why the border enforcement approach is wrongheaded, but it does not explain why a wrongheaded policy is persistent and largely popular. One might posit that the ideal/reality gap is a deliberate failure, because the U.S. power elite actually wants a heavily policed, exploitable undocumented population. There is a thread of truth in this, but it is too simplistic as a whole-cloth explanation, as we shall see. Rather, I will argue, the impulse to fail and fail again at the border emerges from intersecting struggles in the politics, economics, and culture of the contemporary United States.

THE VIRTUAL WALL: BUILT IN MILLENNIAL AMERICA

In the aftermath of the failure of comprehensive immigration reform in 2006 and again in 2007, the already substantial flow of resources into "border security" has sped up, and interior immigration enforcement has also increased, perhaps momentarily. We can understand these actions by exploring the current state of affairs in the United States, and some of the history through which we have come to this point. In this regard, the United States' crucial characteristics include widening inequality and many households with moderate to high material prosperity compared to the working poor of the nation and the world. Specific American legacies of racism and citizenship also influence the scenario. The obsession with imposing definite order, and using police and military tools to do it, arises in this context.

Our understanding of the mindset of defensive prosperity is imperfect, yet it is crucial to the contemporary United States. We should examine and critique it. One element might be a fear of sharing prosperity with others, including immigrants and their children (let alone the rest of the world). Leo Chavez (2001) has pointed out the concern in anti-immigration rhetoric about women and children coming across the Mexican border. One might also note the strong theme of closing the door to public benefits, including health care, municipal services, and public schooling. (I will discuss citizenship and law as idioms for this shortly.) Another motif is distaste, possibly hiding a sense of guilt and shame, at the hard, sweaty, unremunerative work of immigrant laborers. If such people are racially and culturally foreign, from beyond the wall, one does not need to identify with their struggles. A final thread is the confusion of prosperity with Americanness, and Americanness with a specific kind of post–World War II assimilation to Anglo-American culture and language, together with a distaste for otherness (a once-punitive lesson that descendents of poor rural Americans and past immigrants appear to have learned all too well).

Yet here come new waves of immigrants, some well educated and prosperous and others quite poor but hardworking, who through their distinctive languages, cultures, and social networks threaten the comfortable cultural correlates of the American dream. Intertwined with xenophobic anxieties is disturbing knowledge of domestic and global environmental, economic, and political problems. There is much to be genuinely worried about in America's old age, and U.S. residents can be the bearers of both realistic concerns and paranoid fantasies all at once. Thus, in the virtual and physical wall, a certain selfish hope emerges for unity, uniformity, and prosperity and against insecurity, dialogue, and change.

In the period before 1940–1980, straight-up racism would have served to impose conceptual and material order in places where Mexicans migrated and lived. Public institutions were often segregated, pay rates were unequal, and immigration laws were applied capriciously to allow workers in, keep them in line, and send them home when not wanted. Capitalist economic logic, ethnocentrism, and the selfish defense of prosperity aligned neatly along the boundaries of race. But Mexican Americans had long struggled for social justice and civil rights. Starting around 1940, they began to make real progress against strict racial inequality. The struggle took many years and is by no means completed, but by 1980, a new pattern had emerged. People of Mexican (and other Latin American, Caribbean, and Asian) origin now can often claim resources, rights, and standing in U.S. society as citizens, using that term in both its legal and its cultural senses. A more precarious status is legal permanent residence (still subject to deportation), but even then, the term *legal* denotes a standing in society as orderly, belonging, and not entirely foreign.

During the same period, however, labor and family-reunification migration from Mexico and Central America has amplified, not only in numbers but also in variety of occupations and locales. This has taken place through both legal and extralegal channels; indeed, the two are often hard to distinguish on the ground. As I discussed earlier, new immigrants, especially Mexicans, are often envisioned as threatening the imagined cultural correlates of prosperity. Yet marking off all Mexicans as outsiders and rendering them powerless is no longer as simple as it was during the period of strict racist hierarchy. A rearrangement of prejudice and victimization has thus emerged. The target now is "illegal immigrants," mistakenly envisioned as always Mexican, with Mexicans often mistakenly envisioned as mainly "illegal" also. "Illegals" are precisely anti-citizens, anti-law, and anti-order. The U.S.–Mexican border distinguishes American law from chaotic outsiderness. The people who cross it without authorization come from a mysterious and disorderly place, and by being in the wrong place for their legal status, they endanger the clarity of the protective categories. Hence we witness the intense concern with an all-knowing, all-seeing virtual wall to ensure the order desired by a wealthy but insecure society.

It is thus important to take seriously the rhetoric of citizenship and legality as many Americans inchoately express their understanding of who should have jobs, health care, college educations, and so forth. These debates are not simple, and not everyone who uses words like *citizenship* aims to reduce immigration and impose iron-fisted controls, but there is undeniably a thrust in the current language of citizenship toward drawing walls

around the sparse sources of redistribution in an era when wealth is becoming more unequal and social benefits smaller and smaller. Struggles over such claims may take place in
Pennsylvania or north Texas, but the border is almost always invoked—as having broken
down, as needing to be repaired. Symbolic politics is not just a phrase; the border wall is a
giant public symbol for a television and Internet era that differentiates those who belong
inside and have claims to public goods (citizens) and those who should remain outside with
no such claims (aliens).

It is also important to take note of the contradictory placement of border residents and
U.S. Latinos generally—on the one hand, pulled toward restrictive citizenship politics as
entrances to and legitimation of prosperity and inclusion, including work for the police
and military arms of the state; and on the other hand, repelled by the barely hidden racist
themes in some border- and immigration-enforcement rhetoric, in particular the widespread confusion of *Mexican* with *illegal outsider*. In border and immigrant communities,
then, it is important that we resist narrow, wall-like definitions of citizenship and strengthen
the alternative citizenship politics of social justice and civil rights. Three reasons should
inform us: (1) so that the subordinate labor position now and in the near future occupied
by most immigrant Latinos and many others will be valued by society and convey a decent
standard of living; (2) so that this subordinate labor position will not become permanent;
and (3) so that immigrants and children of immigrants will participate in and share the
common goods of American life.

CONCLUDING REMARKS

U.S. border-control policy does not consist only of the physical wall, I have argued, but also
of a virtual wall of advanced surveillance technologies and massive police and military
enforcement operations. The "border as wall" would ideally stop harms from coming into
the country from outside, including undocumented migrants, illegal drugs, and terrorists.
This vision assumes that such issues are due solely to bad forces from outside, and that
American society would be safe from these dangers (and scary social changes generally)
were the border to be walled off appropriately. It does not consider such issues as being
deeply rooted inside the U.S. nation, its domestic economy and society, and its foreign
policy, as well as being driven by globalizing changes in other parts of the world. This border solution also assumes that deterrence and interdiction are successful in halting people
and goods from entering the country. However, evidence shows that the border is currently
unsuccessful in these tasks, and more broadly, puts the underlying assumptions of the virtual wall into question.

It is difficult to tell where the question of American borders will go. We live in a great
period of rebirth and entrepreneurship sparked by the post-1965 immigration, as anyone
can see in immigrant neighborhoods of once-declining cities and small towns. At the same
time, about twelve million people suffer deep material and emotional hurt—withering, ex-
hausting fear—every single day because of their status outside the law. The moral and practical threats to the American dream of prosperity, security, and belonging have not and will
not go away because of a wall on the border, for these threats are both more global and more

internal than anything a boundary can control. So far, the capitalist dream of an efficient wall that lets flows in and out muddles forward. But there is no large guest-worker program (there are some small ones), and the quintessential capitalist dream of importing Mexicans as temporary commodity units of labor has not come to pass. Radical capitalist surgery on Mexico and Central America continues, displacing common people left and right. The virtual border wall is just a moment in North American history, giving us no reason to think that it offers an enduring, let alone ideal, solution to our problems. We stagger toward globalization.

There is no simple solution to border controversies. If the virtual wall is not a magic answer, it would be equally wrong to dismiss all order-making functions of this and other borders. We should first separate much more clearly in our minds the distinction between securing civilians from terrorists (homeland security in the proper sense of the word) and immigration policy. Some terrorists were born or have lived inside the United States for many years while others are migrants, but in all cases they are a tiny number of people, with specific ideas and networks that have little or nothing to do with the enormous masses of labor and family migrants who come to work, live decently, raise their children, and enjoy life. It is conceivable, though apparently not yet actually occurring, that terrorists could slip into the United States through a busy Mexican land border port of entry or among the thousands of undocumented entrants crossing by night. Yet the obvious response to this is to reduce the cover for terrorists by creating a comprehensive immigration reform that would slow substantially the flow of unauthorized entrants. We also need to reduce the business created for smuggling organizations and for drugs if the security apparatus of the government is actually to make us secure.

We need to rework the politics of the contemporary United States so that we relax the recurrent political hostility to immigrants and the pressure to impose heavy-handed repression on the basically peaceful Mexican border. Choices about how to handle the border depend greatly on the climate in the national interior and not just on objective assessments of border issues, and the policed-militaristic direction the border is going will not change until we alter these interior fears and impulses. In other words, we cannot just argue about how much sense alternative policies would make, but we need also to figure out what kind of politics will lead us in inclusive rather than paranoid directions. Otherwise, we will again duel over the imaginary perfect wall in a few years. Citizenship, openness, security, and prosperity are indeed important values, so we need to develop alternative meanings and politics around them. They are double-sided, as easily used for repression and restriction as for widening the common good, and we need to think clearly about how to develop their humane and liberatory qualities.[4]

4. I wrote this essay to read fluidly, with few scholarly citations, but I owe a significant debt to a number of scholars, including Jason Ackleson, Peter Andreas, Leigh Binford, Barry Buzan, Kitty Calavita, Leo R. Chavez, Mathew Coleman, Wayne A. Cornelius, Nicholas De Genova, Rodolfo de la Garza, Timothy J. Dunn, Bill Ong Hing, Jef Huysmans, Robert Lee Maril, Douglas S. Massey, Joseph Nevins, Mae M. Ngai, Tony Payan, Alejandro Portes, Mark Purcell, Jorge Santibáñez Romellón, Nandita Sharma, Matthew B. Sparke, Ellwyn R. Stoddard, Daniel J. Tichenor, John Tirman, Ole Wæver, and Aristide R. Zolberg.

WORKS CITED

Ackleson, Jason. 2003. Securing Through Technology? "Smart Borders" after September 11th. *Knowledge, Technology, and Policy* 16: 56–74.

———. 2005. Border Security Technologies: Local and Regional Implications. *Review of Policy Research* 22: 137–55.

Chavez, Leo R. 2001. *Covering Immigration: Popular Images and the Politics of the Nation.* Berkeley and Los Angeles: University of California Press.

Coleman, Mathew. 2007. Immigration Geopolitics Beyond the Mexico–U.S. Border. *Antipode* 38(2): 54–76.

Cornelius, Wayne A. 2001. Death at the Border: Efficacy and Unintended Consequences of U.S. Immigration Control Policy. *Population and Development Review* 27: 661–85.

———. 2006. Impacts of Border Enforcement on Unauthorized Mexican Migration to the United States. Social Science Research Council. http://borderbattles.ssrc.org/Cornelius (last accessed August 17, 2007).

Eshbach, Karl, Jacqueline M. Hagen, and Nestor P. Rodríguez. 2003. Deaths During Undocumented Migration: Trends and Policy Implications in the New Era of Homeland Security. *In Defense of the Alien* 26: 37–52.

Eshbach, Karl, Jacqueline M. Hagen, Nestor P. Rodríguez, Rubén Hernández-León, and Stanley Bailey. 1999. Death at the Border. *International Migration Review* 33: 430–40.

Fuentes, Jezmin, Henry L'Esperance, Raúl Pérez, and Caitlin White. 2007. Impacts of U.S. Immigration Policies on Migration Behavior. In *Impacts of Border Enforcement on Mexican Migration: The View from Sending Communities,* Wayne A. Cornelius and Jessa M. Lewis, eds., 53–73. La Jolla, CA: Center for Comparative Immigration Studies.

Grossman, Michael, Frank J. Chaloupka, and Kyumin Shim. 2002. Illegal Drug Use and Public Policy. *Health Affairs* 21: 134–45.

Koslowski, Rey. 2006. Immigration Reforms and Border Security Technologies. Border Battles: The U.S. Immigration Debates. Social Science Research Council. http://borderbattles.ssrc.org/Koslowski (last accessed August 17, 2007).

Leiken, Robert S., and Steven Brooke. 2006. The Quantitative Analysis of Terrorism and Immigration: An Initial Exploration. *Terrorism and Political Violence* 18: 503–21.

Rotstein, Arthur H. 2008. Virtual Border Fence in Arizona a Failure: Slow Alerts Cause GAO to Scrap $20m Prototype. *Boston Globe,* April 24, 2008. http://www.boston.com/news/nation/articles/2008/04/24/virtual_border_fence_in_ariz_a_failure (last accessed June 9, 2008).

Santa Ana, Otto. 2002. *Brown Tide Rising: Metaphors of Latinos in Contemporary American Public Discourse.* Austin: University of Texas Press.

United States Government Accountability Office. 2008. Secure Border Initiative: Observations on the Importance of Applying Lessons Learned to Future Projects. Report GAO-08-508T. Washington, DC: Government Printing Office.

5

SPECTACLE IN THE DESERT

THE MINUTEMAN PROJECT
ON THE U.S.-MEXICO BORDER

Leo R. Chavez

On April 1, 2005, volunteers began arriving along the Arizona-Mexico border, converging on Tombstone, the site of the historical Wild West shootout at the OK Corral between Wyatt Earp's men and a gang of roughneck cowboys (LoMonaco 2005). These modern-day volunteers came in search of another confrontation, another example of cowboy justice, only this time the scofflaws were "illegal" immigrants. These volunteers came to be part of the Minuteman Project, a name with immediate appeal because it called forth the patriotic volunteers who fought against British rule of the American colonies. The Minuteman Project's ostensible goal was to monitor the Arizona-Mexico border in the hopes of locating clandestine border crossers. However, this surveillance operation also had a larger objective, which was to produce a spectacle that would garner public media attention and influence federal immigration policies.

The Minuteman Project's start date of April 1 is known as April Fool's Day in the United States and is a time to play a joke on someone else. In a sense that is what their spectacle in the desert did. It made the press into the unwitting co-conspirators of the Minuteman Project's attempt to shape public policy. As they were given something—a spectacle—to cover, the media broadcast the Minuteman Project's message about a need for greater border surveillance.

Like many spectacles, this one had costumes. The Minutemen volunteers came equipped with military fatigues, binoculars, bulletproof vests, aircraft, walkie-talkies, even guns, since it is legal to carry firearms in Arizona (Riley 2005; Rotstein 2005). The Minuteman Project had all the trappings of a military campaign, which is not surprising given that many of the volunteers had served in the military, in places such as Vietnam and Iraq (Grillo 2005; Coronado 2005a). Jim Gilchrist, the founder of the Minuteman Project, was himself wounded in Vietnam (Delson 2005).

Leo R. Chavez is professor of anthropology at the University of California, Irvine.
Reprinted with permission of Hurst & Co. (Publishers) Ltd., from "Spectacle in the Desert: The Minuteman Project on the U.S.-Mexico Border," by Leo R. Chavez in *Global Vigilantes*, edited by David Pratten and Atreyee Sen. Copyright © 2008 by Hurst & Co. (Publishers) Ltd.

This chapter attempts to contextualize the pseudo-military operation at the Arizona-Mexico border. The Minuteman Project's April 2005 offensive to monitor the Arizona-Mexico border is examined in relation to Michel Foucault's (1977) contrasting concepts of "spectacle" and "surveillance." The Minuteman Project engaged in practices of both spectacle and surveillance to achieve its goals, especially the larger objective of targeting public opinion and the federal government's immigration policies. The Minuteman Project's border surveillance is viewed here as a practice of power that defines the juridical border between "citizens" and "others," that is, "illegal aliens."

Michel Foucault's concepts of "spectacle" and "surveillance" provide a useful theoretical and analytical framework for assessing the Minuteman Project and its goals. In *Discipline and Punish*, the spectacle is isomorphic with the scaffold, the public execution of prisoners in 18th century France. The spectacle was a public performance that enacted upon the body of the prisoner the power of the sovereign, and thus clarified the distinction between the sovereign and those he governed. "Its [the spectacle's] aim is not so much to re-establish a balance as to bring into play, at its extreme point, the dissymmetry between the subject who has dared to violate the law and the all-powerful sovereign who displays his strength" (Foucault 1977, 48–49). A key to the spectacle of public torture was "above all, the importance of a ritual that was to deploy its pomp in public" (49). These two aspects of the spectacle, that it demarcates power positions and does so in a public way, are central to the activities of the Minuteman Project on the U.S.-Arizona border. In this case, the public performance was one that emphasized the power and privileges of citizenship, which is controlled by the democratic state now standing in place of the sovereign. The subjects in this spectacle were the "illegal aliens" who dared to violate the law and in doing so put the privileges of citizenship into question, at least for the Minuteman organizers and participants.

For Foucault, the move toward fewer public executions is coterminous with the emphasis on surveillance as a means of discipline. Surveillance, especially the totalizing practices represented by Foucault's use of the Panopticon, was a practice of power that instilled discipline in subjects, producing docile bodies. Rather than opposing these two practices, this chapter views the Minuteman Project's border monitoring as a practice that combined both spectacle and surveillance. In short, the Minuteman Project used surveillance to produce a spectacle on the Arizona-Mexico border. Finding clandestine border crossers became part of the "show," and what one might describe as a "media circus." In the final analysis, the success of the Minuteman Project was not in numbers of border crossers found and detained, but in the attention the project received and the disciplining it achieved, that is, the ability to force governmental reaction aligned with its cause.

Before we turn to the events in Arizona, the Minuteman Project must also be contextualized historically. The following section examines the representation of Mexican immigration and the U.S.-Mexico border in public discourse as threats to the nation.

THE U.S.-MEXICO BORDER AS A PLACE OF DANGER

The Minuteman Project must be viewed in relation to decades of public discourse in the United States that has constructed and represented the U.S.-Mexico border as a place of danger and threat to U.S. society and culture. Research on national U.S. magazines covers and their accompanying articles found that alarm is conveyed through images and text that directly or metaphorically invoke crisis, time bombs, invasion, reconquest, floods, war, and border breakdown (Chavez 2001). A few examples will have to suffice.

In December of 1974, the cover of the *American Legion Magazine* depicted the United States being overrun by "illegal aliens." Most of the cartoon people in the image are Mexicans storming, *en masse*, across the U.S.-Mexico border, breaking down a sign that states "USA BORDER" and another one that states "KEEP OUT." Other immigrants are landing by boats along the East coast, flying in and swimming from the Caribbean, parachuting across the Canadian border, and all of them are converging upon, and inundating, the nation's institutions, most notably welfare, education, housing, jobs, and medical aid. Such images would become more frequent on the nation's magazines over the next three decades and they contributed to an increasingly alarmist discourse on Mexican immigration.

It should also be noted that the *American Legion Magazine* serves the U.S. armed services, which underscores the salience of the threat to U.S. society posed by Mexican immigration and the possible need for the military to be ready for action. As noted, the Minuteman Project was a quasi-military action in which ex-military played an important role, as did the ideology of protecting the nation.

On July 4, 1977, *U.S. News & World Report*'s cover again focused attention on Mexican immigration. The cover's text reads, "TIME BOMB IN MEXICO: Why There'll Be No End to the Invasion of 'Illegals.'" The use of "invasion" on the cover of a mainstream national magazine is a noteworthy escalation in the alarmist discourse on Mexican immigration (Chavez 2001). *Invasion* is a word that carries with it many connotations, none of them friendly or indicating mutual benefit. Friends do not invade; enemies invade.

The invasion metaphor evokes a sense of crisis related to an attack on the sovereign territory of the nation. Invasion is an act of war and puts the nation and its people at great risk. Exactly what the nation risks by this invasion is not articulated in the image's message. The war metaphor is enhanced by the prominence of the words *TIME BOMB*. The text conjures up an image of Mexico as a bomb which, when it explodes, will damage the United States. The damage, the message makes clear, will be the unstoppable flow of illegal immigrants to the United States.

The "Mexican invasion" theme was the focus of both *U.S. News & World Report* (March 7, 1983) and *Newsweek* (June 25, 1984). *U.S. News & World Report*'s cover announced, "Invasion from Mexico: It Just Keeps Growing." The image on the cover was a photograph of a line of men and women being carried by men across a canal of water. At the head of the line is a woman being carried to the United States on the shoulders of a man. *Newsweek* had a similar cover, a photographic image of a man carrying a woman across a shallow body of water. The woman is wearing a headscarf and a long shawl. The man carries the woman's handbag, which suggests she is traveling somewhere, moving with a purpose and for an extended amount of time. She holds a walking cane. The text states, "Closing the Door? The Angry Debate over Illegal Immigration. Crossing the Rio Grande."

Featuring women so prominently on the covers of these two national magazines while warning of an "invasion" sends a clear message about fertility and reproduction. Rather than an invading army, or even the stereotypical male migrant worker, the images suggest a more insidious invasion, one that includes the capacity of the invaders to reproduce themselves. The women being carried into U.S. territory carry with them the seeds of future generations. The images signal not simply a concern over undocumented workers, but a concern with immigrants who stay and reproduce families and, by extension, communities in the United States. These images, and their accompanying articles, allude to issues of population growth, use of prenatal care, children's health services, education, and other social services related to reproduction.

Newsweek's June 25, 1984 feature story characterized the public as deeply concerned with undocumented immigration and yet conflicted in their attitudes and views about what to do about it. *Newsweek* alerts us to the "fact" that "America has 'lost control' of its borders" (18). The report cites President Ronald Reagan, who envisioned the nation in grave peril because of this loss of control: "The simple truth is that we've lost control of our own borders, and no nation can do that and survive" (18).

Immigration and "reconquest" came together in *U.S. News & World Report*'s August 19, 1985 cover. Its headline announces, "The Disappearing Border: Will the Mexican Migration Create a New Nation?" The accompanying article, titled "The Disappearing Border," provides a fully embellished rendition of the "reconquest" theme:

> Now sounds the march of new conquistadors in the American Southwest. . . . By might of numbers and strength of culture, Hispanics are changing the politics, economy and language in the U.S. states that border Mexico. Their movement is, despite its quiet and largely peaceful nature, both an invasion and a revolt. At the vanguard are those born here, whose roots are generations deep, who long endured Anglo dominance and rule and who are ascending within the U.S. system to take power they consider their birthright. Behind them comes an unstoppable mass—their kin from below the border who also claim ancestral homelands in the Southwest, which was the northern half of Mexico until the U.S. took it away in the mid-1800s. (30)

In the mid-1980s, the framing of the U.S.-Mexico border as something that is "lost" and across which "invaders" come coincided with calls from prominent political leaders to further militarize the border. In 1986, San Diego's sheriff publicly advocated for Marines to be stationed every 15 or 20 feet, day and night, along the border (Meyer 1986). Then-Senator Pete Wilson also publicly supported this idea, should immigration reform not work to reduce the flow of undocumented immigrants across the border (Gandelman 1986). Duncan Hunter, a member of the House of Representatives from San Diego, suggested that rather than the Marines, the National Guard should be stationed on the border (McDonnell 1986). Not surprisingly, the military's involvement has steadily increased since this initial controversy, with National Guard and U.S. Marines regularly deployed along the U.S.-Mexico border (Andreas 2000; Dunn 1996, 1999; Reza 1997).

The invasion metaphor was subtly referenced in the *Atlantic Monthly*'s May 1992 feature article by William Langewiesche, which is a first-hand account of Langewiesche's travels on the U.S. side of the border. In addition to characterizing the U.S.-Mexico border as an unpleasant and dangerous place, the author includes images of a militarized border and metaphors of war throughout the article. For example, a Border Patrol officer is quoted as he compares his nightly vigilance against illegal border crossers to Vietnam, a war "we didn't win there either" (74). The author describes the high level of technology used along the border to "fight" smuggling, and the various contributions of U.S. military personnel to the anti-drug smuggling effort. In remote deserts, the author finds that the Army carries out training exercises designated in part to intimidate would-be drug smugglers. In southern Arizona, the National Guard, the reserve army, searches vehicles. A frustrated Customs agent also compares his work trying to stop the entry of drugs to his Vietnam experience: "It's a civilian version of Vietnam. That makes it the second losing war I've fought" (84). The recurring Vietnam metaphor not only helps to characterize the U.S.-Mexico border region as a war zone, but also heightens the level of frustration and anxiety over problems associated with the region. It suggests a deep sense of hopelessness about the government's ability to successfully secure the borders and protect citizens from the various "problems" (immigrants, drugs, now terrorists) that manage to cross it clandestinely. The ideology (below) of the Minuteman Project also expresses the despair inherent in the Vietnam analogy. At the very least, in relation to Mexican immigration, raising the Vietnam analogy challenges us not to lose another "war."

The problem of moving from the metaphor of the border as a war zone to acting as if this were actually the case became painfully obvious on May 20, 1997. On that day, a Marine corporal shot to death 18-year-old Esequiel Hernandez Jr., an American citizen, who had been herding his family's sheep on a hilltop near his family's home on the U.S. side of the border near Redford, Texas. The corporal and three privates were stationed along the border to help the Border Patrol detect drug smugglers under an agreement with a federal agency called Joint Task Force Six, which was established in 1989. The Marines were to observe and report to the Border Patrol. However, Esequiel Hernandez Jr. carried a .22-caliber rifle and was shooting at rocks as he passed the time guarding his sheep. Feeling themselves under attack, the Marines, who were hidden from view, observed the young man for 23 minutes, determined that he was tending his flock, but then killed Hernandez when he looked as if he was going to fire his .22 again. Controversy developed over the length of time the Marines watched Hernandez, and the fact that Hernandez was shot in the side, not in the chest, indicating he was not facing the Marines as he shot his rifle. In addition, the Marines never identified themselves, nor did they render first aid to the dying Hernandez. Medical assistance was not called until the Border Patrol arrived 20 minutes later, but by then it was too late for intervention (Prodis 1997).

Despite the inherent problems raised by the militarization of the U.S.-Mexico border, pundits continued to portray the border as under assault. In 2000, Samuel P. Huntington repeated the alarm of a Mexican reconquest. "The invasion of over 1 million Mexican civilians is a comparable threat [as 1 million Mexican soldiers] to American societal security, and Americans should react against it with comparable vigor. Mexican immigration looms as a unique and disturbing challenge to our cultural integrity, our national identity, and potentially to our future as a country" (Huntington 2000, 22).

The harsh reality between the metaphor of a war zone and the actual practice of increased militarization of the border region raises a number of issues, including those of human rights (Dunn 1999). At the very least is the incongruence between military personnel trained for war and the job of the Border Patrol, which more often than not involves servicing unarmed civilians seeking work or to reunite with their family. The idea of untrained civilian border guards or militia, such as the Minutemen, expands these concerns exponentially.

The relationship that must be underscored between the public discourse examined here and the increased militarization of the border region is not that anti-immigrant discourse *caused* this push for militarization to occur. However, the discourse of invasion, the loss of U.S. sovereignty, and the representation of Mexican immigrants as the "enemy" surely contributed to an atmosphere that helped to justify increased militarization of the border as a way of "doing something" about these threats to the nation's security and the American way of life. The Minuteman Project's enlistment of citizens to conduct surveillance along the U.S.-Mexico border in Arizona is a logical consequence of this decades-long maelstrom of rhetoric associating Mexican immigration with narratives of threat, danger, invasion, and destruction of the American way of life.

THE MINUTEMAN PROJECT

In early 2005, Jim Gilchrist put a call out for "citizens" to come to the Arizona-Mexico border to monitor and report "illegal" immigrants (Strohm 2005). Although a resident of California, Gilchrist's motivation for his call to action was the failure of the Bush administration and the U.S. Congress to provide the funds necessary to secure the borders against the "millions of illegal migrants" flowing into the United States from Mexico (Strohm 2005), a powerful theme in the post-9/11 political debate over security. They chose Arizona because, by 2005, this was the area where a disproportionate number of undocumented migrants crossed. Of the 1.1 million unauthorized border crossers apprehended in 2004, one-fifth were caught in one Arizona county, Cochise County, alone (Argetsinger 2005). Such statistics are, as Jean and John Comaroff (2006) put it, part of the "alchemy of numbers" that helps construct the rhetoric of fear discussed above. For example, Mike McGarry, the Minuteman Project's media liaison, commented, "We have something in the neighborhood of three million people from all over the world breaking into the country. And we have an out-of-control—by any definition could be termed an invasion" (democracynow.org 2005). Although such statistics can be used to signify "invasion" and "threat," they do not illuminate the political economy that creates a demand in the U.S. labor market for immigrant labor (Inda 2006). But they are useful to motivate the enlistment of Minutemen.

Gilchrist had the following goals for the Minuteman Project: (a) draw attention to "illegal immigration" and the lack of border security, (b) reduce the number of apprehensions along the border where they monitor, and (c) influence the U.S. Congress to put a 10-year moratorium on illegal immigration and cap the number of legal immigrants to 200,000 per year (Strohm 2005). Although monitoring the U.S.-Mexico border was Gilchrist's immediate objective, the larger goal was to use the "citizen patrols" on the border to draw attention to Gilchrist's aim of influencing public opinion and federal immigration policy.

The government's immediate reaction to the Minuteman Project, before it actually began its operations, was not favorable. President George W. Bush took a strong position: "I'm against vigilantes in the United States of America. I'm for enforcing law in a rational way. It's why we've got the Border Patrol, and they ought to be in charge of enforcing the border" (Strohm 2005). At the time Bush made this statement, he was meeting with Mexico's President Vicente Fox, with whom Bush had discussed immigration reform early in 2001, during his first administration and before the 9/11 attacks (Smith and Chen 2001). The organizers of the Minuteman Project were outraged by Bush's use of the term *vigilantes*, which carries a negative connotation, identifying a group of individuals who operate outside the law, or "rational" law enforcement, by taking action into their own hands. Gilchrist continually stressed that the Minuteman Project was a nonviolent protest along the lines of Martin Luther King Jr. (Kelly 2005a). However, one of the main concerns of the Minuteman Project organizers in the days leading up to April 1 was the possibility for violence, given that many of the volunteers would carry guns. Moreover, one of the organizers, Chris Simcox, had been convicted on federal weapons charges, and the white supremacist group Aryan Nations was recruiting Minuteman volunteers (Marizco 2005). In addition to President Bush's condemnation of the Minuteman Project, Joe Garza, spokesman for the Border Patrol's Tucson, Arizona sector, dismissed the Project's impact, stating that the agency is not planning to change any operations as a result of the Minutemen's activities (Strohm 2005).

Despite such official reservations about the Minuteman Project, Jim Gilchrist was proclaiming success a few days before the Minuteman Project volunteers were even to begin arriving in Arizona: "I struck the mother lode. It has already accomplished what we want to accomplish: nationwide awareness. And we haven't even started the project yet" (Strohm 2005). Gilchrist's emphasis on nationwide awareness underscores the public spectacle nature of the Minuteman Project and its goal of disciplining the federal government.

It is easy to see why Gilchrist was claiming success before the Minuteman Project began operations. On March 30, 2005, two days before the official start date of the Minuteman Project, the Bush administration announced that more than 500 additional Border Patrol agents would be deployed along the Arizona-Mexico border, bringing the total to about 2,900, and additional aircraft. In addition, top Homeland Security officials would be arriving in Tucson to add to the visible display of the administration's efforts to enforce the border (Alonso-Zaldivar 2005). Government officials claimed there was no connection between the Minutemen and this new deployment of resources to the Arizona border (Argetsinger 2005). However, a spokesman for the Minuteman Project, Bill Bennett, pointed to these deployments as a sign of success: "President Bush called the Minuteman Project a bunch of vigilantes—but if it's the case that this [federal crackdown] did start because of the Minuteman Project, then the project is a success. I find it very interesting that this is all coinciding" (Alonso-Zaldivar 2005).

APRIL 2005 ON THE ARIZONA-MEXICO BORDER

Minuteman volunteers officially began operations on April 1, 2005. Organizers expected 1,300 volunteers (LoMonaco 2005). By April 2, however, only about two hundred volunteers had shown up and were stationed in seven outposts along a 23–mile stretch of border (Kelly 2005b). One newspaper described the Minutemen's activities this way: "In four member teams, they rode out caravan-style for several miles along red-dirt roads flanked by rocks and prickly brush. They fanned out hundreds of yards apart along a skimpy barbed wire fence at the Mexico border, eager to catch men and women trying to sneak into the United States" (Talev 2005).

The volunteers' motivations for coming echoed the discourse on Mexican immigration discussed above. "We have an illegal invasion of our country going on now that is affecting our schools, our healthcare system and our society in general. No society can sustain this" (Kelly 2005c). Another said about immigration, "It's destroying America" (Talev 2005). Another noted, "I'd like to see my brother get a wheelchair lift rather than an illegal alien get a free education. I just think you've got to take care of your own" (Talev 2005). Yet another noted, "I think all of this will put the federal government on notice as to where we stand as citizens" (Kelly 2005b). Such comments clearly delineate simple dichotomies, such as us/them, invaders/invaded, destroyers/victims, illegal/"our own" or legitimate members of society, and citizens/noncitizens, that define both citizens and those in a position of "illegality" (Ngai 2004).

Although the number of Minutemen was less than anticipated, the media turned up in full force. In fact, as the *Los Angeles Times* observed, "The number of media members here Friday to cover the volunteer border patrols nearly outnumbered the Minutemen. Reporters from around the world descended on Tombstone, population 4,800. Along with journalists came some filmmakers working on documentaries about the U.S.-Mexico border" (Kelly 2005a). Ironically, Chris Simcox, editor of the *Tombstone Tumbleweed* and one of the organizers of the Minuteman Project, seemed to blame the media for manufacturing the event: "The media has created this frenzy and this monster. They are looking for Bigfoot, the Loch Ness monster, the vigilante" (Kelly 2005a). However, Jim Gilchrist was more candid: "We have already accomplished our goal a hundredfold in getting the media out here and getting the message out" (Kelly 2005a). As Gilchrist's comment indicates, the Minuteman Project's goal of creating a spectacle was clearly elevated above other objectives originally elaborated for the Minuteman Project. Indeed, the other goals seemed to have been forgotten, perhaps reflecting the fewer than expected volunteers. Or perhaps this lays bare the point being made here, that media attention was their only real objective in staging this spectacle.

On April 3, the media reported on still larger increases in surveillance power along the Arizona-Mexico border. The Department of Homeland Security upped the ante to more than 700 additional border patrol agents to the area (Levine 2005). In addition, the U.S. Senate approved an amendment to hire 2,000 border patrol agents, a direct affront to President Bush's 2006 budget, which called for only an additional 216 new border patrol agents (Levine 2005). Both the new deployments of agents and new hiring goals come just as Minutemen were beginning to monitor the border.

By April 5 there appeared to be fewer clandestine border crosses in the areas monitored by the Minutemen. Chris Simcox was quick to claim another success: "We've shut down the whole sector. That's success" (Coronado 2005b). However, the reduced numbers of clandestine border crossers was also influenced by other factors, not the least of which was the Mexican police force Grupos Beta, patrolling the Mexican side of the border, warning would-be migrants of the Minutemen's presence (Coronado 2005b). Two weeks into the project, the Border Patrol had apprehended about the same number of clandestine border crossers as during the same period the year before (Richard 2005). However, such considerations did not deter Jim Gilchrist from bragging: "None of this would have happened if it wasn't for the Minuteman action. This thing was a dog and pony show designed to bring in the media and get the message out and it worked" (Kelly 2005a).

Although the Minuteman Project was to be a month-long monitoring exercise, Jim Gilchrist claimed "victory" and formally ended the project's border monitoring on Wednesday, April 20, 2005 (Coronado 2005c). Border monitoring was to continue, however, under the guise of Civil Homeland Defense, headed by Chris Simcox. Also, the Minuteman Project spawned related projects along the U.S.-Mexico border in Texas, New Mexico, California, and far from the border in Idaho and Michigan (Carroll 2005; Seper 2005). The fallout from the Minuteman Project also had other ramifications. On April 19, Arnold Schwarzenegger, Governor of California, caused quite a political furor when he announced that closing the borders was a good idea. "Close the borders in California and all across, between Mexico and the United States . . . because I think it is just unfair to have all these people coming across," adding that border enforcement was "lax" (Sample 2005). In mid-August (August 12 and 15, respectively), the governors of New Mexico and Texas went even further, declaring their respective counties along the U.S.-Mexico border "disaster areas," thus freeing up government funds to spend in the region (Gaguette 2005). Although the Minuteman Project's April offensive ended prematurely, it helped to turn the public debate on immigration reform decidedly toward increased border enforcement, eclipsing guestworker programs, legalization programs, and other issues.

Jim Gilchrist managed to turn his 15 minutes of fame into an extended spotlight on "illegal aliens" and the U.S.-Mexico border by running as the American Independent Party's candidate for U.S. Congress in Orange County, California. The 48th Congressional District is solidly Republican, but Gilchrist managed to use his one-issue campaign to stir up politics. His campaign attracted media attention and a war chest of about $500,000, both of which helped him win third place in the November 29, 2005 primary election, with 15 percent of the vote (Pasco and Weikel 2005). Gilchrist still came in third in the final election on December 6, 2005, but he increased his share of the electorate to 25 percent (Pasco 2005). In the course of the campaign, the favorite candidate and eventual winner, John Campbell, had to insist that he too was tough on immigration. Two votes Campbell cast as a member of the California legislature became favorite Gilchrist targets. One vote allowed undocumented students who grew up in California to pay in-state tuition rather than the more costly tuition charged students from foreign countries when attending public colleges and universities. The other vote concerned Mexican consulate cards and their use as valid identification in California. By the time of the final election, Campbell had repudiated these votes and joined Gilchrist in opposing a guestworker program and other moderate immigration reforms (Barabak and Pasco 2005). Immediately following his defeat at the polls, Jim Gilchrist assured his followers of his intentions to continue to seek elected office and to focus attention on "illegal immigration" (Barabak and Pasco 2005). In other words, he would continue to use the spectacle of surveillance to garner media attention.

THE SPECTACLE REVISITED

Renato Rosaldo has observed, "The U.S.-Mexico border has become theater, and border theater has become social violence. Actual violence has become inseparable from symbolic ritual on the border—crossings, invasions, lines of defense, high-tech surveillance, and more" (1997, 33). To this list I would add the Minuteman Project. The border theater that occurred in Arizona was indeed a symbolic ritual of surveillance.

However, the Minutemen's monitoring may not have provided a great deterrent to clandestine border crossers in the long run. First of all, the demand for immigrant labor continues to act as a magnet for Mexicans and others. This demand results from a complex set of interacting factors, none of which are carefully examined in the Minuteman Project's public discourse. For example, rarely if ever discussed are the effects of low fertility rates and an aging U.S. population, especially during periods of economic expansion; middle and upper class Americans' desire for cheap commodities, food, and services; economic pressures related to globalization and low-wage production in developing countries; or the economic benefits of immigration, not the least of which is their consumption of U.S. goods, or as *Businessweek* magazine put it on its July, 18, 2005 cover, "Embracing Illegals: Companies Are Getting Hooked on the Buying Power of 11 Million Undocumented Immigrants." Simply increasing surveillance along the U.S.-Mexico border does little to address these salient factors creating a demand for the type of labor supplied by undocumented migrants. Consequently, the Minuteman Project's monitoring of a small area along the U.S.-Mexico border probably resulted in potential unauthorized border crossers moving elsewhere, seeking less guarded areas.

Without a doubt, however, the spectacle of surveillance was very effective in reaching the target audience, the public. The Minuteman Project's April "offensive" on the Arizona-Mexico border was a media success, or as one newspaper put it, "Sifting hoopla from hard facts can be tricky, but Minuteman Project has succeeded in key goal—shifting nation's eyes to illegal immigration" (Richard 2005). Not only did the media turn out in full force, but stories on the Minuteman Project saturated newspapers nationwide.

From the perspective of critical cultural analysis, the spectacle in the desert has many connotations. The Minuteman Project grew out of a sense of frustration with new global realities that reduce the power of national borders to delimit the nation-state as an autonomous territory. Anthropologists have been arguing that these flows reflect the unmoored or deterritorialized nature of contemporary post-nation-state realities that make national borders permeable in many ways (Gupta and Ferguson 1997). Indeed, the world is now on the move as capital, culture, people, and information flow across once ponderous national borders at an increasingly rapid pace (Appadurai 1996; Inda and Rosaldo 2002). The organizers and sympathizers of the Minuteman Project viewed its activities as a stand against the destruction of the nation-state symbolized by the inability of the state to control the flow of unauthorized border crosses. For the Minutemen, the "breakdown" of border, as they perceived it, was an empirical assertion that the border was, for all practical purposes, a legal fiction (Coutin 2005). Their dramatics were an attempt to reaffirm the contours of the nation-state, which from their perspective was in danger of being "lost." Through their actions, the Minutemen hoped to restore the nation-state's clearly defined border around its territory. The spectacle of surveillance on the Arizona-Mexico border drew the line, as it were, along the U.S.-Mexico border.

The Minuteman Project engaged in a performance that inscribed citizenship and the nation similar to the way anthropologists have shown for gender (Butler 1993; Cassell 1997). Through the dramatics of their "hunt" for noncitizen "prey," the Minutemen enacted a rite of policing noncitizens, an act of symbolic power and violence that defined their own citizen-subject status. At the same time, the spectacle in the desert was a nation-defining performance. Unauthorized border crossers, those "space invaders," as Puwar (2004) might put it, were kept in their own national territory. For a couple of weeks, in a small area along the 2,000-mile U.S.-Mexico border, the danger to the nation posed by people out of place was averted (Douglas 1966). The Minutemen's monitoring of the border was a corporal spectacle and for many the Minutemen came to embody the citizen exerting power to preserve the privileges, and purity, of citizenship and the integrity of the nation-state.

WORKS CITED

Alonso-Zaldivar, Ricardo. 2005. "U.S. to Bolster Arizona Border Security." *Los Angeles Times*, March 30.

Andreas, Peter. 2000. *Border Games: Policing the U.S.-Mexico Divide.* Ithaca: Cornell University Press.

Appadurai, Arjun. 1996. *Modernity at Large: Cultural Dimensions of Globalization.* Minneapolis: University of Minnesota Press.

Argetsinger, Amy. 2005. "Immigration Opponents to Patrol U.S. Border: Rights Groups Condemn 'Minuteman Project.'" *Washington Post*, March 31.

Barabak, Mark Z., and Jean O. Pasco. 2005. "Election as Immigration Bellwether." *Los Angeles Times*, December 8.

Butler, Judith. 1993. *Bodies That Matter: On the Discursive Limits of "Sex."* New York: Routledge.

Carroll, Susan. 2005. "Border Watch to Widen: Minuteman Project Plans to Patrol More States." *Republic Tucson Bureau*, April 19.

Cassell, Joan. 1997. "Doing Gender, Doing Surgery: Women Surgeons in a Man's Profession." *Human Organization* 56 (1): 47–52.

Chavez, Leo R. 2001. *Covering Immigration: Popular Images and the Politics of the Nation.* Berkeley: University of California Press.

Comaroff, Jean, and John L. Comaroff. 2006. "Figuring Crime: Quantifacts and the Production of the Un/Real." *Public Culture* 18 (1): 209–246.

Coronado, Michael 2005a. "Volunteers Arrive to Monitor Border." *Orange County Register*, April 2.

———. 2005b. "Wary Groups in Border Watch." *Orange County Register*, April 5.

———. 2005c. "Minutemen Quit Patrol Early but Declare Victory." *Orange County Register*, April 19.

Coutin, Susan Bibler. 2005. "Being En Route." *American Anthropologist* 107 (2): 195–206.

Delson, Jennifer. 2005. "Profile of James Gilchrist." *Los Angeles Times*, April 11.

democracynow.org. 2005. "Vigilantes or Civilian Border Patrol? A Debate on the Minuteman Project." September 22.

Douglas, Mary. 1966. *Purity and Danger.* London: Routledge & Kegan Paul.

Dunn, Timothy J. 1996. *The Militarization of the U.S.-Mexico Border, 1978–1992: Low-Intensity Conflict Doctrine Comes Home.* Austin, TX: Center for Mexican American Studies Books.

———. 1999. "Military Collaboration with the Border Patrol in the U.S.-Mexico Border Region: Inter-Organizational Relations and Human Rights Implications." *Journal of Political and Military Sociology* 27 (2): 257–277.

Foucault, Michel. 1977. *Discipline and Punish: The Birth of the Prison.* London: Tavistock.

Gaguette, Nicole. 2005. "Border Troubles Divide U.S. States." *Los Angeles Times,* August 18.

Gandelman, Jose. 1986. "Wilson Would Back Marines on Border If Reform Move Fails." *San Diego Union,* April 6.

Grillo, Ioan. 2005. "Minute Patrol Off to a Slow Start." *Houston Chronicle,* April 2.

Gupta, Akhil, and James Ferguson. 1997. "Culture, Power, Place: Ethnography at the End of an Era." In *Culture, Power, Place: Explorations in Critical Anthropology,* edited by Akhil Gupta and James Ferguson, 1–29. Durham, NC: Duke University Press.

Huntington, Samuel P. 2000. "The Special Case of Mexican Immigration: Why Mexico Is a Problem." *The American Enterprise* 11 (8): 20–22.

Inda, Jonathan Xavier. 2006. *Targeting Immigrants: Government, Technology, and Ethics.* Malden, MA: Blackwell.

Inda, Jonathan Xavier, and Renato Rosaldo. 2002. *The Anthropology of Globalization.* Malden, MA: Blackwell.

Kelly, David. 2005a. "Border Watchers Capture Their Prey—the Media. *Los Angeles Times,* April 5.

———. 2005b. "Citizens Border Patrols Hurry Up . . . and Wait." *Los Angeles Times,* April 3.

———. 2005c. "Minutemen Prepare to Lay Down the Law." *Los Angeles Times,* April 2.

Levine, Samantha. 2005. "Border Guard Shift Questioned." *Houston Chronicle,* April 3.

LoMonaco, Claudine. 2005. "Minutemen Gather in Tombstone for Border Watch." *Tucson Citizen,* April 1.

Marizco, Michael. 2005. "Abusive Acts vs. Entrants Are Ignored, Activists Say." *Arizona Daily Star,* March 29.

McDonnell, Patrick J. 1986. "Hunter Asks for National Guardsmen Along Border." *Los Angeles Times,* June 24.

Meyer, J. Stryker. 1986. "Sheriff Urges Posting Marines Along Border." *San Diego Union,* April 6.

Ngai, Mae M. 2004. *Impossible Subjects: Illegal Aliens and the Making of Modern America.* Princeton, NJ: Princeton University Press.

Pasco, Jean O. 2005. "Campbell Wins Seat; Gilchrist Takes 3rd." *Los Angeles Times,* December 7.

Pasco, Jean O., and Dan Weikel. 2005. "O.C. Race a Border Skirmish." *Los Angeles Times,* December 4.

Prodis, Julia. 1997. "Texas Town Outraged at Marines over Shooting of Goat Herder." *Orange County Register,* June 29.

Puwar, Nirmal. 2004. *Space Invaders: Race, Gender and Bodies Out of Place.* Oxford, UK: Berg.

Reza, H. G. 1997. "Patrols Border on Danger." *Los Angeles Times,* June 29.

Richard, Chris. 2005. "The Buzz on the Border." *The Press-Enterprise,* April 14.

Riley, Michael. 2005. "1,000 Activists to Patrol Arizona Border for Migrants." *Denver Post,* March 31.

Rosaldo, Renato.1997. "Cultural Citizenship, Inequality, and Multiculturalism." In *Latino Cultural Citizenship,* edited by William V. Flores and Rina Benmayor, 27–38. Boston: Beacon Press.

Rotstein, Arthur H. 2005. "Volunteer Border Watchers Cause Concern." *Ventura County Star,* March 27.

Sample, Herbert A. 2005. "Governor Talks of Closing Mexico Border." *Sacramento Bee,* April 20.

Seper, Jerry. 2005. "Border Patrols Inspire Imitation, Other Civilians Take Up Cause." *Washington Times,* April 16.

Smith, James F., and Edwin Chen. 2001. "Bush to Weigh Residency for Illegal Mexican Immigrants." *Los Angeles Times*, September 7.

Strohm, Chris. 2005. "Activists to Flock to Border, Set Up Citizen Patrols." *National Journal Group*, March 28.

Talev, Margaret. 2005. "Minuteman Volunteers Give Motives: Middle Aged Whites Express Frustrations with Illegal Crossings." *Modesto Bee*, April 4.

6

BARE LIFE

BORDER-CROSSING DEATHS AND SPACES OF MORAL ALIBI

Roxanne Lynn Doty

Deep tensions strain at the edges of the nation-state and the contemporary mobilities that continually contradict presumptions of stability and stasis which underpin conventional notions of a world of sovereign entities which are willing and able to control movements across and within their territories. Foremost amongst the many tensions is the one created by the relative ease with which human beings traverse the numerous spaces demarcated as sovereign, most notably those whose movements are deemed "unauthorized," "undocumented," "irregular," and "illegal." States throughout the world have responded to this form of human mobility with restrictions meant to make unauthorized border crossings difficult and dangerous and thus to discourage them. Nowhere is this more powerfully exemplified as in the US border control strategy of "prevention through deterrence," which was put into practice in the 1990s and which remains the cornerstone of US border enforcement policy. The result in too many cases has not been deterrence but tragedy and a skyrocketing death rate of migrants crossing the US–Mexico border in increasingly dangerous and remote areas. Over the past decade or so, writers, both academic and nonacademic, have created a large body of literature on this topic (see Annerino, 1999; Jimenez, 2009; Nevins, 2010).

The borderlands of the world are particularly appropriate sites for examining contemporary instances of states of exception and the creation of "bare life" (see Jones, 2009). Geographic border areas are the prototypical margins of "the state," i.e., spaces where law and order are simultaneously rigorously enforced and elided and where tensions are often the most obvious and the most extreme. An essential task of statecraft is thus to manage the tensions that are inherent at the borders. Such management takes place against particular historical, social, and political backgrounds. In terms of unauthorized migration, this background includes issues of race and class as illustrated by the fact that poor, relatively unskilled, but often highly sought after, Third World migrants have at various times been both

Roxanne Lynn Doty is associate professor of Politics and Global Studies at Arizona State University.

wanted and unwanted—wanted for their labor but unwanted as human beings. In a word, they are perfect candidates for being reduced to bare life. In this chapter I examine the issue of migrant border-crossing deaths around the US–Mexico border and the policies that have led to the drastic increases in these fatalities. Scholars across a number of disciplines have, in recent years, turned their attention to the concepts of biopower and bare life, offering insights into how power is exercised and statecraft practiced. This chapter contributes to this conversation in three ways. (1) I highlight the fact that biopower is exercised differentially across different populations. It is thus important to raise the question of who is the subject population of biopolitics/biopower. The subject population here consists of human beings who cross the US–Mexico border without documentation. This implicitly calls attention to the relevance of Foucault's writings on biopolitics for the international realm. While Foucault's focus often seems to be on very local operations of power, these are not unconnected to the international, and indeed, when it comes to border politics, local practices of power are inextricably linked to the international or the external. I argue that Foucault's work has much relevance for understanding border politics, whose fundamental purpose is the construction of boundaries demarcating the internal versus the external. Further, I suggest that race is significant to this process and that Foucault's writings are extremely suggestive and helpful in illuminating important aspects of border politics. (2) I call attention to the significance of geographic space/landscape in the process of obscuring official state responsibility for the moral consequences of the bare life that is made possible by the creation of spaces of exception. I thus draw explicit attention to the ethical/moral implications of biopower. Drawing upon the works of Foucault and Agamben as well as recent discussions of their work, I highlight the significance of geographic space to this particular practice of statecraft in the borderlands circa the US–Mexico divide. I suggest that the spatial landscapes in these areas have been essential to the workings of statecraft during the past twenty years and that these spaces have functioned to provide a *moral alibi* for any responsibility on the part of the United States for the deaths of undocumented migrants. (3) Finally, in the conclusion I briefly raise the question of agency in the context of bare life and the state of exception. Often discussions implicitly seem to presume the absence of agency, thus precluding the possibilities for resistance. To be sure, official government responses to the tension between sovereignty and human mobility have created "exceptional" spaces in which human beings are subject to being reduced to bare life. However, these spaces, while ripe with that potential, do not always result in an actualization of bare life. Possibilities for resistance inhere in exceptional politics.

There are numerous dangerous border areas in the world, such as the Strait of Gibraltar, the minefields between Greece and Turkey, the Indian Ocean, and remote sections of the Greek–Bulgarian border (Weber, 2009; Carling, 2007). The focus of this study is on one such place, the southwestern deserts that make up the borderland areas separating the United States and Mexico, which contains some of the harshest terrain in the United States as well as some of the most extreme temperatures. In these extreme locales we find an intersection of biopower and the creation of a space of exception, which produces bare life that can be taken without apology, classified as neither homicide nor sacrifice. Biopower, so conceived, is not solely a politics of making life live but also a politics of making life die. The case at hand illustrates one way that these phenomena play out on the ground. I do not attempt to make arguments as to the superiority of, for example, Agamben's versus Foucault's conceptualization of biopower. Belcher et al (2008) make the important observation that Agamben's affinity with Foucault is often lost in the various interpretations of these two theorists. For the purposes of this chapter, it is not necessary or even desirable to come down on one side or the other, but rather to look for insights that can illuminate the wielding of contemporary forms of power and the consequences that ensue. My goal here is to let the situation and practices contribute to our understandings of how biopower works and how some human beings are turned into bare life. As noted above, it is also important to appreciate that, like everything else, biopower and the politics of exceptionalism are not monolithic fortresses of power. Rather, they are characterized by tensions and cracks within which human beings practice various forms of resistance.

BIOPOWER AND BARE LIFE IN THE US–MEXICO BORDERLANDS

On Friday, July 6, 2007, volunteers with two local humanitarian groups in Tucson, Arizona, Humane Borders and Samaritans, went in search of Prudencia Martin Gomez, age 18, from Guatemala. She was headed to Oakland, California, to join her boyfriend/fiancé and had been missing since June 11 in the Ironwood Forest National Monument, a 129,000-acre expanse of land, in the Sonoran Desert 25 miles northwest of Tucson. There are no facilities in the Ironwood Forest, and visitors are warned of the hazards of the extreme heat. Human beings simply cannot survive in this part of the southwestern deserts for as long as Prudencia had been missing, so there was no pretense that they would find her alive, and they did not. The official location of her body was recorded as GPS: N 32'25.455/W111'307.80 (*Arizona Daily Star* 2010). Prudencia had fallen ill and had been unable to continue. Her fellow travelers had left her with water, but it was not enough. She was only a mile south of a Humane Borders water station, but a mile can be a very long way in the desert, in the month of June, when one has already walked a long distance. Authorities determined that Prudencia had died on June 15. The recorded high temperature on that day was 115°F. Prudencia was a contemporary version of what Agamben (1998) refers to as bare life, life that can be taken without apology, classified as neither homicide nor sacrifice. She was US border policy stripped to its essence. And hers, tragically, is not an isolated example. In 2004, Mario Alberto Diaz, 6 feet tall with a black belt in karate and working on a master's degree in biology, crossed the border near Sasabe, Arizona. His body was discovered twenty days later in a creek in the foothills of the Sierrita Mountains (Bourdeaux, 2004). In the summer of 2005 the Pima County medical examiner in Tucson, Arizona, had to rent a refrigerated tractor-trailer to store the bodies of migrants due to the record number of deaths that year (*Arizona Republic* 2005). The deadly trend continues. Even as apprehensions have steadily declined, deaths continue to rise (McCombs, 2009). The migrant death count for fiscal year 2009 was the third highest since 1998. In the fifteen-year period since "prevention through deterrence" was first introduced, approximately 5,000 migrants have died, though near universal agreement exists that estimates of migrant deaths are undercounts and the actual number is likely much higher (Coalición de Derechos Humanos, 2007).

When they debated, formulated, and put into effect the various border control operations collectively known as prevention through deterrence, policymakers likely had never
heard of GPS: N 32'25.455/W111'307.80 or the Ironwood Forest or the Sierrita Mountains or the many other locations at which migrant bodies have been, and continue to be,
found. However, it is arguably inconceivable that they did not know of the harsh conditions to which migrants would be subjected under this border strategy. The Border Patrol's own blueprint for one of the early and well-known manifestations of the new
operations, Operation Gatekeeper, noted that it would channel migrants to locations
where "the days are blazing hot and nights freezing cold" (ACLU, 2009). In this section, I
argue that the prevention through deterrence border control strategies exemplify Foucault's theoretical writings on how biopower, sovereign power, and racism can be articulated with one another thus to function in concert. While biopolitics, as formulated by
Foucault, is generally understood as being concerned with the governance and regulation
of a population in matters such as health and sexuality, it is also consistent with what
Agamben refers to as bare life. For Foucault the emergence of the "problem of the population" coincided with the development of an art of government wherein the main concerns
of government were on the wealth, longevity, health, and sexuality of the population,
giving rise to the notion of biopower as "making life live" (Foucault, 1991). Through regulations in these matters, subjects become entangled in the practices of statecraft. Agamben
has critiqued what he calls Foucault's "progressive disqualification of death" (i.e., the cir-
cumscription of the issue of death to discussions of classical sovereign power), offering a
conceptualization of biopower which focuses on the ways in which sovereign power produces a radical exposure, abandoning subjects, stripping their identities to that of bare
life, and thereby creating spaces of exception or a "juridical void" which permits abuses
and killings without punishment.[1] While Agamben's theorizations of biopower and its
relation to bare life are invaluable for understanding how modern power works, he arguably draws a bit of a straw man when it comes to Foucault. In *Society Must Be Defended*,
Foucault poses the following question: How can biopower, whose function is to improve
life and prolong its duration, kill? "How can the power of death, the function of death, be
exercised in a political system centered upon biopower?" (2003, page 254). His definition
of "killing" is not "simply murder as such, but also every form of indirect murder: the
fact of exposing someone to death, increasing the risk of death for some people, or, quite
simply, political death, expulsion, rejections, and so on" (page 256). Clearly Foucault recognizes that biopower does not preclude the taking of life. He responds to his own question by turning to race, suggesting that race performs two functions: (1) it introduces a
break in the domain of life under power's control between what must live and what must
die, thus fragmenting the field of the biological that power controls; and (2) it establishes
a relationship between life and death. "If you want to live, you must take lives, you must
be able to kill" (2003, pages 254–255).

---

1. Agamben critiques Foucault for not giving sufficient attention to bare life, i.e., to circumscribing the problem of death to the realm of sovereign power and ignoring or understudying/underelaborating on how death may
figure in biopolitics. For an excellent discussion of the concept of biopolitics, and specifically comparisons and
contrasts between Foucault and Agamben, see Coleman and Grove (2009). Also see Coleman (2007).

Before considering how this phenomenon has played out in US border control strategies, I want to highlight two interrelated issues that are addressed somewhat peripherally or implicitly by Foucault but that are key when it comes to examining border politics and policies. First is the issue of citizenship. Foucault's writings refer to the population, but clearly the population is not a monolithic, all-encompassing entity. Foucault's writings on biopolitics can and have been interpreted to mean the local or national population, thus lending credence to the criticism of his neglect of the international. However, as noted earlier, when his ideas are put to work in the arena of border policies, the international looms large, and it becomes clear that the definition of who is part of the "population" and who is not is to a great extent what is at stake. So the issue of citizenship and the citizen is vitally important (see Nyers, 2010). For the citizen to live, the undocumented must be permitted to die. Those lacking citizenship are potentially bare life.[2] The second issue that warrants consideration is how Foucault understands race. Foucault asks, "What in fact is racism?" and refers to the appearance of distinctions, a hierarchy amongst races, and racism's inscription within the state (Foucault, 2003, page 254). However, he is vague on precisely what race is. I am not suggesting that this imprecision needs to be corrected or that it is a lacuna in Foucault's writings. I call attention to this so as to maintain a space for an understanding of race that can incorporate "differentialist" or "neoracism," which is highly significant in understanding how race enters into contemporary border politics. Nation, citizen, and race have been historically intertwined in complex ways that are virtually impossible to unravel. This is clearly illustrated in contemporary immigration policies in the United States and throughout the world.

The origins of the "prevention through deterrence" strategy nicely illustrate connections between the local, national, and global/international and highlight how policies designed for the management of populations at local levels cannot always be considered solely local or national issues. More than this, though, the very distinctions between local, national, and international can be a key aspect of such policies. Three government efforts of the early 1990s that can arguably be considered examples of biopolitics were key to the beginnings of the US border blockade: (1) Operation Blockade/Hold the Line in El Paso, Texas, in 1993; (2) the passage of Proposition 187 in California in 1994; and (3) Operation Gatekeeper in the San Diego/Tijuana area in 1994.[3] All of these were, in various ways, focused on issues pertaining to the population and were ostensibly very local in nature. However, they were ultimately intimately connected to the international and to reinforcing the boundaries between the two. The process of enacting such a reinforcement involved attempts to define precisely who constituted the population. Operation Blockade began far from the center of sovereign US power, in the relatively isolated area of El Paso, Texas, which is located at the tip of West Texas. Surrounded by desert, this area in 1993 was the second busiest sector for undocumented border crossings. The busiest was the San Diego sector. Silvester Reyes, the Border Patrol chief of the El Paso sector, unilaterally launched Operation Blockade on September 19, 1993, deploying 400 agents and their vehicles along a 20-mile stretch of the

2. This is clearly evident in U.S. border policy. See Darling (2009) for a study of how asylum seekers in Britain have been rendered bare life as a result of their lack of citizenship.

3. Much of the background information on these three policies comes from the classic and recently updated study of Operation Gatekeeper in Nevins (2010) and from Dunn's (2009) excellent study of Operation Blockade.

border between El Paso and Ciudad Juarez, Mexico (Nevins, 2010, page 111). Prior to this, the border patrol strategy had been to apprehend unauthorized entrants *after* they had crossed the border. This meant that hundreds of thousands who were suspected of being undocumented migrants were stopped every year. Most of those stopped were El Paso residents of Hispanic appearance. Not surprisingly, this led to charges of racial profiling (Dunn, 2009, page 12). With Operation Blockade, apprehensions dropped 80–90%. The strategy received much favorable national publicity and was quickly replicated in October 1994 with Operation Gatekeeper in San Diego, California (Nevins, 2010, page 111). The local situation in California was also a significant factor leading up to Operation Gatekeeper, specifically the debates over and eventual passage of Proposition 187, also known as the Save Our State ballot initiative. Proposition 187 was an anti-immigrant measure that proposed to deny public education from elementary to postsecondary levels, social services, and public health care (excluding emergencies) to unauthorized immigrants. It was passed by 59% of California's electorate. The proposition resulted from the efforts of local immigration control groups in California as well as the national anti-immigrant organization, Federation for American Immigration Reform (FAIR).[4] National-level politics were also key factors leading to the border build up of the early 1990s. The anti-immigrant backlash loomed as a potential threat to then President Bill Clinton's reelection. Gatekeeper was followed by Operation Safeguard in central Arizona in 1995, which "redirected illegal border crossings away from urban areas near the Nogales port-of-entry to comparatively open areas" (National Border Patrol, 2000). Operation Rio Grande was launched in south Texas in 1997, which encompasses McAllen, Brownsville, and Laredo (National Border Patrol, 2000).

Border Patrol agents are not the only aspect of US border control strategy. The strategy also includes technology and infrastructure (see Heyman, this volume).[5] Prevention through deterrence has thus expanded to include virtual fencing, a planned 670-mile-long physical border fence/wall, and various high-tech surveillance devices on or near the border. More recently called "Secure Border Initiative," the latest strategy continues and expands prevention through deterrence, focusing on even more border patrol agents; upgrading technology, including increased manned aerial assets; expanded use of UAVs (unmanned aerial vehicles); and increased investment in infrastructure, with additional "physical layers" of security and more access roads for the border patrol to facilitate quicker responses.[6] As Foucault notes, apparatuses of security associated with biopower have a tendency to expand. Such apparatuses are centrifugal, allowing for the development of ever-wider circuits (2009, page 45). This has certainly been the case with "prevention through deterrence."[7] The US Border Patrol is now the US federal government's largest law enforcement agency. This expansion consists not only of broadening the range of strategies for controlling the border

4. On FAIR, see Doty (2009). Proposition 187 was later declared unconstitutional.

5. Presentation by Jeanne Ray-Condon, Division Chief for Operational Support, Tucson Sector Headquarters, Tucson, AZ, January 8, 2010.

6. Secure Border Initiative was unveiled by then Secretary of Homeland Security Michael Chertoff on November 2, 2005. See "ICE plays key role in Secure Border Initiative," Inside ICE: Volume 2, Issue 3, November 14, 2005.

7. The latest border strategies also include interior enforcement, which consists of increased detention, workplace enforcement, as well as state and local partnerships.

on the part of the US government, but also the expansion of surveillance and monitoring of the border into the ostensibly "private" realm. A major aspect of the Secure Border Initiative is SBI*net*, which consists of a network of surveillance towers with radar and cameras. In September 2006 the Boeing Corporation won the $70 million Department of Homeland Security contract to develop and build the towers and monitor its subcontractors. Putting these into practice involves Boeing personnel in the actual monitoring of the border (Logan, 2007).[8] As the various surveillance mechanisms, from agents to high-tech equipment, have been put into place, they have collectively contributed to the increase in migrant deaths. Robin Hoover of Humane Borders has measured the locations where migrant bodies have been found, and they are further and further away from populated areas. "The migrants are walking in more treacherous terrain for longer periods of time, and you should expect more deaths," he says (Rotstein, 2009).

The significance of prevention through deterrence in terms of the techniques of bio-power can be found in the fact that it has not *completely* eliminated, nor arguably was it ever intended to eliminate, unauthorized immigration (Nevins, 2010, page 114). Like the border policies prior to it, prevention through deterrence was in part a "border game," rife with symbolic power which functioned to reaffirm the significance of the boundary between Mexico and the United States and at the same time asserted/reasserted the sovereignty of the latter.[9] However, it inaugurated a new intensity in that US border policies became much more than a symbolic game, in the sense that crossing the border without authorization now became an extremely dangerous proposition in which death lurked in every new migrant crossing route, through formidable mountain ranges and along desolate, heat-scorched desert lands. In terms of the operations of power, the significance of this new border strategy lies in a subtle shift from the dominance of sovereign, juridical power to biopower. I say "subtle" because I do not mean to suggest that juridical power and biopower are opposed to one another. Clearly, they work together in this case, and it is a matter of emphasis that I am suggesting here. Juridical power intensified the US border enforcement regime. However, biopower is clearly evident as the newly intensified enforcement regime produced a radical exposure for migrants which stripped them of their humanity and permitted their killing without punishment.

In an effort to reduce the probability of some migrants successfully crossing the border and thereby deter others from attempting to cross, prevention through deterrence depended on some human beings being constituted as bare life. The key division involves the creation of bare life, i.e., the differentiation between those who can be sacrificed for the well-being (or perceived well-being) of others and those whose well-being is ostensibly promoted. Those whose well-being is promoted are the ones who claim that migrants are swamping their country and who clamor for "control of our borders," as well as those who benefit directly and indirectly from the labor of the migrants who successfully cross. Juridical power obviously does not recede completely but, rather, works in tandem with biopower. Foucault's distinction between the population and the multiplicity of individuals is relevant

8. The author also witnessed Boeing personnel in the Border Patrol control room at the headquarters of the Tucson sector of the U.S. Border Patrol, January 2010.

9. Andreas's argument on border policies as symbolic games is key here. See Andreas (2000).

here. The multiplicity of individuals will "only be pertinent to the extent that, properly managed, maintained, and encouraged, it will make possible what one wants to obtain at the level that is pertinent" (Foucault, 2009, page 44). Prevention through deterrence seeks to do just this with the multiplicity of individuals who attempt to cross the US–Mexico border without authorization. "Management" is simply not the concentrated, focused kind of management found with disciplinary power, but is more consistent with Foucault's notion that the apparatus of security "lets things happen," albeit after certain policies/strategies are in place (page 45). After the apparatuses of security fabricate and organize a *milieu*—i.e., after physical barriers, increased numbers of border patrol agents, and high-tech surveillance are put in place—agents of security can just let things take their "natural course."[10] Biopolitics works on probabilities, of minimizing what is inconvenient or risky as opposed to absolute suppression. "Instead of a binary division between the permitted and the prohibited, one established an average considered as optimal on the one hand, and, on the other, a bandwidth of the acceptable that must not be exceeded" (Foucault, 2009, pages 6 and 19). This "bandwidth of acceptability" does not consist solely of statistics but includes the totality of border control efforts necessary to give the appearance of a border securely under control. We see both sovereign power and biopower at work, with the latter creating a distinction between those who can be sacrificed and those for whom such sacrifice is regarded as necessary. Clearly, the US economy has always needed immigrant labor and, notwithstanding various periods of economic downturn, will continue to do so. As Cornelius (2005, page 792) notes, this tends to lock "in the current policy mix, under which unauthorized immigrants bear most of the costs and risks of "control" while benefits flow impressively to employers and consumers." In fact, many unauthorized immigrants bear the ultimate cost in terms of their being sacrificed without consequence. Prevention through deterrence functions simultaneously as evidence that the United States is serious about controlling its borders and as assurance that some will survive and make it to the agricultural fields, the meat-packing factories, and the restaurants of El Norte.

How does race figure into all of this? Foucault (2003, page 294) points to racism in response to his own question, "How can the function of death be exercised in a political system centered upon biopower?" For Foucault, racism makes it possible to "establish a relationship between my life and the death of the other that is not a military or warlike relationship of confrontation, but a biological-type relationship" (page 259). The death of the other does not guarantee increased physical safety, but rather is something that "will make life in general healthier: healthier and purer" (page 255). Foucault's use of the phrase "biological-type relationship" makes possible the interpretation that his conceptualization of race is a biological one. However, it seems questionable to me that, given the overall complexity of Foucault's thinking, he would be using "biological" in a simplistic way that refers to some objective, neutral classification of humanity in terms of physical markers of difference. His ideas on racism are pertinent to the multiple ways in which identities have been racialized. Race, in its various guises from simplistic biological notions to more nuanced notions, has

---

10. A milieu is understood here as "a set of natural givens—rivers, marshes, hills—and a set of artificial givens," which appear as a field of intervention; see Foucault (2009, page 21). In this study the southwestern deserts make up the relevant milieu.

been significant for immigration policies both past and present. Race, culture, and illegality have become thoroughly intermeshed in contemporary anti-immigrant arguments. Indeed, the very designation of the adjective "immigrant" is often reserved for poor workers from "Third World" countries (Calavita, 2003). In the United States we have witnessed, in recent years, a widespread demonization of undocumented migrants in both official circles and more broadly throughout civil society (Chavez, 2008; Doty, 2009). In its numerous guises, race has figured prominently in this process. As Hing (2009) points out, such demonization can lead to dehumanization where the migrant is not even treated as human.

Race, as it pertains to immigration policies, is relevant to the criticisms and questions that have been raised about Foucault's neglect of the international realm and specifically his lack of attention to the operations of power beyond the local and national realms of the West. Jabri (2007, page 74) points to the contemporary relevance of race, arguing that it is just as much a part of the "late modern intervention into the societies of others" as it was in the colonial past. When it comes to contemporary US border enforcement strategies, biopolitics is implicated in the very construction of the boundaries that create a national realm as distinct from an international realm, and race is clearly implicated in this. The racialized underpinnings of various contemporary local legislations such as Proposition 187, discussed above, as well as the long history of overt and structural racism in US immigration policies culminate in the undocumented migrant as bare life, a subject whose very existence is synonymous with illegality and is therefore deemed a threat to US sovereignty and governance. The unauthorized migrant becomes socially undesirable, and ultimately one who can be killed without consequence. De Genova (2002, page 433) observes that "the sociopolitical category 'illegal alien' . . . has come to be saturated with racialized difference and indeed has long served as a constitutive dimension of the racialized inscription of 'Mexicans' in the United States." This is consistent with Balibar's (2005) exploration of the phenomenon of racism and his argument that the categories of difference, otherness, and exclusion are crucial to an examination of racism, especially in its multiple forms, notably pertaining to what has been labeled differentialist racism or neoracism. Balibar (2005, page 20) notes that "globalization as such has, at least in principle, no exterior" and that such exterior, as it exists to any degree, "is only reinforced by the working of political boundaries as mainly instruments of security and control of the flows of populations with absolutely unequal status and rights." The unequal status and rights of populations frequently break down along racialized lines.

SPACE AS MORAL ALIBI

Geographic space clearly figures prominently in prevention through deterrence as it does in any strategy for controlling the territory of a sovereign nation-state. However, space, including geographic space, is not a fixed, apolitical, or neutral object that is simply there. Rather, landscapes and the geographic spaces in which they are situated are implicated in the use of power and are themselves products of coercion, struggle, and resistance (see Mitchell, 1996; Price, 2005). That said, I believe that it is important to acknowledge that while space itself and the significance attributed to it may be the result of social and political practices, the raw physicality of some natural environments has an inherent power which can be put to use and can function to mask the workings of social and political power. In the case of US border control strategy, geographic space has made it possible to suggest that the consequences in the form of migrant deaths result from "natural causes"—e.g., extreme heat, dehydration, thirst, or exposure to the elements—thus deflecting official responsibility. Prevention through deterrence created numerous spaces of exceptionalism that relied heavily on such geographic spaces. US border control strategies have turned and continue to turn much of the southwestern border areas into spaces of exception, and those who traverse them, potentially into bare life. Many of these areas are commonly referred to as "killing fields." The US Customs and Border Patrol itself uses the term "corridor of death" to describe parts of the Sonoran Desert that extends from Mexico's state of Sonora into the US state of Arizona (*Customs and Border Protection Today* 2003). Most of these spaces are located far from the urban areas that in the past had been popular crossing spots—e.g., San Diego and El Paso—though many of these spaces are amazingly close to centers of population.[11] For example, Ana Rosa Segura-Marcial, a fifteen-year-old girl, crossed the border near Agua Prieta, Mexico/Douglas, Arizona, on August 9, 2002. Her body was found three days later in an orange grove south of Gilbert, Arizona, on the outskirts of Phoenix, one of the major metropolitan areas in the United States (Stern, 2002). The "Yuma 14" who perished in May of 2001 were at various times during their journey amazingly close to population centers, though they would have had no way of knowing this.[12] Thus, Agamben's "camp" becomes the vast and varied migrant crossing areas, not limited to any specific demarcated or confined space though "grounded," so to speak, in specific geographic terrains.

The natural geography of migrant crossing areas provides a convenient moral alibi in terms of where to locate responsibility for the deaths. State officials can simply let "nature take its course." As Cornelius points out, the logic of US immigration policy was that if the major gateways such as the El Paso and San Diego areas could be controlled, "geography would do the rest" (Doris Meissner, former INS commissioner, in Cornelius, 2005, page 779). Policymakers would argue that the deaths that have resulted from prevention through deterrence are "unintended consequences" and that the intention was to deter migrants from crossing, not to subject them to the high probability of death. However, an argument can be made that the concept of "unintended consequences" functions much as geography does, i.e., as a moral alibi to shun official responsibility for migrant deaths. The logic of the policy actu-

11. Distance, like many other things, can be a complex and relative concept. Migrants have died a few miles from cities and towns. I have personally traveled with humanitarian groups on numerous occasions into remote and desolate locations of potential death that in terms of spatial distance are not too far from cities (e.g., Tucson and Marana, Arizona). The Ironwood Forest National Monument is one example of this. See Doty (2006a). The proximity of a population center has little meaning if migrants do not know the town is near, and many, if not most, are clearly unfamiliar with the geography in which they travel. Migrants die in very remote places and also in places that seem remote but are fairly close to population centers.

12. The "Yuma 14" were fourteen Mexican nationals between the ages of 16 and 35 who died in May 2001 in the area of El Camino del Diablo. El Camino del Diablo, or the Devil's Highway, consists of approximately 100 miles of unpaved road stretching from the U.S.–Mexico border through the Sonoran desert to an area near the town of Yuma, Arizona. It is the historic route of Francisco Vasquez de Coronado, who travelled the road in 1540 in his expedition from Mexico City to the Southwest United States searching for gold. The road is desolate, to put it mildly, and temperatures can reach well over 120?F. According to the U.S. Fish and Wildlife Service, in the summer a person requires two gallons of water a day just to survive in this region. See Urrea (2004).

ally depends on the possibility of deaths and would be meaningless in the absence of this possibility. Johnson (2007, page 112) argues that this border control operation "was deliberately formulated to maximize the physical risks for Mexican migrant workers, thereby ensuring that hundreds of them would die." Behind the theory lay a technology of the human body and the limits of its physical endurance. While this may have remained unspoken, the horrors of a human body without sufficient water was absolutely essential to the success of prevention through deterrence. Other hazards, such as the terrain itself and the difficulty of traversing it, the extreme cold of the desert nights, drowning in the water that rushes through canals, and so on, could also act as deterrents, but the summer heat is the big killer. It is physically impossible for most people to carry a sufficient amount of water. Writer John Annerino recorded his own body's requirement for fluid when he made a 130-mile trek along El Camino del Diablo for six days. The minimum he consumed in one day was two gallons but on several days he drank as much as five gallons (Annerino, 1999).

In 1999 the American Civil Liberties Union of San Diego and Imperial Counties and the California Rural Legal Assistance Foundation filed a petition before the Inter-American Commission on Human Rights on behalf of 350 migrants who had died in unauthorized entries into the United States during the implementation of Operation Gatekeeper (Jimenez, 2009). The petition argued that US authorities were aware that US border enforcement strategies placed migrants in mortal danger and that they had failed to develop any effective response to the mounting death toll.[13] There is a distinctly racial element to this bare life so constructed by US immigration enforcement. In fiscal year 2005, a record year for migrant deaths in the desert, the Coalición de Derechos Humanos in conjunction with the Consular offices of Mexico, Guatemala, El Salvador, Honduras, and Brazil issued a report on border-crossing deaths. Of the 282 recorded deaths, 138 were from Mexico, 2 were from Guatemala, and the rest were unknown (Coalición de Derechos Humanos, 2007). While one may argue that it stands to reason that the number of deaths of Mexicans and Central Americans would be high in that they constitute the majority of unauthorized border crossers, this does not negate the fact that certain racialized groups suffer the most severe consequences of US border policies which have dehumanized them and denied them "the right to have rights."[14] Unauthorized migrants have come to constitute what Balibar refers to as the "radically excluded" who are denied the material conditions of life and recognition of their humanity (Balibar, 2001). They are, in a word, bare life, life that does not deserve to live and that is taken in remote hinterlands of the vast southwestern deserts of the United States. The geographic spaces offer a potentially endless deferral of human responsibility.

CONCLUSION

In this chapter I have examined how geographic space has figured prominently in the border control strategy of prevention through deterrence. Space was conceived as a deterrent to unauthorized border crossers, but instead this strategy has led to dramatic increases in

13. It is important to note that this was 1999, and the death toll has continued to climb.

14. The "right to have rights" comes from Hannah Arendt's *The Origins of Totalitarianism* and is discussed in Balibar (2001).

the number of migrant deaths over the past 16 years. Migrants have been rendered as bare life, and their deaths considered of little consequence. Space has also served as a moral alibi permitting policymakers to deny responsibility for the deaths. However, as has been often noted regarding Foucault's conceptualization of power, where there is power there is always resistance. "The reason why we have seen the development of so many power relations, so many systems of control, and so many forms of surveillance is precisely that power has always been impotent" (Fontana and Bertani, 2003, page 280). Impotent should not be taken to mean without consequence, and clearly that is not what Foucault is suggesting. In the case examined here, the consequences of the power exercised by the United States at its southern border have been dire for some. Still, we can find resistance in numerous forms (see Walsh, this volume).

Prevention through deterrence illustrates an instance in which biopower is operative in constructing/reconstructing the very population that is the subject of government. This of course entails the delineation of those who are *not* the population, and this is where we find spaces of exception and bare life. However, while prevention through deterrence did and continues to create spaces in which human beings may be reduced to bare life and killed without consequence, these spaces only create the conditions of possibility. They do not guarantee that those possibilities will actually come to be. Human beings may resist. Many migrants die in the spaces of exception created in the southwestern deserts of the United States. However, some survive, often against all odds, and the very fact of survival is itself a form of resistance. Even those who die arguably exercise something of a counterpolitics, sparking projects such as that of forensic anthropologist Lori Baker of Baylor University in Texas who works to identify the remains of migrants who have perished in the deserts of Arizona, the scrublands of Texas, and the waters of the Rio Grande in order to reunite them with their relatives (Doty, 2006b). In addition, there are numerous groups such as Humane Borders and No Más Muertes whose presence and practices create alternative spaces of human empathy and redeem/reassert the full humanity of migrants. The survival of those migrants who successfully negotiate the dangerous crossings and elude border control authorities attests to the potential for a refusal to be captured in the sovereign state of exception which has relegated them to bare life. In doing so they exercise agency and resistance, though such resistance is admittedly often very fragile. Still, their survival and arrival at their destinations signals a subversion, at least temporarily, of both the state's exercise of sovereign power as well as biopower. This subversion may be short-lived, or it may last for a very long time. In their discussion of the academic field of geography's use of Agamben's work, Belcher et al (2008) foreground the concept of potentiality, i.e., the tension between actuality (materialization) and the potential not to be. The notion of potentiality is consistent with the idea that resistance is possible and, I would argue, creates an opening for us to imagine some kind of agency on the part of those who are potentially bare life.

Perhaps the ultimate irony, which can be considered a form of what might be called "intrinsic resistance," can be found in the fact that the border patrol itself is officially tasked with rescuing migrants in distress in the desert, thus highlighting the very complicated nature of a biopolitics that, on the one hand, renders the unauthorized as bare life, exposing them to death without consequence, and, on the other hand, attempts to prevent the very same subjects from dying. BORSTAR (Border Patrol Search, Trauma, and Rescue) was launched in 1998 as part of the Border Safety Initiative, whose two main objectives were to reduce injuries to migrants and prevent deaths in the southwest border region (*Customs and Border Protection Today* 2004). It consists of specially trained border patrol agents who seek out migrants in distress. The existence of BORSTAR might ostensibly seem to undermine my arguments that US border enforcement policy produces migrants as bare life. However, I would argue that what it points to is the inherent instability of any set of practices—even those that create bare life. The official practice of pushing migrants to extremely dangerous crossroads of death and then attempting to rescue some of them indicates that spaces of exception are not hermetically sealed, either physically or in terms of social norms and values. I would argue that spaces of exception are always incomplete, with numerous fissures and cracks that hold the possibility of letting in some light, however dim and wavering that light may be.

WORKS CITED

Agamben G, 1998, *Homo Sacer: Sovereign Power and Bare Life*, translated by D Heller-Roazen (Stanford University Press, Stanford, CA)

American Civil Liberties Union, 1999, "Petition challenges deadly U.S. Border Enforcement Strategy," press release, February 10, ACLU, New York

Andreas P, 2000, *Border Games: Policing the U.S.-Mexico Divide* (Cornell University Press, Ithaca, NY)

Annerino J, 1999, *Dead in Their Tracks: Crossing America's Desert Borderlands* (Four Walls Eight Windows, New York)

Arizona Daily Star, 2010, "Bodies of illegal border crossers found over the weekend," February 8

Arizona Republic, 2005, "Country rents truck to use as morgue," September 2, page B10

Balibar E, 2001, "Outlines of a topography of cruelty: Citizenship and civility in the era of global violence," *Constellations* 8 15–29

Balibar E, 2005, "Difference, otherness, exclusion," *Parallax* 11 19–34

Belcher O, Martin L, Secor A, Simon S, Wilson T, 2008, "Everywhere and nowhere: The exception and the topological challenge to geography," *Antipode* 40 499–503

Bourdeaux R, 2004, "Deadly journey of hope," *Los Angeles Times*, October 10, page 5

Calavita K, 2003, "A reserve army of delinquents," *Punishment and Society* 5 399–413

Carling J, 2007, "Migration control and migrant fatalities at the Spanish-African borders," *International Migration Review* 41 316–343

Chavez L, 2008, *The Latino Threat: Constructing Immigrants, Citizens, and the Nation* (Stanford University Press, Stanford, CA)

Coalición de Derechos Humanos, 2007, "Arizona Recovered Human Remains Project," www.derechos humanosaz.net

Coleman M, 2007, "Review of *State of Exception*," Environment and Planning D: Society and Space 25 187–190

Coleman M, Grove K, 2009, "Biopolitics, biopower, and the return of sovereignty," *Environment and Planning D: Society and Space* 27 489–507

Cornelius W, 2005, "Controlling 'unwanted' immigration: Lessons from the United States, 1993–2004," *Journal of Ethnic and Migration Studies* 31 775–794

Customs and Border Protection Today, 2003, "Operation Desert Safeguard—U.S. and Mexico cooperate to prevent migrant deaths," August, http://www.cbp.gov/xp/CustomsToday/2003/august/op_desert_safeguard.xml

Customs and Border Protection Today, 2004, "Border Safety Initiative," June, http://www.cbp.gov/xp/CustomsToday/2004/June/bsi_falfurrias.xml

Darling J, 2009, "Becoming bare life: Asylum, hospitality, and the politics of encampment," *Environment and Planning D: Society and Space* 27 649–665

De Genova N, 2002, "Migrant 'illegality' and deportability in everyday life," *Annual Review of Anthropology* 31 419–447

Doty R, 2006a, "Fronteras compasivas and the ethics of unconditional hospitality," *Millennium: Journal of International Studies* 35 53–74

Doty R, 2006b, "Crossroads of death," in *Living, Dying, Surviving: The Logics of Biopower and the War on Terror*, Eds E Dauphinee, C Masters (Palgrave Macmillan, New York)

Doty R, 2009, *The Law into Their Own Hands: Immigration and the Politics of Exceptionalism* (University of Arizona Press, Tucson, AZ)

Dunn T, 2009, *Blockading the Border and Human Rights: The El Paso Operation That Remade Immigration Enforcement* (University of Texas Press, Austin, TX)

Fontana A, Bertani M, 2003, "Situating the Lectures," in Foucault's *Society Must Be Defended* (Picador, New York)

Foucault M, 1991, "Governmentality," in *The Foucault Effect: Studies in Governmentailty*, Eds G Burchell, C Gordon, P Miller (University of Chicago Press, Chicago IL)

Foucault M, 2003, *Society Must Be Defended: Lectures at the Collège de France 1975–1976* (Picador, New York)

Foucault M, 2009, *Security, Territory, Population* (Palgrave Macmillan, London)

Hing B O, 2009, "Institutional racism, ICE raids, and immigration reform," *University of San Francisco Law Review* 44 1–50

Jabri V, 2007, "Michel Foucault's analytics of war: The social, the international, and the racial," *International Political Sociology* 1 67–82

Jimenez M, 2009, "Humanitarian crisis: Migrant deaths at the U.S.–Mexico border," ACLU of San Diego and Imperial Counties and Mexico's National Commission of Human Rights

Johnson K, 2007, *Opening the Floodgates: Why America Needs to Rethink Its Border and Immigration Laws* (New York University Press, New York)

Jones R, 2009, "Agents of exception: Border security and the marginalization of Muslims in India," *Environment and Planning D: Society and Space* 24 879–897

Logan T, 2007, "Virtual Fence Project puts Boeing in the hot seat of immigration debate," *St. Louis Post-Dispatch* 26 November, page 1

McCombs B, 2009, "No signs of letup in entrant deaths," *Arizona Daily Star* December 27

Mitchell D, 1996, *The Lie of the Land: Migrant Workers and the California Landscape* (University of Minnesota Press, Minneapolis)

National Border Patrol, 2000, "The National Border Patrol Strategy," August 31, https://www.hsdl.org/?view=docs/dhs/nps06-1000903-02.pdf&code=972f638868718f0cc0be321f1f7f1d20

Nevins J, 2010, *Operation Gatekeeper and Beyond: The War on "Illegals" and the Remaking of the U.S.–Mexico Boundary* (Routledge, New York)

Nyers P, 2010, *Securitizations of Citizenship* (Routledge, New York)

Price P, 2005, *Dry Places: Landscapes of Belonging and Exclusion* (University of Minnesota Press, Minneapolis)

Rotstein, A, 2009, "Border deaths up despite apparent dip in crossings," *San Diego Union-Tribune* April 8

Stern R, 2002, "The tragic journey of Ana Rosa Segura-Marcial," *Easy Valley Tribune* December 15, pages 1–4

Urrea L, 2004, *The Devil's Highway: A True Story* (Little, Brown, Boston, MA)

Weber L, 2009, "Knowing and yet not knowing about European border deaths," *Australian Journal of Human Rights* 15 35–58

III   POLICING THE INTERIOR

Along with the continued expansion of border enforcement, political and other authorities have placed increasing emphasis on the interior policing of the nation. Indeed, in the post-9/11 period, interior enforcement has become a central component of the border fight against "terror" and "illegal" immigration. What has happened is that the border, as a regime of security and immigration control, has been deterritorialized and projected into the nation's interior. Put otherwise, there has been a "disaggregation of border functions"—basically the policing and control of mobility—away from the physical border. As part of this border disaggregation, certain spaces of everyday life—workplaces, homes, neighborhoods, and a variety of public spaces—have been identified as strategic sites and become subject to intensified policing. Thus, numerous locales across the interior of the United States have been turned into border zones of enforcement. The border is thus no longer simply (if it ever really was) a location at the nation's edge where the regulation of movement takes place, but also a mobile technology—a portable, diffused, and decentered control apparatus interwoven throughout the nation. Indeed, we are in the presence of the border at any time and in any space where immigration policing and control take place.

The chapters in this section focus on interior policing at three levels of government: the federal, the state, and the local. Chapter 7, by David Bacon and Bill Ong Hing, draws attention to the federal government's use of "silent raids" to police the nation's workplaces. Normally, a raid is a practice whereby immigration authorities, sometimes with the help of other policing agencies, descend *en masse* on specific places, often worksites, with the express purpose of apprehending individuals believed to be in the country illegally. Such raids were popular during the administration of George W. Bush. They resulted in the deportation of thousands of immigrant workers, the separation of families, and damage to communities where raids took place. This type of raid has generally ceased under the Barack Obama administration and been replaced by what some call "silent raids." A silent raid is a procedure in which immigration authorities audit workplaces—for example, checking to make sure that workers are using valid Social Security numbers—in order to "weed out" undocumented immigrants. Such raids do not lead to deportation. However, they do result in the firing of workers who cannot prove that they have a legal right to work in the United States. Bacon and Hing's chapter examines the detrimental consequences of silent raids. The authors reveal how such practices deprive immigrant workers of a means to earn a living, and undermine union efforts to improve the wages and working conditions of all workers. They also highlight how exploitative employers often escape punishment by cooperating with immigration authorities and receiving immunity from prosecution for their assistance.

Importantly, interior immigration policing is not just taking place under the auspices of the federal government. Utah, Alabama, Georgia, Arizona, and other states have also recently passed tough immigration laws. Chapter 8, by Rogelio Sáenz, Cecilia Menjívar, and San Juanita Edilia García, focuses on the most visible state effort to manage migrant illegality: that of Arizona. On April 23, 2010, Governor Jan Brewer signed into law SB 1070, at the time considered the most punitive piece of immigrant legislation in the nation. The law requires police officers to determine a person's immigration status during the course of a "lawful stop, detention, or arrest" when there is "reasonable suspicion that the person is an alien and is unlawfully present in the United States." In their discussion of SB 1070, Sáenz, Menjívar, and García highlight the fact that the law has created the condition for multiple violations of human rights, not only those of immigrants but also those of U.S. citizens. Specifically, they explore how measures like SB 1070, which legitimate racial profiling, have served to instill fear in Latino communities, creating a climate that hampers the ability of both immigrant and native-born Latinos to participate meaningfully in quotidian life.

Chapter 9, by Liette Gilbert, focuses on immigration policing at the local level. Since 2006, hundreds of cities and towns across the nation—from Escondido, California, and Farmer's Branch, Texas, to Hazleton, Pennsylvania, and Prince William County, Virginia— have passed ordinances or strategically deployed existing laws to manage the presence of undocumented immigrants in their localities. Some of these ordinances are not outwardly focused on immigration but are used tactically to constrain the life prospects and conduct of undocumented immigrants. In Escondido, for example, city officials have targeted Latino immigrants, who tend to live in poorer neighborhoods, through a crackdown on dilapidated homes, illegal garage conversions, graffiti, abandoned vehicles, and other violations of city regulations. Other ordinances are explicitly meant to regulate immigration. Gilbert's chapter focuses on one such case, that of Hazleton. In July 2006, the city council approved a municipal measure that made it illegal for employers to hire undocumented immigrants and for landlords to rent to them. Gilbert highlights how the goal of this local measure is essentially to incapacitate unwanted residents. The idea is to penetrate the everyday spaces that unauthorized residents inhabit (such as homes, neighborhoods, streets, workplaces, and so on) in order to deprive them of "the ability to participate in a regular life by imposing additional control and regulation on their presence and mobility." The ultimate effect is to erode the civil rights of immigrants.

SUGGESTIONS FOR FURTHER READING

Allegro, Linda. 2010. "Latino Migrations to the U.S. Heartland: 'Illegality,' State Controls, and Implications for Transborder Labor Rights." *Latin American Perspectives* 37 (1): 172–184.

Armeta, Amada. 2012. "From Sheriff's Deputies to Immigration Officers: Screening Immigrant Status in a Tennessee Jail." *Law & Policy* 34 (2): 191–210.

Brettell, Caroline B., and Faith G. Nibbs. 2011. "Immigrant Suburban Settlement and the 'Threat' to Middle Class Status and Identity: The Case of Farmers Branch, Texas." *International Migration* 49 (1): 1–30.

Coleman, Mathew. 2007. "Immigration Geopolitics Beyond the Mexico-U.S. Border." *Antipode* 39 (1): 54–76.

———. 2012. "The 'Local' Migration State: The Site-Specific Devolution of Immigration Enforcement in the U.S. South." *Law & Policy* 34 (2): 159–190.

Hing, Bill Ong. 2009. "Institutional Racism, ICE Raids, and Immigration Reform." *University of San Francisco Law Review* 44: 1–49.

Luna, Guadalupe T., and Fran Ansley. 2009. "Global Migrants and Access to Local Housing: Anti-Immigrant Backlash Hits Home." In *Global Connections and Local Receptions: New Latino Immigration to the Southeastern United States,* edited by Fran Ansley and Jon Shefner, 155–193. Knoxville: University of Tennessee Press.

Romero, Mary. 2011. "Keeping Citizenship Rights White: Arizona's Racial Profiling Practices in Immigration Law Enforcement." *Law Journal for Social Justice* 1 (1): 97–113.

Stumpf, Juliet P. 2008. "States of Confusion: The Rise of State and Local Power over Immigration." *North Carolina Law Review* 86: 1557–1618.

Thronson, David B. 2008. "Creating Crisis: Immigration Raids and the Destabilization of Immigrant Families." *Wake Forest Law Review* 43 (2): 391–418.

Varsanyi, Monica W., ed. 2010. *Taking Local Control: Immigration Policy Activism in U.S. Cities and States.* Stanford, CA: Stanford University Press.

Winders, Jamie. 2007. "Bringing Back the (B)order: Post-9/11 Politics of Immigration, Borders, and Belonging in the Contemporary U.S. South." *Antipode* 39 (5): 920–942.

7 | THE RISE AND FALL OF EMPLOYER SANCTIONS

David Bacon and Bill Ong Hing

INTRODUCTION

Ana Contreras would have been a competitor for the national tai kwon do championship team in 2009. She was fourteen years old. For six years she went to practice instead of birthday parties, giving up the friendships most teenagers live for. Then in October 2009, disaster struck. Her mother, Dolores, lost her job. The money for classes was gone, and not just that. "I only bought clothes for her once a year, when my tax refund check came," Dolores Contreras explains. She continues:

> Now she needs shoes, and I had to tell her we didn't have any money. I stopped the cable and the Internet she needs for school. When my cell phone contract is up next month, I'll stop that too. I've never had enough money for a car, and now we've gone three months without paying the light bill.[1]

Dolores Contreras shared her misery with eighteen hundred other families. All lost their jobs when their employer, American Apparel, fired them for lacking immigration status. For months she carried around the letter from the Department of Homeland Security (DHS), handed to her by the company lawyer. It says the documents she provided when she was hired were no good, and without work authorization, her work life was over.

Of course, it was not really over. Contreras still had to keep working if she and her daughter were to eat and pay rent. So instead of a job that barely paid her bills, she was forced to find another one that would not even do that.

Contreras is a skilled sewing machine operator. She came to the United States thirteen years earlier, after working many years in the garment factories of Tehuacan, Puebla, Mexico. There, companies like Levi's make so many pairs of stonewashed jeans that rumor has

David Bacon is a journalist, photographer, and associate editor at Pacific News Service. Bill Ong Hing is professor of law at the University of San Francisco.

Reprinted with permission of the authors, from "The Rise and Fall of Employer Sanctions," *Fordham Urban Law Journal* 38: 77–105, by David Bacon and Bill Ong Hing. Copyright © 2010 by David Bacon and Bill Ong Hing.

1. Interview with "Dolores Contreras" (name changed for this chapter), in L.A., Cal. (Dec. 15, 2009).

it the town's water has turned blue. In Los Angeles, Contreras hoped to find the money to send home for her sister's weekly dialysis treatments, and to pay the living and school expenses for four other siblings. For five years she moved from shop to shop. Like most garment workers, she did not get paid for overtime, her paychecks were often short, and sometimes her employer disappeared overnight, owing weeks in back pay.

Finally Contreras got a job at American Apparel, famous for its sexy clothing, made in Los Angeles instead of overseas.[2] She still had to work like a demon. Her team of ten experienced seamstresses turned out thirty dozen tee shirts an hour. After dividing the piece rate evenly among them, she would come home with $400 for a four-day week, after taxes. She paid Social Security too, although she will never see a dime in benefits because her contributions were credited to an invented number.

Now Contreras is working again in a sweatshop at half what she earned before. Meanwhile, American Apparel took steps to replace those who were fired. Contreras says they are mostly older women with documents, who cannot work as fast. "Maybe they sew 10 dozen a day apiece," she claims. "The only operators with papers are the older ones." Younger, faster workers either have no papers, or if they have them, they find better-paying jobs doing something easier. "President Obama is responsible for putting us in this situation," she charges angrily. "This is worse than an immigration raid. They want to keep us from working at all."[3]

Contreras is right. The White House website says, "President Obama will remove incentives to enter the country illegally by preventing employers from hiring undocumented workers and enforcing the law."[4] In June 2009, he told Congress members that the government will be "cracking down on employers who are using illegal workers in order to drive down wages—and oftentimes mistreat those workers."[5]

The law Obama is enforcing is the 1986 Immigration Reform and Control Act, which requires employers to keep records of workers' immigration status, and prohibits them from "knowingly hiring" those who have no legal documents, or "work authorization."[6] In effect, the law made it a crime for undocumented immigrants to work. This provision, employer sanctions, is the legal basis for all the workplace immigration raids and enforcement for a quarter century and now for Obama's auditing of employment records. The end result is the same: workers lose their jobs. Sanctions pretend to punish employers, but in reality, they punish workers.

OBAMA'S INTERIOR ENFORCEMENT STRATEGY

Workplace Immigration and Customs Enforcement (ICE) raids by gun-wielding agents resulting in the mass arrest of dozens and sometimes hundreds of employees that were com-

---

2. Jim Straub, *Who's Your Daddy*, CLAMOR MAG., Fall 2006, *available at* http://clamormagazine.org/issues/38/aa/straub.php.

3. Interview with "Dolores Contreras," *supra* note 1.

4. *See Immigration*, WHITE HOUSE, http://www.whitehouse.gov/issues/immigration (last visited Sept. 27, 2010).

5. Katherine Brandon, *Working Together for Immigration Reform*, THE WHITE HOUSE BLOG (June 25, 2009, 6:45 PM), http://www.whitehouse.gov/blog/Working-Together-for-Immigration-Reform

6. 8 U.S.C. § 1324a (2005).

mon under the George W. Bush administration appear to have ceased under the Obama administration.[7] Legally questionable mass arrests continue to occur in neighborhoods under the pretext of serving warrants on criminal aliens. However, disruptive, high-profile worksite raids appear to have subsided. When a Bush administration-style ICE raid took place in Washington State in February 2009 soon after Janet Napolitano took the helm as Secretary of the DHS, she expressed surprise and ordered an investigation. These types of raids were not in her strategy plan, she noted; instead, enforcement in her regime would focus on employers who hire undocumented workers, not on the workers themselves.[8]

Make no mistake, although deportations related to worksite operations may have decreased under the Obama approach in contrast with that under George W. Bush, actual deportation numbers are not down. According to the *Washington Post*, the Obama administration is deporting record numbers of undocumented immigrants, with ICE expecting to remove about 400,000 individuals in 2010.[9] The total is nearly ten percent above the Bush administration's 2008 sum and twenty-five percent more than were deported in 2007. According to ICE, the increase has been partly a result of deporting those persons picked up for other crimes and expanding the search through prisons and jails for deportable immigrants already in custody.[10] "Unlike the former worksite raids that led to arrests and deportation, the 'silent raids,' or audits of companies' records by federal agents, usually result in firings."[11] "Just 765 undocumented workers have been arrested at their jobs in 2010 through early summer, compared with 5,100 in 2008, according to Department of Homeland Security figures."[12]

However, as we see from the Contreras family's plight, the Obama administration's focus-on-employers-rather-than-workers strategy in fact falls squarely on the shoulders of the workers. Immigration raids at factories and farms have been replaced with a quieter enforcement strategy: sending federal agents to scour companies' records for undocumented immigrant workers. "While the sweeps of the past commonly led to the deportation of such workers, the 'silent raids,' as employers call the audits, usually result in the workers being fired, although in many cases they are not deported."[13] The idea is that if the workers cannot work, they will self-deport, leaving on their own. However, they actually do not leave, because they need to work. They become more desperate and take jobs at lower wages. Given the increasing scale of enforcement, this can lead to an overall reduction in the average wage level for millions of workers, which is, in effect, a subsidy to employers. Over a twelve-month period, ICE conducted audits of employee files at more than 2,900 compa-

7. *See generally*, Bill Ong Hing, *Institutional Racism, ICE Raids, and Immigration Reform*, 44 USF L. REV. 307 (2009).

8. *Secretary Seeks Review of Immigration Raid*, N.Y. TIMES, Feb. 26, 2009, at A19, *available at* http://www.ny times.com/2009/02/26/washington/26immig.html

9. Peter Slevin, *Deportation of Illegal Immigrants Increases Under Obama Administration*, WASH. POST, July 26, 2010, at A01.

10. *See id.*

11. Roy Maurer, *Undocumented Workers Fired, Firms Audited in 'Silent Raids,'* SOC'Y FOR HUMAN RESOURCE MGMT. (July 22, 2010), http://www.shrm.org/hrdisciplines/global/ Articles/Pages/SilentRaids.aspx

12. *Id.*

13. Julia Preston, *Illegal Workers Swept from Jobs in "Silent Raids,"* N.Y. TIMES, July, 9, 2010, at A1, *available at* http://www.nytimes.com/2010/07/10/us/10enforce.html

nies.[14] "The agency levied a record $3 million in civil fines [in the first six months of 2010] on businesses that hired unauthorized immigrants, according to official figures."[15] Thousands of workers were fired.

Employers say the audits reach more companies than the worksite roundups of the Bush administration. The audits force businesses to fire every suspected undocumented worker on the payroll—not just those who happened to be on duty at the time of a raid—and make it much harder to hire other unauthorized workers as replacements. Auditing is effective in getting unauthorized workers fired for sure.

Consider other examples. An audit of Gebbers Farms in the orchard town of Brewster, Washington, yielded results that were similar to what happened at American Apparel. Immigration inspectors scoured the records of Gebbers Farms and found evidence that approximately 550 of its workers, mostly immigrants from Mexico, did not have proper documentation.[16] So, those workers were fired. ICE officials also pressured one of San Francisco's major building service companies, ABM, into firing hundreds of its own workers in the spring of 2010.[17] ICE agents told ABM that they had flagged the personnel records of those workers. Weeks earlier, the agents sifted through Social Security records and the I-9 immigration forms all workers have to fill out when they apply for jobs. They then told ABM that the company had to fire 475 workers who were accused of lacking legal immigration status. Similar ICE actions resulted in the firing of 1,200 ABM janitors in Minneapolis, and 100 janitors in Seattle in the fall of 2009.[18]

Echoing President Obama's theme of focusing on employers who use undocumented workers to "drive down wages" and "mistreat" workers, ICE chief John Morton says the agency is looking primarily for "'egregious employers' who commit both labor abuses and immigration violations."[19] But American Apparel, ABM, and Gebbers Farms do not appear to fit that profile.

While American Apparel is a huge corporation that makes hundreds of millions of dollars a year, the workers dismissed were "long-term employees being paid decent wages."[20] "The company is proud of their 'Made in America' labels" and had a reputation for paying more than most garment shops.[21] Before the audit, its CEO, Dov Charney, took to the streets

14. *See id.*

15. *Id.*

16. *See* Melissa Sanchez, *Massive Firings in Brewster, and a Big Debate about Illegal Immigration*, SEATTLE TIMES, Feb. 13, 2010, http://seattletimes.nwsource.com/html/localnews/2011069760_brewster14.html

17. Lauren Smiley, *Janitors Descend from Skyscrapers to Protest Immigration Raids*, SFWEEKLY BLOG (Apr. 27, 2010, 5:59 PM), http://blogs.sfweekly.com/thesnitch/2010/04/janitors_descend_from_skyscrap.php

18. *See* Lornet Turnbull, *Illegal Workers Quietly Let Go*, SEATTLE TIMES, Nov. 23, 2009, http://seattletimes .nwsource.com/html/localnews/2010333876_firedjanitors23m.html; Sasha Aslanian, *1,200 Janitors Fired in 'Quiet' Immigration Raid*, MINNESOTA PUBLIC RADIO (Nov. 9, 2009), http://minnesota.publicradio.org/display/web/2009/11/09/immigrants-fired

19. Preston, *supra* note 13.

20. Ben Johnson, *Crackdown on American Apparel Workers Another Wasted Effort*, ALTERNET.ORG (Oct. 6, 2009), http://www.alternet.org/immigration/143116/crackdown_on_american_apparel_workers_another_wasted_effort

21. *Id.*

and stood shoulder to shoulder with workers in protesting and demanding legalization for workers who have been "victimized by our broken immigration system."[22]

Similarly, Gebbers Farms had a general reputation for "doing right by their employees."[23] "It built housing and soccer fields for its workers and, unlike many other growers, provides stable year-round work."[24] "After the firings, Gebbers Farms advertised hundreds of jobs for orchard workers. But there were few takers in the state."[25] Finally, the employer applied to the federal guest worker program to import about 1,200 legal temporary workers—most from Mexico. "The guest workers, who can stay for up to six months, also included about 300 from Jamaica."[26] This was an implementation of the Chertoff strategy, "open the front door and you shut the back door."[27] The unspoken rationale for the audits is revealed—force employers to use guest worker programs.

As for ABM, the building service has been a union company for decades, and many of the workers had been there for years. According to Olga Miranda, president of Service Employees Local 87, "They've been working in the buildings downtown for fifteen, twenty, some as many as twenty-seven years. They've built homes. They've provided for their families. They've sent their kids to college. They're not new workers. They didn't just get here a year ago."[28]

The audit-and-fire strategy was initiated early in the Obama administration. For example, in May 2009, 254 workers at Overhill Farms in Los Angeles were fired under similar circumstances.[29] The company, with over 800 employees, was audited by the Internal Revenue Service earlier that year. According to John Grant, Packinghouse Division Director for Local 770 of the United Food and Commercial Workers, which represents production employees at the food processing plant, "they found discrepancies in the Social Security numbers of many workers. Overhill then sent a letter . . . to 254 people—all members of our union—giving them thirty days to reconcile their numbers."[30]

On May 2, the company stopped the production lines and sent everyone home, saying there would be no work until "they called us to come back."[31] For 254 people that call never came. According to a spokesman for Overhill Farms, "the company was required by federal law to terminate these employees because they had invalid Social Security numbers. To do otherwise would have exposed both the employees and the company to criminal and civil prosecution."[32]

22. *Id.*

23. Preston, *supra* note 13.

24. Sanchez, *supra* note 16.

25. Preston, *supra* note 13.

26. *Id.*

27. *See* Michael Chertoff, Remarks at University of Southern California National Center for Risk and Economic Analysis of Terrorism Events (Aug. 13, 2008), *available at* http://www.hsdl.org/?view&did=236243

28. Interview with Olga Miranda, president, Service Employees Local 87, in S.F., Cal., (May 3, 2010).

29. *See* Tiffany Ten Eyck, *Immigration Reform: What's Labor Up To?*, LABOR NOTES (June 5, 2009), http://labornotes.org/node/2310

30. Interview with John Grant, Packinghouse Div. Dir., United Food and Commercial Workers Local 770, in L.A., Cal. (Dec. 15, 2009).

31. Interview with Isela Hernandez, in L.A., Cal. (Dec. 10, 2009).

32. Interview with Alex Auerbach, Director, Overhill Farms, in L.A., Cal. (Dec. 10, 2009).

BACKGROUND ON EMPLOYER SANCTIONS

The softer, gentler approach to employer sanctions enforcement implemented by the Obama administration may appear more humane on the surface. After all, auditing and firing is accomplished without guns, handcuffs, or detention. However, the result—loss of work—is not necessarily softer or gentler for the thousands of fired workers who have been working to support their families.

Employer sanctions are of relatively recent vintage in the nation's immigration laws. In the climate of heightened concerns over the number of undocumented workers (predominantly Mexican) in the United States in the 1970s and early 1980s, estimates of up to nine million undocumented people residing in the country were offered to demonstrate that immigration enforcement efforts were ineffectual.[33] Policymakers proposed addressing the situation from a new angle—by penalizing employers who were hiring undocumented workers, through what came to be called "employer sanctions."[34] "By 1986, employer sanctions had become part of the nation's immigration laws. The passage of the Immigration Reform and Control Act (IRCA) represented the culmination of years of social, political, and congressional debate about the perceived lack of control over the U.S. southern border."[35] "The belief that something had to be done about the large numbers of undocumented workers who had entered the United States from Mexico in the 1970s was reinforced by the flood of Central Americans who began to arrive in the early 1980s."[36] While the political turmoil of civil war in El Salvador, Guatemala, and Nicaragua drove many Central Americans from their homeland, they, along with the Mexicans who continued to arrive, were generally labeled "economic migrants" by the Reagan administration, the Immigration and Naturalization Service, and the courts.[37]

The idea of employer sanctions was not new.

In 1952—when the immigration laws were overhauled to clamp down on subversives and Communists—a provision outlawing willful importation, transportation, or harboring of undocumented aliens was debated; one amendment proposed imposing criminal penalties for the employment of undocumented aliens if the employer had "reasonable grounds to believe a worker was not legally in the United States."[38]

Not only was the amendment soundly defeated, but the following language was added to the final legislation: "for the purposes of this section, employment (including the usual and normal practices incident to employment) shall not be deemed to constitute harboring."[39]

---

33. Bill Ong Hing, *The Immigration and Naturalization Service, Community-Based Organizations, and the Legalization Experience: Lessons for the Self-Help Immigration Phenomenon,* 6 GEO. IMMIGR. L.J. 413, 470 (1992) [hereinafter Hing, *Lessons for the Self-Help*].

34. BILL ONG HING, DEFINING AMERICA THROUGH IMMIGRATION POLICY 179–82, 196–97 (2004).

35. *Id.* at 155.

36. *Id.*

37. Susan Gzesh, *Central Americans and Asylum Policy in the Reagan Era,* MIGRATION INFO. SOURCE (Apr. 1, 2006), http://www.migrationinformation.org/Feature/display.cfm?id= 384

38. HING, DEFINING AMERICA, *supra* note 34, at 155.

39. Act of Mar. 20, 1952, Pub. L. No. 283, 66 Stat. 26.

For the time being, we were not about to punish U.S. employers who might be benefiting from the labor of low-wage, undocumented workers. "Beginning in 1971, legislative proposals featuring employer sanctions as a centerpiece reappeared and were touted as the tool needed to resolve the undocumented alien problem."[40] Resolving the "problem" of undocumented people essentially meant forcing them to leave the country by denying them the ability to work, and therefore to eat, pay rent, or support themselves and their families. By the end of the Carter administration in 1980, the Select Commission on Immigration and Refugee Policy portrayed the legalization of people already here as a necessary balance to sanctions, which, presumably, would discourage more undocumented people from coming in the future.

Within thirty years of the 1952 rejection of employer sanctions, Congress believed that most Americans were convinced that a crisis over undocumented immigration—especially undocumented *Mexican* migration—existed and that something had to be done.[41] By 1986, federal employer sanctions were enacted as the major feature of reform. By a bare swing vote of only four members of the House of Representatives, legalization (or amnesty) provisions were also made part of the package to address the undocumented immigrant issue.[42]

> Although on paper it appeared that a deal involving employer sanctions for amnesty had been struck, there was not political trade-off; IRCA would have gone forward if legalization were dropped by the House, and its effective implementation in the hands of an inept Immigration and Naturalization Service was seriously in doubt.[43]

The efficacy of employer sanctions in reducing undocumented migration is hotly debated. Proponents of increased enforcement note that few employers have been fined or punished since 1986. That view, however, fails to note that hundreds of thousands of workers have been fired. In fact, punishing employers, or threatening to do so, was always simply a mechanism to criminalize work for the workers themselves, and thereby force them to leave the country, or not to come in the first place.

In addition to the many social and economic phenomena that historically cause undocumented migration to the United States from Mexico, we now know that the North American Free Trade Agreement (NAFTA) and the effects of globalization create great migration pressures on Mexicans.[44] The push-pull factors are strong. As the Mexican consul from Douglas, Arizona once noted, the border could be "mined" and migrants would still attempt to cross.[45] As Renee Saucedo points out, "So long as we have trade agreements like NAFTA that create poverty in countries like Mexico, people will continue to come here, no matter how many walls we build."[46] Consider Ismael Rojas, who left his family in Mexico

---

40. HING, DEFINING AMERICA, *supra* note 34, at 156.

41. *See* Hing, *Lessons for the Self-Help, supra* note 33, at 475–76.

42. *See id.* at 480.

43. HING, DEFINING AMERICA, *supra* note 34, at 156.

44. *See generally* BILL ONG HING, ETHICAL BORDERS: NAFTA, GLOBALIZATION, AND MEXICAN MIGRATION (2010).

45. Interview with Jennifer Allen, Exec. Dir., Border Action Network, in Nogales, Ariz. (June 15, 2007).

46. Interview with Renee Saucedo, Dir., San Francisco Day Labor Program, in S.F., Cal. (May 3, 2010).

many times over a twenty-five-year period to work in the United States as an undocumented worker. In his words, "you can either abandon your children to make money to take care of them, or you can stay with your children and watch them live in misery. Poverty makes us leave our families."[47] Utilizing employer sanctions to address the phenomenon of Mexican migration in this context of poverty and globalization causes misery for workers, but does not reduce migration. Arresting and deporting workers for working without authorization as a means of discouraging them from coming here for a better life simply cannot be effective in the face of such grave economic and social forces. We also need to ask ourselves whether we can really justify punishing workers who are here because of the effects of many U.S. economic policies.

Another problem with employer sanctions is the discrimination that results. Long before the recent evaluation of the discriminatory effects of the E-Verify program,[48] discrimination was rampant. In its final report to Congress on employer sanctions in 1990, the General Accounting Office estimated that of 4.6 million employers in the United States, 346,000 admitted applying IRCA's verification requirements only to job applicants who had a "foreign" accent or appearance.[49] Another 430,000 employers only hired applicants born in the United States or did not hire applicants with temporary work documents in order to be cautious.[50]

Direct and indirect recruitment of Mexican workers has continued in spite of the implementation of employer sanctions legislation in 1986. In 2001, researchers continued to identify organized groups of farm labor contractors who travel to Mexican cities and towns, where they offer loans and work guarantees to convince potential farm workers to cross the border into the United States.[51] The process involves well-organized networks of contractors and contractor agents representing major U.S. agricultural companies. The headhunters are themselves often Mexicans who recruit in their own hometowns and farming communities where earning the trust of eager farm hands is not difficult. One of the contractors' favorite tactics to attract workers is to offer them loans to help pay off debts, coupled with a pledge to find work for the person north of the border. Many U.S. companies rely on these networks of recruiters.[52]

Even a cursory review of the ICE raids in the past few years reveals an obvious disparity in the targeting of undocumented workers over the employers who hire them. Anyone

47. Ginger Thompson, *Mexican Leader Visits U.S. with a Vision to Sell*, N.Y. TIMES, Aug. 24, 2000, at A3, *available at* http://www.nytimes.com/2000/08/24/world/mexican-leader-visits-us-with-a-vision-to-sell.html

48. E-Verify is a federal, web-based program through which U.S. businesses can attempt to verify the work authorization of new hires. *See* IMMIGR. POL'Y CTR., DECIPHERING THE NUMBERS ON E-VERIFY ACCURACY (Feb. 11, 2009), *available at* http://www.immigrationpolicy.org/sites/default/files/docs/Deciphering%20 the%20Numbers%20on%20E-Verify%20Accuracy.pdf

49. Michael Fix & Frank D. Bean, *The Findings and Policy Implications of the GAO Report and the Urban Institute Hiring Audit*, 24 INT'L MIGRATION REV. 816 (1990).

50. Laura C. Oliveira, Comment, *A License to Exploit: The Need to Reform the H-2A Temporary Agricultural Guest Worker Program*, 5 SCHOLAR 153, 170 (2002).

51. *See* Dan Herbeck, *Family Charged with Keeping Workers in Illegal Conditions*, BUFFALO NEWS, June 19, 2002, http://www.highbeam.com/doc/1P2-22459482.html

52. *See* MARY BAUER & SARAH REYNOLDS, S. POVERTY L. CTR., CLOSE TO SLAVERY: GUEST-WORKER PROGRAMS IN THE UNITED STATES (Mar. 2007), *available at* http://www. sharedprosperity.org/splcenter.org.SPLCguestworker.pdf

who sympathizes with the undocumented workers' position but feels that "the law is the law" must hold employers to that same standard. That means demanding the enforcement of labor laws against unscrupulous employers who take advantage of low-income workers—documented or undocumented. All too often, the undocumented workforce that has been paid less than minimum wage for work conditions that violate health and safety standards is hauled away, and the employer receives no punishment. Instead of deporting the workers, we should remove the barriers that stand in the way of their efforts to place pressure on the employers to improve wage and work conditions. In the process, the jobs may, in fact, become more attractive to native workers—something that, ironically, anti-immigrant forces want.

In 2009, Ken Georgetti, president of the Canadian Labour Congress, and John Sweeney, president of the AFL-CIO, wrote to President Obama and Canadian Prime Minister Harper, reminding them that

> the failure of neoliberal policies to create decent jobs in the Mexican economy under NAFTA has meant that many displaced workers and new entrants have been forced into a desperate search to find employment elsewhere. . . . We believe that all workers, regardless of immigration status, should enjoy equal labor rights. . . . We also support an inclusive, practical and swift adjustment of status program, which we believe would have the effect of raising labor standards for all workers.[53]

While employer sanctions have little effect on migration, they have made workers more vulnerable to employer pressure. Because working is illegal for them, undocumented workers fear protesting low wages and bad conditions. Employer sanctions bar them from receiving unemployment and disability benefits, although they make payments for them. If they get fired for complaining or organizing, it's much harder to find another job. Despite these obstacles, immigrant workers, including the undocumented, have asserted their labor rights, organized unions, and won better conditions.[54] But employer sanctions have made this harder and riskier.

Using Social Security numbers to verify immigration status has led to firing and blacklisting many union activists.[55] Even citizens and permanent residents feel this impact, because in our diverse U.S. workplaces immigrant and native-born workers work together.[56] Making it a crime for one group to enforce the law or use their rights has simply created obstacles for everyone else. Unions now have greater difficulty defending the rights of their

53. Letter from Ken Georgetti, President, Canadian Labour Cong., and John Sweeney, President, Am. Fed'n Labor and Cong. of Indus. Orgs., to Barack Obama, President, U.S., and Stephen Harper, Prime Minister, Can. (Feb. 18, 2009), *available at* http://ebookbrowse.com/jjs-kg-letter-to-obama-and-harper-021809-pdf-d51436061

54. *See* Justin Akers Chacón, *Out from the Shadows, into the Street: The New Immigrant Civil Rights Movement*, 47 INT'L SOCIALIST REV. (2006), *available at* http://www.isreview.org/issues/47/newmovement.shtml

55. David Bacon, Labor & Emp't Comm., Nat'l Lawyers Guild, Talking Points on Guest Workers (July 6, 2005), *available at* http://www.nlg-laboremploy-comm.org/media/documents/nlg-laboremploy-comm.org_77.pdf

56. National Commission on ICE Misconduct and Violation of 4th Amendment Rights investigations of ICE raids reveal that citizens as well as immigrants were held in custody. *See* NAT'L COMM'N ON ICE MISCONDUCT & VIOLATIONS OF 4TH AMENDMENT RIGHTS, RAIDS ON WORKERS: DESTROYING OUR RIGHTS (2009), *available at* http://www.icemisconduct.org/docUploads/UFCW%20ICE%20rpt%20FINAL%20150B_061809_130632.pdf?CFID=908 3458&CFTOKEN=87909032

own members or organizing new ones. The exploitation of the undocumented workforce will only end if workers are free to make complaints and organize.

Eliminating the undocumented workforce without providing an avenue for their labor to be utilized in the United States also would have devastating economic consequences. Data reveal many U.S. job categories that rely on the undocumented workforce.[57] Gordon Hanson's findings for the Council on Foreign Relations support these arguments. He notes that between 1960 and 2000 the number of U.S. residents with less than twelve years of schooling fell from fifty percent to twelve percent.[58]

Arizona stands to see the negative effects of massive exclusion of an undocumented workforce (see Sáenz et al., this volume). Before the state's enactment of its "Legal Arizona Workers Act" in 2007, the state experienced decades worth of growth, boosted by its estimated twelve percent undocumented labor force.[59] The new law caused many headaches and loss of production for Arizona employers who need workers. Also, we should not lose sight of the fact that immigrants are consumers as well. Their consumption creates demand for certain goods and services, which in turn creates jobs.

UNION FOCUS—COINCIDENCE OR INTENTIONAL

President Obama says employer sanctions enforcement targets employers "who are using illegal workers in order to drive down wages—and oftentimes mistreat those workers."[60] An ICE Worksite Enforcement Advisory claims "ICE . . . investigates employers who employ force, threats or coercion . . . in order to keep the unauthorized alien workers from reporting substandard wage or working conditions."[61] One has to wonder whether firing or deporting workers who endure employer sanctions actually helps to cure such conditions. Also, consider the workers whom ICE has been targeting under the Obama approach. Workers at Smithfield were trying to organize a union to improve conditions. Overhill Farms has a union. American Apparel pays better than most garment factories. The ABM workers in San Francisco, and another 1,200 fired janitors in Minneapolis, were union members who were receiving a higher wage than non-union workers—and they had to strike to win it.[62]

ABM is one of the largest building service companies in the country, and it appears that union janitorial companies are the targets of the Obama administration's immigration enforcement program. A frustrated union official points out that

Homeland Security is going after employers that are unions. . . . They're going after employers that give benefits and are paying above the average. . . . What kind of economic recovery

57. *See* BILL ONG HING, DEPORTING OUR SOULS: VALUES, MORALITY, AND IMMIGRATION POLICY 12–14 (2006). The categories include construction, food preparation, grounds maintenance, agriculture work, janitorial work, housekeeping, and sewing.

58. Gordon H. Hanson, *The Economic Logic of Illegal Immigration* 14 (Council on Foreign Rel., CSR No. 26, 2007).

59. Faye Bowers, *Employers Risk Little in Hiring Illegal Labor*, CHRISTIAN SCI. MONITOR, Apr. 18, 2006, http://www.csmonitor.com/2006/0418/p01s01–usec.html

60. *See* Brandon, *supra* note 5.

61. *Worksite Enforcement*, U.S. IMMIGR. AND CUSTOMS ENFORCEMENT, http://www.ice.gov/worksite/index.htm (last visited Oct. 8, 2010).

62. *See* Aslanian, *supra* note 18.

goes with firing thousands of workers? Why don't they target employers who are not paying taxes, who are not obeying safety or labor laws?[63]

The 1,200 fired janitors in Minneapolis belonged to the Service Employees International Union Local 26, the 475 janitors in San Francisco were from Local 87, and 100 janitors working for Seattle Building Maintenance fired in November 2009 belonged to Local 6.[64]

And despite Obama's contention that sanctions enforcement will punish those employers who exploit immigrants, employers are rewarded for cooperating with ICE by being immunized from prosecution. Javier Murillo, president of SEIU Local 26, says, "[t]he promise made during the audit is that if the company cooperates and complies, they won't be fined. So this kind of enforcement really only hurts workers."[65]

Workers fired at Overhill Farms accuse the company of hiring replacements, classified as "part timers," who do not receive the benefits in the union contract.[66] By firing regular workers who were being paid benefits, the company was able to save "a lot of money."[67]

The history of workplace immigration enforcement is filled with examples of employers who use audits and discrepancies as pretexts to discharge union militants or discourage worker organization. The sixteen-year union drive at the Smithfield pork plant in North Carolina, for instance, saw a raid, and the firing of fifty workers for bad Social Security numbers.[68] ICE's campaign of audits and firings, which SEIU Local 26's Murillo calls "the Obama enforcement policy," targets the same set of employers the Bush raids went after— union companies or those with organizing drives.[69] If anything, ICE seems intent on punishing undocumented workers who earn too much, or become too visible by demanding higher wages and organizing unions.

This growing wave of firings is provoking sharp debate in unions, especially those with large immigrant memberships. Many of the food processing workers at Overhill Farms and ABM's janitors have been dues-paying members for years. They expect the union to defend them when the company fires them for lack of status. "The union should try to stop people from losing their jobs," protests Erlinda Silerio, an Overhill Farms worker. "It should try to get the company to hire us back, and pay compensation for the time we've been out."[70] At American Apparel, although there was no union, some workers had actively tried to form one in past years. Jose Covarrubias got a job as a cleaner when the garment union was helping them organize. "I'd worked with the International Ladies' Garment Workers and the Garment Workers Center before," he recalls, "in sweatshops where we sued the owners when they disappeared without paying us. When I got to American Apparel I joined right

63. Interview with Olga Miranda, *supra* note 28.

64. *Id.*

65. Interview with Javier Murillo, President, SEIU Local 26, in S.F., Cal. (May 3, 2010).

66. Interview with Lucia Vasquez, in L.A., Cal. (Dec. 10, 2009).

67. *Id.* An Overhill spokesman claimed that the replacements are paid at the same rate, although he acknowledged they lack benefits. Interview with Alex Auerbach, *supra* note 32.

68. Julia Preston, *Immigration Raid Draws Protest from Labor Officials*, N.Y. TIMES, Jan. 26, 2007, http://www.nytimes.com/2007/01/26/us/26immig.html

69. Interview with Javier Murillo, *supra* note 65.

70. Interview with Erlinda Silerio, in L.A., Cal. (June 18, 2009).

away. I debated with the non-union workers, trying to convince them the union would defend us."[71]

The Obama approach ends up promoting a guest worker program akin to his predecessor's vision. As we have seen, at Gebbers Farms, there really were no takers among the native workforce, and guest workers were brought in. Remarks by President Bush's DHS Secretary, Michael Chertoff, in 2008 were revealing: "[T]here's [an] obvious . . . solution to the problem of illegal work, which is you open the front door and you shut the back door. . . ."[72] "Opening the front door" allows employers to recruit workers to come to the United States, giving them visas that tie their ability to stay to their employment. And to force workers to come through this system, "closing the back door" criminalizes migrants who work without "work authorization."[73] As Arizona governor, DHS Secretary Janet Napolitano supported this arrangement, signing the state's own draconian employer sanctions bill, while supporting guest worker programs.[74]

In its final proposal to "shut the back door," the Bush administration announced a regulation requiring employers to fire any worker whose Social Security number did not match the Social Security Administration's database.[75] Social Security no-match letters do not currently require employers to fire workers with mismatched numbers, although employers have nevertheless used them to terminate thousands of people. President Bush would have made such terminations mandatory.

Unions, the ACLU, and the National Immigration Law Center got an injunction to stop the rule's implementation in the summer of 2007, arguing it would harm citizens and legal residents who might be victims of clerical mistakes.[76] In July 2009, the Obama administration decided not to contest the injunction.[77] But while dropping Bush's regulation, DHS announced it would beef up the use of the E-Verify electronic database, arguing that it's more efficient in targeting the undocumented.[78]

Social Security, however, continues to send no-match letters to employers, and the E-Verify database is compiled, in part, by sifting through Social Security numbers, looking for mismatches.[79] DHS Secretary Janet Napolitano called on employers to screen new hires using E-Verify, and said those who do so will be entitled to put a special logo on their products stating "I E-Verify."[80] And although the final regulations never took effect, DHS says an

71. Interview with Jose Covarrubias, in L.A., Cal. (Dec. 16, 2009).

72. *See* Chertoff, *supra* note 27.

73. *Id.*

74. *See* Matthew Benson, *Napolitano Signs Immigrant Bill Targeting Employers*, ARIZ. REPUBLIC, July 2, 2007.

75. *See* Jacqueline McManus, *No-Match Letters from the Feds*, MONTEREY COUNTY HERALD, July 23, 2010.

76. *See* Memorandum from Alan Berkowitz and Carolyn Hall, Bingham McCutchen LLP, Federal Judge Enjoins Implementation of Homeland Security's "No-Match Letter" Regulation (Oct. 12, 2007), *available at* http://www.martindale.com/business-law/article_Bingham-McCutchen-LLP_330958.htm

77. *See* Memorandum from Kate Kalmykov, Klasko, Rulon, Stock & Seltzer, LLP, DHS Does Away with the Social Security No-Match Rule in Favor of E-Verify (July 16, 2009), *available at* http://blog.klaskolaw.com/2009/07/16/dhs-does-away-with-the-social-security-no-match-rule-in-favor-of-e-verify

78. *Id.*

79. McManus, *supra* note 75.

80. Press Release, Department of Homeland Security, Secretary Napolitano, ICE Assistant Secretary Morton and USCIS Director Mayorkas Announce New Campaign to Recognize Employers Committed to Maintaining a Legal Workforce (Nov. 19, 2009), *available at* http://www.dhs.gov/ynews/releases/pr_1258640944663.shtm

employer's failure to adequately follow up on a no-match letter can constitute evidence of or contribute to an employer's knowledge of an employee's unauthorized status.[81]

The twelve million undocumented people in the United States, spread across factories, fields, and construction sites throughout the country, encompass lots of workers. Many are aware of their rights and anxious to improve their lives. National union organizing campaigns, like Justice for Janitors and Hotel Workers Rising, depend on the determination and activism of these immigrants, documented and undocumented alike. That reality finally convinced the AFL-CIO in 1999 to reject the federation's former support for employer sanctions and call for repeal.[82] Unions recognized that sanctions enforcement makes it much more difficult for workers to defend their rights, organize unions, and raise wages.

Opposing sanctions, however, puts labor in opposition to the current administration, which it helped elect. Some Washington, D.C. lobbying groups have decided to support the administration's policy of sanctions enforcement instead. One of them, Reform Immigration for America, says, "any employment verification system should determine employment authorization accurately and efficiently."[83] Verification of authorization is exactly what happened at American Apparel and ABM, and inevitably leads to firings. The AFL-CIO and the Change to Win labor federation this spring also agreed on a new immigration position that supports a "secure and effective worker authorization mechanism . . . one that determines employment authorization accurately while providing maximum protection for workers."[84]

Jose Covarrubias, one of the fired American Apparel workers, is left defenseless by such protection, however. Instead, he says, "we need the unity of workers. There are 15 million people in the AFL-CIO. They have a lot of economic and political power. Why don't they oppose these firings and defend us?" he asks. "We've contributed to this movement for 20 years, and we're not leaving. We're going to stay and fight for a more just immigration reform."[85]

CONCLUSION

Wanting more blood, some on the right complain that the Obama employer sanctions' "silent raid" approach is too soft, because although the workers get fired, they do not get deported.[86] They claim that "there is no drama, no trauma, no families being torn apart, no handcuffs."[87] No trauma? Consider the fired San Francisco janitors who faced an agonizing

81. *See* McManus, *supra* note 75.

82. David Bacon, *Justice Deported: Tuesday's Immigration Raids on Meatpacking Plants Weren't About Curbing Identity Theft, They Were About Union-Busting*, AM. PROSPECT, Dec. 14, 2006, available at http://nationalimmi grationreform.org/media/articles/12-14-06American%20Prospect%20Online%20-%20Justice%20Deported.pdf

83. *About Reform Immigration for America*, CAMPAIGN TO REFORM IMMIGR. FOR AM., http://reform immigrationforamerica.org/blog/about (last visited Oct. 8, 2010).

84. Press Release, Change to Win, Change to Win and AFL-CIO Unveil Unified Immigration Reform Framework (Apr. 14, 2009), *available at* http://www.seiu.org/2009/04/change-to-win-and-afl-cio-unveil-unified-immi gration-reform-framework.php

85. Interview with Jose Covarrubias, *supra* note 71.

86. *See* Preston, *supra* note 13 (citing Sen. Jeff Sessions) ("This lax approach is particularly troubling . . . at a time when so many American citizens are struggling to find jobs").

87. *Id.* (citing Mark Reed, president of Border Management Strategies, a national consulting firm based in Tucson that advises companies across the country on immigration law).

dilemma. Should they turn themselves in to Homeland Security, who might charge them with providing a bad Social Security number to their employer, hold them for deportation, and even send them to prison, as was done with workers in Iowa and Howard Industries in Mississippi?[88] For workers with families, homes, and deep roots in a community, it simply is not possible to just walk away and disappear. As SEIU Local 87 president, Olga Miranda, points out, "I have a lot of members who are single mothers whose children were born here. I have a member whose child has leukemia. What are they supposed to do? Leave their children here and go back to Mexico and wait? And wait for what?"[89]

Union leaders like Miranda see a conflict between the rhetoric used by the president and other Washington, D.C. politicians and lobbyists in condemning the Arizona law, and the immigration proposals they make in Congress. "There's a huge contradiction here," she says. "You can't tell one state that what they're doing is criminalizing people, and at the same time go after employers paying more than a living wage and the workers who have fought for that wage."[90]

Renee Saucedo, attorney for La Raza Centro Legal and former director of the San Francisco Day Labor Program, is even more critical. "Those bills in Congress, which are presented as ones that will help some people get legal status, will actually make things much worse. We'll see many more firings like the janitors here, and more punishments for people who are just working and trying to support their families."[91]

Nevertheless, whether or not they are motivated by economic gain or anti-union animus, the current firings highlight larger questions of immigration enforcement policy. Nativo López, director of the Hermandad Mexicana Latinoamericana, a grassroots organizer who organized protests against the firings at Overhill Farms and American Apparel, puts it this way:

> These workers have not only done nothing wrong, they've spent years making the company rich. No one ever called company profits illegal, or says they should give them back to the workers. So why are the workers called illegal? Any immigration policy that says these workers have no right to work and feed their families is wrong and needs to be changed.[92]

Whatever President Obama or Secretary Napolitano may claim about punishing exploitative employers, employers who cooperate with the audit initiative seem to evade sanctions. ICE threatened to fine Dov Charney, American Apparel's owner, but then withdrew the threat.[93] As a result, it's the fired workers who are punished, as the employers escape fines in exchange for cooperation.[94]

And the justification for hurting workers is also implicit in the policy announced on the

---

88. *See, e.g.,* Lynda Waddington, *Raids on Swift, Agriprocessors Highlighted in Immigration Policy Critique,* IOWA INDEP., June 22, 2009, http://iowaindependent.com/16282/raids-on-agriprocessors-swift-highlighted-in -new-immigration-policy-critique

89. Interview with Olga Miranda, *supra* note 28.

90. *Id.*

91. Interview of Renee Saucedo, *supra* note 46.

92. Interview with Nativo López, Dir., Hermandad Mexicana Latinoamericana, in L.A., Cal. (June 18, 2009).

93. *See* Interview with Peter Schey, in L.A., Cal. (Dec. 16, 2009).

94. *See* Interview with Javier Murillo, *supra* note 65.

White House website, "remove incentives to enter the country illegally."[95] This was the original justification for employer sanctions in 1986—if migrants cannot work, they will not come. Of course, people did come, because at the same time Congress passed IRCA, it also began to debate NAFTA. That virtually guaranteed future migration. Since NAFTA went into effect in 1994, millions of Mexicans have been driven by poverty across the border.[96] The real questions we need to ask are what uproots people in Mexico, and why U.S. employers rely so heavily on low-wage workers.

Arguably, no one in the Obama or Bush administrations, or the Clinton administration before them, wants to stop migration to the United States or imagines that this could be done without catastrophic consequences. The very industries they target for enforcement are so dependent on the labor of migrants they would collapse without it. Instead, immigration policy and enforcement consigns those migrants to an "illegal" status, and undermines the price of their labor. Enforcement is a means for managing the flow of migrants and making their labor available to employers at a price they want to pay (see De Genova, this volume).

In 1998, the Clinton administration mounted the largest sanctions enforcement action to date, in which agents sifted through the names of 24,310 workers in forty Nebraska meat-packing plants.[97] They then sent letters to 4,762 workers, saying their documents were bad, and over 3,500 were forced from their jobs. Mark Reed, who directed "Operation Vanguard," claimed it was really intended to pressure Congress and employer groups to support guest worker legislation.[98] "We depend on foreign labor," he declared. "If we don't have illegal immigration anymore, we'll have the political support for guest workers."[99]

Increased ICE raids, stepped up border enforcement, and employer sanctions have not reduced undocumented immigration to the United States.[100] The failure of these harsh efforts must teach us something. The enforcement-only approach has resulted in human tragedy, increased poverty, and family separation, while undocumented workers continue to flow into the United States (see Boehm, this volume; Coutin, this volume). This is a challenge that requires us to understand why workers come here and to address the challenge in a more sensible manner.

The inhumanity of the situation is apparent to many. As Tom Barry puts it,

> we are wasting billions of dollars at home in what has become a war on immigrants. The collateral costs of this anti-immigrant crackdown—including labor shortages, families torn apart by deportations, over-crowded jails and detentions centers, deaths on the border, courts clogged with immigration cases, and divided communities—are also immense.[101]

---

95. *See Immigration, supra* note 4 and accompanying text.

96. *See generally* HING, ETHICAL BORDERS, *supra* note 44.

97. David Bacon, *The Political Economy of Immigration: Reform the Corporate Campaign for a U.S. Guest Worker Program*, MULTINATIONAL MONITOR (Nov. 2004), *available at* http://multinationalmonitor.org/mm2004/112004/bacon.html

98. *Id.*

99. *Id.*

100. *See* HING, *supra* note 44, at 116–32.

101. *See* Tom Barry, *Paying the Price of the Immigration Crackdown*, AMÉRICA LATINA EN MOVIMIENTO, May 23, 2008, http://alainet.org/active/24228&lang=es

And the *New York Times* mourns that after we get through this period of the "Great Immigration Panic,"

> someday, the country will recognize the true cost of its war on illegal immigration. We don't mean dollars, though those are being squandered by the billions. The true cost is to the national identity: the sense of who we are and what we value. It will hit us once the enforcement fever breaks, when we look at what has been done and no longer recognize the country that did it.[102]

It's time to come to our senses and realize that the enforcement plus guest worker approach has failed. The rise of employer sanctions enforcement causes hardship for our fellow human travelers who only seek an opportunity to work to feed their families at an honest day's wage. While employer sanctions enforcement has risen, we pray for its fall. Undocumented migration is the result of factors and phenomena way beyond the control of intimidation, guns, and militarization. The time to get smart has arrived; we must begin considering more creative approaches by understanding the forces at work.[103]

Our current policies produce displaced people in Mexico, criminalize them once they arrive in the United States, and view them simply as a source of cheap labor for employers. We need to see migrants as human beings first and then formulate a policy to protect their human and labor rights, along with those of other working people in this country. Repealing employer sanctions is critical in moving us in that direction.

102. Editorial, *The Great Immigration Panic*, N.Y. TIMES, June 3, 2008, http://www.nytimes.com/2008/06/03/opinion/03tue1.html

103. This would include considering open labor movement between NAFTA countries as is the case among European Union countries, revising trade policies so that Mexico can compete with United States and Canadian companies, creating immigrant enterprise zones for certain parts of the United States, broadening the permanent visa system to allow more needed workers from Mexico to lawfully immigrate, and investing heavily in Mexico's infrastructure so that more jobs are created in Mexico. *See* HING, *supra* note 44, at 133–59.

8 ARIZONA'S SB 1070

SETTING CONDITIONS FOR VIOLATIONS OF HUMAN RIGHTS HERE AND BEYOND

Rogelio Sáenz, Cecilia Menjívar, and San Juanita Edilia García

The United States has been experiencing major shifts in the racial and ethnic composition of its population over the last half century. In particular, due to a variety of demographic patterns alongside globalization forces stimulating the international movement of capital, goods, and people, the presence of the Latino population has increased dramatically over the last several decades. Indeed, Latinos represent the engine of the U.S. population—without Latinos, the country would be much older and would be growing at a slower rate. While the Latino population has moved into places where historically they have been absent (dubbed new-destination areas), they continue to be concentrated along the Mexico-U.S. border. As Latino immigration has expanded in the country, a common reaction has been the implementation of measures to halt it and to criminalize the immigrants' presence, and to round up and deport Latino undocumented (and, in some cases, documented) immigrants already in the country. It is in this region where we have seen the militarization of the border through increasing governmental and vigilante surveillance and the erection of walls and fences to keep immigrants out (see Heyman, this volume; Chavez, this volume).

Arizona is the latest, perhaps most visible, state to initiate draconian policies to apprehend and deport undocumented immigrants and to deter others from coming into the state. In 2007, Arizona passed the Legal Arizona Workers Act, a measure to identify and punish businesses that "knowingly" and "intentionally" hire unauthorized workers. The U.S. Ninth Circuit Court of Appeals upheld this policy in March 2009. More recently, Arizona passed Senate Bill 1070 (SB 1070) in April 2010. This policy requires law enforcement agents of the state of Arizona and its political subdivisions (counties, cities, and towns) to enforce and completely comply with federal immigration policies. In essence, Arizona law enforcement

Rogelio Sáenz is Peter Flawn Professor of Demography and dean of the College of Public Policy at the University of Texas, San Antonio. Cecilia Menjívar is Cowden Distinguished Professor in the School of Social and Family Dynamics at Arizona State University. San Juanita Edilia García is a doctoral student in the Department of Sociology at Texas A&M University.

agents are required to carry out the functions of Immigration and Customs Enforcement (ICE) agents associated with checking the immigration status of individuals. The policy outlines the numerous offenses pertaining to SB 1070 (see below), including requiring law enforcement agents to check the legal status of an individual during a routine stop or during any "legal contact," as well as the hiring and transporting of undocumented immigrants. While many in Arizona and in other parts of the country have voiced support for the policy, many others have expressed major concerns related to the potential violation of basic human rights embedded in this law. In July 2010, Judge Susan Bolton blocked key parts of SB 1070 involving the requirement to check the immigration status of persons suspected of being undocumented. Although the more controversial portions of the law have been temporarily blocked, the effects of signing the law have reverberated through neighborhoods and meeting halls, as other states consider passing similar legislation and immigrants and their families throughout the country wait and hope that this will not be the case.

This chapter provides an overview of the policy and how it creates conditions for multiple violations of human rights, not only of immigrants but of U.S. citizens as well. The chapter has three sections. First, we discuss the demographic context in which policies such as SB 1070 in Arizona have been constructed. Second, we provide an overview of SB 1070, discuss its implications for the violation of human rights, and illustrate fears and actions that it has already generated in Arizona. Third, we suggest that the "long arm" of SB 1070 reaches beyond the confines of Arizona by illustrating how persons in other parts of the country are already facing fears and distress due to the rising anti-immigrant sentiment taking hold in the country.

LATINOS AND WHITES AND THE
SHIFTING DEMOGRAPHY OF ARIZONA

The United States, since its inception, has been a white country. Indeed, for over 150 years beginning in 1790 and ending in 1952, by barring nonwhites from citizenship, U.S. immigration policy essentially stipulated that only whites were eligible for U.S. citizenship. While many European immigrants who arrived in the United States during this period were initially viewed as nonwhite socially, there was no question that they were white legally and thus eligible for U.S. citizenship. Nonwhite racial and ethnic groups who were ineligible for U.S. citizenship but who were incorporated into the country through aggressive and forced immigration were eventually granted U.S. citizenship through the "back door." This was the case for African Americans (Fourteenth Amendment to the Constitution in 1868), Mexican Americans (Treaty of Guadalupe Hidalgo in 1848), Puerto Ricans (Jones Act of 1917), and Native Americans (Indian Citizenship Act of 1924). Other groups who were not considered white fought in the courts for whiteness and for eligibility to become U.S. citizens (see López 2006).

In this environment, to be white has meant to be included, incorporated, welcomed, and to essentially be part of mainstream of American society across its institutions. Even when groups were excluded and received with hostility, such as the case of the Irish, once they were deemed white, they became incorporated and "assimilated" into the mainstream.

Thus, to be white is to be part of the "club" where one feels comfortable in one's environment; it signifies to be "normal." Indeed, whites often do not see themselves as having a race; rather, it is nonwhites (read: those who are outside the mainstream) who have a race and are preoccupied with issues of race. Whites are comfortable in the space where they are the dominant group in terms of numbers, power, and leadership, for this is what is "normal." Indeed, while blacks and other persons of color regularly report that they would prefer to live in integrated settings alongside a significant portion of whites, whites prefer to live mostly with other whites. Many places, including our societal institutions, are "white space," where whites feel comfortable and welcome (see Moore 2008). White space then is a precious commodity for whites because it supports and sustains their power and, importantly, reproduces racial inequality.

When whites feel that this environment is altered, they feel invaded, and forces are set in motion to maintain white space and white benefits. For example, whites felt threatened by the passage of civil rights legislation in the mid- to late 1960s. Quickly we saw policies and actions taken to circumvent school desegregation, affirmative action, fair housing, and so forth. In a short period of time, gains that persons of color made through civil rights legislation were overturned. Indeed, today public schools are as segregated as they were prior to civil rights legislation, the term *affirmative action* has become taboo, and the standard inclusion of the "Affirmative Action/Equal Opportunity Employer" statement in job ads rings hollow.

It is in this context that we have seen the rise of policies and actions directed against Latinos in Arizona and throughout the country. For instance, in 2005 there were 300 bills introduced and 38 immigration-related laws passed throughout the country; by 2007 the numbers had increased to 1,562 bills and 240 laws (Hegen 2008). These actions have come in the form of policies involving English as the official language, attacks on bilingual education, Propositions 187 and 209, anti-affirmative action legislation, and municipal policies such as making it illegal for landlords to rent to undocumented immigrants (see Gilbert, this volume) or for day laborers, presumably undocumented immigrants, to seek work on street corners. The hallmark of these pieces of legislation is their aim to debilitate the "magnet" for immigration by relying on enforcement and the criminalization of an ever wider range of immigrant behaviors and practices (see Stumpf, this volume). In doing so, they bar undocumented immigrants (and their families) from a wide range of public spaces where their presence is visible and people are reminded that the demographic landscape of the country is changing. We now turn to the shifting demography of the state of Arizona.

The Shifting Demography of Arizona

The population of Arizona has grown significantly over the last several decades. Indeed, the state's population more than doubled from 2.7 million in 1980 to 6.5 million in 2008. During this period, Arizona rose from the 29th to the 14th most populous state in the country. The state's population expansion has increasingly been tied to growth in its Latino population. Over the period from 1980 to 2008, Latinos made up two fifths of the nearly 3.8 million people that were added to the Arizona population during this time. The Latino population more than quadrupled, from nearly 441,000 in 1980 to almost 2 million in 2008 (Hobbs and Stoops 2002; U.S. Census Bureau 2010).

Furthermore, the magnitude of the Latino population in the growth of the Arizona population has expanded progressively over time. For example, of the approximately 947,000 people added to the Arizona population between 1980 and 1990, whites constituted nearly two thirds of the change and Latinos accounted for about one fourth (Hobbs and Stoops 2002; U.S. Census Bureau 2010). More recently, however, of the nearly 1.4 million persons added to the state population between 2000 and 2008, Latinos accounted for nearly half of the growth compared to less than two fifths among whites.

These differences in the growth rates of Latinos and whites have led to major changes in the share of each of these groups in the Arizona population over time. The percentage of Arizonians who are Latino rose from 16 percent in 1980 to 30 percent in 2008 (Hobbs and Stoops 2002; U.S. Census Bureau 2010). In contrast, the share of the state's inhabitants who are white fell from 75 percent in 1980 to 58 percent in 2008.

The shifting demography of Arizona has been produced by variations in the age structure of Latinos and whites as well as by the increasing levels of internal and international immigration in the state.

Youthful Latinos and Aging Whites

The age structure of a population is one of the most important demographic factors associated with the magnitude and direction of population change. Populations that are young tend to produce rapid population growth as a large share of persons in the population are in or will be entering the period associated with family formation and childbearing. By way of contrast, populations that are older generally grow at slow rates or may even decline in numbers as deaths and births tend to approximate each other, or deaths outnumber births.

The Latino and white populations of Arizona differ significantly on the basis of the age structure. The median age of Latinos is 17 years younger than that of whites, with the median age of Latinos being 26 and that of whites being 43. Indeed, there is a major demographic divide between Latinos and whites across Arizona's age spectrum. Whites account for over half of the state's population beginning at age 35 and comprise at least 80 percent across elderly age categories (Ruggles et al. 2010a). In contrast, Latinos outnumber whites in the two youngest age cohorts (0–4 and 5–9). This bodes a greater presence of Latinos in the coming decades.

The varying pace of future growth between Latinos and whites in Arizona is evident in one other way—the ratio of births to deaths for Latinos and whites. In 2006, while there were 1.2 births to every 1 death among whites, there were 8.9 births to every 1 death among Latinos, reflecting the much greater youthfulness of Latinos (Center for Disease Control and Prevention 2010; Martin et al. 2009; see also Haub 2006). As such, Latinos are growing much more rapidly than whites due to natural increase (births minus deaths).

Rising Latino Immigration

The Latino population is also growing disproportionately due to rising levels of immigration. Nonetheless, it is important to point out that a significant majority of Latinos in Arizona were born in the United States, with two of every three born in this country. Still, the percentage of Latinos who are foreign born increased from 18 percent in 1980 to 33 percent in 2008 (Ruggles et al. 2010a, 2010b, 2010c, 2010d).

A variety of factors have contributed to Arizona's rising immigration. For example, the passage of the North American Free Trade Agreement (NAFTA) in 1994 stimulated immigration to the United States as many farmers in rural areas of Mexico could not compete effectively with U.S. agriculture. In addition, starting in the early to mid-1990s, the Immigration and Naturalization Service (INS) formed blockages in California and Texas to avert the entry of immigrants in these areas, with the result being that the main entry point shifted to Arizona (see Eschbach et al. 1999; see also Doty, this volume). This movement of the main entry point to Arizona can be seen in the fact that more than half of foreign-born Latinos living in Arizona in 2008 have entered the United States since 1994. Moreover, the weakening California economy has also pushed many Latino immigrants to other states, many to Arizona. While California's share of all foreign-born Latinos in the four border states (Arizona, California, New Mexico, and Texas) declined from 71 percent in 1980 to 60 percent in 2008, that of Arizona rose from 3 percent in 1980 to 7 percent in 2008. It is still apparent that the large majority of foreign-born Latinos in the four border states are concentrated in California and Texas.

In sum, these demographic patterns have upset the comfortable white space of Arizona for many whites. As the Latino population has expanded in Arizona, we have seen the creation of practices and policies, such as SB 1070, and the patrolling of its border by vigilante and reputed neo-Nazi groups (Amster 2010). The goals of these actions have been to halt immigration to Arizona and to round up and deport those already in the state. We now turn to our discussion of SB 1070 in Arizona, its implications for the violation of human rights, and the fears and actions that it has already generated in the state and beyond.

SB 1070 AND VIOLATIONS OF HUMAN RIGHTS

After a string of laws passed in recent years that have sought to penalize the activities and behaviors of undocumented immigrants in the state, Arizona Senate Bill 1070 was signed by Governor Jan Brewer on April 23, 2010, as an attempt to get the state to cooperate with federal immigration agencies in enforcing federal law. The objective was to make "attrition through enforcement" the local policy, meaning that conditions for immigrants in the state were going to be so inhospitable that they were going to deter and discourage immigrants from coming in, and create enough of a disincentive for those already in the state to leave voluntarily. Those already in the state would "self deport." And though not the first (or last) attempt to criminalize the presence and activities of undocumented immigrants (in Arizona or in other states), SB 1070 is unique in its reach and in its inclusion of a variety of behaviors and actions associated with Latino immigrants.

The law, temporarily blocked just before it was supposed to go into effect on July 29, 2010, requires police officers to verify a person's immigration status in the course of "lawful contact" when "practicable" if there is "reasonable suspicion" that the person is an undocumented immigrant. The law included the provision that officers may not solely consider race, color, or national origin in complying with this law. House Bill 2162 amended the law;

it eliminated the word *solely* (from "solely consider race") and changed "lawful contact" to "lawful stop, detention, or arrest." The law also makes it illegal for undocumented workers to seek work in public places and for employers to stop on a street to pick up and hire undocumented workers (the last two are directed at day laborers). The law specifies that in addition to committing a federal violation, a person is guilty of trespassing if the person is present on any public or private land and cannot produce an alien registration card. According to the law, it is unlawful to transport an "alien" in Arizona, and the means of transportation is subjected to vehicle immobilization or impounding. Furthermore, it would allow law enforcement agents to arrest a person without warrant if there is probable cause to believe the person has committed a public offense that makes the individual removable from the United States (Arizona State Senate 2010).

SB 1070 and the state-level laws that preceded it have a direct impact on human rights, whether directly violating them or indirectly creating conditions that lead to violations. Thus, one must remember that SB 1070 does not stand alone, as previous laws that were passed since 2004 in Arizona are still in place, as are those at the federal level, particularly the Illegal Immigration Reform and Immigrant Responsibility Act (IIRIRA) of 1996 that has facilitated the deportation of thousands (see Chacón, this volume). Indeed, Maricopa County (the most populous county in the state) has been one of the most vigorous users of the 287(g) agreement, a federal program that seeks to identify for deportation undocumented immigrants who have committed crimes, but that has been used mostly to conduct raids in businesses where Latino immigrants work or to carry out traffic stops in the neighborhoods in which they live. SB 1070 was passed within this backdrop, not to supersede any of these laws or independent of them but to exacerbate the effects of what was already there. It is this multipronged legal context that is ripe for the infringement of rights.

Some of the most noted local-level laws in Arizona include Proposition 200 ("Protect Arizona Now" or "Arizona Taxpayer and Citizen Protection Act"), a voter-approved initiative passed in 2004 to require proof of eligibility to receive social services such as retirement, welfare, health, disability, public or assisted housing, postsecondary education, food assistance, unemployment, or similar benefits that are provided with appropriated funds of state or local governments, and to require state and local workers to report immigration violations to federal authorities in writing. In 2006, Arizona voters approved Proposition 100, which denies bail to undocumented immigrants accused of felonious crimes; Proposition 102, which bars undocumented immigrants from collecting punitive damages in civil lawsuits; Proposition 103, which makes English the official language of the state; and Proposition 300, which denies in-state college tuition to immigrants who cannot produce proof of permanent legal residence or citizenship, and bars undocumented immigrants from accessing subsidized child care and adult education programs (Arizona Legislative Council 2006). And then in January 2008, the Legal Arizona Workers Act went into effect; it seeks to punish businesses that hire undocumented workers with severe penalties, including the suspension of a business license or its revocation for a second offense.

According to the Universal Declaration of Human Rights, a basic right of individuals is to be able to secure employment and to not be deprived of means of subsistence; it also includes the right to wages sufficient to support a minimum standard of living, equal pay for equal work, and the opportunity for advancement. Furthermore, the United Nations International Convention on the Protection of the Rights of All Migrant Workers and Members of Their Families, adopted in 1990 but not ratified by the United States (or any of the wealthy nations that receive immigrants today), stipulates that migrant workers and members of their families should have the right at any time to enter and remain in their country of origin and that migrant workers or members of their families should not be subjected to arbitrary or unlawful interference with their privacy, family, home, correspondence, or other communications, or to unlawful attacks on their honor and reputation. It affirms that migrant workers and members of their families shall have the right to the protection of the law against such interference or attacks, and that they are not to be subjected individually or collectively to arbitrary arrest or detention (Menjívar and Rumbaut 2008). This convention also stipulates that migrant workers and their children should have access to a range of social services, such as educational institutions, vocational guidance, placement services, and training on the basis of equality of treatment for their children.

There are several provisions of SB 1070 that directly infringe on individuals' universal rights, but in the interest of space we will only address those that directly affect workers. The Arizona laws that target, on the one hand, the business owners who hire undocumented immigrant workers (Legal Arizona Workers Act 2007) and, on the other, the workers themselves who seek employment (SB 1070) directly infringe on this right. SB 1070 goes further, as it penalizes different activities associated with day labor work, a specific kind of employment that is common among Latino immigrants. Thus, it does not penalize all workers in the same way but seeks to be particularly punitive toward day laborers, a group mostly composed of immigrant and/or Latino workers. The multipronged legal system in place today has created conditions that impinge directly and indirectly on the rights of immigrants as workers, and it has done so from multiple angles in a way that slowly asphyxiates the efforts of those who are seeking dignified employment in the state.

In addition to addressing the "supply side" (by seeking to deter immigrants from coming to or staying in Arizona) as well as "the demand" (by penalizing employers who hire immigrants, an action that was already punishable under federal law, the Immigration Reform and Control Act of 1986), SB 1070 creates conditions for immigrants to become more vulnerable and to live more clandestine lives. Fear of detection, for instance, is a powerful force that can keep immigrants from reporting abuses and crime, from seeking services and help when needed, and even from sending their children to school. Importantly, even though the law cannot overtly target Latinos, by going after the jobs that they are likely to take and focusing on neighborhoods where they live, the law essentially aims to drive out Latino immigrants. And it does so by creating a climate of fear and insecurity for them. As Olivas (2007) argues in a critique of these "pigtail ordinances in modern guise, . . . the blowback in affected communities, and the resultant prejudice sure to follow from [them] . . . are sure signs of an ethnic and national origin 'tax' that will only be levied upon certain groups, certain to be Mexicans in particular, or equally likely, Mexican Americans."

Immigrant workers in Phoenix live with this sense of insecurity on a daily basis. A Guatemalan woman in Phoenix told Cecilia Menjívar that when they go clean model homes at night, she and her husband never ride together in the same car for fear that they might be stopped and sent to a detention center, and separated from their children. In her words:

> Look, Cecilia, this situation is scary; it gives us fear. Every day, I don't lie to you, it's constant. So no, we don't drive together. What if we are stopped and we get deported? We'll be taken to jail, right? And the kids, what? Who'll care of them? Who's going to stay with them? We worry; we live anguished. So he goes in one car, with our neighbor, and I go in another one, with my cousin. The same when we go to the market. He goes in one car and I go in another. So no, we try to never, no, we're never in the same car. Never. Who knows what can happen. We need to be careful. We must take precaution.

In addition, workers become more vulnerable to abuses. Even though they recognize abusive practices, such as not getting paid overtime, not being paid what was agreed for a job, or receiving regular threats of being fired, they know they have few places to go. They are cognizant that reporting an abusive employer will bring them to the attention of the authorities, and thus, they do not take the risk. A Salvadoran woman recounted the time when her husband was told to stop by and pick up what he was owed by his boss. "'On Thursday, I'll pay you on Thursday.' But Thursday, there was nothing. And another Thursday went by and nothing." When asked if she was afraid her husband would not be paid at all, the woman said, "That's the thing. You never know because there are people who work and don't get paid. The boss closes the business or says that he has no money. And what can one do? Go to the police to file a complaint? Go to the sheriff [laughs]?" Obviously, unscrupulous employers are well aware that in today's climate, very few of these workers, if any, will turn them in to the authorities.

Thus, the context that a law like SB 1070 creates violates immigrant workers' rights by closing options for work, by making the context so inhospitable that workers will leave, but also by pushing the workers into more vulnerable situations ripe for abuse. However, SB 1070 has attracted the attention of politicians in other states, and even in other countries, who quickly started to contemplate whether similar policies could be implemented in their jurisdiction. Indeed, a few days after the governor of Arizona signed SB 1070 into law, legislators in approximately 22 other states, including Alabama, Colorado, Delaware, Florida, Idaho, Indiana, Maryland, Michigan, Minnesota, Mississippi, Missouri, Nevada, North Carolina, Ohio, Oklahoma, Oregon, Pennsylvania, Rhode Island, South Carolina, Texas, Utah, and Virginia, declared their intent to introduce similar legislation (Waslin 2010). In the process, just the consideration of implementing such laws sends a message to Latino immigrant communities across the country. Thus, the fear and insecurity that immigrants experience in Arizona are not contained within the state's borders; SB 1070 is creating similar experiences in states where it is being considered.

THE REACH OF SB 1070 BEYOND ARIZONA

The anti-immigrant movement and sentiment that abounds perpetuates racism and the devaluation of immigrants or even those who *appear* to be immigrants (Romero 2006). In the current anti-immigrant climate, being an undocumented immigrant, or just an immigrant, has major implications for immigrants and their families. The meaning, stigma, and experiences of undocumented immigrants especially today may also affect not only the immigrant community but the Latino community overall, including U.S.-born Latinos/Latinas (Romero 2006). Given the rise of anti-immigrant sentiment coupled with the increase of enforcement as evidenced by the augmentation of raids, deportations, and anti-immigrant legislation, we argue that this further excludes and marginalizes undocumented immigrants by putting daily strains and structural barriers in their lives. Moreover, we argue that these constant pressures ultimately have a significant impact on their mental health, specifically contributing to feelings of distress.

In this section, we present the voices of undocumented Mexican immigrant women to illustrate how policies such as SB 1070 send a widespread message that causes distress in immigrant communities throughout the United States. The voices of these women portray sentiments of fearing the police and immigration officials, or of being separated from their families due to deportations. They fear being apprehended or questioned by police or immigration officials. This constant fear, similar to the experiences of the couple in Phoenix mentioned above, contributes to feelings of living in the shadows, imprisoned, secluded, limited, and hidden.

These findings from Houston, Texas, have implications for the mental health of immigrants, particularly with respect to how anti-immigrant hostility contributes to feelings of fear and subjugation. More specifically, our observed patterns reveal the social significance of undocumented status and how the unequal social structure of the United States prevents the integration of these women. We now provide data from interviews conducted with undocumented Mexican immigrant women in Houston to show that the effects of policies like SB 1070 are not contained solely in the states where they are passed but become a powerful message sent to immigrants across the United States.

Take, for instance, Zenaida, a 23-year-old immigrant from Guanajuato. Her words capture the fear she constantly lives with due to her undocumented status. Living in an anti-immigrant climate in a society where racism is ingrained and shapes other dynamics creates fear and distress that affect the lives and minds of individuals. An increase in hate crimes toward immigrants, the militarization of the border, draconian legislative policies, and so forth demonstrate how the current climate further pushes to the margins an already marginalized community. Zenaida shares the following:

> I feel sadness and fear at the same time. I'm always with that fear that something may happen, like if the police stops me, or that immigration will be there and I won't be able to make it home or if I'm not with my kids. . . . I'm scared. . . . I'll always be with that fear, sadness, and frustration. . . . You become frustrated because you can't do anything . . . like you can't fix your papers to be here legally.

Living with constant fear is a daily reality for undocumented immigrants, as well as for their documented and U.S.-born relatives. Study participants in Houston spoke about a fear of being apprehended by immigration or police officials—they expressed feeling closed in, limited, or imprisoned. They described the raids, mass deportations, roadblocks in immigrant communities, and the militarization of the border enforced by the U.S. government.

For example, Liliana, a 28-year-old woman who migrated to the United States as a tourist, overstayed her visa, and was then considered an undocumented immigrant but later obtained legal residency via marrying a third-generation Mexican American, provides an example of living with fear. When asked to describe retrospectively how she felt when she was undocumented, she stated the following:

> You don't go to many places, like to other states, because you think you'll get stopped. In other words, you stay in the same circle, doing the same thing. It's sadder. You feel like you're in prison but bigger because you drive to go buy groceries, you take the kids to school, and you bring them back but you continue to feel like you don't belong here.

Liliana describes what it was like living as an undocumented immigrant. She describes feelings of isolation and seclusion and not being able to live worry-free. She relates her experiences of living in the United States as an undocumented immigrant to living in a prison, describing how she must remain within the same circle, such as going to buy groceries and taking her children to and from school. She also describes feeling as if she is not wanted in the United States. Later in her interview, she vocalized the existence and presence of anti-immigrant views, particularly against Mexican immigrants.

Liliana's description, along with other respondents' similar sentiments, are reminiscent of a song titled "La Jaula de Oro" by Los Tigres del Norte (The Tigers of the North). Los Tigres del Norte, a *norteño* genre group, represent the voice of the working-class communities in Mexico and of Latino immigrants in the United States (Ragland 2009). "La Jaula de Oro" is about an undocumented Mexican immigrant man who has been in the United States for 10 years. In this song, the United States is portrayed as a great but confining nation, a "golden cage." This metaphor relates to feeling confined in a golden cage that remains a prison, particularly for the undocumented population or for those who hold uncertain legal statuses and find themselves in legal limbo. This song personifies the ways in which respondents described what it meant to live in the United States as an undocumented immigrant.

Going further in describing what it means to live in constant fear among immigrants is Deyanira from Nuevo León, who states, "You're fearful. You feel scared like if the police stop you, like lately even the police officers can ask for people's Social Security [number]." Although policies like SB 1070 are not in effect in Houston, they nevertheless send a chilling message to the city. Since July 20, 2008, the Harris County Sheriff's Office has agreed to enforce the 287(g) program in Houston (U.S. Immigration and Customs Enforcement 2010, n.d.). Section 287(g) allows local law enforcement officials to question the immigration status of the community, working in conjunction with ICE agencies. The implications of legislative policies such as these are discomforting for the Latino community, and especially for the undocumented population.

Anti-immigrant legislation demonstrates intolerance and racism. Furthermore, legislation such as SB 1070 and similar laws will only increase and legitimize racial profiling. It is evident that individuals who appear to be of Latino descent are likely to be stopped and questioned about their citizenship or residency status. As is reminiscent in Deyanira's quote, the fear of being apprehended by local law enforcement is fierce, a concern that is likely to heighten tension and distrust between the undocumented immigrant community and law enforcement.

The fear of being stopped and questioned by police or immigration officials is a reality for many immigrants. Participants regularly reported being scared of police and immigration officials who have conducted raids, roadblocks, and deportations in the Houston area. Zenaida, one of the immigrants mentioned above, stated that living as an undocumented immigrant is living "with fear, fear that they'll get you in a roadblock, for instance, that they'll be outside the apartment complex asking for your papers, for your Social Security [number]. One feels like you are always hiding, like you always live with fear of going anywhere." She actually lived through that experience when she was driving to her apartment. She described the logistics and location of the roadblock:

> There were about four cop cars on the corner. . . . I was coming through here and the police was right here [as she drew the logistics of the situation] and then the cars came this way and the cops signaled them to go over where they were at. Another car and I were signaled to keep going. . . . Yes, I have been so close to those roadblocks, and yes, I am extremely scared because I don't have a license. I only have my [Mexican] consulate ID card. . . . I was so scared and frightened because I had my 3 children with me. I felt so scared and said I will never drive through that route. I will never go through there anymore because there are too many cops.

This fear of being stopped by police officers expressed numerous times by respondents indicates how legislation like the 287(g) agreements heightens tension between local police enforcement officials and the undocumented population. This has major implications for a number of contacts with authorities, including reporting crimes. Crime reporting is already a problem in minority communities as individuals do not always trust authorities (Menjívar and Bejarano 2004). This legislation exacerbates this situation and may prevent undocumented immigrants from calling the police for fear of being deported. For example, Zenaida had been a victim of domestic violence, and she shared that she never reported her husband even though he had hit her numerous times before. She believes her neighbor called law enforcement officials because she never sought help from them due to the fear of being deported. Her husband had been deported to Mexico three weeks prior to the date she was interviewed. Zenaida was struggling to decide what would be the best outcome for her and her children given her undocumented status, as a single mother, and as having only limited family support in the United States. Given these circumstances, she was contemplating returning to Mexico. This is only one example that shows how restrictive policies can heighten fear of authorities and the police among the undocumented population.

Consistent with the sentiment of being fearful of having their undocumented status discovered, Daniela, a 31-year-old immigrant, states the following:

> You feel secure [with papers] but since I don't have papers you have to put up with things because the last thing you want is to be noticed. You don't want this country to find out that you are here. You don't want anyone to find out. It's like they say: We live in the shadows. We live in the shadows so that no one, not police officers, not immigration, not the government, not anyone, should know that we do not have papers.

Again the theme of feeling isolated and constrained reappears. Daniela makes the comparison to living in the shadows or in confinement. She describes living life as far from public view as possible. She also makes a connection to having to endure certain things for the fear of being found out. This type of seclusion could lead to a worse situation, particularly when these immigrants have been the victims of crime.

Eugenia, a 39-year-old undocumented immigrant from the state of Coahuila, also described being undocumented as living in the shadows. In her words,

> Living in the shadows is living with fear . . . living in, like they say, in the shadows and darkness. . . . It means you cannot live freely. . . . You can't even go out freely to the stores, to run errands, because you are always fearful that they will deport you.

Again we see how prevalent the fear of being deported is and what it means to live in the United States as an undocumented person. This constant fear has been intensified especially in the post-9/11 enforcement era. What it means to be an undocumented immigrant now, in a negative, anti-immigrant context of reception, has major implications for all immigrants, undocumented or not. For instance, there are serious implications from living in a constant state of fear for individuals' mental health and overall health. Additionally, these implications play a major role in the integration process of immigrants and their children. Feelings of having to hide and fear on a routine basis can have detrimental health consequences. Living with constant fear and internalizing social injustices without being able to speak up or challenge them is similar to the concept of "racial battle fatigue," which has been found to have severe health impacts (Smith, Allen, and Danley 2007).

Smith and colleagues (2007) introduce the concept of "racial battle fatigue" to addresses "the physiological and psychological strain exacted on racially marginalized groups and the amount of energy lost dedicated to coping with racial microaggressions and racism" (p. 555). Moreover, the feelings immigrants experience today, described in the above quotes, impact the ways in which immigrants integrate into U.S. society. These quotes show the fear that undocumented immigrants face daily, a fear of being deported and of the consequences should they were deported.

CONCLUSION

Over the last couple of decades, communities and states have created policies to deter immigrants from migrating into these areas and to encourage those already in place to leave due to the fear of being apprehended and deported. The state of Arizona is the latest to establish such policy with the signing of SB 1070 in April 2010. This chapter has provided an overview of the context in which SB 1070 and related policies have been constructed. We have argued that the disproportionate growth of the Latino population has led to whites feeling that their comfort associated with white space, where they are in control and where inequality is reproduced, is being assaulted. As a way to reconstruct white space and to protect the privileges that come with whiteness, policies such as SB 1070 have been put in place. The rabid anti-immigrant sentiments in the country, along with the expansion of the Latino population in areas away from the Mexico-U.S. border, will likely lead to the enactment of similar policies elsewhere.

We have also provided an overview of SB 1070. As we have shown, this law did not emerge in isolation in Arizona but has been part of a larger effort beginning a few years earlier to make Arizona an uncomfortable and unwelcoming place for immigrants and, more generally, Latinos. We have shown the fear that SB 1070 has already generated in the local Latino community, and we have emphasized the potential it has for violating the basic human rights of Latinos in Arizona. Moreover, we have argued that SB 1070 and similar policies have a long reach as their effects are felt beyond the confines of the states in which they are formed. In particular, we have provided an illustration of the fear and apprehension that Mexican immigrant women in a setting outside of Arizona—Houston, Texas—report as they lead their daily lives in an environment that increasingly targets them for apprehension and deportation.

Thus, we have shown how anti-immigrant and draconian policies such as the recent SB 1070 serve to dehumanize unauthorized immigrants and their families. The constant fear felt by undocumented immigrants and even U.S.-born Latinos is a social reality that violates human and constitutional rights. Fear is a form of oppression that limits, belittles, and confines Latino immigrants. Policies such as SB 1070 send a national and even international message, one that relates and paints the United States as a nativist, racist, and anti-immigrant country, particularly targeting Latino immigrants. In this sense, the current immigration regime and its implementation can be conceptualized as "legal violence" (Menjívar 2009).

This chapter has shown how immigrants are racialized, and it has demonstrated the social costs associated with undocumented immigrants living in a nativist and racist society and how this ultimately affects their psychological well-being. The chapter contributes to a timely reality that Arizonians and, even more broadly, Latino immigrants are facing given their marginalized position in the social structure. This group endures discrimination at every turn, but heightened nativism among anti-immigrant groups, alongside enforcement policies, makes undocumented immigrants much more vulnerable for deportation. In this hostile context, the Mexican-origin population is particularly at risk for negative mental health outcomes. Yet scant attention has been given to the relationship between this social environment and ethnic minority mental health outcomes (Vega and Rumbaut 1991; Viruell-Fuentes 2007). Particular attention needs to be placed on a vulnerable group that continues to be marginalized and oppressed (Viruell-Fuentes 2007).

Specifically, in addressing the social ills that contribute to a system of inequality where currently undocumented Mexican immigrants are targeted, we encourage scholars to focus on the unequal and racist society that immigrants enter and on how undocumented immigrants are not provided with the necessary resources to successfully integrate into society. Therefore, by failing to consider the larger social factors that impact people's lives differently depending on their social locations—their structurally unequal position in society based on their undocumented status, along with their race/ethnicity, class, gender, sexual orientation, and so forth—our discourse holds people of color responsible for their positions in society and reinforces prevailing ideas of individualism and meritocracy (Romero 2008). It is imperative to focus on the structural factors and ideological processes that have limited and continue to limit the opportunities for groups of color in the United States.

WORKS CITED

Amster, Randall. 2010. "Climate of Fear: SB 1070 and the Extremist Violence on the Arizona Border." *Common Dreams*, July 27. Retrieved January 15 (http://www.commondreams.org/view/2010/07/27-12).

Arizona Legislative Council. 2006. "2006 Ballot Proposition Analyses." Retrieved January 10, 2011 (http://www.azleg.state.az.us/2006_Ballot_Proposition_Analyses).

Arizona State Senate. 2010. "Fact Sheet for S.B. 1070." January 15. Retrieved September 5, 2010 (http://www.azleg.gov/legtext/49leg/2r/summary/s.1070pshs.doc.htm).

Center for Disease Control and Prevention. 2010. "Compressed Mortality File, Underlying Cause of Death: Mortality for 1999–2006 with ICD 10 Codes." Atlanta, GA: Author. Retrieved July 21, 2011 (http://wonder.cdc.gov/mortSQL.html).

Eschbach, Karl, Jacqueline M. Hagan, Nestor Rodriguez, Ruben Hernández-León, and Stanley Bailey. 1999. "Death at the Border." *International Migration Review* 33:430–40.

Haub, Carl. 2006. "Hispanics Account for Almost One-Half of U.S. Population Growth." Washington, DC: Population Reference Bureau. Retrieved July 21, 2010 (http://www.prb.org/Articles/2006/HispanicsAccountforalmostOneHalfofUSPopulationGrowth.aspx).

Hegen, Dirk. 2008. "2007 Enacted State Legislation Related to Immigrants and Immigration." Washington, DC: National Conference of State Legislatures.

Hobbs, Frank, and Nicole Stoops. 2002. "Demographic Trends in the 20th Century, Census 2000 Special Reports, Series CENSR-4." Washington, DC: U.S. Census Bureau.

López, Ian Haney. 2006. *White by Law: The Legal Construction of Race*. Revised and updated 10th Anniversary ed. New York: NYU Press.

Martin, Joyce A., Brady E. Hamilton, Paul D. Sutton, Stephanie J. Ventura, Fay Menacker, Sharon Kirmeyer, and T. J. Matthews. 2009. "Births: Final Data for 2006." *National Vital Statistics Reports* 57(7). Hyattsville, MD: National Center for Health Statistics.

Menjívar, Cecilia. 2009. "Latino Immigrant Workers and Legal Violence in Phoenix, Arizona." Paper presented at the "Migration During an Era of Restriction Conference," University of Texas, Austin, November 4–6.

Menjívar, Cecilia, and Cynthia Bejarano. 2004. "Latino Immigrants' Perceptions of Crime and of Police Authorities: A Case Study from the Phoenix Metropolitan Area." *Ethnic and Racial Studies* 27(1):120–48.

Menjívar, Cecilia, and Rubén G. Rumbaut. 2008. "Rights of Migrants." Pp. 60–74 in *The Leading Rogue State: The United States and Human Rights*, edited by Judith Blau, David L. Brunsma, Alberto Moncada, and Catherine Zimmer. Boulder, CO: Paradigm.

Moore, Wendy Leo. 2008. *Reproducing Racism: White Space, Elite Law Schools, and Racial Inequality.* Lanham, MD: Rowman & Littlefield.

Olivas, Michael A. 2007. "Lawmakers Gone Wild? College Residency and the Response to Professor Kobach." Public Law and Legal Theory Series, 2007-A-51, University of Houston, TX. Retrieved January 10, 2010 (http://ssrn.com/abstract=1028310).

Ragland, Cathy. 2009. *Música Norteña: Mexican Migrants Creating a Nation Between Nations.* Philadelphia: Temple University Press.

Romero, Mary. 2006. "Racial Profiling and Immigration Law Enforcement: Rounding Up of Usual Suspects in the Latino Community." *Critical Sociology* 32(2):447–73.

Romero, Mary. 2008. "Crossing the Immigration and Race Border: A Critical Race Theory Approach to Immigration Studies." *Contemporary Justice Review* 11(1):23–37.

Ruggles, Stephen, J., Trent Alexander, Katie Genadek, Ronald Goeken, Matthew B. Schroeder, and Matthew Sobek. 2010a. "Integrated Public Use Microdata Series: Version 5.0" [Machine-readable database: 2008 American Community Survey Sample]. Minneapolis: University of Minnesota. Retrieved July 21, 2010 (http://usa.ipums.org/usa/index.shtml).

Ruggles, Stephen, J., Trent Alexander, Katie Genadek, Ronald Goeken, Matthew B. Schroeder, and Matthew Sobek. 2010b. "Integrated Public Use Microdata Series: Version 5.0" [Machine-readable database: 1980 5% Public Use Microdata Sample]. Minneapolis: University of Minnesota. Retrieved July 21, 2010 (http://usa.ipums.org/usa/index.shtml).

Ruggles, Stephen, J., Trent Alexander, Katie Genadek, Ronald Goeken, Matthew B. Schroeder, and Matthew Sobek. 2010c. "Integrated Public Use Microdata Series: Version 5.0" [Machine-readable database: 1990 5% Public Use Microdata Sample]. Minneapolis: University of Minnesota. Retrieved July 21, 2010 (http://usa.ipums.org/usa/index.shtml).

Ruggles, Stephen, J., Trent Alexander, Katie Genadek, Ronald Goeken, Matthew B. Schroeder, and Matthew Sobek. 2010d. "Integrated Public Use Microdata Series: Version 5.0" [Machine-readable database: 2000 5% Public Use Microdata Sample]. Minneapolis: University of Minnesota. Retrieved July 21, 2010 (http://usa.ipums.org/usa/index.shtml).

Smith, William, Walter R. Allen, and Lynette L. Danley. 2007. "Assume the Position . . . You Fit the Description: Psychosocial Experiences and Racial Battle Fatigue Among African American Male College Students." *American Behavioral Scientist* 51(4):551–78.

U.S. Census Bureau. 2010. "2008 American Community Survey 1-Year Estimates, Detailed Tables." Retrieved July 21, 2010 (http://factfinder.census.gov/servlet/DTGeoSearchByListServlet ?ds_name=ACS_2008_1YR_G00_&_lang=en&_ts=303827884148).

U.S. Immigration and Customs Enforcement. 2010. "Fact Sheet: Delegation of Immigration Authority Section 287(g) Immigration and Nationality Act." Washington, DC: Department of Homeland Security. Retrieved January 20, 2011 (http://www.ice.gov/news/library/factsheets/287g.htm).

U.S. Immigration and Customs Enforcement. N.d. "Memorandum of Agreement." Retrieved January 20, 2011 (http://www.ice.gov/doclib/foia/memorandumsofAgreementUnderstanding/r_287g harriscountyso111609.pdf).

Vega, William A., and Rubén G. Rumbaut. 1991. "Ethnic Minorities and Mental Health." *Annual Review of Sociology* 17:351–83.

Viruell-Fuentes, Edna A. 2007. "Beyond Acculturation: Immigration, Discrimination, and Health Research Among Mexicans in the United States." *Social Science & Medicine* 65:1524–35.

Waslin, Michele. 2010. "SB 1070-Inspired Activity Continues in the States." Washington, DC: Immigration Policy Center. Retrieved September 26, 2010 (http://immigrationimpact.com/2010/08/19/ sb1070-inspired-activity-continues-in-the-states).

9   IMMIGRATION AS LOCAL POLITICS

RE-BORDERING IMMIGRATION THROUGH DETERRENCE AND INCAPACITATION

Liette Gilbert

INTRODUCTION

One of the most aggressive challenges to national immigration policies has recently emerged from small town governments. The increasing settlement of migrants in suburbs, small towns, and rural communities that have had little exposure to social diversity has sparked an intense public debate about the impacts of immigration on local and national identity. Overwhelmed by the presence and service needs of (unauthorized) migrants,[1] and questioning federal ability to regulate national borders, local governments have increasingly felt pressured to control the presence and conduct of newcomers in their territories. In the US, more than 100 immigration-related municipal ordinances were introduced or considered in small towns, townships, and counties (in 31 different states) only a few months following the historical pro-immigration mobilizations in the streets of dozens of larger US cities in spring 2006 (see Cisneros, this volume).

This unprecedented level of local mobilization around immigration issues is inscribed in a larger and very polarized public debate between those who want a path to citizenship for the estimated 12 million "unauthorized" migrants living in the US and those who demand more border control and wish to deport all of those they see as being "illegally" in the country. At the onset of the debate, hard-line Republican proposals (such as HR 4437) sought to further criminalize undocumented migrants by increasing security and deportation measures. Other bi-partisan and comprehensive reform proposals, allegedly more "immigrant-friendly," were debated in the Senate and attempted to reconcile increased bor-

Liette Gilbert is associate professor at the Faculty of Environmental Studies at York University.

Reprinted with permission of John Wiley and Sons, from "Immigration as Local Politics: Re-Bordering Immigration and Multiculturalism Through Deterrence and Incapacitation," *International Journal of Urban and Regional Research* 33 (1): 26–42, by Liette Gilbert. Copyright © 2009 by John Wiley and Sons.

    1. The word "unauthorized" is preferred to "illegal" and is used interchangeably with "undocumented" to describe people in the US without any official immigration status. The word is sometimes used in parentheses because most of the ordinances and laws target "illegal" migrants but the consequences are not limited to this group alone.

der enforcement infrastructure, temporary guest worker programs (pushed by former President Bush) and paths to citizenship (i.e., legalized status) for undocumented migrants. After months of intense public and congressional debates, the prospect of any comprehensive immigration reform was abandoned, partly due to the nearing end of Bush's second term in office and the irreconcilable tensions between national security and the civil rights of migrants.

While municipal measures emulated the discourse of criminalization of immigration promoted by federal authorities, local proponents saw in the failed national reform additional arguments to legitimate their actions. Local governments argued that given the incapacity of the federal government to enforce immigration law and to control the US-Mexico border's (unauthorized) crossings, they had no other choice than to enact their own measures to protect the rights of local residents from the adverse effects of (unauthorized) immigration. In a matter of months, local elected officials became immigration policy entrepreneurs and "professional manager[s] of unease" (Bigo, 2002: 74). They legitimized their actions in the face of the inefficiencies of national governments in the control of their borders and local impacts of unwanted populations. In drafting municipal immigration-related ordinances, local officials sought to deter the presence of (unauthorized) migrants by discouraging some from settling in small towns or incapacitating others through fear, law enforcement, and registration programs so that they would relocate elsewhere. In entering the realm of immigration politics and border/internal security, which have previously been exclusively a federal domain, local leaders not only appealed to the larger anti-immigrant masses and conservative media elated by the promises of more fencing along the US-Mexico border, they also reaffirmed the construction of (unauthorized) migrants as security threats to both local and national identity.

This chapter argues that immigration-related municipal ordinances, resolutions, and declarations are some of the latest neoliberal strategies deployed in the governance of immigration, the delocalization of border control, and the re-bordering of state power (Nevins, 2002; Andreas, 2003; Coleman, 2005; Walters, 2006). Not only are these municipal ordinances and declarations re-bordering the inclusion/exclusion of (unauthorized) migrants by expanding the territorial and political rationality of immigration control to small towns, they are also imposing and dispersing new mechanisms of control into the everyday spaces and practices of those regarded as undesirable or ungovernable (Coleman, 2007). Municipal measures to control im/migrants are not only a constitutional challenge to the federal preemption in matters of immigration law (the ineptitude of which they purport to redress), they expand what Bigo (2002) called a "governmentality of unease," where migration is increasingly rationalized as a security problem—and which, in turn, legitimizes mechanisms of exclusion (see also Chacón, this volume). Using municipal measures, the local re-bordering of immigration politics is accomplished through the expansion and juxtaposition of disciplinary and control regimes where both criminality and undesirability intersect in the current climate of in/security and are unperturbedly linked to the decline of the social and the rise of neoliberal regimes of rule.

DISCIPLINING/CONTROLLING BORDERS/SOCIETIES

By merging criminalizing aspects of immigration law, legitimacy of local power and social control, and anti-"illegal" immigration rhetoric, immigration-related urban policy highlights the tensions between criminal justice and social control (Kanstroom, 2004; Legomsky, 2007; see also Stumpf, this volume), between border enforcement policies and municipal social "sorting" politics (Walters, 2006), and between federal pre-emption of immigration law and local governance and accountability (Bigo, 2002). Immigration-related municipal measures illustrate what Walters (2006: 191) describes as a "shift in the spatiality of power" of state borders from a Foucauldian interpretation of "disciplinary societies," where the form of governance instituted particular sites and technologies of confinement and punishment, to a Deleuzian paradigm of "control societies" formed by decentralized networks of monitoring and management of risk. In a dispersed regime of control, conduct is regulated through physical and social structures rather than disciplined by institutionalized compliance.

Municipal attempts to enforce immigration laws therefore expand border politics into the interior. Rose (1999: 236) argues that such a post-disciplinary logic of control "makes power more effective . . . less obtrusive—thus diminishing its political and moral fallout . . . [and] possibilities for resistance." Such control management strategies seek to act preemptively upon potentially problematic populations so as to reduce the risk of undesirable circumstances (Rose, 1999). Risk control and social management (or biopolitics) are therefore not solely enacted by the state but are rather dispersed to individuals, institutions, and communities, and by doing so give rise to new forms of control and cooperation between public and private networks (Bigo, 2002). Such social dispersion does not amount to the reduction of control but rather to "a widening of the net of control whose mesh simultaneously became finer and whose boundaries became more invisible as it spread to encompass smaller and smaller violations of the normative order" (Rose, 1999: 238). This regulatory net, or what Bigo (2002) aptly called the governmentality of unease, is maintained by various mechanisms of exclusion, which, in the particular case of local politics of immigration, attempt to keep im/migrants as outsiders inside the boundaries of a state/society.

Although immigration is clearly framed and characterized by a larger shift in the spatiality of power of state borders (to airports, consulates, transport carriers, employers, and computer systems, among many other places), immigration politics has juxtaposed disciplinary and control regimes (Walters, 2002). Immigration policy has long contained both disciplinary and control dimensions, blending criminal justice and social control. A disciplinary regime of detention and deportation continually looms over the vulnerability of (unauthorized) migrants as control is increasingly and intricately woven throughout administrative processes (for example, in the definition of immigration programs, categories, and selection criteria) and acts as deterrence and incapacitation outside and within national boundaries. The juxtaposition of disciplinary and control practices originated from the border itself.

In the mid-1990s, the development of an intense policing apparatus along the US-Mexico border secured the disciplinary and control powers of the state and sought to deter (unauthorized) crossings. A deterrence ideology was implemented through a series of gate-keeping operations deploying miles of fencing infrastructure, sophisticated surveillance and information technology, and additional personnel (Andreas, 2002; Nevins, 2002; Kil and Menjivar 2006; see also Heyman, this volume). This unprecedented level of border "impermeability" sought to secure control of the US-Mexico border. Preventive deterrence ideology was seen as more effective than the dominant policing mode of apprehension in appeasing official and public concern about the ability of the US government to prevent the so-called "illegal" immigration from Mexico. The result of this increased border enforcement enacted to deter migrants from entering the US was the displacement of crossings from urbanized areas to remote and perilous areas and a somber 4,000 crossing-related fatalities between 1994 and 2006 (Nevins, 2007; see also Doty, this volume). Yet, in the views of the border patrol authorities, the strengthening of border control efforts were deemed successful considering the overall (30%) decline of border apprehensions along the US southern border (Customs and Border Protection, 2007). Interestingly, deterrence as a control process is still measured by the disciplinary outcome of apprehensions. Unsurprisingly, deterrence as control and security risk management comes to legitimize the endless demand for wall technologies separating the US and Mexico.

Border deterrence assumes that increased border enforcement and stiffer penalties would dissuade migrants from entering "illegally" into the US (Legomsky, 2007). Such a view, however, underestimates the importance of transboundary migratory linkages and the appeal of employment opportunities in a socioeconomic context of globalized free trade agreements and growing instability and inequality within and between the US and Mexican economies. Deterrence does not stop at borders; it constantly follows migrants in their clandestinity through variable productions of fear, anxiety, and risk of incapacitation (such as in/voluntary removal). Yet, as unambiguous as deterrence can be in theory, its practices are even more unsettling. This is seen in the origins of the tensions on the US-Mexican border, which, paradoxically, date back to the 1960s' liberal reforms that dismantled the racist immigration quotas. Less acknowledged, though, is the fact that the legislation established an annual quota to restrict migration from the Western Hemisphere (which previously had never been quantitatively restricted) and had the severe effect of restricting "legal" migration from Mexico. The historical interplay between unlimited demands for Mexican labor and easy deportability (rendering Mexican labor distinctly disposable) in immigration law instituted the legal production of Mexican/migrant illegality (De Genova, this volume; Ngai, 2004). "Illegality" as an administrative process embedded in immigration law has therefore been historically managed to favor the US economy but it has grown increasingly uncontrollable and unjust as it imposes "legal nonexistence" on 12 million people being physically, socially, and economically active in civil society but lacking legal and political recognition (Coutin, 2000; 2005).

The failure to link (unauthorized) migration to a condition of globalization and labor needs/demands leads to the intensification of the criminalization of (unauthorized) immigrants, as seen in the 1980s and 1990s with a series of federal policies that created new immigrant-related crimes, increased penalties for existing crimes, and amplified prosecutions (Miller, 2003; Kanstroom, 2004; Legomsky, 2007). Under the Reagan administration, the 1986 Immigration Reform and Control Act sought to prohibit employers from hiring unauthorized workers and to criminalize workers for using false documents. However, employers' sanctions were rarely enforced. The 1990 Immigration Act starkly increased criminal fines for certain immigration-related crimes. Under the Clinton government, the 1996 Illegal Immigration Reform and Immigrant Responsibility Act created new federal crimes linked to false claims in application, squarely shifting criminality to migrants and (unauthorized) workers. In addition, the 1996 Antiterrorism and Effective Death Penalty Act enhanced the role of law enforcement by expanding the grounds for removal in the case of aggravated felony, which used to be limited to charges of murder, drugs, or firearms trafficking, and now has been extended to charges of bribery, perjury, and forgery (rendered almost inescapable by restrictive laws).

Since September 11, antiterrorism statutes enacted under the Bush government have been laden with immigration-related criminalizing provisions in the name of national security (see Chacón, this volume). There has been a proliferation of immigration-related criminal convictions and removals through the expansion of "deportability" in the 2001 PATRIOT Act. The numbers of individuals subjected to mandatory and discretionary preventive detention (pending criminal procedures) and indefinite detention on grounds of national security have significantly increased (Kanstroom, 2004). The Department of Homeland Security's discretionary power of detention on national grounds of security has been particularly controversial given the conflation of im/migrants and terrorists, and the racial and religious profiling of communities. The contentious 2005 Sensenbrenner's Border Protection, Antiterrorism, and Illegal Immigration Control Act (HR 4437) proposal (which triggered the massive pro-immigration street protests) would have pushed the coupling of discipline and control management to an unprecedented level by proposing preventive detention pending removal proceedings for anyone attempting illegal entry into the US. Furthermore, the proposal would have gone as far as considering being present in the US unlawfully or assisting undocumented migrants a felony, i.e., denying current constitutional rights to due process and expanding the net of immigration control to the whole society.

DETERRENCE AND INCAPACITATION AWAY FROM THE BORDER

The reconfiguration of immigration policy includes a number of actors operating at subnational scales. While the US Constitution grants the federal government the exclusive authority to regulate immigration, many states and municipal legislative proposals have challenged the Supremacy Clause precluding lower levels of government from taking action in immigration matters. There are longstanding tensions in the opposition of federal responsibility for immigration to state and local responsibilities to ensure the health, welfare, and safety of residents (Wells, 2004). Legislatures of states along the US-Mexico border were the first to denounce the additional expenses incurred for immigration-related services by filing lawsuits against the federal government. In the 1990s, the border states of Texas and California voted drastic measures to ban public education, public health care services, and other social services to undocumented migrants. Such measures, as in the case of the infamous California Proposition 187, were ultimately ruled unconstitutional by courts that reaffirmed the sole authority of the federal government in matters of immigration. Yet the 1996 package of welfare and immigration reform laws spurred state and local legislation to limit immigration-related services or limit the access by migrants to such services within their jurisdictions, and to establish compensation for migrants' exclusion from federal social services. This trend has continued to the point that, according to the US National Conference of State Legislatures (2007), 1,562 pieces of legislation were proposed in 2007 in relation to education, employment, identification (driver's license), law enforcement, public benefits, trafficking, legal assistance, and voting reform—244 of them became law in 46 different states. It is in this dynamic legislative context of immigration reform that municipal ordinances also developed.

According to a FIRM (Fair Immigration Reform Movement) (2007) database, 135 local governments have introduced or have considered anti-immigration measures to regulate the presence of (unauthorized) migrants since spring 2006. Although the status of these immigration ordinances has fluctuated greatly as local governments have attentively monitored the many pending constitutional and legal disputes (FIRM, 2007), most of them draw from an omnibus ordinance prepared by Joseph Turner of Save Our State, a grassroots "anti-illegal" organization named after the controversial California Proposition 187. Turner's initiative marked the first attempt to use the municipal government powers to mitigate the impacts of (unauthorized) immigration. Turner (2006) initially prepared his "anti-illegal" immigration initiative for San Bernardino, California, and "wanted to provide a template for local elected officials to demonstrate the ability of local governments to mitigate the harmful impacts of illegal immigration" (Menlo Park City Council, 2006). His particular measure for the city of San Bernardino focused on day laborers and prohibited the funding of hiring centers using taxpayer money. Turner's proposed ordinance also made it illegal to rent housing to undocumented migrants, denied business permits and licenses to businesses that aid and abet undocumented migrants, and instituted an English-only policy. His "Illegal Immigration Relief Act" was rejected by the San Bernardino city council in May 2006 and was disqualified from a special election ballot for lack of sufficient signatures. Yet Turner's initiative was soon replicated by many towns across the US.

Variations of Turner's failed "Illegal Immigration Relief Act" were developed by 50 different local governments—almost half of them located in eastern Pennsylvania (FIRM, 2007). Other ordinances focused exclusively on (unauthorized) workers. Specific employment ordinances (presented in 34 municipalities) sought to prevent the hiring of (unauthorized) migrants by businesses, homeowners, and city agencies (*ibid.*). They would also deny licenses to businesses that knowingly hire unauthorized migrants or would require employers to submit affidavits saying that they do not employ undocumented workers—even though such provisions are already contained in federal law (US Code, title 8, section 1324a) and in the 1986 Immigration Reform and Control Act (IRCA), which established an employment eligibility verification process and increased sanctions program for worksite enforcement (see Bacon and Hing, this volume). Some local ordinances went beyond federal provisions by establishing a municipal registration program for day laborers. Local ordinances also problematically extended employment control measures from the work to the housing spheres. Fourteen local governments came up with housing ordinances that would require landlords to verify immigration status of potential tenants (and, in some cases, to make such information available to health officials and police) or face penalties ranging from $1,000 per day to $1,000 per tenant or up to 6 months' imprisonment (*ibid.*). Some housing ordinances also sought to regulate the maximum occupancy of bedrooms and single dwellings or to adopt a legal definition of family limited to the nuclear family. An additional 15 local governments proposed ordinances combining both provisions to bar undocumented migrants from renting and working (*ibid.*). Another type of ordinance, passed in combination with housing and/or employment or separately, sought to make English the official or only language of a town/city. Language ordinances were developed in 16 municipalities (*ibid.*). Finally, six municipal ordinances sought to authorize local police officers to enforce immigration laws by verifying the immigration status of people suspected of crimes (*ibid.*). Under the Department of Homeland Security, such collaboration is already in place between Immigration and Customs Enforcement (ICE) and local and state agencies, notably in correctional services.

Municipal governments seized the dispersed logic of control to legitimate socio-spatial exclusion. From suspicion to denial of access to public benefits and social services (entitled under federal laws), the rationale of local deterrence measures purport to incapacitate the unwanted residents. Incapacitation is not used here in its strict disciplinary and penal imprisonment sense but rather in a managerial sense that draws on social, spatial, and structural exclusion mechanisms. In considering incapacitation as "isolation of the undesirable offender from society" (Legomsky, 2007: 514), incapacitation of im/migrants penetrates the everyday life and places of (unauthorized) residents (e.g., workplaces, homes, neighborhoods, streets, etc.), depriving them of the ability to participate in a regular life by imposing additional control and regulation on their presence and mobilities. As a result, (unauthorized) migrants and their families, particularly Latinos/as, have retreated from community and public life to avoid being detected and deported. They have avoided shopping in "ethnic" stores and participating in school meetings. They have altered their driving routes to avoid arrests, fees, and deportations, and have devised emergency family plans in case of one member not returning from work. They have closed their businesses and relocated to larger cities in search of relative anonymity. In this sense, incapacitation defined by Gilmore (2007: 24) as a "geographical solution," which purports to solve social problems by dislocating people, extends from the border itself and, as at the border, local deterrence and incapacitation displace and deepen problems rather than solve them. Moreover, this incapacitation strategy is entirely consistent with a control mode of power that seeks to diffuse the visibility of a problem by managing risk and legitimizing a neoliberal discourse "stressing the need for individuals and communities to take more responsibility for their own security" while a migrant is "made to accept his or her moral culpability" (Rose, 1999: 239).

Asserting a discourse of self-reliance and self-management (Raco and Imrie, 2000), municipal immigration politics expresses distrust of traditional, large, and inefficient state institutions, and celebrates market freedoms, individual liberty, self-responsibility, and local accountability. Entrenched in a moralistic distinction between "legal" and "illegal," earned and unearned citizenship, deserving and nondeserving residents, local governments (under the neoliberal and egregiously oversimplified credo "illegal is illegal") see themselves as protectors of local and national culture, responsible for risk management, and enablers of law and order. Drawing from Weber's (1947) classical sociological theory of state and bureaucracy, local governments legitimized their authority by using their political power to confront federal regulation, their traditional police power to construct migrants and their practices as public nuisance, and their charismatic power by capitalizing on a climate of national insecurity. The following section examines a specific case of "governmentality of unease" where the local government expresses its local control over im/migrants through a mix of practices of incapacitation and deterrence and, by doing so, imposes its "definition of who and what inspires fears" (Bigo, 2005: 12).

LOCAL POLITICS OF INCAPACITATION AND DETERRENCE: HAZLETON, PENNSYLVANIA

The most scrutinized and comprehensive local immigration ordinance was drafted by Hazleton, Pennsylvania. The city, self-described as the toughest city on "illegal" immigration, approved an Illegal Immigration Relief Act (IIRA) Ordinance composed of two main provisions: making unlawful the hiring and the harboring of undocumented migrants (City of Hazleton, 2006a). Hazleton officials created a related ordinance establishing a tenant registration program, requiring dwellers to obtain an occupancy permit by proving their legal status in the country (City of Hazleton, 2006c). They also put forward an English-only ordinance (City of Hazleton, 2006b). Hazleton's council initially adopted its IIRA Ordinance and its Tenant Registration Ordinance in July 2006. Less than a month later, a legal action led by local Latino residents and organizations challenged the validity of the ordinances, and a court order temporarily restrained Hazleton from enforcing the ordinances. The dispute was brought to court in March 2007 and Hazleton's IIRA and Tenant Registration Ordinances were ruled unconstitutional by a federal judge in July 2007. In a verdict long awaited by other small towns considering Hazleton-like legislation, the US District Court concluded that the City of Hazleton did not have the authority to enact ordinances that regulate the presence and employment of undocumented migrants.

Hazleton's ordinances were based first and foremost on the perceived negative impacts of (unauthorized) immigration on their territories. Directly drawing from Turner's original omnibus initiative, Hazleton's anti-"illegal" Immigration Relief Act contends "that illegal immigration leads to higher crime rates, subjects our hospitals to fiscal hardship and legal residents to substandard quality of care, contributes to other burdens on public services, increasing their cost and diminishing their availability to legal residents, and diminishes our overall quality of life" (City of Hazleton, 2006a: 2.C). When repeatedly asked to provide data, the mayor of Hazleton, Lou Barletta, stated he did not (have or) need data to prove such negative impacts.[2] In doing so, he was asserting his traditional authority

---

2. Hazleton's main argument for the need for an immigration law was that undocumented migrants were committing crimes and costing a lot of money in social services. Mayor Barletta has repeatedly cited the shooting of 29-year-old Derek Kichline as the impetus for his ordinances, but, in July 2007, prosecutors dropped homicide charges against the two undocumented migrants, who are to remain jailed until their deportation to the Dominican Republic (Associated Press, 2007).

while also defending a commonsense perspective "disguising real problems under cultural prejudices" (Harvey, 2005: 39).

Negative consequences of immigration were cunningly linked to the municipality's responsibility to curb such impacts insofar as it "is authorized to abate public nuisances and empowered and mandated by [its] people ... to abate the nuisance of illegal immigration by diligently prohibiting the acts and policies to facilitate illegal immigration in a manner consistent with federal law and the objectives of Congress" (City of Hazleton, 2006a: 2.D). While public nuisance is indeed within the realm of municipal responsibility to regulate public health, safety, and welfare under the authority of police power (Talmadge, 2000), the presumption of "illegal" immigration as public nuisance creates a tension between local police powers and federal preemption. In ruling that Hazleton's IIRA and Tenant Registration Ordinances were in violation of federal law and due process protections, Judge James Munley (2007: 185) estimated that there was no need to establish the validity of police powers since the unconstitutionality of the ordinances represented in itself a violation of police power. Munley (*ibid.*) further indicated that the local police power delegated by the state to a municipality should be used to promote public health, safety, and general welfare and must not invade the fundamental liberties of citizens. In his ruling's conclusion, Munley (*ibid.*: 188–89) unravels any tension between local and federal powers:

> Whatever the frustrations officials of the City of Hazleton may feel about the current state of federal immigration enforcement, the nature of the political system in the United States prohibits the City from enacting ordinances that disrupt a carefully drawn federal statutory scheme. ... Hazleton, in its zeal *to control the presence of a group deemed undesirable*, violated the rights of such people, as well as others within the community [emphasis added].

In recognizing unauthorized migrants as persons to which due process of law is guaranteed, the court rejected the authority of Hazleton's ordinances to protect the quality of life of certain residents by excluding others. Hazleton had argued for the "right [of existing, i.e., 'lawful' residents] to live in peace free of the threat of crime, to enjoy public services provided by this city without being burdened by the cost of providing goods, support and services to aliens [sic] unlawfully present in the United States" (City of Hazleton, 2006a: 2.F). Local governments solemnly believe that they would not have an immigration problem on their hands if the federal government would enforce their laws in the first place and prevent unauthorized migrants from entering the country, but Munley (2007) made very clear that Hazleton's ordinances could not reassert the rights of particular residents over the rights of others. This particular point of Munley's ruling might be the most contentious because local governments probably never presumed violating any person's civil rights, since they considered undocumented migrants as "illegal" citizens in the first place. Hence, local ordinances presumed that "criminality" justified undesirability.

Witnessing demographic and material transformations of their community, Hazleton's officials saw undocumented migrants as bringing unwanted changes, disturbing the "idyllic life of America," and perturbing Hazleton's "quality of life" (Barletta quoted in Ludden, 2007). Hazleton's Mayor Barletta repetitively insisted that his ordinance was indeed designed to drive the undocumented population from his town. Commenting on the exodus of Latinos, despite an early federal court block preventing the law from taking effect, Barletta states: "I don't want them here, period. . . . We have literally seen people loading mattresses and furniture and leaving the city en masse. . . . That was our goal, to have a city of legal immigrants who are all paying taxes" (quoted in Barry, 2006). Such a statement clearly demonstrates that the ordinances acted as mechanisms to deter and incapacitate unauthorized migrants in Hazleton, justified, in the officials' view, by a defense of place sentiment attempting to preserve Hazleton and, by extension, the US as it is/was (or perceived to be by local leaders). For many supporters of local immigration legislation, undocumented immigration represents nothing short of a threat to their local/national identity, culture, and security.

This exclusionary discourse led pro-immigration groups and supporters, and notably the American Civil Liberties Union, who filed the initial legal challenges, to argue that municipal ordinances encourage or even require people to discriminate against undocumented migrants, particularly Latinos. Ordinances were specifically seen as encouraging racial profiling of darker skins and foreign accents and generating a climate of fear and suspicion. Opponents to the ordinances contended that a housing registration program, as proposed in Hazleton, would force migrants to go away or underground, and/or rely on false documentation. In his final court ruling, Munley (2007) rejected the allegations of discrimination based on race, ethnicity, or national origin and the argument that Hazleton's ordinance violated the procedural protections required under the Uniform Residential Landlord and Tenant Act of 1972.

Despite the dismissed argument of discrimination, civil liberties organizations and pro-immigration advocates hailed the Hazleton ruling as a victory for Latino residents and civil and immigrant right activists. The ruling established a national precedent and sent a resounding warning to other local governments and anti-illegal immigration proponents who had been waiting for a legal decision on the constitutionality of local anti-immigration measures. However, the Munley verdict did not dissuade Hazleton's Mayor Barletta, who has publicly vowed to appeal the Pennsylvania District Court ruling and to defend his ordinances all the way to the Supreme Court if necessary. Barletta maintains:

> This fight is far from over. I have said it many times before: Hazleton is not going to back down. We are discouraged to see a federal judge has decided—wrongly, we believe—that Hazleton and cities like it around the nation cannot enact legislation to protect their citizens, their services, and their budgets [quoted in Fears, 2007].

Immigration ordinances do not come cheaply for small local governments with limited resources. Hazleton has spent $100,000 on early legal battles and has established a legal defense fund for the proposed appeal of Munley's ruling to the Supreme Court. To enable his crusade, Barletta has already gathered $300,000 through the Small Town Defenders' website (2006) appealing to the solidarity of "thousands of small towns and cities across America like Hazleton." Barletta's success and popularity shows that the unconstitutional ruling of Hazleton's ordinances did not hinder the frustrations of anti-immigration proponents blaming (unauthorized) migrants for all the social ills diminishing their local quality of life. To the contrary, attempting to control immigration at the local level provided a supportive climate for municipal immigration policy entrepreneurs defending the local impacts of what they perceived as excesses of "openness and tolerance" (Small Town Defenders, 2006).

Local immigration ordinances were drafted and pushed by individuals with strong immigration views and backing by conservative politicians or constituencies. In the US, some local politicians appealing to populist and Republican values have attracted the support of neoconservative anti-immigration organizations such as FAIR (the Federation for American Immigration Reform) and local Minutemen groups (see Chavez, this volume). In a matter of months, leaders such as nonelected Joseph Turner and Mayor Lou Barletta, among many others, have become local and national celebrities of the anti-"illegal" immigration movement, conservative media, and neoconservative Internet blogs. They have used their political and charismatic authority to propel their anti-("illegal") immigration opinions and to secure public support for their causes—and, in response, local politicians have kept emphasizing the incontestable accountability to their constituents. This is clearly expressed in the words of Mayor Barletta when he maintained, "I am doing this for the citizens of Hazleton. I took an oath to protect them and that's what we're doing" (quoted in Reynolds, 2006). The sense of representivity often spread quite widely, as in the case of non-elected Turner, who claims to speak for the whole country: "Americans are tired of pressing one for English. They're tired of feeling like foreigners in their own country. And they're tired of watching their communities turn into third world cesspools, period" (KCET, 2006). Local immigration policy entrepreneurs hold high ambitions for their convictions and immigration ordinances. Hazleton's mayor Barletta admits being "very proud of the immigration law and predicts someday it will become America's law" (quoted in Reynolds, 2006).

Local politicians sought to legitimize their unease toward (unauthorized) immigration by capitalizing on accountability, law and order, and distrust of large and inefficient state institutions. In that sense, local immigration measures did not only present a constitutional challenge to federal law, they also constructed a locally grounded discourse of illegality and undesirability based on fears and insecurities—which, in turn, authorized local laws and technologies of exclusion deterring and/or incapacitating (unauthorized) migrants. In arguing that "some people have taken advantage of America's openness and tolerance" (Small Town Defenders, 2006), local governments in the US extended illegality and criminality constructed by border enforcement to a larger problem of undesirability and ungovernability of migrants.

CONCLUSION: "ILLEGAL" IS *NOT* ILLEGAL

In entering the realm of immigration politics, which had previously been exclusively a federal domain, local governments have taken a wide range of measures designed to deter and incapacitate (unauthorized) migrants from settling within national borders. Municipal ordinances in the US reiterated some of the most punitive federal statutes, while also attempting to implement even more control over the lives of (unauthorized) migrants through housing and employment registration programs. In his July ruling on Hazleton's ordinances, Judge James Munley (2007: 130) made clear that municipal "ordinances burden aliens [sic] more than federal law by prohibiting them from residing in the city although they may be permitted to remain in the United States." In addition to being in conflict with federal law and preemptive, municipal measures "seem to associate Latino political activity with illegality" and thus have created "a climate of fear which causes people to avoid association with groups that express interest in the rights of immigrants and Latinos" (*ibid.*: 25). In their ordinances and numerous public appearances, small town defenders have made eminently clear that illegality warrants undesirability.

While the federal level has sought to reassert its power over immigration, pro-immigration protests and anti-immigration ordinances underscore the fact that political debate about immigration is also embedded in towns, cities, and regions (Ellis, 2005). Pro- and anti-immigration proponents have both, in very different ways, highlighted the same tension between federal control over the regulation of immigration and residency, and the devolution of welfare responsibilities to states and cities. While the neoliberal devolution of immigration and integration responsibilities and expenses have indeed been problematically shifted to many localities, it remains, however, that localities have had very different ways of expressing their frustrations. For some, the fiscal challenge of immigration has presented a way to express their discomfort about the increasing presence of newcomers in their social and physical landscapes. Local immigration measures have been used to legitimize the political authority of some elected officials to control the presence and mobility of im/migrants and to protect their local quality of life against demographic, political, and cultural change. In the borderless field of in/security, some local politicians (and not others) have seized the interpretation of immigration as a security problem to express their own fears about losing symbolic control over their territorial boundaries. These fears have also found resonance with local conservative constituencies, national media, vigilante groups patrolling the border areas, and the larger security agenda (Bigo, 2002). In reproducing the discourse of in/security, local politicians have, through immigration ordinances, presented themselves as accountable and dedicated managers of law and order and quality of life. Contrary to what local leaders would like the larger public to believe, "illegal" is not illegal. "Illegal" in the sense of "unauthorized" simply and quite conveniently obfuscates hegemonic domination, economic dependence, and civil rights in immigration policy. The most alarming aspects of anti-immigration municipal measures are that they seek to authorize the legitimacy of socio-spatial exclusion, the denial of racism, and the erosion of civil rights—in the name of a governmentality of unease (*ibid.*).

WORKS CITED

Andreas, P. (2002) *Border games: policing the US-Mexico divide.* Cornell University Press, Ithaca.

Andreas, P. (2003) A tale of two borders. In P. Andreas and T. J. Biersteker (eds.), *The rebordering of North America.* Routledge, New York.

Associated Press (2007) Hazleton immigrants' charges failed. *Los Angeles Times* 7 July. URL http://www.latimes.com (accessed 7 July 2007).

Barry, E. (2006) Two communities are sued over strict immigration laws. *Los Angeles Times* 16 August. URL http://www.boston.com (accessed 7 June 2007).

Bigo, D. (2002) Security and immigration: toward a critique of the governmentality of unease. *Alternatives* 27 February, 63–92.

Bigo, D. (2005) Globalized (in)security: the field and the ban-opticon. *Traces: A Multilingual Series of Cultural Theory* 4, 1–33 [WWW document]. URL http://www.wmin.ac.uk/sshl/pdf/CSDBigo 170106.pdf (accessed 16 December 2006).

City of Hazleton (2006a) Ordinance 2006–18 Illegal Immigration Relief Act Ordinance. URL http://www.hazletoncity.org (accessed 7 July 2007).

City of Hazleton (2006b) Ordinance 2006–19 Official English Ordinance. URL http://www.hazleton city.org (accessed 7 July 2007).

City of Hazleton (2006c) Ordinance 2006–13 Landlord Tenant Ordinance. URL http://www.hazleton city.org (accessed 7 July 2007).

Coleman, M. (2005) US statecraft and the US-Mexico border as security/economy nexus. *Political Geography* 24.2, 185–209.

Coleman, M. (2007) Immigration geopolitics beyond the Mexico-US border. *Antipode* 95.1, 54–76.

Coutin, S.B. (2005) Contesting criminality: illegal immigration and the spatialization of legality. *Theoretical Criminology* 9.10, 5–33.

Coutin, S.B. (2000) *Legalizing moves: Salvadoran immigrants' struggle for U.S. residency.* University of Michigan Press, Ann Arbor.

Customs and Border Protection (2007) Apprehensions down 30 percent along southern border, 7 December [WWW document]. URL http://www.cbp.gov (accessed 18 June 2008).

Ellis, M. (2005) Unsettling immigrant geographies: US immigration and the politics of scale. *Tijdschrift voor Economische en Social Geografie* 97.1, 49–58.

Fears, D. (2007) Judge blocks city's ordinances against illegal immigration. *Washington Post*, 27 July. URL http://www.washingtonpost.com (accessed 16 December 2007).

FIRM—Fair Immigration Reform Movement (2007) Database of recent local ordinances on immigration. Updated 16 January 2007. URL http://www.fairimmigration.org (accessed 20 July 2007).

Gilmore, R.W. (2007) *Golden gulag: prisons, surplus, crisis and opposition in globalizing California.* University of California Press, Berkeley, CA.

Harvey, D. (2005) *A brief history of neoliberalism.* Oxford University Press, Oxford.

Kanstroom, D. (2004) Criminalizing the undocumented: ironic boundaries of the post-September 11th "Pale of Law." *North Carolina Journal of International Law and Commercial Regulation* 29.4, 639–70.

KCET (2006) Life and times transcript, 18 May [WWW document]. URL http://www.kcet.org (accessed 7 June 2007).

Kil, S.H. and C. Menjivar (2006) The "war on the border": criminalizing immigrants and militarizing the US-Mexico border. In R. Martinez Jr. and A. Valenzuela Jr. (eds.), *Immigration and crime*, New York University Press, New York.

Legomsky, S.H. (2007) The new path of immigration law: asymmetric incorporation of criminal justice norms. *Washington and Lee Law Review* 64.2, 493–530.

Ludden, J. (2007) Hazleton's anti-illegal immigrants law challenged. NPR All Things Considered, 12 March [WWW document]. URL http://www.npr.org (accessed 7 June 2007).

Menlo Park City Council (2006) Menlo Park City Council email log, 6 July [WWW document]. URL http://ccin.menlopark.org (accessed 10 April 2006).

Miller, T.A. (2003) Citizenship and severity: recent immigration reforms and the new penology. *Georgetown Immigration Law Journal* 17.4, 611–66.

Munley, J. (2007) *Lozano vs. City of Hazleton*. United States District Court for the Middle District of Pennsylvania, No. 3:06cv1586, 26 July.

National Conference of State Legislatures (2007) 2007 enacted state legislation related to immigrants and immigration, 29 November. URL http://www.ncsl.org/programs/immig/2007immigration final.htm (accessed 16 December).

Nevins, J. (2002) *Operation gatekeeper: the rise of the "illegal alien" and the making of the US-Mexico boundary*. Routledge, New York.

Nevins, J. (2007) Dying for a cup of coffee? Migrant deaths in the US-Mexico border region in a neoliberal age. *Geopolitics* 12.2, 228–47.

Ngai, M.M. (2004) *Impossible subjects: illegal aliens and the making of modern America*. Princeton University Press, Princeton, NJ.

Raco, M. and R. Imrie (2000) Governmentality and rights and responsibilities in urban policy. *Environment and Planning A* 32.12, 2187–204.

Reynolds, B. (2006) Barletta signs immigration law, 14 July. URL http://www.wned.com (accessed 20 March 2007).

Rose, N. (1999) *Powers of freedom: reframing political thought*. Cambridge University Press, Cambridge.

Small Town Defenders (2006) Homepage: welcome to Small Town Defenders! [WWW document]. URL http://www.smalltoendefenders.com/public (accessed 16 December 2007).

Talmadge, P.A. (2000) The myth of property absolutism and modern government: the interaction of the police power and property rights. *Washington Law Review* 75.3, 857–909.

Turner, J. (2006) City of San Bernardino Illegal Immigration Relief Act Ordinance. URL http://www.campaignsitebuilder.com (accessed 10 April 2007).

Walters, W. (2002) Deportation, expulsion, and the international police of aliens. *Citizenship Studies* 6.3, 265–92.

Walters, W. (2006) Border/control. *European Journal of Social Theory* 9.2, 187–203.

Weber, M. (1947) *Theory of Social and Economic Organization*. Free Press, New York.

Wells, M.J. (2004) The grassroots reconfiguration of US immigration policy. *International Migration Review* 38.4, 1308–47.

IV DETENTION AND DEPORTATION

This part of the book focuses on detention and deportation. Ultimately, today's stepped-up immigration enforcement climate, both at the border and in the interior, has resulted in the massive detention, incarceration, and deportation of immigrants. A stated goal of the Department of Homeland Security (DHS) has been to remove all removable "aliens" from the nation. Although this objective is highly unrealistic because the federal government simply cannot arrest and remove all 10.8 million undocumented migrants estimated to be residing in the United States, the number of deportations has gone up significantly in the post-9/11 period, part of a steep upward trend that began in the 1990s. To facilitate this deportation drive, the DHS has developed a vast complex of carceral spaces in which to detain immigrants pending their removal from the United States. The growth of the carceral complex has been such that DHS's Immigration and Customs Enforcement (ICE) now runs the largest detention operation in the nation. The United States has thus been turned not only into a fortified enclave in its zeal to police immigration, but also into a space of confinement and expulsion.

The authors in this section highlight the impact of detention and deportation practices on the Latino community. Chapter 10, by David Manuel Hernández, provides a genealogy of Latino detention. Hernández suggests that although immigrant detention may have gained notoriety in the post-9/11 period as a result of its widespread use, the practice has long been deployed to manage Latinos. Between World Wars I and II, for example, fears about diseased Mexican bodies entering the United States prompted governmental authorities to institute medical detention and quarantine along the U.S.-Mexico border; and in the 1980s, Central American refugees fleeing political upheaval and violence were detained, often in overcrowded conditions, until the final adjudication of their asylum cases. Today, "criminal aliens"—noncitizens detained for having been convicted of deportable offenses—constitute the largest share of all immigrants in custody. This current wave of detention, which has disproportionately affected Latinos, stems from increased policing, the reclassification and expansion of deportable crimes, and the reduction of avenues for relief from detention. Ultimately, Hernández demonstrates that the detention of Latinos is not simply a contemporary affair, but a recurring phenomenon. Indeed, he shows that Latinos have long suffered the consequences of immigrant detention, a suffering that has only worsened in the post-9/11 context.

The next two chapters deal with what is generally the inevitable outcome of detention: deportation. Specifically, they focus on two Latino groups that have been highly impacted by contemporary removal practices: Mexicans and Salvadorans. Chapter 11, by Deborah A. Boehm, reflects on the deportation of Mexican nationals, concentrating on migrants from a small rural community in the northern Mexican state of San Luis Potosí that has links to several locations in the U.S. West and Southwest. Specifically, Boehm traces the imagined futures of deportees. Although the U.S. government deports Mexican migrants with a sense of finality, the deportees themselves are less certain as to what the future holds, whether it is staying "home" or returning to the United States. A common refrain among Mexican deportees is "¿Quien sabe?" (Who knows?). This refrain captures the sense that many aspects of transnational migration are driven by broader forces (or simply cannot be controlled) and thus that there is really no definiteness to a migrant's deportation to Mexico. Due to global economic crisis, agricultural hardship in rural communities, and increasing violence throughout country, it seems that staying home is not really an option for many deportees. Their future prospects thus more than likely lie in continued migration.

Chapter 12, by Susan Bibler Coutin, focuses on the deportation of "criminal aliens"—specifically former gang members—to El Salvador. She notes that in the United States deportation has emerged as an ostensibly benign technique for ridding the social body of seemingly problematic noncitizens. However, Coutin argues that this technique is far from benign. Deportation is actually a violent practice that wreaks havoc on individuals, families, and communities. For example, removal legally strips individuals of their membership (that is, legal residency) in the United States. They are then shipped back to El Salvador, where they are citizens by law but where, as long-term émigrés convicted of crimes, many lack social connections and clearly recognized legal rights, and are often stigmatized as criminals. The result is that noncitizens who have been found guilty of crimes face a transnational ban of sorts in that they are not really allowed to exist anywhere. Having been deported from the United States, they are not welcome back; and in El Salvador they are generally regarded with contempt—by government officials, the police, and the general public—and routinely subjected to violence. Deportees' lives, Coutin concludes, have thus been rendered inviable as it is almost impossible to carry on a normal existence.

SUGGESTIONS FOR FURTHER READING

Bosworth, Mary, and Emma Kaufman. 2011. "Foreigners in a Carceral Age: Immigration and Imprisonment in the U.S." *Stanford Law and Policy Review* 22 (1): 101–126.

Camacho, Alicia Schmidt. 2010. "Hailing the Twelve Million: U.S. Immigration Policy, Deportation, and the Imaginary of Lawful Violence." *Social Text* 28 (4): 1–24.

Chacón, Jennifer M. 2007. "Unsecured Borders: Immigration Restrictions, Crime Control, and National Security." *Connecticut Law Review* 39 (5): 1827–1891.

Coleman, Mathew, and Austin Kocher. 2011. "Detention, Deportation, Devolution, and Immigrant Incapacitation in the U.S., Post 9/11." *Geographical Journal* 177 (3): 228–237.

Coutin, Susan Bibler. 2010. "Confined Within: National Territories as Zones of Confinement." *Political Geography* 29 (4): 200–208.

De Genova, Nicholas, and Nathalie Peutz, eds. 2010. *The Deportation Regime: Sovereignty, Space, and the Freedom of Movement*. Durham, NC: Duke University Press.

Golash-Boza, Tanya Maria. 2012. *Immigration Nation: Raids, Detentions, and Deportations in Post-9/11 America*. Boulder, CO: Paradigm.

Hagan, Jacqueline, Brianna Castro, and Nestor Rodriguez. 2010. "The Effects of U.S. Deportation Policies on Immigrant Families and Communities: Cross-Border Perspectives." *North Carolina Law Review* 88: 1799–1823.

Kanstroom, Daniel. 2007. *Deportation Nation: Outsiders in American History*. Cambridge, MA: Harvard University Press.

Martin, Lauren L. 2012. "'Catch and Remove': Detention, Deterrence, and Discipline in U.S. Noncitizen Family Detention Practice." *Geopolitics* 17 (2): 312–334.

Welch, Michael. 2004. "Quiet Construction in the War on Terror: Subjecting Asylum Seekers to Unnecessary Detention." *Social Justice* 31 (1–2): 113–129.

Zilberg, Elana. 2011. *Space of Detention: The Making of a Transnational Gang Crisis Between Los Angeles and San Salvador*. Durham, NC: Duke University Press.

PURSUANT TO DEPORTATION

LATINOS AND IMMIGRANT DETENTION

David Manuel Hernández

This chapter explores the contemporary terrain of Latino immigrant detention outside of the shadow cast by the events of September 11, 2001, and within the context of a larger genealogy of Latino detention. Although one of the most distinctive features of the post-9/11 era is the continual avowal of its inimitability, immigrant detention in the US is a long and continuing story, which, when understood historically and comparatively, more properly contextualizes the alarming trends in immigrant detention today. In so doing, it allows us to move beyond the exceptionalist rhetoric found in the government's construction of the "war on terror" to a clearer understanding of what the *New York Times* termed the "fastest-growing form of incarceration" (Berestein, 2007, A1). Further, this chapter seeks to explore the racialized features of immigrant detention, in particular its long-term effects on Latino noncitizens and citizens, who prior to 9/11 suffered the consequences of immigrant detention as it expanded throughout the last century. Immigrant detention, as a process related to the deportation of noncitizens, is thus part of a larger history of federal, local, and individual practices that criminalize immigrants, especially nonwhite immigrants. The incarceration of noncitizens is thus related to their surveillance, punishment, and overall inequality in the areas of labor, education, public health, political representation, and everyday mobility.

Although the histories of Latinos in detention differ in many respects from the experiences of the racially targeted group of Arabs, Muslims, and South Asians who were detained immediately after 9/11, critical features of their collective detentions such as racial profiling, legal vulnerabilities stemming from their immigrant status, deplorable and punitive detention conditions, and an unchecked detention authority, reveal commonalities and long-term patterns in detention history. Further, the legal and institutional changes resulting from the "war on terror" have a scope that reaches all noncitizens in the US, undocumented and documented, and will expand the detention infrastructure for the foreseeable future. 9/11

David Manuel Hernández is assistant professor of Latina/o Studies at Mount Holyoke College.

has inspired new and old forms of enforcement that target immigrants comprehensively, well beyond the "war on terror." As Kevin Johnson argues, "Although Arab and Muslim noncitizens felt the brunt of the civil rights deprivations in the immediate aftermath of September 11, *immigrants in general* will suffer the long-term consequences of the many measures taken by the federal government in the name of fighting terrorism" (2003, 849–850, emphasis added). The contemporary expansion of immigrant detention, a key enforcement initiative, especially in the context of national security crises, should be understood within the complex genealogy of noncitizen detention. Latino experiences with immigrant detention, in particular, pose a unique history, one that is complex, recurring, and escalating today.

EXCEPTIONALISM AND THE WAR ON IMMIGRANTS

One of the greatest challenges to the examination of immigrant detention has been the widespread exceptionalism that surrounds 9/11. It became commonplace after 9/11, and as the major tenets of the "war on terror" were formulated, to read or hear proclamations from various segments of society that "everything had changed" and that this was a time of crisis without precedent. Then Attorney General John Ashcroft announced, for example, "On September 11, the wheel of history turned and the world will never be the same" (2001). Similarly, President Bush told the nation, "We have entered a new era, and this new era requires new responsibilities, both for government and for our people" (2001). The post-9/11 construction of "homeland security," which enveloped and expanded the federal authority to detain noncitizens, also necessitated legislative and policy changes, produced new judicial rulings, and triggered changes in governmental bureaucracies designed to meet the challenges of President Bush's "new era." On the surface, many aspects of immigrant detention indeed appeared to be new and catalyzed by 9/11.

While the pace and scope of these changes, like the ensuing debate, drew attention to US immigrant detention practices, such an awareness was long overdue. Prior to 9/11, legal professionals and immigrant advocates engaged with and provided services to detainees and confronted the large-scale expansion of the detention infrastructure, especially the rapid growth in detention mandated by antiterrorist and immigration legislation which passed in 1996 (see Chacón, this volume). Yet the critical work of this focused group of immigrant advocates was often overshadowed by anti-prison activists and scholars, confronting the mammoth incarceration of over two million persons within the US "prison industrial complex." Moreover, the issue of immigrant detention, often invisible as a transitional space between apprehension and deportation, was also marginalized by the major foci of the national immigration debate: expanding or restricting "legal" immigration, border militarization, undocumented immigration, labor competition, amnesty, etc. As a result, as much as the post-9/11 anti-terror initiatives initiated a "new" awareness of immigrant detainees, the larger history of immigrant detention was burdened with the exceptionalist shadow of 9/11. Any historical perspective about US detention practices and detainees themselves—who in the fall of 2001 were considered "suspected terrorists"—was overwhelmed by fear and sensationalism, as well as by institutionalized and popular hostility and violence. Although detention as a means of effecting racial expulsions has been a cornerstone in US immigration policy and history, what the public did learn about noncitizen detention dealt specifically with the detention of a racially conflated group of Arabs, Muslims, and South Asians, who bore the initial brunt of new anti-terrorist programs and institutions.

Whereas widespread knowledge of US detention practices seems to have begun on 9/11 and would later, after the invasions of Afghanistan and Iraq, be disproportionately represented by grisly photos and unsettling narrative accounts from Abu-Ghraib prison in Iraq and Guantánamo Bay Naval Base in Cuba, the stigma of criminal foreignness and "illegality," and what I term the "undue processes" (Hernández, 2005) of detention and deportation, are facets of immigration policy with which many immigrant communities, in particular Latino communities, have been intimately acquainted for generations. It is important to stress the continuity of such practices. For instance, six months after 9/11, Roberto Martínez of the American Friends Service Committee told the *Los Angeles Times*, "Muslim detainees are complaining in New York, and that's nothing new for us. They are going through the fear factor that Mexicans have undergone for years" (Serrano, 2002). Martínez' observation relates the Mexican immigrant community's longstanding relationship with immigrant detention, and highlights the pervasive anxiety which the ever-present possibilities of deportation and detention engender.

Such fears are not limited to noncitizen detainees. As a broad group of racialized persons in the US, Latino citizens also become fixed to Latino immigrants through their widespread and centuries-old criminalization as "illegals." Contributing to and in turn affected by the detention process, examples of criminalization are ubiquitous, occurring in popular culture, in administrative and local enforcement practices targeting Latinos, and within the law. The conflation of whole groups of Latinos as criminals occurs despite Latinos' profound diversity of incorporation into US society. According to Renato Rosaldo (1999, 255–256), "By a psychological and cultural mechanism of association all Latinos are thus declared to have a blemish that brands us with the stigma of being outside the law. We always live with that mark indicating that whether or not we belong in this country is always in question." As a result of this criminal "blemish" and categorical racialization, Latino citizens and noncitizens have been central figures in detention history. From lengthy and large-scale detention and deportation operations targeted at Mexican nationals throughout the 20th century, to the detention of Latin American asylum-seekers in the Cold War, to contemporary Puerto Rican US citizen and so-called "enemy combatant" José Padilla, we can observe that there are many types of detainees meeting at the nexus of Latino racialization and criminalization.

The post-9/11 "war on terror" contributed to the ongoing history of racial discrimination against noncitizens, initiating a variety of legal and administrative changes directly affecting US immigration policy. For example, after 9/11, there was an immediate suspension of asylum adjudications, entrapping some migrants in detention domestically, or abroad, unable to seek refuge from persecution. In addition, it derailed a serious public discussion, and bilateral negotiations with Mexico about a potential amnesty or "regularization" of status for then-over ten million undocumented migrants, a discussion that would remain muted for nearly five years. Latino noncitizens, and their families and communities, were affected by these and other federal and local enforcement initiatives emerging after 9/11. According to Steven Bender (2002, 1153), Latinos' "negative societal construction made their targeting inevitable as the fervent, amorphous war on terrorism took shape." Racial profiling in law enforcement, a practice that had been broadly criticized over the last decade, received a shot in the arm after 9/11 and was used widely to apprehend Arabs, Muslims, and South Asians in the wake of 9/11, with detrimental effects on Latino and African American communities (Bender, 2002; Johnson, 2003). While racial profiling in immigration enforcement received limited endorsement by the Supreme Court in *US v. Brignoni-Ponce* in 1975,[1] its resurgence after 9/11 signals the return of racial profiling as a "common sense" law enforcement practice that disproportionately affects immigrants and people of color.

The emergent post-9/11 discourse of national security cross-fertilized with existing anti-immigrant sentiment, both of which rely historically on racialized and criminalized constructions of migrants, of whom Latinos for decades have represented the prototypical example and overwhelming majority. Much like other national crises in US history, fighting a war against terrorism came to mean fighting immigrants, even though empirical data on the criminality of immigrants has consistently reflected noncitizens' lawfulness. As a result, such fears of immigrant and Latino criminality have been called erroneous and a "myth" by scholars of immigration and crime (Martínez and Valenzuela, 2006). According to Rubén Rumbaut and Walter Ewing (2007, 1), "In fact, data from the census and other sources show that for every ethnic group without exception, incarceration rates among young men are lowest for immigrants, even those who are the least educated. This holds true especially for the Mexicans, Salvadorans, and Guatemalans who make up the bulk of the undocumented population." Presumptions of immigrant criminality, however, in particular Latino criminality, are resilient and are maintained by politicians, the media, and a misinformed general public. As a result, the legal statutes, administrative strategies, and popular suspicions of noncitizens embedded in detention history serve as a critical prologue to understanding the contemporary detention and deportation of Latino immigrants, which expanded prior to and has expanded since 9/11.

Adding the specter of terrorism to an already contentious immigration debate exacerbated what Juliet Stumpf (this volume) has termed the "crimmigration crisis"—that is, the merger of criminal and immigration law. According to Stumpf, "Criminal and immigration law primarily serve to separate the individual from the rest of US society through physical exclusion and the creation of rules that establish lesser levels of citizenship." Margaret Taylor and Ronald Wright echo this criticism, writing, "However badly these two systems operate by themselves, they work even more poorly when they are haphazardly combined" (2002, 2). The domestic "war on terror," while relying on the prosecutorial advantages of immigration law, has also been used to advance a broader war on immigrants. Through the discourse of national security, the "war on terror" has augmented criminal and immigration enforcement at the federal, state, and local levels, drawing these apparatuses closer together after 9/11, duplicating efforts, and doubling the punishment of noncitizens.

---

1. *United States v. Brignoni-Ponce*, 422 US 873 (1975). The Court found that the "reasonable suspicion" requirement is not met "when the *only* ground for suspicion is that the occupants appear to be of Mexican ancestry" (emphasis added).

WHAT IS IMMIGRANT DETENTION?

The Immigration and Nationality Act enacted in 1952 and amended to the present authorizes the Attorney General to detain noncitizens, including persons seeking asylum, pending their deportation or exclusion hearings before an immigration judge (Immigration and Nationality Act, 1952, Section 236). Detention ensures that immigrants will attend deportation hearings by preventing their ability to abscond, and restricts mobility if the detainee is determined to be a danger to society. In 2004, there were over 23,000 immigrants in detention daily within the US; over 230,000 immigrants were detained during the fiscal year (USICE, 2004). Estimates since that time have ranged from between 20,000 and 30,000 detainees daily.[2] While length of stay can range from days to years, the average adult detainee was held in custody 37.6 days in 2007. The annual population of detainees has risen by nearly 100,000 persons since 2001 to 283,115 in 2006. This continual growth is facilitated by the Department of Homeland Security's (DHS's) increased capacity to detain 30,000 persons daily at 330 adult detention facilities nationwide in 2007 (GAO, 2007).

In general terms, detention is the practice of incarcerating noncitizens who are apprehended at ports of entry or within the nation's interior. Maintained in custody until they are released, bonded and paroled, or deported from the United States, detainees consist of undocumented immigrants, lawful permanent residents, and at times, particular groups of citizens.[3] To maintain the government's claim that detention is an "administrative process"—and not a punitive one—detention is theoretically utilized exclusively as a non-criminal procedure pursuant to deportation. But in practice immigrant detention is employed as a tool for law enforcement, and as witnessed after 9/11, the detention authority is used preventively—in which immigrants can be detained for the purposes of discovering after-the-fact charges that justify long-term detention and facilitate deportation. According to Margaret Taylor and Ronald Wright, "In response to the September 11 attacks, the government has relied on immigration enforcement tools as a pretext for investigative techniques and detentions that would be suspect under the criminal rules" (2002, 2). Underscoring this observation, legal scholar Peter Schuck argues, "But the detention authority is more than a programmatic resource, ancillary to the power to exclude and deport. Detention is also an awesome power in its own right" (1998, 36).

Formerly managed by the Immigration and Naturalization Service under the Department of Justice, custody of detainees is administered at present by Immigration and Customs Enforcement's (ICE) Office of Detention and Removal (DRO)[4] within the DHS.[5]

---

2. In its January 25, 2007, report, "Immigration-Related Detention: Current Legislative Issues," the Congressional Research Service (Siskin 2007) reported 20,000 detainees in fiscal year 2005 whereas detainee advocate organization Detention Watch Network reports over 27,000 detainees daily in 2007. See http://detentionwatchnet work.org/dwn_map (accessed August 2, 2007). The *Los Angeles Times* reported that daily detainees surpassed 30,000 nationally (Gorman, 2007).

3. The most notorious example of the detention of citizens is that of Japanese Americans incarcerated during World War II. In addition, among immigrant detainees today are persons who do not know they possess US citizenship (usually because their parents naturalized when they were minors, thus naturalizing the noncitizen children as well). Such persons carry the burden of proving this fact to the government. Lastly, US citizen children of detainees are often taken into custody during the apprehension of their parents.

4. The DRO was renamed Enforcement and Removal Operations (ERO) in June 2010.

5. On March 1, 2003, the functions of several border and security agencies, including the US Customs Service

Immigrant detainees are incarcerated throughout the nation in three types of facilities: federal detention centers managed by ICE, privately contracted prison facilities, and state and municipal jails subcontracting bed space for immigrant detainees. The latter two non-federal sites, comprising over 300 facilities, are responsible for incarcerating the majority of all detainees nationwide. Because of the variance in standards, conditions, and oversight at the different facilities, federal detention policy is implemented unevenly among the sites. According to Timothy Dunn (1996, 49), "The severity of INS detention practices varie[s] widely across its various districts along the border, depending largely on the availability of detention space and immediate budget resources."

Long preceding the emerging evidence of torture and abuses of power associated with post-9/11 detainees, gross mistreatment, from sexual abuse and rape to overcrowding and denial of medical attention and religious freedom, has been registered at all three types of detention facilities. Yet due to the lack of federal oversight and evaluation, privately con-tracted facilities and local jails have received the most criticism. "The worst abuses were inflicted in the prisons run by contractors," writes Robert Kahn (1996, 15), in his study of Central American refugee detention in the 1980s. Poor detention conditions have come under increased scrutiny, especially after it was reported, in June 2007, that 62 persons had died in ICE "administrative" custody since 2004 (Berestein, 2005). "They get treatment that you might see in a Third World country, and it's really a stain on our system of justice to treat detainees this way," said Adele Kimmel, attorney for a criminal alien detainee suing ICE for delays in medical treatment that allowed a cancer to spread to his penis, resulting in amputation (Fears, 2007, A4).

Among the key reasons for the unevenness in detention conditions are the weak guide-lines that establish detention standards for nonfederal facilities, where over 60% of de-tainees are held. According to the Government Accountability Office (2007, 9), "The standards are not codified in law and thus represent guidelines rather than binding regula-tions. According to ICE officials, ICE has never technically terminated an agreement for noncompliance with its detention standards." The latter point further suggests that viola-tions of detention conditions have negligible consequences for private and contracted detention facilities.

Detainees' experiences with detention are mediated by the unequal treatment at these sites as well as within the immigration court system, affecting access to counsel and visita-tion, the pace of legal proceedings, and the length of stay in detention. For example, a report by Syracuse University's Transactional Records Access Clearinghouse (TRAC, 2006) deter-mined that immigration judges' decisions in asylum cases vary widely: some judges deny asylum as much as 98% of the time, and some as little as 10%. Unlike the criminal courts, the constitutional right to legal counsel is not guaranteed in immigration proceedings. As a result, as few as 11% of immigrant detainees have legal representation in the immigration courts (Miller, 2002, 215). In asylum court, for example, the failure rate for an asylum-seeker without legal representation is 93.4% (TRAC, 2006).

---

and the Immigration and Naturalization Service (INS), were transferred to the US Department of Homeland Secu-rity (DHS). After years of pressure and anticipation, the INS was "split" into three agencies: Immigration and Cus-toms Enforcement (ICE), Citizenship and Immigration Services (CIS), and Customs and Border Protection (CBP).

Immigrant advocates, citing problems with detainees' access to legal representation and lawyers' access to their clients, insist that detainees' due procedural rights are in turn further denied or infringed upon through numerous administrative mechanisms within the detention apparatus. A recent review of telephone access at detention centers nationwide, for example, revealed "pervasive" problems. The Government Accountability Office (2007) concluded, "Without sufficient internal control policies and procedures in place, ICE is unable to offer assurance that detainees can access legal services, file external grievances, and obtain assistance from their consulates." Ironically, for those detainees fortunate to obtain legal representation—oftentimes legal permanent residents with significant ties to their community—their length of stay in detention is prolonged as they fight deportation.

In considering detention's far-reaching effect on Latino communities, one must also more broadly examine the intersections of race, gender, class, and sexuality in the detention experience. Migration, as we know, is a complex process, and gender, sexuality, race, and class background have an enormous effect on the outcomes and experiences of migration, just as migration reshapes these intersecting factors in the workplace, in the family structure, and in the detention experience. When considering Latino detainees, gender, for example, can be located as a factor in immigrant detention, in the criminalization of immigrants, the conditions of detention, and the broader effects on family and community structures which are reorganized due to the absence of detained family members. Among immigrant detainees, it is estimated that 7–10% of detainees are women, reflecting a gendered profile to the criminalization of male immigrant detainees. Of the 9/11 detentions, for example, the prototypical "suspected terrorist" was an Arab, Muslim, or South Asian man. The predominance of male detainees creates a set of conditions for women in detention, in which facilities and services are severely lacking. In addition to the numerous documented cases of sexual abuse (Patel and Jawetz, 2007), services for other vulnerable populations of detainees, such as gay-lesbian-bisexual-transgender detainees, detainees with health problems, and children, are often nonexistent or hazardous.[6]

Further complicating matters is the fact that detainees are a transient prison population—"one of the most highly transient and diverse populations of any correctional or detention system in the world," according to the Government Accountability Office (2007). With the exception of a smaller category of long-term detainees called "lifers," they cycle in and out of immigrant detention at various individual rates. As a result, statistics detailing the national origins of detainees, much like prisoners in general, are difficult to obtain. A survey conducted by the American Correctional Association, Inc. and published in its journal, *Corrections Compendium* (2006), addressed the difficulties of accounting for the number of foreign inmates in US and Canadian correctional facilities. Confirming that little has changed in determining these figures over the last decade, the survey cited its own conclusion from its previous report 11 years prior: "The statement that summarized the 1995 survey still describes corrections' accounting for foreign inmates: 'Until a reliable informa-

6. An escalating problem has been the increased detention of unaccompanied minors who are captured at ports of entry or in the interior of the country. In 2005, 6,460 underage undocumented migrants from Central America were detained, an increase of 35% from the previous year (Aizenman, 2006, A1).

tion system is developed and uniformly applied across the country, it will be impossible to know how many . . . beds are occupied by foreign nationals and illegal immigrants. . . .'"

Owing to the prominence of Latinos among the undocumented who are subject to investigations and deportations by the DRO, most experts agree that Latino immigrants, Mexicans in particular, are the vast majority of detainees.[7] Most recently, the DHS Office of Inspector General reported that between 2001 and 2004, 345,006 criminal aliens—the largest detainee category[8]—were apprehended by ICE. Over 250,000, or 75%, were from Mexico, thus dominating the criminal alien category, from which persons are least likely to be released from detention prior to deportation (OIG, 2006, 7). In the early 1990s, the General Accounting Office (1992, 124) estimated that 51% of detainees were Latinos. This figure, a rate for Mexican detention which remains to this day, was estimated before the unprecedented tripling of detention bed space, and the considerable leap in annual detention as a result of the "war on drugs" and major immigration legislation in 1996. During this time, funding for detention and removal grew to 37% of INS enforcement spending (Dixon and Gelatt, 2005, 5).

While the "war on terror" and the increased detentions of Arab, Muslim, and South Asian immigrants has resulted in a significant increase in the detention infrastructure, the majority-Latino category of criminal alien detainees still represents the largest share of immigrant detainees. The DRO estimated that for fiscal year 2007, there would be 605,000 foreign-born persons admitted to local and state correctional facilities and that half would be removable aliens (OIG, 2006, 2). These persons, who include many long-term legal permanent residents, represent *future* detainees, who will be reincarcerated on immigration charges after completion of their criminal sentences. The expansion of bed space to accommodate these detainees is central to the long-term expansion of immigrant detention and reflects the increased coordination of the criminal justice system with the immigration court system.

New initiatives and administrative changes within the Departments of Homeland Security and Justice have increased the capacity to detain noncitizens and have facilitated longer periods of detention. For example, the DRO's "Strategic Plan 2003–2012: Endgame" seeks a "100% removal rate" of deportable immigrants in order "to maintain the integrity of the immigration process and protect our homeland" (Tangeman, 2003). Because detention is a central part of any individual or mass deportation effort, "Endgame's" "operational focus on fugitive apprehension," according to former DRO director Anthony Tangeman (2003) "will require significant increases in detention and removal operations and resources." Responding to this need for detention space, Congress approved the addition of 8,000 detainee beds per year from 2006 to 2010 as part of the Intelligence Reform and Terrorism Prevention Act (2004), effectively tripling detention bed space for the second decade in a row. Although the Department of Homeland Security's Office of Inspector General reported in 2007 that "ICE

---

7. It is estimated that there are over 11 million undocumented residing in the US, with 500,000 arriving annually (Siskin *et al.*, 2006, 1). The DHS reports that Mexicans represent the largest portion of undocumented, at over six million, or 57%, with the next largest groups arriving from El Salvador and Guatemala. These nations account for 65% of all undocumented while South American migrants account for an additional 8%. Asia accounts for 12% of undocumented immigration (Hoefer *et al.*, 2006, 1).

8. The large majority of detainees are criminal aliens who are undergoing removal proceedings (Siskin et al., 2006, 20).

is not well positioned to oversee the growing detention caseload that will be generated by DHS' planned enhancements to secure the border" (2007, 1), proposed immigration legislation in 2006 and 2007 also included further expansions in detention bed space, an increase of 20,000 detention beds. This expansion, buoyed by the bureaucratic shift to a national security context, occurs even though the majority of detainees, Latino criminal alien detainees, have nothing to do with terrorism.

A BRIEF GENEALOGY OF LATINO DETENTION

With its near-mythic status in the formation of the United States as a "nation of immigrants," immigration history, as it is generally known in the US, has also served as a repository for historical amnesia. Unlike the heralded experiences of European immigrants whose racial inscription was nonexistent or temporary, permitting descendant generations to achieve social advancement, immigration for Latinos has been a far more vexed process, in which Latinos' racialization, criminalization, and constant threat of detention and deportation maintain their racialized foreignness before the law and society. In coming to terms with the contemporary detention of Latino immigrants, it is critical to confront this historical erasure and develop a more complex understanding of the continuity of detention policy over the last century. The capacity for the detention of Latino immigrants has been made possible by its genealogical precursors and judicial and legislative precedents. A variety of discourses of exclusion and Latino criminality, reinvented through the detention process, has served to naturalize Latino immigrants' "illegality." As De Genova (this volume) argues, "Indeed, the legal production of 'illegality' has made an object of Mexican migration in particular, in ways both historically unprecedented and disproportionately deleterious." Mexican and other Latino immigrants have, thus, long lived with the consequences of their degraded citizenship status in the US. Detained as a result of biological reasoning and fears of contagion, for ideological motives as refugees, or persistently as criminalized noncitizens, Latino experiences with detention are recurring, and not isolated, episodes in the 20th century. They provide the historical context for understanding today's escalation of detention, deportation, and degradation of Latino immigrant communities.

Medical Detention: Several major episodes in detention history, some of them ongoing and which coincide with the construction of national crises, have led to the large scale detention of Latino immigrants. The first such episode for Latinos occurred between World Wars I and II, during a time when Mexican immigrants and Mexican Americans contended with what Natalia Molina has called "medicalized nativism" (Molina, 2006, 58). Motivated by emerging questions of public health, which were steeped in racialized presumptions about contagious diseases that were believed to inhabit the bodies and cultures of arriving migrants, medical detention and quarantine were instituted along the US–Mexican border from 1917 until the onset of World War II (Stern, 2005, 65). Medical detentions occurred at a time when there was no military threat with which to rationalize the scapegoating or detention of Latino migrants. While an entire discourse of contagion specifically targeted at Asian immigrants emerged on the West Coast, for Mexicans, who were exempt from racial exclusion laws and later the racist national quota system, medical rationales were even more critical to the restriction of Mexican immigration, as the quarantine and medical detention of border-crossers "became the status quo on the border" (Stern, 2005, 70), lasting nearly 20 years.

Detention, Repatriation, and Operation Wetback: During the same period as the border quarantine, concerns over Mexican criminality as well as economic competition in the 1930s Depression-era, led to a nationwide repatriation campaign which effected the removal and voluntary departure of a conservative estimate of one half million Mexicans and their children, many of them citizens, in what Francisco E. Balderrama and Raymond Rodríguez called "the first major contingent of displaced refugees in the twentieth century" (2006, 329). Mexican "illegality," which was established with the criminalization of undocumented entry in 1929 (Nevins, 2002, 54), has dominated public anxieties for three quarters of a century. Statutory notions of "illegality" are sustained by popular conceptions of criminality, as both the popular and the statutory constructions of "illegality" shape each other. According to Steven Bender (2003, 1), who traces Latino criminalization to the 19th century construction of the Mexican "greaser," "For Latinas/os and certain other groups, stereotypes actually drive their distressing legal and societal treatment."

In the 1950s, concerns about Mexican immigrant criminality would again lead to record-setting detentions and deportations.[9] On June 9, 1954, the INS initiated what was officially termed Operation Wetback, a nationwide deportation campaign to round up, detain, and deport Mexican nationals. The operation led to the highest number of persons ever held in detention by the INS in a single year, at over one-half million (Swing, 1954, 31, 36). Although Operation Wetback resulted in outrage from Mexican American communities and organizations regarding harassment of citizens, the break-up of families, and widespread fear of law enforcement, the INS hailed Operation Wetback a huge success. "For the first time in more than ten years, illegal crossing over the Mexican border was brought under control," after "the backbone of the wetback invasion was broken," proclaimed the INS commissioner (Swing, 1955, 10, 14, 17).

Refugee Detentions: In the 1980s, the detention of Latino refugees was a distinguishing feature of the decade, set in motion in 1980 when 125,000 Cuban *marielitos* fled Cuba, departing through the port of Mariel. In addition, roughly one million Salvadoran, Guatemalan, and Nicaraguan refugees entered the US during the decade, fleeing political upheaval and violence, which was maintained by US Cold War policies and extralegal actions in Central America. The exodus from the Caribbean and Central America fueled a racial panic about refugee streams which were feared to be black and Latino, criminal, ideologically left, and diseased. Fearing a criminal class of Cuban immigrants among the mostly young and male refugees, the US broke with its former policy of proactive acceptance as several thousand Cubans were detained *en masse* in the early 1980s, leading to severe overcrowding and riots at detention centers in Georgia and Louisiana (Hamm, 1995).

Refugees from Central America further clogged detention centers during the decade, especially after the attorney general ordered, in 1981, that all undocumented refugees be detained until the final adjudication of their asylum cases (Kahn, 1996, 16). According to

9. By 1954, Mexican deportations represented 84% of all deportation proceedings, and Mexican immigrants were the largest national group in 10 of the 13 deportation categories listed in the INS annual report. The remaining three categories were noncriminal reasons for deportation (Swing, 1954, Table 24).

historian María Cristina García (2006, 91), "Detention centers along the United States–Mexico border filled to capacity with people the Border Patrol called the OTMs (other than Mexicans)." As a result, the Port Isabel immigration prison in South Texas expanded, through tent construction, its bed capacity from 425 to 10,000 (Kahn, 1996, 13). In addition, there was also an expansion of contracted facilities all along the US–Mexico border, and a reopening of a federal facility once used to detain Japanese Americans (Kahn, 1996, 20). Encumbered with pervasive allegations of human rights abuses—from denial of legal counsel and translated legal material to invasion of private correspondence and sexual abuse—the newly expanded detention infrastructure facilitated Cold War foreign policy objectives, defined differently for various countries of origin. While the asylum applications of Salvadorans and Guatemalans fleeing US-backed administrations were rejected 97–99% of the time, Nicaraguans fleeing a socialist government which the US opposed were granted either asylum, at rates as high as 84% in 1987, or a suspended deportation, leading to release from detention (Kahn, 1996, 21).

Criminal Aliens: While refugees were being detained at ports of entry in the 1980s, domestic criminalization and detention policy initiatives during the "war on drugs" shifted the enforcement focus inside the nation, to "criminal aliens." Detained for having been convicted of deportable offenses, "criminal aliens" represent the largest share of all immigrant detainees today. Any noncitizen, whether undocumented or a lawful permanent resident, can be detained as a "criminal alien" and placed into deportation proceedings. Constituting what border expert Timothy Dunn called a "historic change in INS detention practices" (1996, 73), the increased detention of "criminal aliens" resulted from increased policing, the reclassification and expansion of deportable crimes such as drug or gun trafficking, mandatory drug sentencing, and reduction of avenues for relief from detention. According to the Congressional Research Service, by 2002, of the 202,000 immigrants detained, over 51% had criminal records (Siskin, 2004, 12).

As legal status generated inequality in criminal law in the 1980s and 1990s, the largest group of immigrants, Mexican nationals, suffered disproportionately from "criminal alien" enforcement. Like African Americans, Mexican and Mexican American communities were already targeted for criminal enforcement of drug crimes, contributing to the massive prison expansion taking place nationwide. Such criminal enforcement has a direct effect on increases in detention, as noncitizens convicted of deportable crimes are placed in detention and deportation proceedings at the completion of their criminal sentences. Noting that Hispanic incarceration rates have risen 43% since 1990, Marc Mauer and Ryan King state, "While the disproportionate rate of incarceration for African Americans has been well documented for some time, a significant development in the past decade has been the growing proportion of the Hispanic population entering prisons and jails" (2007, 1–2). As they were in the 1950s, Mexican nationals are again the largest number of detainees held each year, representing 50% of persons in detention, or 101,000, in 2002 (Siskin, 2007, 12).

A forerunner to the detentions stemming from the "war on terror," this pre-9/11 episode in detention growth in the 1990s transpired by means of a combination of new legislation that targeted immigrants by reducing their due procedural rights, and the reintroduction and codification of "national security" in the wake of foreign and domestic terrorism in the mid-1990s (see Chacón, this volume). Two laws were passed in 1996 in the wake of the 1995 Oklahoma City bombing that dramatically increased noncitizens' vulnerability to detention and deportation. The Antiterrorism and Effective Death Penalty Act (AEDPA), enacted near the one-year anniversary of the Oklahoma City bombing, was drafted as antiterrorism legislation, but instead had its greatest impact on noncitizen criminal offenders, making them easier to deport, and mandating their detention pursuant to their deportation. Five months later, Congress passed the Illegal Immigration Reform and Immigrant Responsibility Act (IIRIRA), elaborately facilitating "criminal alien" detention through a sweeping denial of due process to noncitizens. According to Taylor, "IIRIRA amended some of AEDPA's most controversial immigration provisions, but overall made things worse for noncitizen criminal offenders" (2005, 353). By reinforcing "mandatory detentions" for immigrants facing deportation, removing avenues for judicial relief, and expanding the category of "aggravated felony" which triggers mandatory detention and deportation proceedings, IIRIRA is responsible for the tripling of immigrant detention in the 1990s.

The episodic development of Latino immigrant detention discussed above reflects different constructions of national security in a variety of social, political, and historical contexts. Discourses of national security in these eras cross-fertilize with anti-immigrant sentiment and the legal and social inequalities of noncitizens, and result in the expansion of immigrant detention during periods of national crisis. National security is threatened, so it is argued, by the very presence of immigrants. From fears of disease and particular ideologies from abroad, to concern about refugee streams, and to the constant fear of criminal activity among immigrants, detention has served as an operational nexus for these fears and the construction of Latinos as criminals and undesirables. As Jonathan Inda has argued, "a variety of immigration 'experts'—social scientists, INS/DHS bureaucrats, policy analysts, immigration reform organizations, and the popular press—have constructed 'illegal' immigrants—typically imagined as Mexican—as anti-citizens incapable of exercising responsible self-government and thus as threats to the overall well-being of the social body" (2006, 63–64). Latino immigrants—with diminished legal rights as noncitizens and limited social benefits as racialized subjects—have borne the lasting burden of expanding detention policies, which have articulated the boundaries of Latino citizenship over the last one hundred years.

CONTEXTUALIZING LATINO DETENTION

As briefly articulated at the outset of this chapter, it has been useful to disaggregate Latino immigrant detainees from the sensational and extraordinary post-9/11 detention period, in order to shed light on the pervasive history of Latinos in detention, as well as on the key role of immigrant detention in the criminalization, immobilization, and racial expulsion of noncitizens from the US. These histories are part of a broad and complex set of racist experiences that Latinos have endured at all stages of the processes of immigration and settlement, ranging from policies and practices at the federal, local, and popular level, which impinge on Latinos' civil rights, cultural practices, and economic advancement. This strategic move notwithstanding, I want to suggest that it is critical to understand Latino detention in a comparative racial frame. The detention of noncitizens in the United States, as it has developed over the last one hundred years, has entrapped a variety of racialized groups in very different political and social contexts. This is because the convergence of national security, race, and noncitizenship is an episodic occurrence in US history, and a comparative racial analysis better reveals the systemic arrangements and institutionalized racism in detention policy.

In addressing Latino immigrant detention in this chapter, it has been difficult to speak only of Latinos. With a heterogeneous background, Latinos in and of themselves already have a complex and vexed history of incorporation into the US: as former colonial subjects, as refugees, as victims of direct military conquest, or as persons displaced by US global economic power. Correspondingly, and as I hope this chapter has shown, Latinos have inhabited nearly every category of detainee across an entire century, including medical detainees at the border prior to World War II, persons entrapped in large-scale deportation campaigns in the 1930s and 1950s, refugees and criminal aliens detained because of the Cold War and "war on drugs," and lastly, as a result of the contemporary enforcement of the "war on terror," we should also include so-named "enemy combatant" José Padilla. As the prominence and complexity of Latino experiences with detention demonstrate, the detention of immigrants can affect all noncitizens and their families and communities, in particular historically racialized groups.

Immigrant detention thus underscores the structural inequality of all noncitizens in the US, and therefore it is vital that we come to know Latino detainees alongside similarly positioned persons. Critical episodes of immigrant detention also include Chinese and Chinese Americans detained for biological and eugenic reasoning; Japanese and Japanese American citizen detainees during World War II; immigrant laborers occupying the margins of whiteness, detained during the early 20th century Red Scare and the Cold War; Haitian detainees since the 1970s; and most recently, 9/11 detainees. These racialized episodes of immigrant detention are related directly and indirectly to contemporary Latino detention because they have created legal prerequisites, diminished legal avenues for relief, and generated the construction and escalation of the detention infrastructure. While this chapter centers on the detention of Latino immigrants, the larger scale of its impact occurs beyond detainees and their families, and extends to the creation of severe legal inequalities for all noncitizens. As the largest of this group today, Latino immigrants and their families and communities are extremely vulnerable to the hardships created by this process. Unless it is challenged, Latinos will suffer disproportionately from the government's domestic "war on terror."

The trends of escalating detentions and deportations, in particular the expansion of the detention infrastructure established with the dramatic changes in immigration and detention law in 1996, have continued into this new century. More than eleven years after 9/11, national security anxieties continue to occupy the popular imagination and serve to generate political energy for politicians invoking the security threat presented by immigration. According to Heather MacDonald, a fellow at the conservative Manhattan Institute, 9/11 was a "freebie" for persons whose real agenda is to halt undocumented immigration. "Talking about security makes it easier to talk about immigration without being called a racist," says MacDonald (Corcoran, 2006, 4S). Merging traditional arguments for and against immigration with fears of international terrorism, politicians from both sides of the aisle have reframed the immigration debate, suggesting that immigrants are the cause of the nation's security vulnerabilities. Candidates in both the Republican and Democratic parties have campaigned on the professed links between terrorism, security, and undocumented workers, reinforcing these connections in campaign advertisements, and signaling the merger of discourses of immigration control with national security and terrorism (Corcoran, 2006, 4S; see also Chacón, this volume).

In today's context of an ever-expanding "war on terror," the provision of "homeland" security substantiates a vast, secretive, and racially driven security state, domestically and internationally. Thus, while terrorism prosecutions have dropped (Eggen, 2006, A6), older methods of enforcement, such as immigrant detention, have intensified as the array of issues surrounding detention, asylum, undocumented immigration, and border security, are couched in their so-called threat to national security. According to Border Patrol Chief David V. Aguilar, "The nexus between our post-Sept. 11 mission and our traditional role is clear. . . . Terrorists and violent criminals may exploit smuggling routes used by immigrants to enter the United States illegally and do us harm" (Archibold, 2006, 26). This restructuring of immigration control policies, and the current and heated struggles over "enforcement-only" legislation, testify to the ascendancy of this terror context. As legislative mandates continue to limit the judicial protections and sources of relief for detainees as well as immigration judges' ability to grant such relief or maintain legal safeguards, the trend in detention policy is to advance a variety of "undue processes" against noncitizens and detainees by depriving them of their due procedural rights, both statutorily and through administrative minutiae.

Latino migrants and US-born Latinos—demographically the largest of all migrant groups and US minority populations—will bear the burden of the US's increased capacity to surveil, control, and detain noncitizens and persons perceived to be immigrants. According to Kevin Johnson, "Ultimately, persons of Mexican ancestry—citizens and non-citizens—will be disparately affected by the legal changes triggered by September 11" (2003, 852). Popular sentiment supports this trend; the political currency it generates for politicians and pundits makes it possible; and history has provided the legal precedents and historical trajectory to execute this punitive tendency. As the huge increases in federal funding and private investment that will triple detention capacity by the end of the decade make obvious, the federal government has unbridled its enforcement initiatives in the wake of 9/11, collaborating with local and international governments and the domestic criminal justice system, and formulating highly problematic information-sharing networks. These efforts at protecting the "homeland" through scapegoating, burdening, and reducing the rights of immigrants, have distorted the meaning of national security, producing long-term challenges and adverse human consequences for a vital and permanent segment of our society.

WORKS CITED

Aizenman, Nurith Celina. 2006. Young Migrants Risk All to Reach US. *Washington Post*, August 28, A1.

American Corrections Association, Inc. 2006. Foreign Inmates: Survey Summary. *Corrections Compendium* 31(2): 10–21.

Archibold, Randal C. 2006. Border Patrol Draws Increased Scrutiny as President Proposes an Expanded Role. *New York Times*, June 4, 26.

Ashcroft, John. 2001. Prepared Remarks for the US Mayors Conference (speech at the US Mayors Conference, Washington, DC). October 25. Available at http://www.justice.gov/archive/ag/speeches/2001/agcrisisremarks10_25.htm (accessed April 10, 2005).

Balderrama, Francisco E. and Raymond Rodríguez. 2006. *Decade of Betrayal: Mexican Repatriation in the 1930s*, Revised Edition. Albuquerque: University of New Mexico Press.

Bender, Steven W. 2002. Sight, Sound, and Stereotype: The War on Terrorism and Its Consequences for Latinas/os. *Oregon Law Review* 81: 1153–1178.

Bender, Steven W. 2003. *Greasers and Gringos: Latinos, Law, and the American Imagination.* New York: New York University Press.

Berestein, Leslie. 2005. Woman in Detention Alleges Rape. *San Diego Union-Tribune*, January 18. Available at http://www.signonsandiego.com/news/metro/20050118-9999-1m18assault.html (accessed August 12, 2007).

Bernstein, Nina. 2007. New Scrutiny as Immigrants Die in Custody. *New York Times*, June 26, A1.

Bush, George W. 2001. President George W. Bush's Address to America Before Representatives of Firemen, Law Enforcement Officers, and Postal Workers in Atlanta, Ga. November 8. Available at http://www.september11news.com/PresidentBushAtlanta.htm (accessed June 6, 2005).

Corcoran, Katherine. 2006. Mexican Immigrants Caught in Backlash of Terror Anxiety. *San Jose Mercury News*, September 10, 4S.

Dixon, David and Julia Gelatt. 2005. Immigration Enforcement Spending Since IRCA. Report No. 10, Migration Policy Institute, November.

Dunn, Timothy J. 1996. *The Militarization of the US–Mexico Border: Low Intensity Conflict Doctrine Comes Home, 1978–1992.* Austin: CMAS Books.

Eggen, Dan. 2006. Terrorism Prosecutions Drop. *Washington Post*, September 4, A6.

Fears, Darryl. 2007. Illegal Immigrants Received Poor Care in Jail, Lawyers Say. *Washington Post*, June 13, A4.

García, María Cristina. 2006. *Seeking Refuge: Central American Migration to Mexico, the United States, and Canada.* Berkeley: University of California Press.

General Accounting Office. 1992. Immigration Control: Immigration Policies Affect INS Detention Efforts. Report to the Chairman, Subcommittee on International Law, Immigration, and Refugees, Committee on Judiciary, House of Representatives. General Accounting Office, June.

Gorman, Anna. 2007. Immigration Detainees are at Record Levels. *Los Angeles Times*, November 5. Available at http://www.detentionwatchnetwork.org/node/461 (accessed November 27, 2007).

Government Accountability Office (GAO). 2007. Alien Detention Standards: Telephone Access Problems Were Pervasive at Detention Facilities; Other Deficiencies Did Not Show a Pattern of Noncompliance. GAO-07-875, Government Accountability Office, July.

Hamm, Mark S. 1995. *The Abandoned Ones: The Imprisonment of the Mariel Boat People.* Boston: Northeastern University Press.

Hernández, David Manuel. 2005. Undue Process: Immigrant Detention, Due Process, and Lesser Citizenship. Ph.D. dissertation, University of California, Berkeley.

Hoefer, Michael, Nancy Rytina and Christopher Campbell. 2006. Estimates of the Unauthorized Immigrant Population Residing in the United States: January 2005. Office of Immigration Statistics, Department of Homeland Security, August.

Immigration and Nationality Act. 1952. INA § Section 236, 8 U.S.C. §1226.

Inda, Jonathan Xavier. 2006. *Targeting Immigrants: Government, Technology, and Ethics.* Malden, MA: Blackwell.

Johnson, Kevin R. 2003. September 11 and Mexican Immigrants: Collateral Damage Comes Home. *DePaul Law Review* 52: 849–870.

Kahn, Robert S. 1996. *Other People's Blood: US Immigration Prisons in the Reagan Decade.* Boulder, CO: Westview Press.

Martínez Jr., Ramiro and Abel Valenzuela Jr., eds. 2006. *Immigration and Crime: Race, Ethnicity, and Violence.* New York: New York University Press.

Mauer, Marc and Ryan S. King. 2007. Uneven Justice: State Rates of Incarceration by Race and Ethnicity. Washington, DC: The Sentencing Project, July.

Miller, Teresa A. 2002. The Impact of Mass Incarceration on Immigration Policy. In *Invisible Punishment: The Collateral Consequences of Mass Imprisonment,* eds. Marc Mauer and Meda Chesney-Lind, 214–238. New York: New Press.

Molina, Natalia. 2006. *Fit to Be Citizens? Public Health and Race in Los Angeles, 1879–1939.* Berkeley: University of California Press.

Nevins, Joseph. 2002. *Operation Gatekeeper: The Rise of the "Illegal Alien" and the Making of the US–Mexico Boundary.* New York: Routledge.

Office of Inspector General (OIG). 2006. Detention and Removal of Illegal Aliens. Department of Homeland Security, April.

Office of Inspector General. 2007. ICE's Compliance with Detention Limits for Aliens with a Final Order of Removal from the United States. Department of Homeland Security, February.

Patel, Sunita and Tom Jawetz. 2007. Conditions of Confinement in Immigration Detention Facilities. Briefing Paper. Available at http://www.aclu.org/pdfs/prison/unsr_briefing_materials.pdf (accessed August 11, 2007).

Rosaldo, Renato. 1999. Cultural Citizenship, Inequality, and Multiculturalism. In *Race, Identity, and Citizenship: A Reader,* eds. Rodolfo D. Torres, Louis F. Miron, and Jonathan Xavier Inda, 253–261. Malden, MA: Blackwell.

Rumbaut, Rubén G. and Walter Ewing. 2007. *The Myth of Immigrant Criminality and the Paradox of Assimilation: Incarceration Rates Among Native and Foreign-Born Men.* Washington, DC: Immigration Policy Center, Spring.

Schuck, Peter H. 1998. *Citizens, Strangers, and In-Betweens: Essays on Immigration and Citizenship.* Boulder, CO: Westview Press.

Serrano, Richard A. 2002. Arrests on Border Fall After 9/11. *Los Angeles Times,* March 2, A1/A8.

Siskin, Alison. 2004. Immigration-Related Detention: Current Legislative Issues. CRS Report for Congress, Congressional Research Service.

Siskin, Alison. 2007. Immigration-Related Detention: Current Legislative Issues. CRS Report for Congress, Congressional Research Service, January 25.

Siskin, Alison, Andorra Bruno, Blas Nunez-Neto, Lisa M. Seghetti and Ruth Ellen Wassem. 2006. Immigration Enforcement Within the United States. CRS Report for Congress. Congressional Research Service, April.

Stern, Alexandra Minna. 2005. *Eugenic Nation: Faults and Frontiers of Better Breeding in Modern America.* Berkeley: University of California Press.

Swing, Joseph M. 1954. *Annual Report of the Immigration and Naturalization Service.* Washington, DC: Government Printing Office.

Swing, Joseph M. 1955. *Annual Report of the Immigration and Naturalization Service.* Washington, DC: Government Printing Office.

Tangeman, Anthony S. 2003. Memorandum for Deputy Assistant Director, Field Operations Division and Field Office Directors: Office of Detention and Removal Strategic Plan 2003–2012: Endgame. Office of Detention and Removal, June 27.

Taylor, Margaret H. 2005. *Denmore v. Kim:* Judicial Deference to Congressional Folly. In *Immigration Stories*, eds. David A. Martin and Peter H. Schuck, 344–376. New York: Foundation Press.

Taylor, Margaret H. and Ronald F. Wright. 2002. The Sentencing Judge as Immigration Judge. Research Paper No. 02–15, Public Law and Legal Theory Research Paper Series, Wake Forest University School of Law, September.

Transactional Records Access Clearinghouse (TRAC). 2006. Report: Immigration Judges. Syracuse University.

U.S. Immigration and Customs Enforcement (USICE). 2004. Fact Sheet: ICE Office of Detention and Removal. May 4.

11 | "¿QUIEN SABE?"

DEPORTATION AND TEMPORALITY AMONG TRANSNATIONAL MEXICANS

Deborah A. Boehm

INTRODUCTION: *LOS DEPORTADOS*

"You've heard, haven't you, about *los deportados* [the deportees]? There are many who have returned—Chucho, Beny, Juan.[1] It seems you are sending us all back!" Mariela was tidying the house as we spoke. She walked into the courtyard, threw some food to the dogs there, and came back inside. Her joking tone quickly passed: "*Quien sabe que van a hacer . . . ¿Quien sabe?* [Who knows what they are going to do. . . . Who knows?]" When I first went to rural Mexico to conduct fieldwork in 2001, everyone in the community was talking about migration north: a family member who was there, plans for one's own migration, life on the other side. Years later, in the summer of 2008, the conversation had notably shifted. Now as people welcomed me into their homes and chatted with me at community gatherings, they had a common topic on their minds: return to the *rancho* and the experiences of deportees who had arrived in the past months. As Mariela described, the future of the town's deportees was indeed uncertain, though continued migration north—of family and community members, and even of deportees themselves—seemed likely.

Responding to Nathalie Peutz's call for an "anthropology of removal" (2006), I trace narratives of temporality and un/certainty among deportees, undocumented (im)migrants,[2] and individuals from the broader binational networks and communities within which de-

Deborah A. Boehm is assistant professor of Anthropology and Women's Studies at the University of Nevada, Reno. Reprinted with permission of the author, from "'¿Quien Sabe?': Deportation and Temporality Among Transnational Mexicans," *Urban Anthropology and Studies of Cultural Systems and World Economic Development* 38 (2–4): 345–374, by Deborah A. Boehm. Copyright © 2009 by Deborah A. Boehm.

1. To protect migrants in the United States without the state's authorization, I use pseudonyms, for individuals and their home community, throughout the chapter.

2. Because of the difficulties of categorizing and distinguishing between migrants and immigrants, as well as the way that the category of "immigrant" is "posited always from the standpoint of the migrant-receiving nation-state, in terms of outsiders coming in" (De Genova 2002: 421), I utilize "(im)migrant" and "(im)migration" and/or use the terms "migrant/migration" and "immigrant/immigration" interchangeably. Similarly, I employ the terms "unauthorized" and "undocumented" to describe migrants who are labeled by the DHS and in public discourse as "illegal" (see De Genova 2002).

portees are embedded to examine the effect of deportation and "deportability" (De Genova 2002) in the daily lives of transnational Mexicans. The aims of this research are twofold: to write against processes that "render individuals invisible" (Peutz 2006: 231), highlighting particular experiences of Mexican migrants, the largest group of documented and undocumented immigrants living in the United States; and to consider the complex, contradictory, and intersecting scales of time and unpredictability that permeate threats of deportation and processes of removal. This project studies an emergent order of social injustice in the United States and its local/transnational effects.

The doubts and insecurity described by deportees and those without papers who could potentially be deported—those who are, in the language of the U.S. Department of Homeland Security (DHS) (2008), "deportable"—can be traced to the presence of the state in individual lives. The words and experiences of migrants provide a particular and telling view of state policies and the work of state agents. Given that such state processes often gain strength through their obscurity, a focus on the everyday lives of deportees and those fearing deportation makes visible (albeit partially) the character of state actions. Such ethnographic research demonstrates the potency of state power in everyday lives and suggests potential directions for comprehensive immigration reform.

TEMPORALITY AND REMOVAL:
SITUATING DEPORTATION IN TIME AND PLACE

My analysis is based on longitudinal, binational research among a transnational community with ties to a small, rural town or *rancho* in the state of San Luis Potosí, Mexico, that I call San Marcos, and several locales in the U.S. West, primarily in California, Nevada, New Mexico, Oregon, and Texas. The study has included more than a decade of fieldwork in multiple sites where members of the network are situated. My findings are based on qualitative, ethnographic research, including interviews and life histories, participant observation, visual methodologies such as photography and videography, and work with local grassroots immigrant rights organizations. The community has a long history of migration to and from the U.S. West, a pattern of male-led migration that was established beginning with the Bracero Program (1942–1964), through which the U.S. government contracted with (male) laborers to work in the agricultural sector.

Since the inception of the Bracero Program, movement has been shaped by gendered migration (Boehm 2008a) to and from the United States through transnational "circuits" (Rouse 1991), with male labor migrants returning to Mexico seasonally to plant or harvest pinto beans grown throughout the area. The history of the region, and Mexico more generally, has been characterized by both migration and return, and current deportations of Mexican nationals must be considered "within a long historical frame" (Kanstroom 2007: 7; see also De Genova this volume) of migration between Mexico and the United States. Previous "returns" to Mexico have been both voluntary, such as the seasonal migration described above, and forced, for example, the "repatriation" of Mexican nationals post-World War I (1920–1923), during the Great Depression (1930s), and through Operation Wetback beginning in 1954 (see discussion in Ngai 2004; also see De Genova 2005; Kanstroom 2007 for research about "returns" in U.S.-Mexico history). Today's deportations are deeply embedded within the state-driven removals of Mexican nationals in the past.

So while return and involuntary removal are not new processes for Mexicans, since the mid-1990s return migration to this region of Mexico has taken on a shifting character from previous decades. According to oral histories I have conducted with migrants, migration and return were relatively open from the late 1970s through the early 1990s, and many migrants received amnesty through the Special Agricultural Worker provisions (SAW I and II) of the Immigration Reform and Control Act (IRCA) of 1986. However, the U.S. Illegal Immigration Reform and Immigrant Responsibility Act (1996) and the events of 9/11 have set the stage for the increased control of undocumented migration (see Stumpf this volume; Chacón this volume). The U.S. crackdown on undocumented migration in recent years has been implemented through a progressively more militarized border (see Heyman this volume; Chávez this volume), federal immigration raids in locations throughout the United States (e.g., Capps et al. 2007), deportations of undocumented migrants with U.S. citizen children (Preston 2007), state laws and local ordinances and practices aimed at curbing undocumented migration (see Saénz et al. this volume; Gilbert this volume), and a growing number of U.S. permanent residents who are being denied citizenship or deported during the naturalization process (Preston 2008).

Over the past decades, deportations of foreign nationals from the United States have been on the rise (U.S. DHS 2008: 95). Mexican nationals make up the largest number of individuals identified as "deportable." For example, Mexican nationals were 854,261 of the 960,756 "deportable aliens" located by the DHS in 2007 (2008: 92). The DHS distinguishes between "removals" and "returns." A removal is what is commonly understood as deportation, a legal process with "administrative or criminal consequences placed on subsequent reentry owing to the fact of removal," while return is "not based on an order of removal" (2008: 95). According to the DHS, the majority of these "voluntary returns" are of Mexican nationals who are apprehended by U.S. Border Patrol agents and then returned to Mexico (2008: 95). Notably, these ostensibly "voluntary" returns have declined since a peak of 1,675,876 in 2000 to 891,390 in 2007, while "removals" or formal deportations were at a record high of 319,382 in 2007 (2008: 95). In other words, "returns" are decreasing while deportations or "removals," with their accompanying legal ramifications, are on the rise.

The context of such deportation statistics (a story that is much more difficult to tell through statistical data) is the population of Mexican nationals who are undocumented or unauthorized (im)migrants living in the United States. The number of unauthorized immigrants living in the United States is estimated to be 11.9 million (Passel and Cohn 2008), 7 million of whom are from Mexico (Passel and Cohn 2009: i). However, as Nicholas De Genova posits, "there are no hermetically sealed communities of undocumented migrants" (2002: 422), further complicating demographic portraits of unauthorized migration. Indeed, undocumented migration, deportability, and removal by the U.S. state must be considered within a frame that recognizes the permeability and shifting character of the supposedly rigid categories that delineate documented and undocumented migrants.

Of course, not all transnational Mexicans are undocumented, but within binational families and communities, all migrants, regardless of status, are impacted by deportability and processes of removal, albeit in diverse ways and to varying degrees. The familial and community relationships within which one is embedded—groupings of individuals with mixed statuses vis-à-vis the U.S. state—mean that "deportability" has a broad effect in transnational Mexican lives. Essentially every family from San Marcos is a mixed-status family, made up of individuals with different legal immigrant statuses within the United States. Through social relations, deportability can be transferred to those who are "legally" in the United States, including U.S. permanent residents and even U.S. citizens. Those who are documented, such as the U.S. citizen children of unauthorized migrants, may be constructed as "alien" by association (Boehm 2011), precisely through social and familial relations, by state agents, and within public discourse. Similarly, the presumed "permanence" and security of U.S. permanent residency held by foreign nationals can also be undermined by deportability and deportation.

The racializing dimensions of state power—a "racial governmentality" (Rosas 2007: 99)—also extend to transnational Mexicans regardless of individual "legal" immigrant statuses, demonstrating the slippery boundaries of U.S. state-defined membership for Mexican nationals or those perceived to be Mexican, Latino, foreign, other. U.S. citizens of color, while not legally "deportable," are subject to the racial logic of "deportability" and the racism that guides surveillance and deportation (e.g., Chávez 2008; De Genova 2005; Rosas 2007). The shifting and racialized character of deportability and deportation underscores the complexities of studying "undocumented migration" and points to the significance of ethnographic research in the analysis of both migration and return.

This work draws on and contributes to different bodies of literature, including emergent scholarship about "illegality," "deportability," state power, and return migration, as well as ongoing discussions about transnational movement within the field of migration studies. Recent scholarship focuses on the construction of "(il)legality" and "illegal" subjects as people cross nation-state borders (e.g., Chávez 2008; Coutin 2000, 2007; De Genova 2002, 2005; Ngai 2004). These scholars emphasize the historical, political, and social context within which states define migrants as "illegal" and the effect of such processes of categorization. Collectively, this body of work demonstrates how categories linked to "illegality" are produced and maintained.

Here, deportation and "deportability" figure prominently: research has focused on, among other topics, how exclusion and return have been tied to the development of the nation (Kanstroom 2007; Ngai 2004); the racialized character of policing within the United States and at the U.S.-Mexico Border (Chávez 2008; De Genova 2005; Rosas 2007); the ways that "criminality" is constructed within processes of deportation (Coutin, this volume; Peutz 2006; Zilberg 2004); and the character of state power as national governments create policies, patrol borders, and implement removals (Coutin 2007; Heyman 1995, 1999; Peutz 2006; Peutz and De Genova, 2010). My research contributes to the work on illegality and deportability by extending analysis of deportation to migrants' nations of origin or current nations of residence (see also Coutin 2007; Peutz 2006; Zilberg 2004), studying the impact of legal categories formulated in the United States among a population central to U.S. immigration processes and policies: migrants from and/or currently residing in Mexico.

Through a focus on the everyday lives of transnational Mexicans, my work also augments ethnographic study of the ways that state regimes, institutions, and agents interpret, implement, and/or extend immigration laws (Coutin 2000, 2007; Heyman 1995, 1999). Ethnography among deportees, those who have moved through state systems of immigration control and removal, is fruitful in explicating processes which may be difficult for researchers to "reach" (Rhodes 2006), including "vast institutional machinery—consisting of local jails, prisons, detention centers, INS and FBI surveillance and interrogation, transport, and more" (Rhodes 2006: 235). The perspective of transnational Mexicans, a view from those directly impacted by U.S. policies and practices, contributes to our understanding of the complexity of state structures and multiple state actors.

In addition, my analysis links to the body of work on "return migration," scholarship that examines the processes through which (im)migrants and/or their descendants go back to their or their family's country of origin. This research typically focuses on second (or later) generations and processes of voluntary return (e.g., Tsuda 2003), although the return migration of Mexican nationals has not been a primary focus. Similarly, research about different forms of first-generation return (Markowitz and Stefansson 2004), including work about refugees and exiles returning to their homelands, has not included comprehensive study of Mexican return or "reverse" migration. My research expands notions of north-south movement by including different forms of forced returns: those labeled "voluntary" by the DHS (U.S. DHS 2008: 95) as well as formal "removals" or deportations. Above all, the project adds to the emergent body of research on return migration by focusing specifically on Mexican nationals and by looking at an understudied yet crucial aspect of "return migration": first-generation, involuntary return.

Significantly, this project also engages a growing literature that incorporates and revisits previous work on transnationality and globalization, situating the study of deportation within interdisciplinary migration studies. The "removal" of undocumented Mexican migrants is entwined with international migration and must be considered within a transnational frame (Coutin 2007; Zilberg 2004). While much of the research about Mexican migration has considered movement from a transnational perspective (e.g., Kearney 2004; Rouse 1991; Stephen 2007), including my own (Boehm 2012), there has not been comparable ethnographic, binational study of deportation and forced return, largely because these are processes-in-the-making.

Previous studies of transnationalism have been criticized for an overemphasis on the weakening of the state (see Aretxaga 2003), although as Begoña Aretxaga argues, globalization "is not only compatible with statehood; it has actually fueled the desire for it" (2003: 393). In response to such critique, recent scholarship theorizes transnational encounters as "friction" (Tsing 2005), laden with "growing inequality" and "exclusion" (Appadurai 2006: x). Reconsiderations of state power capture the erosion of state power as well as reformulations of state control (e.g., Rosas 2007). This chapter, then, draws on this shift in research foci, situating an understudied aspect of U.S.-Mexico migration—deportation or forced north-south movement—within the context of "transmigration" (Glick Schiller et al. 1995). The research also captures the unstable, durable, and developing character of state power in transnational context, underscoring how deportation and removal are always intertwined with past and future transnational flows.

The narratives of un/certainty that I focus on in this chapter point to the inherently temporal dimensions of global movement. Both migration and deportation are understood in terms of time and are "temporally complex" (Yngvesson and Coutin 2006: 181); these transnational processes represent a convergence of temporal scales, a collapsing and/or interdependence of past, present, and future (see also Yngvesson and Coutin 2006: 184). Migration is clearly linked to the past through the historical factors that have shaped movement. Another connection to the past is the fact that family and community members, from previous and current generations, have migrated, whether it was as unauthorized migrants last month or as Braceros in the 1940s. Migration is also in the present, especially as it provides subsistence for families through remittances. Finally, Mexican migration to the United States is nearly always focused on that which is yet to come: people repeatedly equate migration with their hopes for a secure future, for themselves, but especially for their families and children (Boehm 2008b).

Deportation, on the other hand, is nearly void of future imaginings, except as expressions of the future as unknown or a definitive dead-end. Here, too, past individual experiences collide with present events and future trajectories. Previous actions that seemed insignificant or at least commonplace, such as obtaining a social security card, can have a lasting, calamitous effect. Life in the United States, and/or the support provided by labor migrations, is understood as fleeting, since one can be deported at any time, while deportation and the threat of removal are persistent, a perpetual state of unpredictability that frames unauthorized migration. In this chapter, I focus on how these different dimensions of time and insecurity are expressed in the narratives of undocumented migrants. By placing discourses of temporality—particularly those of un/certainty, im/permanence, and un/predictability—at the center of my analysis, I emphasize how the unknown aspects of individual trajectories are, paradoxically, accompanied by a sense of surety, as persistence, permanence, or finality, for deportees and unauthorized (im)migrants.

Un/certainty, then, frames discourses about migration, but especially discussions of deportations: in the refrain, "¿*Quien sabe?* [Who knows?]," a phrase that is peppered throughout nearly every conversation about migration and return, there is a recognition of the many aspects of transnational movement that cannot be controlled or are driven by broader forces. Migrants hope for "*suerte* [luck]" and acknowledge the limits to individual agency, "*Así es la vida* [That's life]." While such tropes can be read as fatalistic, I understand them to be expressions of social reality, or what Maria Tapias has termed the "embodiment of social suffering" (2006). Such statements point to the vast "gulf between who is in and who is out" (Bhabha 1998: 612), the expulsion or attempted erasure of undocumented (im)migrants.

DEPORTABLE: THE UN/CERTAINTY OF DEPORTABILITY

The tension was thick, as families filled the room for an information session about immigrant rights. There had recently been raids at several fast-food franchises and insecurity among the immigrant community was growing. The meeting, held in Reno, Nevada, had been coordinated by activists and community organizations, and featured a panel of attorneys, service providers, and a representative from the Mexican consulate. The attorneys focused on steps to take in the event that a migrant is arrested, preparations *in case of* detention and possible deportation. Migrants expressed concerns, some specific to their individual cases and others that applied to the collective. As the panelists took questions from the audience, a reality became clear: there is a predictable, if not inevitable, path should undocumented migrants be detained. As the attorneys explained, exceptions are rarely granted, so it was especially important to prevent, if at all possible, arrest and detention.

Here, lives in the present are repeatedly shaped by preparations to stave off potential risks in the future. Attorneys explained to (im)migrants what they could legally do if the police or immigration officials came to their home or work, or stopped them in a public place. The organizers handed out booklets explaining immigrant rights and outlined the limited preventative steps immigrants could take now: locate an attorney and always have her/his phone number on hand, carry an immigrant rights card stating the desire to contact an attorney if taken into custody, make copies of important documents, and most disturbing to parents, make arrangements for the care of children in the event of an arrest. But how does one prepare for deportation, a legal process that devastates families, turns lives upside-down, or as one man described, "is the end of your world"? One cannot anticipate the finality of deportation and its limited options: the reality is that most undocumented migrants have no legal recourse, no prospect for alternative trajectories should they be arrested and detained.

In this section, I consider "deportability" (De Genova 2002), the possibility of deportation and the accompanying fear that it is imminent: "Migrant 'illegality' is lived through a palpable sense of deportability—which is to say, the possibility of deportation, the possibility of being 'removed' from the space of the state" (De Genova 2002: 439). Those without documents articulate the uncertainty associated with going outside of their homes and support networks, describing trips to the grocery store, meetings at their children's schools, and especially time at work as risky, alarming, or dangerous. As Daniel, an unauthorized migrant, explained:

> Life as an undocumented immigrant is uncertain . . . When I go to work, to buy groceries, to pay bills, I'm afraid. It's dangerous for my family to go out, wondering if *la migra* [U.S. Immigration and Customs Enforcement] is going to come. . . . We all fear deportation, we live this way . . . the fear of leaving the house to work each day—it's annihilating, destructive.

In communities throughout the United States, workplace raids, Immigration and Customs Enforcement (ICE) agents serving warrants at people's homes, arrests at the Department of Motor Vehicles (DMV) or after "routine" traffic stops, and racially motivated violence targeting undocumented migrants have increased, creating a climate of uncertainty and fear.

Deportability can define the daily lives of Mexican migrants living in the United States without papers. Even the most quotidian of activities (going to work or the grocery store) includes fear and danger, the conscious awareness of possible risk, in the distance and close to home, today or sometime in the future. Workplace raids and exchanges with law enforcement are realities, experienced by migrants and those close to them. For example, in Reno, Nevada, over the past year, ICE agents have carried out raids at places of employment as well as audits of I-9 forms (the forms required by the federal government to verify an employee's eligibility to work in the United States) at several companies. The audits resulted in the dismissal of hundreds of employees, and the impact rippled throughout the community. Nearly everyone was touched by the raids and audits.

The bind is clear: while the likelihood of being among the relatively small number of those deported is slim, deportation is actualized in communities, and all unauthorized migrants, whether or not they themselves have experienced deportation, have certainly witnessed it: the deportation of a family member, a community member, a child's friend, a coworker, a parent from their children's school. Similarly, documented transnational Mexicans feel the effects of "deportability." For example, U.S. citizen children experience fear that a parent will be deported while U.S. permanent residents can feel the insecurity that accompanies the threat of a partner's deportation. So, while deportation does not effectively reduce undocumented migration, it is very effective at controlling migrants, their families, and broader communities: "Some are deported in order that most may remain (un-deported)— as workers, whose particular migrant status may thus be rendered 'illegal'" (De Genova 2002: 439). This is a form of disciplining on the part of the state, "generalized punishment" (Foucault 1977: 73) to monitor individuals, and by extension, the social body.

But as Susan Bibler Coutin describes, in these "spaces of nonexistence" (2000: 27), one takes precautions, yet also goes on with life. For example, a man who had lived in the United States for nearly two decades without papers, Felipe, needed to renew his vehicle registration, but feared going to the DMV because of rumors that ICE agents were arresting undocumented migrants when they came in to apply for a driver's license or register their automobile. Felipe considered not registering his vehicle, but thought it important to follow the laws in the United States and went ahead with it. Concerned that his undocumented status might be discovered, Felipe decided to have a friend, a U.S. permanent resident, register the vehicle in her name. He accompanied her to the DMV, and when the DMV representative suggested they include both names, Felipe agreed. After waiting several hours (Felipe and his friend thought that this was the standard wait time) five ICE agents appeared and arrested Felipe. Here, Felipe's fears were actualized through his experience of the everyday; the seemingly mundane act of registering his vehicle and, poignantly, what he understood to be his duty as a responsible community member, resulted in this event that changed his life course.

In an attempt to ward off the risks of deportability, migrants have responded as they are able, although there are limits to one's countering of the uncertainty of deportability. For example, phone trees, e-mail and text messages, and hushed conversations communicate potential dangers. As Susana explained, she credits a phone call from a friend with securing her family's safety on one particular day:

> A coworker had warned me not to go outside. Her friend worked for *la migra* [U.S. Immigration and Customs Enforcement] and tipped her off that raids were to take place that morning. She initially called people she knew, and then we all starting calling and texting everyone we knew. I had my children stay home. We didn't go out. That day, the raids took place.

However, Susana's sense of security was fleeting: "What about the next time?" she asked. "We must be vigilant, the possibility that we will be caught . . . it doesn't end."

Similarly, raids and audits, whether or not one is directly affected by them, sow uncertainty and can change future plans in an instant. For example, the day following an I-9 audit at a major employer in Nevada, many community members, concerned with their safety and that of their family members, did not leave their homes or allow their children to go out, even for school or work. Some of the migrants, especially those dismissed from positions because of the I-9 audits, felt it necessary to move from their homes to further protect themselves and their families; told by their former employers that ICE officials had lists of employees without required documentation, individuals and families picked up and moved to new residences in the area or left the state entirely. This tangible "deportability," as assigned by the state, underscores what Coutin (this volume) has termed the "inviability of life." Here, lives are constructed as "expendable" (Coutin, this volume), underscoring the heaviness, the un/certainty of living lives deemed dispensable.

DEPORTED: THE IM/PERMANENCE OF DEPORTATION

"It was very humiliating. . . . There I was in an orange jumpsuit, handcuffed. It was awful." As Pedro retold the details of his detention and deportation, he stared at the ground and spoke softly. Pedro was one of the first deportees to tell me his story when I was in San Marcos in 2008. Pedro recounted how, ashamed of the experience of being deported, he decided he would not attempt return to Dallas; instead, his wife and youngest children came to Mexico while his adult children chose to remain in Texas. Pedro's father's death was the impetus for a chain of events that ended with his deportation. When his father died, explained Pedro, he felt it was his responsibility to return to the *rancho* to support his mother and siblings during such a difficult time. He had been gone for more than 12 years when he returned to San Marcos. He went back to the *rancho* for several months, making arrangements for the burial and helping his mother move into his sister's home. But when Pedro tried to go back to his family, crossing into the United States turned out to be a challenging, and ultimately impossible, endeavor. Pedro tried to cross five times: once in Laredo, twice in the desert of Sonora, and twice near Ciudad Juárez. The first four crossings resulted in being picked up by Border Patrol agents and then "returned" to Mexico. The fifth attempt at crossing into the United States, however, altered Pedro's trajectory, indefinitely from his perspective.

The fifth and final crossing took place at Ciudad Juárez/El Paso. Pedro went to the border with his nephew and they arranged to cross with *coyotes* (individuals paid to facilitate entry into the United States). The larger group, which included 27 people, was stopped. Pedro's nephew was returned without formal proceedings, but Pedro was arrested and transported to Dallas, because of, he was told, an outstanding warrant for his arrest. Pedro had been arrested the prior year as he was driving to work. When he was pulled over, the police officer said he had turned without signaling; he was put in jail for a brief time, given a date for a court appearance, and then released. To this day, Pedro remains uncertain about why he was initially arrested for a minor traffic infraction and believes he was racially profiled by police. Because he was undocumented and feared deportation, Pedro never appeared at his hearing. In federal detention, he was given a "choice:" wait up to 18 months for a trial or be deported immediately. Dreading even another week in detention, he opted for deportation, but was told that he would not be able to return to the United States for at least 10 years. Agents said that if he did return and was caught, he would be imprisoned for a minimum of a decade. For Pedro, 18 months seemed an eternity, and so he signed, and was "removed."

In this section, I examine detention and deportation itself, focusing on several cases in which deportation was actualized. Detention in local jails, transport to and detention in federal immigration facilities, and the process of "removal" are described as harrowing and shameful. Whether it is time at a county jail, solitary confinement in federal detention, or even one's "release" while awaiting trial, migrants' narratives emphasize the temporal aspects of removal, a sense of im/permanence that accompanies forced return. Migrants speak of being "caught," both when they are arrested and as they imagine limited future trajectories, though discourses describing deportation also focus on its contradictory elements. Transnational Mexicans tell of both the enduring and temporary aspects of removal: they express the finality of deportation but also its fleeting, less certain dimensions.

As with deportability, migrants' temporal understandings of removal are framed by uncertainty and confusion. Is deportation a permanent or a temporary state? Through processes of removal, there is a presentation of certainty or permanence on the part of immigration officials, and yet for migrants, deportation is defined by obscurity and confusion. Virtually every conversation I have had with deportees about the process of "removal" includes bewilderment or perplexity about what precisely happened, the process through which they were removed, how they ended up back in Mexico, and the permanence of removal. Of course, there is no preparing for deportation and its paradoxical effects: even as one fears its imminence it is difficult to imagine in concrete terms; if deportation is actualized, it has unreal, murky dimensions as well as tangible consequences. Expelled from the United States, deportees describe finality, a dead-end of return, and yet, deportation can be a temporary state.

The experience of Felipe, whom I discussed above, captures the un/certainty and im/permanence of removal. When Felipe was arrested at the DMV, it was a confusing process that directly threatened his family's security. First, the family was unable to locate him. Scared to contact ICE officials because they themselves were undocumented, family members asked friends who were U.S. permanent residents or U.S. citizens to call and inquire about his whereabouts. These calls resulted in further confusion, when administrators of the county jail did not have Felipe on their records and calls to ICE went directly to voicemail. Felipe was essentially erased from the community (see Coutin 2000: 35): one day he was registering his vehicle, the next he had been taken from his daily life, unable to contact family and/or be located by family and friends. Although he was clearly rooted in the United States (he had spent the majority of his life in the country, 19 years after arriving at age 14), he was instantly taken away. Soon after his arrest, family members put together the funds to retain an attorney, though the lawyer was not hopeful about Felipe's chances of staying in the United States. Deportation was likely, and as the attorneys had explained at the information session earlier in the year, given the current laws it was essentially permanent. There was little that could be done to prevent Felipe's removal and there were few chances for his "legal" return to the United States anytime in the future.

Another case of deportation involved the Hernandez family. I met Flora when I was in Mexico in 2001. At the time, Flora's husband Enrique was living in Fresno, California, working at a restaurant with several men from the *rancho,* including Flora's brothers. Flora and her children had financial security: Enrique sent money regularly and Flora was overseeing the addition of a third bedroom to their home. When I was in San Marcos again in 2007, I met Enrique for the first time. He was living in the *rancho* after an encounter with U.S. immigration officials several months earlier. Like Pedro, Enrique was arrested while attempting to cross back into the United States; in Enrique's case, he was just east of Tijuana/San Diego. As he explained his interactions with U.S. Border Patrol agents, Enrique expressed uncertainty about what precisely had happened when he was, as he described, "sent back." And as with Pedro, Border Patrol agents conveyed finality: Enrique was told that he could not return to the United States for "a very long time." "How many years?" I asked. Enrique paused, "Maybe five years, seven years?" He could not be certain. Was he, I asked, deported or "returned"? Did he appear before a judge? Did he have a trial? Again, Enrique could not be sure. Yes, he explained, he spoke with someone . . . perhaps the man was a judge, or maybe an attorney? "*¿Quien sabe?* [Who knows?]" Enrique shrugged. "Honestly, I just don't know."

This is a point of confusion for nearly all individuals who have interacted with immigration officials, whether in detention or at the border, and been subsequently sent back to Mexico. Such obscurity serves the state in its implementation of "deportability." It also perpetuates an undocumented migrant's status as outside legal processes—and therefore without legal rights—further marginalizing migrant communities. For those who have been "removed" from the United States, whether they have been deported or "returned," there is an enduring, seemingly permanent dimension: this is a return to a tangible reality, the economic suffering that led to unauthorized migration in the first place. It is from this place that it is difficult to imagine an out, although, as I discuss in the conclusion, repeat or "return" migration to the United States may be one's only option.

Consider, finally, the experiences of Rodrigo, a migrant whose parents and adult siblings are U.S. residents. In the 1980s, Rodrigo had been living in the United States, though he returned to Mexico because of health problems, and therefore he did not receive amnesty as several of his family members did. Years later, however, he was able to obtain a tourist visa, which allowed him to visit his parents and siblings (who are U.S. permanent residents), adult children (who are undocumented migrants), and grandchildren (with mixed statuses) in New Mexico. Prior to his "removal" from the United States in 2006, Rodrigo and his wife had traveled twice using the tourist visa without difficulties, each time careful to return to Mexico within the six-month period for which they were granted permission to be in the United States. Rodrigo explained to me that he did not want to break any U.S. laws, and so he always came back to Mexico within the allotted timeframe.

On his third trip north, in 2006, Rodrigo's experience was quite different than during previous border crossings. When he arrived at the U.S. port of entry at El Paso, he and his wife were taken aside, each questioned for several hours separately because, as outlined in the "Notice to Alien Ordered Removed/Departure Verification" he was later given, Rodrigo was "suspected of being an intended immigrant." Like the everyday lives of undocumented migrants in the United States, this was a process filled with fear for both Rodrigo and his wife, Tina. Ironically, he experienced "deportability" and was deported without having actually entered the borders of the nation. His Mexican passport, with the U.S. tourist visa inside, was confiscated and he was formally "removed."

The questioning of Rodrigo by a Border Patrol agent reveals intersecting scales of temporality. According to Rodrigo, the agent pressured him to discuss years from the past during which he had worked without papers in the United States. Curiously, this time during the 1970s and 1980s was the precise period when individuals who received amnesty through IRCA were also working without documents. For example, Rodrigo's two brothers, now U.S. permanent residents, both worked with Rodrigo, first in agriculture and then for a construction company in Albuquerque. Here, the past, present, and future converged in unsettling ways. In this moment, this one afternoon, Rodrigo's future trajectory took a certain, seemingly permanent turn based on events from decades ago.

Just prior to his "removal," Rodrigo was given a stack of paperwork, including a transcript of his exchange with Border Patrol agents. Then he walked across the pedestrian bridge at El Paso/Ciudad Juárez and took a cab to the bus station for his eventual return to the *rancho*. Several of the questions in the transcript of Rodrigo's removal documents aim to verify the clarity of the proceedings and his understanding of the events; the transcript ends on a definitive note, with Rodrigo's signature at the bottom of the document indicating that the information is correct and that he understood the ramifications. However, while these documents represent the proceedings as clear and straightforward, they were, for Rodrigo, a source of great confusion. When I spoke with Rodrigo about the experience, there was little certainty, a quite different rendition of that day than the official documents indicate. "I didn't understand it . . . honestly, I'm still not sure what happened. It was all very confusing. My wife was in another room, and so I was worried about her. Also, I was concerned that they would go after my parents and my brothers [U.S. permanent residents] and punish them." He showed me the forms and asked if there was anything that could be done. Could I, he wondered, at least explain to him what it all meant? Could he return to the United States sometime in the future or was he permanently banned from entering?

"WHERE DO WE GO FROM HERE?"
RETURNING AGAIN AND THE UN/PREDICTABILITY OF TRANSNATIONAL MIGRATION

A few days after I spoke with Pedro, who was deported after an attempted crossing into the United States, his wife Lucia invited me over for a visit. That afternoon, sitting next to a shrine to the Virgin of Guadalupe, Lucia told me how much she missed the United States, her home for nine years. She said that, although she never imagined she would, she found herself nostalgic about *los bolillos* [slang for white U.S. citizens, literally white sandwich rolls]. She laughed as she remembered her first weeks in a community outside of Dallas, Texas. "It was awful. . . . I missed Mexico so! I couldn't imagine creating a life for our family there. But that's exactly what happened. Over time we became comfortable there. Our children studied, made friends, my youngest son was born there. It became our home."

As we spoke over the noise of a construction project taking place at the back of the house (they were installing a bathroom), Lucia described the temporal aspects of the family's return: "We have had to start over . . . we're like newlyweds with nothing. When I left years ago, we didn't plan to return. . . . We are starting from the beginning this time." Lucia also described the unpredictability of her and her family's future. "*¿Quien sabe?* [Who knows?]" she asked. Lucia went on:

> Who knows what the future will bring? My husband says he will never return, but I will go if I need to. There hasn't been any rain! If we aren't able to plant, there will be no bean harvest. How can we survive like this? Yes, if I must, I will go. I don't know how, but I will go.

She said that she did not know if she would continue to have the "luck" she had the previous times she had crossed with a *coyote*. It was different then, she explained, but now "it is hard to know. . . . I wonder if the next time I cross it will not be so easy. I crossed twice without problems, but one never knows what will happen." Even as Lucia and Pedro made arrangements for their future in Mexico—cleaning out their home that had been empty for nearly a decade, building a bathroom, buying a refrigerator with remittances from their children, requesting a telephone line—they were both aware that the future was unpredictable.

Their sentiments were similar to that of José, an undocumented migrant contemplating the possibility of deportation. "Where do we go from here?" he had asked, a question that ended our interview and to which there was no adequate response. Deportation presents a void, a vacuum, and yet it is an uncertainty that is concrete and palpable. Deportees are not alone in assuming futures with limited options; nearly all undocumented migrants present an understandably narrow view of future individual and collective transnational lives. While hope for comprehensive immigration reform and a possible amnesty remains, it is overshadowed by the immediacy of increasing deportations and the multiple factors that continue to drive migration from Mexico to the United States. Undocumented migrants and deportees, caught between processes of migration and forced return, articulate the ways they are slotted into an underclass. As Lucia declared, "You [Americans] want us in your country, but then you throw us out!" Paradoxically, while the future trajectories of deportees and migrants are vague and unclear, removal—forced return to Mexico—is likely to result in migrants' "return" migration to the United States.

One aspect seems certain for Lucia and Pedro, indeed all migrants impacted by deportation: future trajectories will be linked to ongoing transnational migration, a "chronic, contradictory transnationalism" (Rouse 1992: 46). At the very least, deportees will depend on the remittances of family members living in the United States. Agricultural hardship in home communities, a global economic crisis, increasing violence throughout Mexico, and significantly, a demand for unauthorized labor in the United States (as one woman stated, "We Mexicans are the mules of your country") drive such future migrations and "returns" north. For example, Enrique told me that, regardless of the formalities of his removal, "I'll go back. I have to go back." Rodrigo explained that he would probably return to the United States sometime in the future, above all because "many of my children and grandchildren are there." And while Pedro was adamant that he would stay in Mexico, his wife Lucia was willing to go if needed or, she said, perhaps their 13–year-old son would leave in a couple of years as an undocumented labor migrant like his father. Pedro and Lucia also expect that their four-year-old son, a U.S. citizen, will someday return to "his country." After describing in an interview the gravity and sense of permanence in being returned, one man wished me well on the day of my departure from the *rancho* to the United States: "Safe travels. . . . I might even see you there!"

At the back of the booklet distributed at the information session I described above, there is a small drawing offering hope: A crowd of people are standing in front of the U.S. capitol, smiling and cheering. A banner reads, "*Reforma Migratoria* [Immigration Reform]— Opportunities for All!" Here, an imagined future of security replaces the uncertainty and instability of the present. For now, however, the words of migrants tell another story. As one man described, the temporal frame of deportation and deportability is unending: "There's no freedom . . . day after day, year after year—the fear is damaging." The narratives of deportees, unauthorized migrants, and documented transnational Mexicans capture the contradictions of deportation and deportability: its im/permanence and a persistent or even predictable uncertainty. It seems that in a milieu characterized both by a growing number of removals of Mexican nationals from the United States and the necessity for ongoing transnational migration, there is an uncertainty one can count on.

WORKS CITED

Appadurai, Arjun (2006). Fear of Small Numbers: An Essay on the Geography of Anger. Durham: Duke University Press.

Aretxaga, Begoña (2003). Maddening States. Annual Review of Anthropology 32: 393–410.

Batalova, Jeanne (2008). Mexican Immigrants in the United States. A Report by the Migration Policy Institute, April 2008 (www.migrationinformation.org).

Bhabha, Jacqueline (1998). "Get Back to Where You Once Belonged": Identity, Citizenship, and Exclusion in Europe. Human Rights Quarterly 20: 592–727.

Boehm, Deborah A. (2008a). "Now I Am a Man and a Woman!": Gendered Moves and Migrations in a Transnational Mexican Community. Latin American Perspectives 35 (1): 16–30.

Boehm, Deborah A. (2008b). "For My Children": Constructing Family and Navigating the State in the U.S.-Mexico Transnation. Anthropological Quarterly 81 (4): 765–790.

Boehm, Deborah A. (2011). Here/Not Here: Contingent Citizenship and Transnational Mexican Children. IN Everyday Ruptures: Children, Youth, and Migration in Global Perspective, Cati Coe, Rachel Reynolds, Deborah A. Boehm, Julia Meredith Hess, and Heather Rae-Espinoza (eds.). Nashville, TN: Vanderbilt University Press, pp. 161–173.

Boehm, Deborah A. (2012). Intimate Migrations: Gender, Family, and Illegality Among Transnational Mexicans. New York: New York University Press.

Capps, Randy, Rose Maria Castañeda, Ajay Chaudry, and Robert Santos (2007). Paying the Price: The Impact of Immigration Raids on America's Children. A Report by The Urban Institute. Washington DC: National Council of La Raza.

Cave, Damien (2008). States Take New Tack on Illegal Immigration. New York Times 6/9/2008.

Chávez, Leo R. (2008). The Latino Threat: Constructing Immigrants, Citizens, and the Nation. Stanford: Stanford University Press.

Coutin, Susan Bibler (2000). Legalizing Moves: Salvadoran Immigrants' Struggle for U.S. Residency. Ann Arbor: University of Michigan Press.

Coutin, Susan Bibler (2007). Nations of Emigrants: Shifting Boundaries of Citizenship in El Salvador and the United States. Ithaca: Cornell University Press.

De Genova, Nicholas P. (2002). Migrant "Illegality" and Deportability in Everyday Life. Annual Review of Anthropology 31: 419–447.

De Genova, Nicholas P. (2005). Working the Boundaries: Race, Space, and "Illegality" in Mexican Chicago. Durham: Duke University Press.

Foucault, Michel (1977). Discipline and Punish: The Birth of the Prison. Translated from French by Alan Sheridan. New York: Pantheon Books.

Glick Schiller, Nina, Linda Basch, and Cristina Blanc-Szanton (1995). From Immigrant to Transnational Migrant: Theorizing Transnational Migration. Anthropological Quarterly 68: 48–63.

Heyman, Josiah McC. (1995). Putting Power into the Anthropology of Bureaucracy: The Immigration and Naturalization Service at the Mexico-United States Border. Current Anthropology 36 (2): 261–287

Heyman, Josiah McC. (1999). State Escalation of Force: A Vietnam/U.S.-Mexico Border Analogy. IN States and Illegal Practices, Josiah Heyman (ed.). Oxford: Berg Publishers, pp. 285–314.

Kanstroom, Daniel (2007). Deportation Nation. Cambridge: Harvard University Press.

Kearney, Michael (2004). Changing Fields of Anthropology: From Local to Global. Lanham, MD: Rowman & Littlefield.

Markowitz, Fran and Anders H. Stefansson (2004). Homecomings: Unsettling Paths of Return. New York: Lexington Books.

Ngai, Mae M. (2004). Impossible Subjects: Illegal Aliens and the Making of Modern America. Princeton: Princeton University Press.

Passel, Jeffrey S. and D'Vera Cohn (2008). Trends in Unauthorized Immigration: Undocumented Inflow Now Trails Legal Inflow. Washington, DC: Pew Hispanic Center, October.

Passel Jeffrey S. and D'Vera Cohn (2009). A Portrait of Unauthorized Immigrants in the United States. Washington, DC: Pew Hispanic Center, April.

Peutz, Nathalie (2006). Embarking on an Anthropology of Removal. Current Anthropology 47 (2): 217–241.

Peutz, Nathalie and Nicholas De Genova (eds.) (2010). The Deportation Regime: Sovereignty, Space, and the Freedom of Movement. Durham: Duke University Press.

Preston, Julia (2007). Immigration Quandary: A Mother Torn from Her Baby. New York Times, November 17.

Preston, Julia (2008). Perfectly Legal Immigrants, Until They Applied for Citizenship. New York Times, April 12.

Rhodes, Lorna A. (2006). Comments—Embarking on an Anthropology of Removal by Nathalie Peutz. Current Anthropology 47 (2): 235–237.

Rosas, Gilberto (2007). The Fragile Ends of War: Forging the United States-Mexico Border and Borderlands Consciousness. Social Text 25 (2): 81–102.

Rouse, Roger (1991). Mexican Migration and the Social Space of Postmodernism. Diaspora 1 (1): 8–23.

Rouse, Roger (1992). Making Sense of Settlement: Class Transformation, Cultural Struggle, and Transnationalism Among Mexican Migrants in the United States. IN Towards a Transnational Perspective on Migration: Race, Class, Ethnicity and Nationalism Reconsidered, Linda Basch,

Nina Glick Schiller, and Cristina Blanc-Szanton (eds.). New York: New York Academy of Sciences, pp. 25–52.

Stephen, Lynn (2007). Transborder Lives: Indigenous Oaxacans in Mexico, California, and Oregon. Durham: Duke University Press.

Tapias, Maria (2006). Emotions and the Intergenerational Embodiment of Social Suffering in Rural Bolivia. Medical Anthropological Quarterly 20 (3): 399–415.

Tsing, Anna Lowenhaupt (2005). Friction: An Ethnography of Global Connection. Princeton: Princeton University Press.

Tsuda, Takeyuki (Gaku) (2003). Strangers in the Ethnic Homeland: Japanese Brazilian Return Migration in Transnational Perspective. New York: Columbia University Press.

U.S. Department of Homeland Security (DHS) (2008). 2007 Yearbook of Immigration Statistics. Washington, D.C.: U.S. Department of Homeland Security, Office of Immigration Statistics.

Yngvesson, Barbara and Susan Bibler Coutin (2006). Backed by Papers: Undoing Persons, Histories, and Return. American Ethnologist 33 (2): 177–190.

Zilberg, Elana (2004). Fools Banished from the Kingdom: Remapping Geographies of Gang Violence Between the Americas (Los Angeles and San Salvador). American Quarterly 56: 759–779.

EXILED BY LAW

DEPORTATION AND THE INVIABILITY OF LIFE

Susan Bibler Coutin

A Rampart Division CRASH [Community Resources Against Street Hoodlums] officer pursuing a case against a 15-year-old accused of a fatal double shooting attempted to arrange the deportation of a high-profile activist whose testimony could clear the youth of murder charges, the activist says. . . .

Alex Sanchez, who is being held at the federal immigration detention facility in San Pedro, said his Jan. 21 [2000] arrest by Rampart Officer Jesus Amezcua came after months of threats and harassment against him and other activists in Homies Unidos, a group working to end gang violence. . . .

Sanchez and others say Jose Rodriguez, the teenager accused of murder, was at a Homies Unidos meeting at the time the shooting took place in August. . . .

The arrest of Sanchez—whose detention has made him something of a cause celebre—is the most recent example of what critics say is Rampart Division officers' use of immigration issues to eliminate troublesome witnesses by having them deported. . . .

In an interview, Sanchez said he and Amezcua were well-acquainted by the time the officer arrested him. Last summer, Amezcua stopped him and photographed him, saying he looked suspicious, Sanchez said.

A few weeks later, on Aug. 6, Amezcua kicked open the door at a birthday party for Sanchez's fiancée, along with another officer who shoved a girl's face against the wall several times and hit Sanchez in the head with a baton, Sanchez said.

He said he next saw Amezcua after the slaying, at a Juvenile Court hearing for Rodriguez. After that, according to Sanchez, Amezcua began to stop him routinely on the street and search him, sometimes punching him in the groin, telling him: "We'll see who wins the court trial—his gang or our gang."

Sanchez and others said Amezcua was one of the officers who regularly harassed many

Susan Bibler Coutin is professor of Criminology, Law, and Society and Anthropology at the University of California, Irvine.

Reprinted with permission of Duke University Press, from "Exiled by Law: Deportation and the Inviability of Life," by Susan Bibler Coutin, in *The Deportation Regime: Sovereignty, Space, and the Freedom of Movement*, edited by Nicholas De Genova and Nathalie Peutz. Copyright © 2010 by Duke University Press. All rights reserved.

members of Homies Unidos, stopping them on their way to and from the group's Thursday night meetings at Immanuel Presbyterian Church on Wilshire Boulevard.

He said Amezcua was one of several officers who went to the church in September just hours before state Sen. Tom Hayden (D–Los Angeles) was to hold a nighttime hearing on harassment of the group. . . .

When Amezcua saw Sanchez on the street later, he said "he was going to see me behind bars, and he gave Homies Unidos six months to live," Sanchez alleged. . . .

Not long before his arrest, Sanchez said, Amezcua searched him and a friend, Ricardo Hernandez, who was arrested on a minor charge and then held because of his own illegal immigration status.

Then at 8 P.M., Jan. 21, Amezcua stopped Sanchez and told him he was wanted by the INS, saying: "'It's over. You can take Homies Unidos and shove it' . . . [were his] exact words," Sanchez said. . . .

He said Amezcua refused to let him call a lawyer or Hayden's office. He was taken to Men's Central Jail but not booked, then transported to Parker Center, he said.

—Anne Marie O'Connor, "Activist Says Officer Sought His Deportation"

Alex Sanchez's experience of being arrested and placed in deportation proceedings after having spent most of his life in the United States is unusual in that he was the leader of a gang violence prevention program, he had the support of respected public officials such as California state senator Tom Hayden, and his case became part of the controversy over the Rampart scandal, in which officers in the Los Angeles Police Department (LAPD) were convicted of violence and the falsification of evidence against alleged gang members (Zilberg 2002). At the same time, his experience is not unusual in that deporting aliens with criminal convictions has increasingly been a goal of both immigration and crime control policies in the United States (Coutin 2005). Further, U.S. antigang policies, which assign gang membership based on tattoos, association, and dress style, forbid suspected gang members from congregating in particular areas, and increase penalties for those deemed to be gang members, have been exported to Central American nations and other countries, making life for deported gang members difficult at best (Zilberg 2007a).

In this chapter, I analyze how the transnational conjuncture of immigration and criminal justice policies constitutes "criminal aliens" or émigrés as expendable and indeed exiles them not only from particular legal territories but also from the social domains that make life itself viable. In the United States, removal—the legal term for deportation—has emerged as a seemingly benign technique for extricating seemingly problematic ("illegal," "criminal") noncitizens from U.S. territory. The neutrality of the term hides the violence that removal wreaks on individuals, families, communities, and the law itself. Through removal, individuals are legally stripped of their de facto or *de jure* (i.e., legal permanent residency) membership in the United States and are constituted as fully alien. They are then "returned" to countries where they are *de jure* citizens, but where, as long-term émigrés who were convicted of crimes, many lack social connections or clearly recognized legal rights. In fact, antigang policies in their countries of origin may drive them out—and back to the United States—once more. Such departures are akin to a de facto or unofficial deportation, in that law enforcement policies, lack of economic opportunity, and social stigmatization lead them to leave their "home" countries (Zilberg 2007a). By constituting "criminal aliens" as so-called enemies whose right to exist is in question, nations claim to have bolstered public security. In fact, however, such policies contribute to insecurity by rendering law itself unstable.[1]

To analyze the ways that criminal justice and immigration policies constitute certain noncitizens as expendable others, I interweave accounts of Alex Sanchez's experiences with analyses of U.S. and Salvadoran government policies. I have chosen to focus on Alex Sanchez both because of the variety of his experiences—he was deported to El Salvador in 1994, he returned to the United States in 1996, and he was placed in removal proceedings again in 2000—and because his immigration case draws attention to the violence and persecution experienced by former gang members. I also draw on fieldwork conducted in El Salvador and Los Angeles between 2000 and 2004, consisting primarily of interviews with Salvadoran immigrants in the United States, immigrant rights advocates and government officials in the United States and El Salvador, and deportees affiliated with Homies Unidos in El Salvador. This fieldwork suggests that noncitizens who have been convicted of crimes are facing a transnational injunction of sorts, such that they are not permitted to exist anywhere. Their lives are rendered inviable as they are pushed underground either figuratively, in that they must live as fugitives, or literally, in that they are subjected to violence that can lead to their deaths.

> I [Alex Sanchez] was born in San Salvador. It was a little town, on the outskirts of San Salvador going towards Cojutepeque. From San Martin . . . I remember the scene were I lived. The area, the streets, the railroad tracks and this bridge and the cliff on the back of the house I lived in. So I remember most of that stuff, but in a blur, you know. It was all in a blur. . . .
>
> I mean, the country [of El Salvador] was in conflict, and my dad had family that was involved in the movement. And, well, he had us. He had children. So he wanted something else for us. And then the area right there where we lived was like the spot where they'd throw bodies. You know, so he really wanted to get us out of there. . . .
>
> We flew to, I think, Mexico. From Mexico City, I think, I'm not too sure. I know we went on train from, I guess, Mexico to another place. And then, then there was this other friend. The same people that was taking us, took us across the border in a van. . . . I remember it was real scary. . . .
>
> I started 3rd grade. And I went to the school, Wilshire Crest. And it was really an experience because it was about speaking English and I didn't know anything. But I kind of, I mean there wasn't no ESL classes. And there wasn't, you know, that much help. And there weren't that many people around that were immigrants during that time. You know? It was mostly Chicanos or white. There weren't many blacks around that area. But I hanged around with these Chicanos and started learning English pretty fast. So then I went to 4th grade, I came to Hobart, and by that time I knew a lot of English. . . .
>
> But when I actually really felt it was when I was in 6th grade. When people used to ask me, "Well, where are you from?" And I would say, "El Salvador." And "What place?" And I would say, "San Salvador." "But where in San Salvador?" I would say, "I don't know. I just know that I'm from down there and that's it." I felt kind of frustrated that I didn't know

---

1. Antigang policies, can, for example, encourage police harassment or even, as occurred in the Rampart scandal, fabrications of evidence by authorities. Such policies can thus bolster insecurity rather than security.

where exactly I was from. But at the same time I felt proud of being a Salvadorean. I had pride in it. I would never deny it. . . .

I didn't know the place [El Salvador]. They talk about los Chorros, they talk about Apulo, they talked about la Costa del Sol, all these places. Las piscinas. And I just didn't know. Los volcanes de San Vicente. And so many things they talked about that I just didn't relate to that. And I even ended up, kind of, losing my slang through years. Salvadorean slang. So you lose a lot of things. But during the time that I came, there weren't that many Salvadoreans here in L.A.

So it was, like in . . . '85, '86, the schools were filled with Salvadorean kids by then, you know. There were a lot of people from El Salvador. And so I started kind of getting my slang back. And that's when I found out about this neighborhood, this gang that was a Salvadorean gang! You know, I related, I really related to it. And . . . I liked being with them because they spoke Spanish, they weren't always speaking English. Because I still had a little bit of trouble with pronunciations? So sometimes I'd rather speak Spanish than English. So I felt more comfortable being with these guys and speaking Spanish. It wasn't like they were like the other crowd I was with that only spoke English. In a way it helped me because I learned it faster than anything because, you know, I wasn't speaking Spanish all the time. And I was learning, trying to learn it too so I could have a conversation with them, you know. But that's when I found out about the gang, Mara Salvatrucha, and the relationship with El Salvador. Because I didn't even know what a Salvatrucha was, a mara, you know, I didn't. And I found out and I said, "Wait a minute. This is me. This is the people I belong with." (Interview, May 8, 2001)

The complex belongings that Alex Sanchez described in my interview with him are belied by legal constructs that assign citizenship to a single nation. Noncitizens can be removed from the United States because, even if they are legal permanent residents, they lack incontrovertible membership in the U.S. polity. If they are apprehended by U.S. immigration authorities or if they are convicted of crimes that make them ineligible for legal permanent residency, they can be removed to their site of legal citizenship. In the case of Alex Sanchez, this site was El Salvador, a place that he left at age seven and that he remembered only as "a blur." During his childhood, Sanchez, like many other immigrants, was situated in multiple places and nowhere at the same time. He "lost" something of El Salvador—his memories, his slang—even as he found the United States somewhat unwelcoming. There were few services for immigrant children in the public schools of Los Angeles, and though he learned English quickly, he "still had a little bit of trouble with pronunciations." As a teenager, he found himself most at home with the Mara Salvatrucha, a gang that was made up of people who, like him, were from El Salvador, spoke both Spanish and English, and were somewhat set apart from Anglo and even Chicano or Mexican American society. Such complex positionings—as outsiders within their country of origin and residency, yet members of youth subgroups belonging in some sense to both places—cannot be acknowledged by laws that elevate a legal origin as citizen over other measures of belonging, and that treat the presence of noncitizens as always, in some sense, probationary (Kanstroom 2000).

Officially, removing a noncitizen from the United States is not considered to be a punishment but is deemed merely to place individuals who are not "legally" part of the polity outside of U.S. territory. Unlike incarceration and other criminal penalties, which ostensibly "correct" (i.e., rehabilitate) while also punishing an individual for his or her wrongdoing, removal is simply the consequence of lacking the right to enter or remain within U.S. territory. Therefore, although the United States does not sentence citizens to exile or deportation, noncitizens can, in essence, be exiled. As Daniel Kanstroom points out, "Federal deportation laws based on post-entry criminal conduct require a theoretical explanation for why banishment is a punishment when applied to citizens, but is not a punishment when applied to lawful resident aliens. This explanation . . . derived from the status of alienage being seen as an increasingly tenuous claim to any rights against deportation" (2000, 1909). As individuals who have tenuous claims, noncitizens are placed in the position of supplicant—they must request the right to be present. Removal is the default position and, though it may have devastating consequences for the individuals involved, does not carry the due process protections (such as the right to a state-appointed attorney) that accompany criminal proceedings (Cole and Dempsey 2002).

In the United States, removal has become increasingly common as criminal justice and immigration policies have converged (Welch 2002; see also Stumpf this volume). In 1996 the Antiterrorism and Effective Death Penalty Act (AEDPA) and the Illegal Immigration Reform and Immigrant Responsibility Act (IIRIRA) expanded the definition of aggravated felony for immigration purposes, creating a situation that legal scholar Nancy Morawetz referred to as "Alice-in-Wonderland-like." Morawetz explains, "As the term is defined, a crime need not be either aggravated or a felony. For example, a conviction for simple battery or for shoplifting with a one-year suspended sentence—either of which would be a misdemeanor or a violation in most states—can be deemed an aggravated felony" (2000, 1939). Legal permanent residents who are convicted of such aggravated felonies are stripped of their residency and made deportable. Before 1996, noncitizens with criminal convictions could request waivers by arguing that their equities—relatives, lengthy period of residence, educational history—in the United States weighed against their deportation. The 1996 laws eliminated such challenges, made both detention and removal mandatory, and applied this new policy retroactively, to convictions that occurred prior to 1996 (Hafetz 1998). Noncitizens were made a particular target of law enforcement practices, and criminals were made a target of deportation policies. As Kanstroom points out, "Deportation policy . . . has aimed increasingly at permanently 'cleansing' our society of those with undesirable qualities, especially criminal behavior" (2000, 1892).

The convergence between immigration and criminal justice policies extends the logic of mass-incarceration policies to immigrant populations. Correctional practices have recently moved from a rehabilitation model to what Feeley and Simon (1992) term "risk management." Instead of attempting to reform socially deviant individuals, prisons now attempt to "manage" dangerous persons, who are then "warehoused" as part of ever-growing prison populations. Prisons are conceptualized as a space *outside* society (Schinkel 2002), as evidenced by the increasing use of the term "reentry" to refer to being released from prison (Petersilia 2003). Targeting noncitizens who have been convicted of crimes extends this spatialized logic in that such individuals are physically removed from U.S. society and territory, initially through detention centers and eventually through deportation. Warehousing offenders and deporting noncitizens with criminal convictions also have similar social consequences. In both cases, individuals are removed from communities, family members are subjected to lengthy separations, and populations are excluded from the electoral process (felons are often disenfranchised, and noncitizens cannot vote in the United States). A Bureau of Justice Statistics report attributed 14 percent of the growth in the federal prison population between 1985 and 2000 to increases in the incarceration of immigration offenders (Scalia and Litras 2002). The 1996 laws had an immediate and dramatic effect on the number of noncitizens forcibly removed from the United States, as table 1 shows.

The number of noncitizens forcibly removed increased by a dramatic 37 percent in 1996, when IIRIRA and AEDPA were passed, followed by even larger increases of 64 percent and 51 percent in 1997 and 1998 respectively. Subsequently, removals remained at high levels, with the exception of 2001, which remained stable, and 2002, in which there was a small decrease. Cumulatively, between 1996 and 2007, deportations more than quadrupled. Strikingly, in the year 2007 alone, deportations to El Salvador increased by 81 percent.

Although criminal justice and immigration policies attempt to resituate noncitizens who are convicted of crimes in a space outside of the U.S. territory and polity, such individuals may in fact have myriad ties to the United States, whether or not they are physically present. As Elana Zilberg notes, "Banished though they may be from the U.S., these deported youth and young adults remain linked to that landscape through, among other things, ongoing ties with family. . . . Deportees remain an integral part of the 'structure of feeling' [of] the *barrio*, of its internal relations and the everyday practices of its residents" (2007b, 495). The individuals who are subjected to removal may have relatives in the United States; they may have attended U.S. schools, worked in the United States, developed fluent English skills, acclimated to U.S. culture (particularly to youth subcultures), and envisioned futures within this country. In the earlier interview excerpt, Alex Sanchez names the Los Angeles public schools

Table 1 *Aliens Expelled, 1991–2007*

Year	Formal Removals	Percent Increase	To El Salvador	Percent Increase
1991	33,189		1,496	
1992	43,671	31%	1,937	29%
1993	42,542	−3%	2,117	9%
1994	45,674	7%	1,900	−10%
1995	50,924	11%	1,932	2%
1996	69,680	37%	2,493	29%
1997	114,432	64%	3,900	56%
1998	174,813	53%	5,465	40%
1999	183,114	5%	4,160	−24%
2000	188,467	3%	4,736	14%
2001	189,026	0%	3,928	−17%
2002	165,168	−13%	4,066	4%
2003	211,098	28%	5,561	37%
2004	240,665	14%	7,269	31%
2005	246,431	2%	8,305	14%
2006	280,974	14%	11,050	33%
2007	319,382	14%	20,045	81%

SOURCE: U.S. Department of Homeland Security, *2007 Yearbook of Immigration Statistics,* Tables 36 and 37d, and earlier DHS and INS statistical yearbooks.

that he attended as a young child. The landscape of Los Angeles pervades his personal history. As Judge Learned Hand wrote about a Polish deportation case in 1926, "Whether the relator came here in arms or at the age of ten, he is as much our product as though his mother had borne him on American soil. He knows no other language, no other people, no other habits, than ours; he will be as much a stranger in Poland as anyone born of ancestors who immigrated in the seventeenth century" (quoted in Kanstroom 2000, 1890). Forcible removal requires reconstituting such complexly situated individuals as alien.

> Alan Diamante, Sánchez's attorney, indicated that during his youth his client was involved in a Mara Salvatrucha gang that operated on 8th Street and Normandie Avenue.
>
> He also said that when he was 18 years old, Sánchez already had a criminal record. On his rap sheet there appears a conviction for car theft, accusations of weapons possession and of intimidating witnesses.
>
> "For committing certain crimes and for having a criminal history, they deported him in 1994," stated Diamante.
>
> During his stay in El Salvador, Sánchez received threats, was persecuted and detained, according to his attorney.
>
> Those factors, and the fact that a son of his was born, motivated him to abandon gangs and return to the United States, Diamante noted.
>
> "He supposedly entered in an illegal fashion," he noted, adding that his defense only has two legal avenues.
>
> One, the attorney said literally, is to solicit suspension of removal [from the country], as a political case, and the other is to base the case on international law against torture, which states that a person cannot be sent to a country when there is sufficient proof that if he is returned, he will be tortured at the hands of the government or other groups. (Linares 2000)

The process of removal officially transforms de facto community members into aliens with no right to remain in the United States. Noncitizens who are subjected to deportation may find this transformation shocking. A Homies Unidos member who was interviewed for this project after having been deported to El Salvador could not imagine that he could never return legally to the United States: "You can't just say, 'You're expelled for life. You're deported for life.' I mean, I hope not!" Of course, deportation is not supposed to *transform* individuals. Rather, it is supposed to be a consequence of already being both alien and unauthorized. Note that in Alex Sanchez's case his only legal option when faced with deportation was to demonstrate that he could not safely return to El Salvador, and therefore he had to remain in the United States. Despite having lived in this country for more than two decades and having U.S. citizen relatives (including a wife and son), his criminal convictions, prior deportation, and unauthorized reentry were presumed to define him as alien and his presence as illicit. Nonetheless, there is a sense in which the process of deportation *produces* the very "alienage" and "illegality" from which it is supposed to flow.

The transformative nature of deportation is demonstrated by the experiences of King (a pseudonym), whom I interviewed in El Salvador in 2001. King came to the United States in the early 1980s at age four or five and became a legal permanent resident in the late 1980s, when he was approximately nine or ten. As a teenager, he began to have trouble with the law and served time in juvenile hall, but he was not concerned about immigration consequences:

"Because I had the residency, I figured, oh, shssh, I got it made, you know, a resident." King was incarcerated in 1993, and then in 1996 he learned about the passage of AEDPA and IIRIRA: "I *always* watched the news in prison. . . . And then after that Timothy McVeigh blew up that building? They passed a law, . . . instead of, you know, going after the guys that did that, they decided to wash their hands and throw it out from all the [immigrants] and residents, uh-huh. They called 'em, uh, 'a terrorist threat.' To them, we're a terrorist threat. Just because of what Timothy, Timothy McVeigh did." An immigration hold was placed on King, and when he completed his prison sentence, he was transferred to an immigration detention center, where he unsuccessfully fought his deportation case for six months. Although King had projected a future in the United States, he was ordered deported.

Before being deported, King was transferred to a holding cell, where conditions were difficult: "We were there all night, and we were cold." From the holding cell, he and others were bused to Arizona, where, in shackles, they were flown to Houston, Texas. In Texas, they were processed for deportation and then taken to a county jail, which King described as "messed up. . . . They wouldn't let us buy nothing at the store or nothing, so we didn't have no deodorant, no razor, no toothbrush. And they wouldn't, uh, give us any, because they were treating us like lower, you know what I mean? Like, you're getting deported anyways, you don't need none of that." Being treated as "lower" continued as King was placed in another holding cell: "And it was like hot, moisture. Like everything starts sweating, you know, with the body heat. And the water was no good. There was no drinking water. Only a shower to shower. The toilets were messed up, there was no pressure." King was in the holding cell for four or five days. King found these conditions dehumanizing, telling one of the sergeants, "Look, Sergeant, man, what's going on? We don't get rec, yard, nothing. You know? You're treating us like animals, man!" Finally, King and other deportees were shackled and placed on one of the oldest planes that King had ever seen: "And we took off. Fshshshshoooooooooo! All shackled up. T-t-t-t. And then, like, they give us, like, a tore-up sandwich and stuff? To eat up there? You know, I wasn't hungry, I didn't eat nothing. That's the least thing I had on my mind was food after leaving, you know, the country you were raised in." King found the shackles particularly debasing: "They think they can treat you like you don't know your rights, you know what I mean? Even if you're deportable, you still got rights, human rights."

King's account of deportation is replete with references to humiliating experiences, to being treated as an animal, as debased, as lacking rights. The shackles—which King reported were removed before landing, after flying out of U.S. airspace—were a particularly vivid marker of criminalized "illegality" and alienage. King experienced deportation not as a *return*, but rather as a *departure*, "leaving, you know, the country you were raised in." Deportation officially transformed King in ways that he experienced bodily (heat, cold, shackles, and deprivation). Officially he was not only a noncitizen of the United States but also a citizen of El Salvador. Unofficially, however, deportees' membership in their countries of origin can also be questioned.

> I [Alex Sanchez] just said, "I've always wanted to know how El Salvador looks like." I mean, I could have fought it [deportation] for a while but I still wanted to know where I was from. I wanted to know where exactly in San Salvador I was from. So I signed it [the paperwork] and got deported. . . .

I was anxious to smell the air. I was anxious to go see that curve and the railroad tracks and the bridge that I remembered. I wanted to see the scene from that cliff on the back of where we lived that had the view of the mountains over by San Vincente and el Lago de Apulo en Ilopango. We had that view from up there. And I wanted to, I wanted to go. I mean when I got off there, I was like, riding in the back of a truck. There was nobody waiting for me. Nobody. Nobody knew I was going over there. . . .

I was in the back of this truck going towards this address that I had in this envelope. I was just enjoying the view and everything green and nice and beautiful. You know, you can't ride in a pickup truck standing up in back, here [in the United States]. So I was, like, standing up and getting all that air.

And all of a sudden, you know, I was enjoying the view and I seen like this big rock coming up out of the mountain. And it had some writing on it. And it said, "MS-13." It had my gang name on it. And that's what I said, "I can't get away from them." (Interview, May 8, 2001)

Although they are deported as citizens of El Salvador, Salvadoran deportees who have lived in the United States. for considerable periods may find themselves alienated within El Salvador. In the interview excerpt, Sanchez hoped that being deported would enable him to reencounter places that he remembered only dimly, and thus to know where he was from. He returned, however, without anyone knowing. No one met him at the airport. He only had the address of a relative, written on the back of an envelope. Such experiences are not unusual. King, whose experiences were described earlier, found that when he first returned to El Salvador, "I was *lost*, man! I was like, if I was busted again, if I was in *jail*! Because I was like, I knew a place that, I knew how it was, and I knew I could be there [in the United States], and I knew I had family, and people I know there. I wouldn't face the facts, you know, reality, that I was here [in El Salvador], you know what I mean?" Although they may have childhood memories, and although their networks may span U.S. and Salvadoran territory (as when Sanchez encountered the name of his gang on a rock), El Salvador is also, for many deported long-term U.S. residents, alien territory.

Such alienation assumes a quasi-legal form. Having been deported from the United States for being undocumented, deportees may also, somewhat surprisingly, find themselves undocumented in El Salvador, their country of legal citizenship. Deportees were issued a provisional Salvadoran passport, which was then taken from them at the airport when they arrived. Those who had been outside of El Salvador for many years might lack Salvadoran identity documents. Obtaining such documents could be difficult, as their appearance and language skills might make them appear foreign. One interviewee, who had been adopted by a U.S. family as an infant, then been convicted of crimes and (as his parents failed to apply for his naturalization) subsequently deported, described his difficulties:

Here they wanted ID in order for me to get ID from here. . . . I spent about a *month* trying to get my paperwork. Of running from here to there, waiting in lines, not understanding what they're telling me, buying things that I don't need. I get to the window, "No, this is not what you need. You need to go back and you need to wait in line. And you need to do this again." Every now and then I would find someone who spoke English to help me out a little. But it was a very long process to get your *cédula* [national I.D. card].

Though this speaker's experiences may have been more frustrating than most, problems obtaining Salvadoran identity documents are common among deportees who immigrated to the United States as children. An NGO member who worked with deportees reported, "The authorities don't want to give [them] *cédulas*. . . . In some cases, we have been told that they have to conduct an identity trial. Bring witnesses to say, 'He was born here, he left at a certain age.'" Another NGO member characterized deportees as *doblemente mojados*, doubly "illegal," given their undocumented status in the United States and their difficulties obtaining identity documents in El Salvador.

The alienation and stigmatization that makes officials doubt deportees' Salvadoranness can also exclude deportees from other domains of social life. Within El Salvador, deportees are generally suspected of being criminals and possibly gang members (Zilberg 2007a). Those who have tattoos and wear the baggy clothing typical of U.S. youth cultures are especially stigmatized. Employers may be reluctant to hire such individuals, neighbors may reject deportees, and even relatives are not always welcoming. A lack of cultural and social knowledge exacerbates these problems; as an NGO member reported, "It's like a child who doesn't know, they don't have any idea what the country is like, how it works." By the late 1990s, social programs, such as migrant shelters, limited financial assistance (e.g., bus fare), an orientation course, and vocational training, provided some assistance to returnees; however, the scope of such aid was limited (Coutin 2007; Zilberg 2002). The predominant governmental response to deportees, however, has been subsumed within a broader antigang initiative known as *Super Mano Dura* or "super heavy hand." Instead of welcoming deportees, Super Mano Dura focuses on incarceration (Zilberg 2007a).

> The Chief of Police of San Salvador, Alfonso Linares, arrives today in Los Angeles to testify about the dangers that activist Alex Sánchez can face in the event that he is deported to El Salvador.
>
> Linares will go before the federal court as of Wednesday, July 26, where he will serve as a witness in relation to the assassinations of three members of Homies Unidos. Those crimes occurred in the last 16 months, after they were deported, said Rocky Rushing, chief administrator in the office of Senator Tom Hayden. . . .
>
> According to documents obtained by La Opinión about the testimony of Linares, he will speak about the deaths that have occurred in El Salvador at the hands of death squads.
>
> "It is believed that the assassinations have been the work of . . . those groups, which dedicate themselves to social 'cleansing.' This group is similar to those death squads known as La Sombra Negra, an extremist group that has terrorized the country with its extrajudicial killings," stated Linares' written declaration.
>
> Moreover, this establishes that he considers "it certain that Alex could be killed if he returns to El Salvador. I do not think that the law can protect him."
>
> "Alex Sánchez has the profile of a victim. He is an ex-gang member and currently advocates for the rights of other gang members in his organization Homies Unidos. In fact his photograph has appeared in the paper and he has been characterized as a gang member," stated the declaration that Linares will present to the court next week. (Delgado 2000)

The death squads that San Salvador chief of police Linares referred to in his testimony in Alex Sanchez's deportation case are perhaps the most extreme version of the antigang climate generated by policies adopted in El Salvador in the late 1990s. The Salvadoran government did not condone death squads, but between 1999 and 2005, it criminalized gang membership, increased police presence in areas of high gang activity, mobilized soldiers alongside police in antigang units, rounded up suspected gang members, and increased prison terms for convicted suspects. These policies, known during the presidency of Francisco Flores as "Mano Dura" or "Heavy Hand" and during the presidency of Tony Saca as "Super Mano Dura" or "Super Heavy Hand," responded to a crime wave that struck El Salvador during the postwar years. In 1994 the homicide rate in El Salvador reached 138 per 100,000 residents, as compared to 30 per 100,000 residents in the prewar years (Dalton 2002a; Dalton 2002b),[2] and by 1996, according to World Bank statistics, El Salvador was considered the most dangerous country in the Americas (Dalton 2001a). By 2001, an average of fourteen cars were being stolen and six homicides were being committed daily (Dalton 2001b), and a survey conducted in 2002 found that 25 percent of all Salvadorans reported having been the victim of an assault or robbery in the previous four months (El Diario de Hoy 2002). While crime in El Salvador assumed many forms, including "minor urban crime, private and public corruption, white collar financial embezzlement of large fraudulent financiers, organized crime (like the international bands of car thieves and drug smugglers), intrafamily and youth violence, massacres of entire families, the activities of assassins and the aftermath, pseudo-political or not, of kidnappers who cling to the past" (Bejar 1998, 98), publicly gangs were blamed for the crime problem. In 2004, when Super Mano Dura was launched, newspaper advertisements announced, "¡A los pandilleros se les acabó la fiesta! Hoy sí tenemos Súper Mano Dura" (The gang members' party is over! We now have Super Mano Dura.).[3]

Government antigang policies have made it very difficult for deportees who may be or resemble gang members to survive within El Salvador. These initiatives created a temporary special security regimen to contend with the emergency created by gangs and high crime. Within this regimen, gangs were defined as "illicit associations," making gang membership—as evidenced by displaying tattoos, throwing hand signs, or obeying gang leaders—a crime. Soldiers joined police in the fight against gangs, resulting in the detention of 19,275 suspected gang members (FESPAD and CEPES 2004). This public effort was accompanied by the securitization or militarization of private space. In El Salvador, it was common for businesses, offices, banks, stores, fast-food restaurants, gas stations, pharmacies, car repair shops, and even homes (in the case of affluent individuals) to hire security guards who prominently displayed their guns. Owners of small, street-side shops sometimes sold their products to customers through barred windows (Godoy 2005). Homes were frequently behind walls or, in the case of those who were economically advantaged, behind gates with security systems and armed guards. Public discourse conflated crime with gangs, and gangs with deportation, as one NGO member who worked with deportees noted during an interview: "Here, we [Salvadoran society] blame the deportees for everything bad that happens. For crime, for murders, for drug problems, for gang problems, for everything. There is an

2. By 2002, the homicide rate had declined to 60 per 100,000 residents (Dalton 2002a).

3. See advertisement published by the Ministerio de Gobernación in *La Prensa Gráfica*, September 8, 2004, 21.

extreme stigmatization, which the communication media contribute to as well. There will be an article in the paper—'100 murderers deported,' or '100 gang members deported.' Salvadoran society closes its doors to the reinsertion of deportees."

Such security measures and public discourse made it hard for deportees to pursue such everyday activities as traveling, shopping, working, socializing, or going to school. One deportee interviewed in 2004 explained, "Let's say that you apply for a job and they see that you speak English. Then they won't want to know anything else about the situation here. They'll just say, 'How did you learn English? How long were you there? Oh, you were deported? What for?' and then they think that it's better not to hire you for the job." Another deportee, who worked with Homies Unidos, commented during a 2004 interview that almost all deportees who stay in El Salvador are in prison. "Or," he said, "they stay in prisons of their own, locking themselves in their houses and remaining hidden. They can only be gang members inside their homes. When they go out, they have to wear elegant clothing, get elegant haircuts." In these circumstances, deportees (particularly those with criminal convictions) had few options. Immigrant advocates who worked with deportees in El Salvador estimated that between 40 and 60 percent of deportees returned illegally to the United States, where they faced incarceration if apprehended. The near impossibility of living in the United States or in El Salvador placed deportees with criminal convictions outside of the bounds of the citizenry of each nation, and indeed almost outside the bounds of humanity.

> I [Alex Sanchez] was like stuck during that time, I was stuck in El Salvador. By this time I had been there for 6 months and I was stuck. It was like this warfare [between gangs and death squads]. And I was like, "Man, I've got to get out of here." So yeah, so we had a lot of people being killed. And the target was mostly the guy that had been deported. And the thing was, everything that happened in El Salvador that was a crime, it was blamed on gangs. . . . It's kind of sort of [like] here, you know. Because I mean, which politician doesn't use gangs for their campaign? Or immigration? . . .
>
> Not all the gang members have to carry a gun or shoot people. They don't. Out of ten, probably one or two are the ones that really evolve into serious violence and like really want to put their name up high because they want to be recognized. Probably one out of 10. The rest are just a bunch of followers that do what this person tells them to. With these [Three Strikes] laws that came in [in the United States], yeah, it scared some of these followers, but they weren't doing anything, first of all. The majority were just followers or they were youth at risk and they said, "Oh, my god." But they were not the ones. They probably get arrested for doing drugs, or petty theft or maybe a, stealing a car. Not a car jacking but maybe just stealing a car just for a joy ride. All of a sudden these guys are scared, of course, they're not seriously involved in violence. But what about the one person or that two persons out of that ten? You know, he's been involved with violence all his life. He's hard, you know. All of a sudden, though, this guy's probably getting out of jail, you know, a two-striker. "You get one more strike, you're through, Mister." This guy gets out, you know, what's out there for him? I mean, "Yeah. They threatened me. I'm a two-striker. What the hell am I going to do? There's no jobs. I try to work someplace. They say I'm a two-striker. Been in prison. They're not going to give me the job!" So they have all these problems, you know. They get desperate. They get really desperate, you know. . . .

It gets them into a certain situation, a desperate situation, when they go ahead and get desperate and go and do it. And sell drugs to maintain or to do something or get drunk and get in a fight, you know. And all of a sudden, you know, they're carrying a gun and that's a strike. . . . You put them in situations where—bam! if I get busted. You're not thinking about getting busted, but you're thinking about, "Man, if the police get me, then that's it." So all of sudden you have the police right there, what are you going to do? You're going to try to get away because now all of a sudden you're thinking about the third strike.

I go crazy sometimes just thinking about things like this because I look at 'em in a different way. (Interview, May 8, 2001)

In this interview excerpt, Alex Sanchez details ways that, by making people desperate to avoid additional convictions, harsh criminal justice policies can fuel rather than reduce violence. In the United States, increased penalties for illegal entry, stiffened border enforcement, reductions in means of legalizing, expanded definitions of offenses for which one becomes deportable, and the elimination of waivers that would prevent deportation have given rise to an abject class of individuals who could be deported if apprehended. This abject class includes undocumented individuals, as well as former legal permanent residents who have been deported and who returned "illegally" to the United States. Similarly, in El Salvador, stiffened antigang policies have made life nearly impossible for deportees who have been convicted of crimes in the United States, or who resemble gang members. Whether they are located in El Salvador, the United States, or somewhere in between, members of this class have few legal options. Denied work authorization in the United States, subjected to employment discrimination in El Salvador, and made targets of police activity in both countries, such individuals face great difficulties in entering the legal economy. Members of this subgroup often must work under the table or enter the illicit economy. Such policies affect not only unauthorized immigrants but also, as Sanchez notes above, anyone who develops a criminal record and for whom an additional "strike" can mean a lengthy or perhaps perpetual prison sentence. Policies that deny unauthorized migrants and other excluded individuals access to employment, social domains, and even national territories can fuel the very sorts of lawlessness that they are designed to combat, thus doing violence to the law itself. Such policies also have deadly effects on the unauthorized, pushing them into illicit domains, unlawful activities, and dangerous spaces where their lives are in jeopardy, whether from the hazards of migrating "illegally," the lack of access to health care and social services, or violence at the hands of those (not excluding officials) caught up in networks of illegality. In short, deportation can remove people not only from national territory but also from any legal means of supporting themselves and finally even from life itself.

An immigration judge granted political asylum yesterday to the activist Alex Sánchez, an ex-gang member who now is the director of the program Homies Unidos, who helps young people leave the criminal life.

It is the first time that immigration authorities overlooked or removed the criminal history of an ex-gang member to give him haven in this country, said Alan Diamante, attorney of Sánchez. . . .

Sánchez, Diamante explained, was able to demonstrate to the immigration judge that his life was in danger if he was deported to El Salvador, his country of origin. (Amador 2002)

POSTCRIPT

On June 24, 2009, Alex Sanchez was rearrested and charged with federal racketeering and conspiracy charges. Authorities allege that he failed to sever his ties with Mara Salvatrucha and that he conspired to commit a murder in 2006. Supporters contend that he is innocent of these charges and that he was targeted due to his work as a gang interventionist. Prior to his arrest, Alex Sanchez directed the gang violence prevention group Homies Unidos in Los Angeles, were he counseled youths, gang members, and their families, and advocated for the rights of immigrants and noncitizens convicted of crimes. In the days following his arrest, supporters raised 1.2 million dollars in bond securities and solicited 110 letters attesting to his character. As of March 20, 2012, Sanchez was out on bail, awaiting trial.

WORKS CITED

Amador, Lucero. 2002. "Otorgan asilo político a activista." *La Opinión*, July 11. http://www.laopinion.com (accessed December 6, 2006).

Bejar, Rafael Guido. 1998. "El Salvador de posguerra: Formas de violencia en la transición." In *Violencia en una sociedad en transición*, ed. Renos Papadopoulos et al., 96–105. San Salvador: Programa de las Naciones Unidas para el Desarrollo (PNUD).

Cole, David, and James Dempsey. 2002. *Terrorism and the Constitution: Sacrificing Civil Liberties in the Name of National Security*. New York: New Press.

Coutin, Susan Bibler. 2005. "Contesting Criminality: Illegal Immigration and the Spatialization of Legality." *Theoretical Criminology* 9 (1): 5–33.

———. 2007. *Nations of Emigrants: Shifting Boundaries of Citizenship in El Salvador and the United States*. Ithaca, NY: Cornell University Press.

Dalton, Juan José. 2001a. "Endurecen condenas por delitos graves en El Salvador." *La Opinión*, July 20. http://www.lapinion.com.

———. 2001b. "Pobreza, violencia y corrupción son una realidad en El Salvador." *La Opinión*, July 8. http://www.laopinion.com.

———. 2002a. "Armas y muerta van de la mano en El Salvador." *La Opinión*, April 25. http://www.laopinion.com (accessed August 5, 2002).

———. 2002b. "Reportaje: La violencia no cede en El Salvador." *La Opinión*, March 11. http://www.laopinion.com (accessed August 9, 2002).

Delgado, Hilda Marella. 2000. "Jefe policial salvadoreño testifica en caso de deportación." *La Opinión*, July 22. www.laopinion.com (accessed December 6, 2006).

El Diario de Hoy. 2002. "El 25% tiene al menos un familiar asaltado." June 24. http://www.elsalvador.com (accessed June 24, 2002).

Feeley, Malcolm M., and Jonathan Simon. 1992. "The New Penology: Notes on the Emerging Strategy of Corrections and Its Implications." *Criminology* 30 (4): 449–74.

FESPAD (Fundación de Estudios para la Aplicación del Derecho) and CEPES (Centro de Estudios Penales de El Salvador). 2004. *Informe Anual Sobre Justicia Penal Juvenil El Salvador 2004*. San Salvador, El Salvador: FESPAD.

Godoy, Angelina Snodgrass. 2005. "Democracy, 'Mano Dura,' and the Criminalization of Politics." In *(Un)Civil Societies: Human Rights and Democratic Transitions in Eastern Europe and Latin America*, ed. Rachel May and Andrew Milton, 109–37. Lanham, MD: Lexington Books.

Hafetz, Jonathan L. 1998. "The Untold Story of Noncriminal Habeas Corpus and the 1996 Immigration Acts." *Yale Law Journal* 107 (8): 2509–44.

Kanstroom, Daniel. 2000. "Deportation, Social Control, and Punishment: Some Thoughts About Why Hard Laws Make Bad Cases." *Harvard Law Review* 113 (8): 1890–1935.

Linares, Jesse J. 2000. "Pandilleros deportados corren peligro en El Salvador." *La Opinion*, July 24. http://www.laopinion.com (accessed December 6, 2006).

Morawetz, Nancy. 2000. "Understanding the Impact of the 1996 Deportation Laws and the Limited Scope of Proposed Reforms." *Harvard Law Review* 113 (8): 1936–62.

O'Connor, Anne-Marie. 2000. "Activist Says Officer Sought His Deportation." *Los Angeles Times*, February 17.

Petersilia, Joan. 2003. *When Prisoners Come Home: Parole and Prisoner Reentry.* New York: Oxford University Press.

Scalia, John, and Marika F. X. Litras. 2000. *Immigration Offenders in the Federal Criminal Justice System, 2000: Bureau of Justice Statistics Special Report.* Washington: Office of Justice Programs, U.S. Department of Justice.

Schinkel, Willem. 2002. "The Modernist Myth in Criminology." *Theoretical Criminology* 6(2): 123–44.

U.S. Department of Homeland Security. 2008. *2007 Yearbook of Immigration Statistics.* Washington: U.S. Department of Homeland Security, Office of Immigration Statistics.

Welch, Michael. 2002. *Detained: Immigration Laws and the Expanding INS Jail Complex.* Philadelphia: Temple University Press.

Zilberg, Elana. 2002. "From Riots to Rampart: A Spatial Cultural Politics of Salvadoran Migration to and from Los Angeles." Ph.D. diss., University of Texas, Austin.

———. 2007a. "Refugee Gang Youth: Zero Tolerance and the Security State in Contemporary U.S.-Salvadoran Relations." In *Youth, Globalization and the Law*, ed. Sudhir Venkatesh and Ron Kassimir, 61–89. Stanford, CA: Stanford University Press.

———. 2007b. "Inter-American Ethnography: Tracking Salvadoran Transnationality at the Borders of Latino/a and Latin American Studies." In *Companion to Latino Studies*, ed. Juan Flores and Renato Rosaldo, 492–501. Oxford: Blackwell.

V   IMMIGRANT CONTESTATIONS

This final part focuses on immigrant resistance and contestation. There is no doubt that a criminal dragnet has been cast over the United States in order to manage the putative "dangers" of migrant illegality. However, the nation cannot be reduced to a mere space of policing. It is also most certainly a site of political struggle. Indeed, although the policing of immigrants may have escalated, the undocumented have not stood idly by and accepted the highly punitive treatment to which they have been subjected. Rather, they and their allies have actively sought to challenge the anti-immigrant climate and the governing of immigration through crime. We have called their acts of contestation *migrant counter-conducts*. These are acts or forms of comportment that challenge the criminalization and exclusion of undocumented migrants. The counter-conducts in which migrants have engaged include labor and hunger strikes for justice, advocating for legalization and political rights, the occupation of churches as a way of gaining sanctuary, public demonstrations, and fighting for legal redress for unpaid wages. Such counter-conducts ultimately speak to the political becoming of undocumented migrants and their enactments of citizenship.

The authors in this section highlight several of these forms that pro-immigrant activism has assumed in the United States: mass marches and protests, undocumented student activism, and border activism. Chapter 13, by Josue David Cisneros, focuses on the momentous pro-immigrant marches that took place in the spring of 2006. Across the country, unions, religious institutions, immigrant rights groups, Latino organizations, and the general public banded together that spring to publically protest immigration policing and its drastic effects on migrants and their communities. Cisneros specifically deals with what has come to be known as *La Gran Marcha*, the pro-immigrant demonstration that took place in Los Angeles on March 25. With an estimated half a million people participating, it was one of the largest of the nationwide marches. The main argument that Cisneros makes is that *La Gran Marcha* amounted to an enactment of U.S. citizenship: the protesters simultaneously sought to construct undocumented immigrants as part of the national community and to challenge the popular and political construction of these individuals as alien others who threaten the social body.

Chapter 14, by Roberto G. Gonzales, deals with the political activism of undocumented students. As part of the general growth of the undocumented immigrant population in the United States, there has been an increase in the number of children being raised without the privileges and protections of citizenship. For these children, legal status, poverty, and poor schools have conspired to make social, political, and economic incorporation tremendously difficult; but as Gonzales shows, many undocumented students have refused to be reduced to the status of victims and have instead engaged in civic and political actions. For example, this population was well-represented among the ranks of the spring 2006 marchers. Beyond the marches, they have organized into groups in order to educate the public about the plight of unauthorized youth, as well as to advocate for inclusion. Ultimately, Gonzales suggests that although unauthorized students may leave themselves vulnerable to deportation and hate crimes as a result of their very visible political activities, the precariousness of their situation actually leaves them little choice but to fight for the right to become full citizens.

Chapter 15, by James P. Walsh, focuses on the U.S.-Mexico border as an important site of political struggle. Walsh highlights how activist groups opposed to the extensive securitization of the U.S.-Mexico border have used surveillance to "humanize the border environment." For example, Humane Borders, a faith-based humanitarian group committed to "taking death out of the immigration equation," has been building water stations in the Arizona desert since 2001. These stations—each stocked with food, clothing, first-aid kits, and a 100–gallon water tank—are meant to serve as lifelines for migrants crossing the treacherous desert terrain. The placement of the stations is determined with the help of geographic information systems (GIS) and other locational technologies. Humane Borders uses such surveillance technologies to map desert-crossing routes and the spatial distribution of migrant deaths, and then strategically locates the stations in areas with high rates of fatalities. Walsh's basic argument is that although watching and monitoring may typically be used to enhance and extend state control over territorial borders, such acts are not inherently exclusionary or repressive. They can actually also be employed to contest official gatekeeping strategies and create alternative moral geographies in which the imperatives of social justice and global hospitality prevail over those of sovereignty and national security.

SUGGESTIONS FOR FURTHER READING

Buff, Rachel Ida, ed. 2008. *Immigrant Rights in the Shadows of Citizenship*. New York: New York University Press.

Burridge, Andrew. 2010. "Youth on the Line and the *No Borders* Movement." *Children's Geographies* 8 (4): 401–411.

Casillas, Dolores Inés. 2011. "Sounds of Surveillance: U.S. Spanish-Language Radio Patrols La Migra." *American Quarterly* 63 (3): 807–829.

Chavez, Leo R. 2008. "The Immigrant Marches of 2006 and the Struggle for Inclusion." In *The Latino Threat: Constructing Immigrants, Citizens, and the Nation*, 152–176. Stanford, CA: Stanford University Press.

Coll, Kathleen. 2011. "Citizenship Acts and Immigrant Voting Rights Movements in the U.S." *Citizenship Studies* 15 (8): 993–1009.

Coutin, Susan Bibler. 2005. "Contesting Criminality: Illegal Immigration and the Spatialization of Legality." *Theoretical Criminology* 9 (1): 5–33.

Hondagneu-Sotelo, Pierrette. 2008. *God's Heart Has No Borders: How Religious Activists Are Working for Immigrant Rights.* Berkeley: University of California Press.

Ridgley, Jennifer. 2008. "Cities of Refuge: Immigration Enforcement, Police, and the Insurgent Genealogies of Citizenship in U.S. Sanctuary Cities." *Urban Geography* 29 (1): 53–77.

Rodriguez, Robyn M. 2011. "Fighting for Fatherhood and Family: Immigrant Detainees' Struggles for Rights." In *Gender and Culture at the Limit of Rights*, edited by Dorothy L. Hodgson, 200–217. Philadelphia: University of Pennsylvania Press.

Seif, Hinda. 2004. "'Wise Up!' Undocumented Latino Youth, Mexican-American Legislators, and the Struggle for Higher Education." *Latino Studies* 2 (2): 210–230.

Varsanyi, Monica W. 2005. "The Paradox of Contemporary Immigrant Political Mobilization: Organized Labor, Undocumented Migrants, and Electoral Participation in Los Angeles." *Antipode* 37 (4): 775–795.

Voss, Kim, and Irene Bloemraad, eds. 2011. *Rallying for Immigrant Rights: The Fight for Inclusion in 21st Century America.* Berkeley: University of California Press.

13 (RE)BORDERING THE CIVIC IMAGINARY

RHETORIC, HYBRIDITY, AND CITIZENSHIP IN *LA GRAN MARCHA*

Josue David Cisneros

Persistent public controversy about immigration and its impact on society points to a deep public anxiety about the integrity of the nation. As a recent essay by D. Robert DeChaine argues, "the specter of the border haunts the language of social relations."[1] Obsession over the literal and symbolic border between American and foreigner, between us and them, is motivated in part by fear of the dilution and dissolution of US citizenship. As a result, alienization of the non-citizen is fundamental to the rhetorical maintenance of US identity. Discursive bordering is a "double-edged sword," for in order to make citizenship (or American-ness, in this case) a special and desired identity, it must not only be desirable but also exclusive and difficult to attain.[2]

Migrants and racial and ethnic minorities, among other minority groups, have served as "others" through which US identity is constituted in part. Consequently, many scholars have traced how contemporary mass media discourse, popular culture, and political rhetoric surrounding immigration attempt to "border" the nation, shoring up the demarcations between citizen and alien through constructions of race, culture, and gender.[3] However, while (rhetorical) bordering may be our obsession, it is not totalizing. Discourses of US national identity certainly define the border between citizen and non-citizen and also structure the lives of immigrants, who live in the shadows as "impossible subjects."[4] However, migrants regularly struggle with these dominant logics of the border and of US citizenship;

Josue David Cisneros is assistant professor of Communication Studies at Northeastern University.

Reprinted with permission of Taylor & Francis Ltd. on behalf of the National Communication Association, from "(Re)Bordering the Civic Imaginary: Rhetoric, Hybridity, and Citizenship in *La Gran Marcha*," *Quarterly Journal of Speech* 97 (1): 26–49, by Josue David Cisneros. Copyright © 2011 by the National Communication Association.

1. D. Robert DeChaine, "Bordering the Civic Imaginary: Alienization, Fence Logic, and the Minuteman Civil Defense Corps," *Quarterly Journal of Speech* 95 (2009): 43.

2. Vanessa B. Beasley, *You, the People: American National Identity in Presidential Rhetoric* (College Station, TX: Texas A&M University Press, 2004), 5.

3. For example, see Kent A. Ono and John M. Sloop, *Shifting Borders: Rhetoric, Immigration, and California's Proposition 187* (Philadelphia: Temple University Press, 2002).

4. Mae M. Ngai, *Impossible Subjects: Illegal Aliens and the Making of Modern America* (Princeton, NJ: Princeton University Press, 2004).

they are not merely victims of alienization and exclusion. We know that "citizenship enact-ment necessarily involves hegemonic struggles over the very meaning of the term 'citizen' in a multipublic sphere."[5] Dominant discourses of US citizenship are contested through alter-native attempts to (re)border the civic imaginary. Just as the border is drawn to exclude migrants based on their legal, racial, ethnic, or other "difference," borders can be redrawn to reshape the contours of US citizenship. In this chapter I show how migrants, who embody a "troublesome" ambivalence and ambiguity as transnational subjects, resist and rewrite dominant representations of the ideal US citizen.

I focus on the immigration protests of 2006 as moments that materialized the contesta-tion over the meaning of US citizenship. Throughout the spring and summer of 2006, in cities across the country, immigrant groups organized to protest restrictive federal immi-gration legislation and repressive representations of immigrants in popular culture. Specifi-cally, these protests were organized in response to proposed federal immigration legislation (H.R. 4437—The Border Protection, Antiterrorism, and Illegal Immigration Control Act of 2005) that would have enacted a number of restrictive immigration measures. Latina/o and immigrant communities across the country mobilized in an effort to defeat this drastic shift in federal immigration policy and in an effort to resist the alienating representations of im-migrants circulating in public discourse.[6] *La Gran Marcha* (hereafter LGM), which took place in Los Angeles on March 25, was one of the first and one of the biggest of these na-tionwide demonstrations. LGM saw over half a million people, many documented and un-documented immigrants, participate in the largest protest in LA history.[7]

Research shows that some have interpreted LGM through bordering logics as an "alien" discourse.[8] According to this view, immigrants who took to the streets justified their exclu-sion from US citizenship by embodying their foreignness, criminality, and threat to the nation. Others interpreted LGM as a wholly "American" discourse in which immigrants presented themselves as assimilated members of the nation, deserving full "inclusion." In this view, protestors proclaimed themselves as "good" citizens and demanded rights and recognition on those grounds.[9] I offer a third interpretation of the march in this chapter. Rather than see the protest as wholly "alien," as it was conceived of by anti-immigrant forces, or as purely "American," as an attempt for inclusion, I see LGM as a hybrid perfor-mance of citizenship that fused the alien and the American to (re)border the civic imagi-nary and challenge conventional demarcations between citizen and alien. Following Robert Asen's view that citizenship takes shape through situated and stylized discursive enactments, in this chapter I explore LGM as a rhetorical enactment of US citizenship.[10] I argue that the protest sought neither to entrench border logics ("alienization") nor to al-

5. DeChaine, "Bordering," 45.

6. Leo R. Chavez, *The Latino Threat: Constructing Immigrants, Citizens, and the Nation* (Stanford, CA: Stanford University Press, 2008), 154–5.

7. Adrián Félix, Carmen González, and Ricardo Ramírez, "Political Protest, Ethnic Media, and Latino Natural-ization," *American Behavioral Scientist* 52 (2008): 618–34.

8. Chavez, *Latino Threat*; DeChaine, "Bordering."

9. Beth Baker-Cristales, "Mediated Resistance: The Construction of Neoliberal Citizenship in the Immigrant Rights Movement," *Latino Studies* 7 (2009): 69.

10. Robert Asen, "A Discourse Theory of Citizenship," *Quarterly Journal of Speech* 90 (2004): 189–211.

leviate anxiety concerning the integrity of the nation ("inclusion"). Instead, LGM fused multiple modes of discourse (including verbal, visual, and material rhetoric), transnational political traditions, and racially coded appropriations of US identity to stage a hybrid version of citizenship. In the analysis that follows, I show how LGM contested naturalized borders, challenged national anxiety, and presented an alternative performance of US citizenship.

To this end, this chapter takes shape in five main sections. First, I explain the context of LGM, including the impetus for the movement and the parties that organized the protest. Second and third, I review scholarship concerning the performance of citizenship and explore the discursive dimensions of hybridity, which both serve as theoretical underpinnings of the chapter. In the fourth section, I analyze several discursive fragments of LGM to show how it fused multiple, transnational citizenship traditions and varied forms of discourse into a hybrid enactment of US citizenship.[11] By analyzing a variety of evidence, I show how protestors enacted US citizenship, simultaneously drawing undocumented immigrants into the US national community and challenging the very processes of bordering endemic to citizenship. In the final section, I argue that understanding the hybrid performance of citizenship that took shape in the protest sheds light on the rhetorical process of (re)bordering, the discursive enactment of citizenship, and the democratic possibilities of radical, hybrid rhetoric.

MOBILIZATION OF A MOVEMENT

Scholars and community activists agree that LGM was mobilized—in the most immediate sense—in opposition to Congressional immigration legislation (H.R. 4437) and the anti-immigrant, anti-Latino discourse surrounding this initiative in the popular media.[12] Throughout the fall of 2005, Congress debated proposals for "comprehensive" immigration reform as President Bush toured the country speaking in border states such as Arizona, Texas, and New Mexico. In December 2005 the House of Representatives passed H.R. 4437, a bill that would impose a number of restrictions on federal immigration policy, such as making both undocumented immigration and the aiding of undocumented immigrants felony crimes, mandating the building of a massive border fence, and authorizing the immediate deportation of undocumented immigrants. Concurrent with this legislative debate, numerous vigilante Minutemen groups—spurred on by fears of "illegal immigration"— began to police the border, protest immigration, and purportedly protect the sanctity of the US nation (see Chavez, this volume). Popular discourses of immigration—whether ema-

11. This chapter brings together a number of sources documenting LGM: a fifteen-minute video recording of protestors outside of City Hall recorded by CBS 2/KCAL 9 (a local Los Angeles television station); several short videos taken by protestors or observers, available on the Internet Archive; and photographic images taken from the website of Unity Corp (*Cuerpo de Unidad*)—one of the organizing groups of the protest. "Immigration March Draws Thousands of Protestors," *CBS 2/KCAL 9 Los Angeles*, March 25, 2006, http://cbs2.com/video/?id?15998@kcbs.dayport.com; *Cuerpo de Unidad*, Inc., "La Gran Marcha 2006," 2006, http://www.granmarcha.org; "La Gran Marcha, Los Angeles," *Internet Archive*, http://www.archive.org/details/LaGranMarchaLosAngeles

12. Chavez, *Latino Threat*; Alfonso Gonzales, "The 2006 Mega *Marchas* in Greater Los Angeles: Counter-Hegemonic Moment and the Future of *El Migrante* Struggle," *Latino Studies* 7 (2009): 30–59.

nating from political leaders, mainstream media, or radical groups like the Minutemen—relied on "deeply embedded" stereotypes and dominant logics of immigration as a social problem and of immigrants as threats to the nation.[13]

As Kent Ono and John Sloop's book *Shifting Borders* shows, these dominant logics of immigration are so entrenched in US identity and cultural history that even discourses that champion immigrant rights often employ assumptions of US citizenship as a static identity that must adapt to and/or benefit from the introduction of immigrant "others."[14] In other words, the immigrant is often a "symbol of hope" justifying both US citizenship and US exceptionalism. However, this is only insofar as the immigrant evidences cultural myths of assimilation such as "a nation of immigrants" or "the melting pot." More often than not, the immigrant is "a source of fear" and anxiety, a threat to national unity and the cultural integrity of the nation.[15]

As a result of these exigencies created by Congressional legislation and popular debate about immigration, "diverse organizational constituencies were . . . mobilized," including activists and community leaders, documented and undocumented immigrants, and second- and third-generation Latina/os.[16] A series of summits were held throughout the country which were organized by grassroots groups and "were designed to forge a coalition to confront the Minutemen and to address a growing anti-Latino migrant climate."[17] These organizations ranged from Latina/o and immigrant activist groups, like the *Hermandad Mexicana Nacional* and the National Alliance for Human Rights, to larger labor groups, like the Service Employees International Union and the United Farm Workers (UFW).

After organizing the basic elements of LGM, activists and organizers reached out to Latino media to promote the march and spur discussion about H.R. 4437. Radio DJs in particular played a key role in mobilizing popular support and participation by promoting LGM to both Latina/o citizens and immigrants.[18] Though protests in Chicago and Phoenix in early March (organized by many of the same groups and activists) provided impetus for LGM, the size and scope of the LA march exceeded all expectations. As one organizer—Victor Narro of the UCLA Center for Labor Research and Education—remembered:

> By 7am it was clear that there were more than [the projected] 50 000 [sic] people ready to march. Most of the organizers had not even got there. Some had not even woken up yet. I had to quickly recruit people to do crowed [sic] control. I remember asking random people to help with security as they got off the bus and training them on the spot.[19]

13. Lisa A. Flores, "Constructing Rhetorical Borders: Peons, Illegal Aliens, and Competing Narratives of Immigration," *Critical Studies in Media Communication* 20 (2003): 381.

14. Ono and Sloop, *Shifting Borders*, Chapter 5.

15. Vanessa B. Beasley, "Presidential Rhetoric and Immigration: Balancing Tensions Between Hope and Fear," in *Who Belongs in America: Presidents, Rhetoric, and Immigration*, ed. Vanessa B. Beasley (College Station, TX: Texas A&M University Press, 2006), 14.

16. Matt A. Barreto, Sylvia Manzano, Ricardo Ramirez, and Kathy Rim, "Mobilization, Participation, and *Solidaridad*: Latino Participation in the 2006 Immigration Protest Rallies," *Urban Affairs Review* 44 (2009): 747.

17. Gonzales, "Mega Marchas," 39.

18. Félix et al., "Political Protest, Ethnic Media, and Latino Naturalization."

19. Quoted in Gonzales, "Mega Marchas," 43.

Though ultimate calculations of the protest's size varied widely, even conservative estimates placed LGM at half a million participants.

As a result, LGM was a galvanizing event that sparked a nationwide protest movement. As Alfonso Gonzales argues, anti-immigrant forces saw it as "proof of [immigrants' and Latina/os'] unwillingness to assimilate" while "migrants and their allies" saw the march as "a national wakeup call to action."[20] Many studies of LGM have focused on the mobilization of the protest movement as well as its effects on Latina/o political solidarity and public opinion about immigration.[21] Yet as Richard Pineda and Stacey Sowards argue, the presence of multiple national flags and even the protestors' bodies served as points of contestation in debates about immigration and citizenship.[22] Following on this work, I argue that LGM was a hybrid performance of US citizenship that contested dominant discourses of immigration and (re)bordered the US civic imaginary. In the next section, I explain the theoretical grounding of this argument by elaborating on the performative dimensions of US citizenship.

CITIZENSHIP AND CIVIC PERFORMANCE

Rhetorical scholars have traced the way citizenship is defined through public discourses that ritualize national identity and constitute the borders of the imagined community.[23] This approach to citizenship, which Asen terms a "discourse theory," turns attention to how, why, and to what end citizenship takes shape through public discourses and performances of national belonging. Citizenship shifts, in this perspective, "from a status attribute to a way of acting."[24] In other words, civic belonging is not conceptualized exclusively through a nation's laws, institutions, or myths but instead in individual and group performances of citizenship. Individuals enact citizenship through a host of discursive actions, including consuming information, displaying the flag, engaging in public discussions, participating in public ceremonies, demonstrating, and even voting. Above all else, viewing citizenship as performance entails shifting focus from the category of citizen (and the attributes or qualities that define it) to the individual and situated articulation of citizenship.

This focus on civic performance as a marker of citizenship borrows from performance theory by foregrounding quotidian enactments of citizenship that are, in Robert Hariman and John Louis Lucaites' words, "aesthetically marked, situated, reflexive examples of 'restored behavior' presented to an audience."[25] Like performance art, enacting or performing citizenship—whether through community activism, artistic expression, speeches, conversations, cultural demonstrations, protest, or even economic activity—is "aesthetically marked"

20. Gonzales, "Mega Marchas," 43.

21. Adrian D. Pantoja, Cecilia Menjívar, and Lisa Magaña, (Eds). "The Spring Marches of 2006: Latinos, Immigration, and Political Mobilization in the 21st Century," special issue, *American Behavioral Scientist* 52 (2008).

22. Richard D. Pineda and Stacey K. Sowards, "Flag Waving as Visual Argument: 2006 Immigration Demonstrations and Cultural Citizenship," *Argumentation & Advocacy* 43 (2007): 164–74.

23. Beasley, *You, the People*; Celeste Michelle Condit and John Louis Lucaites, *Crafting Equality: America's Anglo-African Word* (Chicago: University of Chicago Press, 1993); Robert Hariman and John Louis Lucaites, *No Caption Needed: Iconic Photographs, Public Culture, and Liberal Democracy* (Chicago: University of Chicago Press, 2007).

24. Asen, "A Discourse Theory," 204.

25. Hariman and Lucaites, *No Caption Needed*, 33.

because it is staged and framed as a public spectacle, like the flying of an American flag. Civic performances are "situated" enactments of national belonging because they entail, in Asen's words, both "manner" (or intent) and "deed" (or action).[26] That is, civic performances (such as patriotic songs or pledges) not only refashion collective identity but also move a particular audience and motivate political consequences. Enactments of citizenship also necessarily involve what Hariman and Lucaites term "reflexive" and "restored" behavior, or the reiteration and appropriation of accepted practices, norms, rituals, and ideals.[27] The flying of national flags or the appropriation of national myths or slogans necessarily reflects and remakes national values to fit the circumstance in which they are discursively deployed. In other words, though civic performances may problematize conventions of citizenship and national identity, they still affirm commitment to the public, broadly defined.

At the most macro level, citizenship is continually performed through "civic rituals [that] constitute and sustain truths [and] that stabilize normative political identities."[28] In their book *No Caption Needed*, for example, Hariman and Lucaites trace how iconic images serve as national civic performances which provide the vocabulary for public culture and through which citizenship and civic identity are reiterated.[29] Also, in the more formal and ritual setting of presidential inaugurals, Vanessa Beasley argues, American ideals and identity are performed.[30]

Yet we have seen this performative or discursive perspective on citizenship take shape not just in studies of dominant discourses such as photojournalism or presidential rhetoric but also in the vernacular rhetoric of counterpublics. For example, several studies show how, at a time when they were defined as second-class citizens, women enacted citizenship and challenged conventions of belonging through appropriation of ritualized rhetorical acts such as petitions, marches, or attempts to vote in public elections.[31] Scholarship on the African American civil rights movement too shows how individuals and groups reimagined cultural ideographs and/or dominant narratives of American identity through public discourse and protest, all in the struggle for full citizenship.[32] Furthermore, protest movements have unique and far reaching rhetorical significance in attempts to challenge exclusionary dimensions of citizenship based on sexuality and gender.[33] Thus one of the most obvious domains for the vernacular performances of citizenship can be found in the legacy of social protest movements, which both enact and challenge citizenship.

In sum, this performative view of citizenship entails enactment and appropriation of

26. Asen, "A Discourse Theory," 194.

27. Hariman and Lucaites, *No Caption Needed*.

28. Jeffrey A. Bennett, *Banning Queer Blood: Rhetorics of Citizenship, Contagion, and Resistance* (Tuscaloosa: University of Alabama Press, 2009), 6.

29. Hariman and Lucaites, *No Caption Needed*.

30. Vanessa B. Beasley, "The Rhetoric of Ideological Consensus in the United States: American Principles and American Pose in Presidential Inaugurals," *Communication Monographs* 68 (2001): 169–83.

31. Angela G. Ray, "The Rhetorical Ritual of Citizenship: Women's Voting as Public Performance, 1868–1875," *Quarterly Journal of Speech* 93 (2007): 1–26; Susan Zaeske, *Signatures of Citizenship: Petitioning, Antislavery, & Women's Political Identity* (Chapel Hill: University of North Carolina Press, 2003).

32. Condit and Lucaites, *Crafting Equality*.

33. Jeffrey A. Bennett, "Passing, Protesting, and the Arts of Resistance: Infiltrating the Ritual Space of Blood Donation," *Quarterly Journal of Speech* 94 (2008): 23–43.

citizenship and national identity in the discourses and acts of dominant and vernacular groups—from the ritualistic to the quotidian. As Asen summarizes, "when viewed as a mode of public engagement, citizenship appears as a performance, not a possession."[34] This view of citizenship is evident in scholarship on immigration, for what Ono and Sloop call "dominant logics" of the nation are reiterated through large and small scale discourses— from public debates about immigration to the radical vigilantism of the border Minutemen.[35] This is not to say that citizenship is wholly discursive, for laws and institutions granting formal inclusion (or exclusion) still exist. However, viewing citizenship as a way of acting rather than as a status attribute means that even those individuals, like migrants, who are excluded from formal dimensions of citizenship can enact national belonging and challenge the borders of the civic imaginary. In the next section I elaborate on this discursive view of citizenship by discussing the role of hybridity in terms of civic performance and more specifically in relation to migration and citizenship.

HYBRIDITY, CITIZENSHIP, AND MIGRATION

The concept of hybridity has received significant attention from a number of scholars, in part because it speaks to the fragmentation/fusion of culture and identity in the conditions of globalization.[36] However, here I want to provide some conceptual clarity to the term as it relates first to the previous discussion of citizenship and second to literature on migration and border rhetoric. Then, through an analysis of LGM as a performance of hybrid citizenship, I will connect these theoretical strands and suggest new avenues for scholarly inquiry.

Hybridity and Citizenship

A discursive view of national identity necessitates a discussion of hybridity, for, as Asen argues, "acts do not possess intrinsic value" as expressions of citizenship. An act such as buying fair trade coffee can be one of many "hybrid cases" of citizenship because it has a hybrid function; it is at once a performance of citizenship and an act of consumption (which is not an inherently civic act).[37] In the same vein, a political protest may perform citizenship and civic engagement in the public sphere while simultaneously serving to consolidate the solidarity of the protestors and contribute to the group's self-affirmation. Hybridity is a metaphor for the complex and intersecting purposes of many performances of citizenship, which, like other performances, feature a fusion of audiences (both inward and outward-directed) and functions (artistic expression, political statement, entertainment, etc.).

In another sense, Kathleen Hall Jamieson and Karlyn Kohrs Campbell use hybridity as a metaphor to explain the "productive but transitory character of . . . combinations" in genres of discourse.[38] The metaphor of hybridity describes not the function but the multiform

34. Asen, "A Discourse Theory," 203.

35. Ono and Sloop, *Shifting Borders*; DeChaine, "Bordering."

36. Marwan M. Kraidy, "Hybridity in Cultural Globalization," *Communication Theory* 12 (2002): 316–39.

37. Asen, "A Discourse Theory," 206.

38. Kathleen Hall Jamieson and Karlyn Kohrs Campbell, "Rhetorical Hybrids: Fusions of Generic Elements," *Quarterly Journal of Speech* 68 (1982): 147.

nature of discourses that combine multiple generic elements and styles. In a more recent article, Darrel Enck-Wanzer speculates about the radical possibilities of this hybrid (or what he calls "intersectional") rhetorical form, in which "one form of discourse is not privileged over another; rather, diverse forms intersect organically to create something challenging to rhetorical norms." In his discussion of the Young Lords Party's "garbage offensive," Enck-Wanzer shows how a hybrid rhetorical form reshapes community and challenges conventions of "US liberal democracy."[39]

Therefore, performative enactments of citizenship can be called hybrid both in terms of their compound function—as quotidian acts and as acts of civic engagement—and in terms of their hybrid rhetorical form—since many performances of citizenship fuse multiple forms of discourse together. As this review suggests, beyond grounding as situated, staged, and aesthetically marked performance of national belonging, turning scholarly attention to discourses of citizenship and national identity necessitates attention to the hybrid functions and rhetorical forms of this rhetoric.

Hybridity and Migration

More specific to migration and Latina/o identity, however, scholars draw on the term hybridity to discuss the melding of cultures and the fusion of political identities.[40] As discussed above, dominant logics of immigration present a contradictory picture of immigrants and their role in the US. Immigrants are conceived of as physically within our borders yet not within our people, necessary but threatening to the integrity of the nation. There is a "deep ambivalence" about immigrants' role in US society and a conflicting view of immigration.[41] This "troublesome both/and" of migrants is evident in the contradictory public discourses of immigration throughout American history and in the binary interpretations of LGM (as either alien or American) discussed above.[42]

Yet viewing activities like LGM through the discursive or performative perspective on citizenship can focus our attention on how migrants negotiate this productive tension at the heart of US national identity. As scholars such as Homi Bhabha and May Joseph have argued, there is a congruence between the condition of migrants (e.g., a "troublesome both/and") that contributes both to anxiety over immigration and concurrently to the agency of migrants to reformulate national belonging.[43] In other words, the "ambiguous positionality" of migrants—their hybrid status as both "necessary and unwelcome, . . . both visible and invisible, both acknowledged and ignored"—creates anxiety in dominant society because of the very power migrants possess to problematize borders and lay bare the otherization endemic to citizenship.[44] As Joseph explains, there is a radical potential in the "tenuous" condi-

---

39. Darrel Enck-Wanzer, "Trashing the System: Social Movement, Intersectional Rhetoric, and Collective Agency in the Young Lords Organization's Garbage Offensive," *Quarterly Journal of Speech* 92 (2006): 191.

40. For example, see Gloria Anzaldúa, *Borderlands/La Frontera: The New Mestiza* (San Francisco: Spinsters/Aunt Lute, 1987), 205–21.

41. Ono and Sloop, *Shifting Borders*, 72.

42. DeChaine, "Bordering," 50.

43. Homi K. Bhabha, *The Location of Culture* (London: Routledge, 1994); May Joseph, *Nomadic Identities: The Performance of Citizenship* (Minneapolis: University of Minnesota Press, 1999).

44. DeChaine, "Bordering," 50.

tion of migration that "sunders the relationship between passport and citizen and challenges any tidy division between citizen and noncitizen."[45]

In this case, performances of citizenship by immigrants entail not only hybrid rhetorical form and a fusion of rhetorical functions but also the synthesis of political and transnational identities. On the one hand, the hybridity of many migrants and minorities—their status as "both us . . . and not us"—fuels "a deep anxiety about the national project."[46] Hybridity can be threatening to dominant logics, fueling attempts to shore up the borders of national identity. On the other hand, the hybrid position of migrants can challenge sedimented cultural forms by crafting new, diverse, and multi-positional forms of political identity. In sum, appropriation of the conditions that often make migrants abject creates opportunities to (re)border US citizenship and national identity.

I contend that LGM was fundamentally a hybrid performance of citizenship that fused multiple, transnational citizenship traditions and varied forms of discourse into a new vision of the civic imaginary. In the following section I explain how LGM enacted hybrid citizenship through a dynamic discourse involving signs and chants (verbal rhetoric), flags and symbols (visual rhetoric), and physical presence (embodied rhetoric). By coming out in public and staging a multi-discursive performance of US citizenship, protestors in LGM *enacted* US citizenship and civic identity. Yet by flouting their violations of citizenship laws (their violations of the border), celebrating transnational political and cultural traditions, and embodying racial difference, the protestors *problematized* citizenship, creating a hybrid "discursive space."[47] In other words, the protest was simultaneously an act of position (i.e., citizenship) and an act of op-position to dominant logics of immigration.

HYBRID CITIZENSHIP IN *LA GRAN MARCHA*

That LGM was a civic performance—a discursive staging of citizenship—is evident in much of its verbal rhetoric, including its signs and chants. The signs that protestors carried as they marched through the streets of downtown Los Angeles featured a variety of messages that served to perform citizenship for immigrant marchers. For example, "*Amnistía* [Amnesty]! Full rights for all immigrants," read one of the prominent signs carried by protestors. Other prominent signs included "The USA is MADE by IMMIGRANTS . . . and that's it," "*Ya basta de abusar a los migrantes* [Enough with abusing immigrants]," and "We are not the enemy— we are part of the solution." Through signs such as these, protestors pronounced their inclusion as members of the national body. Immigrant protestors appropriated a common cultural myth, that the US is a "nation of immigrants," into a new context. In contrast to conventional understandings of assimilation—a melting pot ideology—these protestors proclaimed their place firmly within the American civic imaginary. In a sense, these signs constructed an enthymeme that drew on the historical narratives surrounding immigra-

45. Joseph, *Nomadic Identities*, 17.

46. Arjun Appadurai, *Fear of Small Numbers: An Essay on the Geography of Anger* (Durham, NC: Duke University Press, 2006), 44.

47. Lisa A. Flores, "Creating Discursive Space Through a Rhetoric of Difference: Chicana Feminists Craft a Homeland," *Quarterly Journal of Speech* 82 (1996): 142–56.

tion. Latina/o immigrants were contributing to the "nation of immigrants"; they too were part of the tired, poor, and huddled masses yearning to breathe free.

Yet the appropriation of common myths of immigration, such as the notion that the US is a "nation of immigrants," was only part of the verbal rhetoric of LGM. In their chants and signs, protestors not only enacted belonging—"The USA is MADE by IMMIGRANTS . . . and that's it"—but also used political slogans and chants from Latina/o and Latin American history, reframing these diverse ethnic and national traditions into a performance of US citizenship. With chants such as "*Sí, se puede*" [Yes, it can be done], "*Palante*" [Onward, Forward], and "*El pueblo unido jamás será vencido*" [A united people will never be conquered], protestors in LGM forged links with Latina/o and Latin American protest movements from the twentieth century. They translated these discourses simultaneously into demands for citizenship and into challenges to the exclusionary dimensions of US civic identity.

For example, a chant like "*Sí, se puede*," which was prevalent throughout LGM, evidences the hybrid nature of the protestors' verbal rhetoric. In one sense, it could be read as "yes, it [full recognition/belonging] can be done." Yet considering the origin and legacy of this simple chant problematizes this interpretation. "*Sí, se puede*" was created by Dolores Huerta and deployed in the context of boycotts and strikes by Huerta, César Chavez, and the UFW for wages and other economic rights.[48] The chant was not merely a call for rights and recognition, but an enactment of solidarity and identity for the marginalized. Similarly, "*Palante*" (from *Para alante*), a rallying cry of the Puerto Rican Young Lords, also presumes the radical rhetoric of Latina/o social movements. The Young Lords, a self-professed radical, socialist organization, used confrontational tactics to oppose racism and segregation against Puerto Ricans in 1960s New York.[49] The Farm Workers and the Young Lords represent not movements for assimilation but confrontational social movements struggling to contest dominant traditions of US identity and its implicit racial and class dimensions. While each group struggled under different circumstances, both *critiqued* traditions of US citizenship; neither wholeheartedly embraced the conventional (white, male) myth of "a nation of immigrants."

Furthermore, appropriation of slogans such as "*Sí, se puede*" and "*Palante*" served an ego function for the protestors in LGM by constructing a narrative history that situated LGM in a long line of (Latina/o) struggles for social inclusion. As Michael McGee notes, constructing a "people" demands producing a "vision of the collective life."[50] This collective life involves both a picture of the past and a plan for the future. Therefore, by drawing on the rhetorical legacies of past protest movements, protestors in LGM worked to construct a mythic basis for their status as a movement. Through these diverse discourses, LGM fused a Latina/o-immigrant people.

To a large degree, the explicit connections made in the protestors' verbal rhetoric between contemporary and historical Latina/o struggles with citizenship are natural charac-

48. Stacey Sowards, "Rhetorical Agency as *Haciendo Caras* and Differential Consciousness Through Lens of Gender, Race, Ethnicity, and Class: An Examination of Dolores Huerta's Rhetoric," *Communication Theory* 20 (2010): 224.

49. Enck-Wanzer, "Trashing the System."

50. Michael C. McGee, "In Search of 'the People': A Rhetorical Alternative," *Quarterly Journal of Speech* 61 (1975): 245.

teristics of social protest movements, which aim to establish a degree of continuity and connection to the past even as they radically challenge the present. Yet protestors in *La Gran Marcha* also struck transnational links between their demands for citizenship and the struggles of Latin Americans across the hemisphere. Reaching across national borders, their verbal rhetoric fused multiple nationalities, political traditions, and identities into, paradoxically, a demand for US national belonging.

For example, protestors in LGM used a number of variations on the well known Spanish chant "*El pueblo unido jamás será vencido*" [A united people will never be conquered]. Some of these adaptations substituted "*Latinos*," "*Familias*" and "*Migrantes*" for "*El pueblo*." This chant, though connected to a variety of South American radical resistance groups, was popularized by Chilean musical groups who used the slogan as a rallying song against Augusto Pinochet's authoritarian government.[51] Drawing on this chant as a rhetorical resource, protestors again enacted hybrid purposes and spoke to multiple audiences. First, the chant constituted protestors outwardly as a united "people" with agency in the American public sphere. Second, it framed a more targeted message directed at Latina/os and immigrants, one which portrayed US immigration and citizenship policy as an authoritarian system and immigrants and Latina/os as defenders of freedom and justice. Third, the deployment of terms such as *Latinos, familias,* and *migrantes* for "the people" created an equivalence between these groups and constituted solidarity between the diverse constituents of LGM. Through the simple appropriation and variation of this slogan, protestors multiply rewrote the narrative of immigration, situating immigrants both as political actors, as a community of families, a united ethnic people, and as insurgents defending freedom and justice against an authoritarian regime. The use of this popular Spanish-language chant constructed both a public enthymeme and an analogy for protestors to understand their struggles and their adversary.

The fusion of these diverse meanings implicit in just a few of the prominent slogans used in LGM attests to the unconventional citizenship enacted therein. In hybrid fashion, at once protestors proclaimed themselves citizens, constituted themselves as a movement, and critiqued structures of exclusion endemic to US identity. "The USA is MADE by Immigrants . . . and that's it," becomes a hybrid proclamation both drawing upon and subverting the myth of a nation of immigrants. Of course, this hybrid verbal rhetoric is no more evident than in the bilingual nature of the protest. By speaking Spanish in their enactments of US belonging, protestors presented a challenge to the conventional expectations of immigrants in the US—that they speak English in the public sphere. The textured nature of these language strategies and appeals represents the hybrid function of the event (as civic performance, political demand, cultural solidarity, and radical critique) and its multiple audiences (the American public, Latina/os and immigrants, and the protestors themselves). In spite of, or perhaps because Anglos may not have understood, the Spanish chants or slogans, the deployment of these discourses in LGM explicitly marked the protest as a "troublesome both/and." For Latina/o immigrants, the verbal rhetoric and the use of Spanish constituted rhetorical and political agency even when situated outside the formal legal channels of recognition.

---

51. Mark Mattern, *Acting in Concert: Music, Community, and Political Action* (New Brunswick, NJ: Rutgers University Press, 1998), Chapter 3.

Turning to the use of visual rhetoric in LGM, protestors used flag waving to construct a similar hybrid enactment of national belonging. We know that flags are symbols of national identity and can form part of a discursive enactment of public values and culture. Civic participation is often communicated through flag waving and flying flags outside one's home. In these cases, public use of the flag becomes a "figural enactment of national identity."[52] In LGM, protestors participated in these discourses of civic identification. In tandem with the performance of US citizenship evident in their signs and chants, the waving of American flags by protestors functioned as a rhetorical enactment of US citizenship. In fact, the use of American flags in the protests was an intentional choice meant to foreground the protestors' self-identification as members of the American national community.[53]

Yet the rhetorical use of flag waving also demonstrates the discursive appropriation of multiple citizenship traditions that took shape in LGM. Certainly protestors waved American flags in performance of US civic identity, but they also prominently displayed Mexican, Guatemalan, or Salvadoran flags, pronouncing their dual national identities and their unique transnational agency. Many political commentators and spectators wondered how under conventional understandings of citizenship a group could demand protection as a member of the US national community but also profess allegiance to another flag.[54] Even some Latina/o organizers lamented the inclusion of foreign flags because it contributed to stereotypes of immigrants as "Mexicans" and "foreigners" rather than Americans; "If we want to live here," said radio DJ Eddie "Piolin" Sotelo, "we want to demonstrate that we love this country and we love the American flag."[55]

Others saw the flying of these foreign flags merely as a cultural expression, akin to the display of shamrocks on St. Patrick's Day.[56] Viewed in tandem with their verbal rhetoric, however, the use of multiple national flags in LGM was more than an appeal to cultural tradition. Instead, by appropriating multiple national symbols and transnational traditions, protestors in LGM were challenging the implicit border logic that demarcates citizen from alien and demands single nation-state identification as part of the compact of citizenship. To paraphrase Bhabha, in their visual rhetoric of flag waving, protestors both evoked and erased the nation's "totalizing boundaries."[57] Protestors proclaimed their national belonging because they were flying the stars and stripes. Yet by flying both US flags and Mexican and other Latin American flags, protestors in LGM enacted belonging in multiple national communities. Like their use of the Spanish language and foreign political traditions, by flying foreign flags in the American public square, protestors appropriated dominant stereotypes concerning unassimilable "aliens" in the service of challenging border logics. They created a civic imaginary that could hold in tension allegiance both to the United States and to other nations.

The verbal and visual rhetoric of the protestors I have discussed above—communicated through signs, chants, and flags—operated in tandem with LGM's embodied elements. By

52. Hariman and Lucaites, *No Caption Needed*, 100.
53. See Chavez, *Latino Threat*, Chapter 7.
54. For examples see Pineda and Sowards, "Flag Waving as Visual Argument," 168–70.
55. Quoted in Chavez, *The Latino Threat*, 158.
56. See Chavez, *The Latino Threat*, 158–9.
57. Homi K. Bhabha, "DissemiNation: Time, Narrative, and the Margins of the Modern Nation" in *Nation and Narration*, ed. Homi K. Bhabha (London: Routledge, 1990), 300.

taking up public space and coming together as a collective body politic, protestors also fused a hybrid performance of citizenship. In the most basic sense, immigrants became visible and marked as bodies out in the open, an unusual circumstance for a group of people whose main goal is to blend indistinguishably into society. As I noted above, the immigrant is conceived in popular society as an ambiguous and sometimes threatening "other" that is "fundamentally outside the national body."[58] As such, undocumented immigrants, by virtue of their legal and social status, are absent from the public sphere. Yet by marching a little over a mile through downtown Los Angeles, from the corner of Olympic and Broadway, where the protest originated, to LA's City Hall, immigrant protestors in LGM physically and visibly took up space in the public square and embodied their role as members of the national community. Through their physical presence, the protestors performed public belonging, for "the capacity to make oneself visible," argues Anne Norton, "is a prerogative, and hence a sign, of power."[59] Like earlier protest movements, immigrant demonstrators in LGM performed their civic belonging through a "coming out" in public.[60] Their embodied rhetoric worked in tandem with their verbal and visual performances of US citizenship, for many of the protestors intentionally wore a quintessentially American outfit consisting of blue jeans and white T-shirts. Much like the function of *presence* in argumentation, which foregrounds certain topics or proofs to make them act on the ongoing deliberation, this embodied rhetoric presenced immigrants' enactments of citizenship in the public sphere. In one sense, by making themselves visible as "Americans," immigrant protestors in LGM constructed a performance of belonging.

LGM was not merely a performance of American-ness, however. Protestors also embodied conventional racial stereotypes of immigrants as abject and threatening, using them in the service of challenging alienization. Attempts to solidify the border often "find a scapegoat" in minorities because of "the threats their racial, financial, linguistic, and cultural border-blurrings pose."[61] Therefore, the non-white bodies of Latina/o and immigrant protestors challenged these conventional racial presumptions of citizenship, performing national belonging in and through racial difference. Racially and ethnically marked bodies took to the streets in numbers, shouting and waving signs in foreign languages, marching to foreign music. Latina/o immigrants in particular drove through the streets blaring Tejano or salsa music and honking their car horns. Protestors congregated on green space as they marched through the streets to converse in Spanish. Their embodied performances were infused with what José Esteban Muñoz calls "affective excess." In contrast to the "white middle-class subjectivity" that structures US citizenship and its "national affect," protestors in LGM appropriated the Latino/immigrant affect of a troublesome and hybrid figure.[62] In a second sense, then, beyond merely coming out of the shadows to demand inclusion, the

58. Flores, "Constructing Rhetorical Borders," 381.

59. Anne Norton, *Republic of Signs: Liberal Theory and American Popular Culture* (Chicago: University of Chicago Press, 1993), 120.

60. Kevin Michael DeLuca, "Unruly Arguments: The Body Rhetoric of Earth First!, ACT UP, and Queer Nation," *Argumentation & Advocacy* 36 (1999): 18.

61. DeChaine, "Bordering," 49.

62. José Esteban Muñoz, "Feeling Brown: Ethnicity and Affect in Ricardo Bracho's The Sweetest Hangover (and Other STDs)," *Theatre Journal* 52 (2000): 69–70.

protestors' rowdy and racialized "coming out" flouted the racial components of US citizenship and demanded recognition of the specifically Latina/o-immigrant citizen. Immigrants enacted citizenship in and through their racially and ethnically marked bodies rather than trying to erase those differences exclusively through performances of assimilation.

Furthermore, protestors appropriated the "fear of small numbers" that minority populations pose to the nation-state.[63] In their physical presence on streets, sidewalks, and public parks, immigrant protestors embodied the sense of uncertainty brought on by racial, ethnic, and cultural minorities, the same anxiety that propels bordering rhetoric. When protestors performed US citizenship through Spanish-language chants, waving diverse national flags, appealing to foreign political traditions, and often physically flaunting national immigration laws, they "disperse[d] the homogeneous" traditions of US national identity that impose these types of difference as conditions for exclusion.[64] Protestors demanded an acknowledgment of their *il*legal US citizenship. They took over public space and symbols of American identity, all the while celebrating other traditions and cultures. The impact of LGM on the fear of minority numbers was evident in the contest over the size of the protest, for while Los Angeles police claimed that "500,000 plus" marched, organizers and activists countered that there were "2 million people" present.[65] Thus there was rhetorical power in both amplifying and minimizing the size of LGM. By taking over public space with a massive group of minorities, immigrants flaunted the fear of numbers that often propels exclusion or assimilation of migrants.

In its embodied rhetoric, as in its verbal and visual elements, LGM turned the process of alienization endemic to nationalism on its head to challenge the boundaries between "us" and "them." On the one hand, LGM physically enacted inclusion into the US civic imaginary. On the other hand, appropriating stereotypes of immigrants as an ever-growing threat to the nation, protestors magnified the differences that would normally exclude them from belonging in the service of performing citizenship. LGM featured a hybrid position for immigrants as simultaneously both citizens and others. What was the embodied "social (dis)ease of the US border problem" became a body of hybrid citizens denaturalizing the borders of the nation.[66] In essence, by embodying and appropriating dominant logics of immigration in a hybrid performance of citizenship, protestors in LGM demonstrated the impossibility of discerning citizens from aliens, exposing the rhetorically constructed roots of US citizenship.

(RE)BORDERING THE CIVIC IMAGINARY

In this analysis, I have argued that LGM represented a hybrid discourse of American citizenship in which migrants fused competing traditions of citizenship in the construction of a broader national identity. The borders between citizens and aliens are rhetorically constructed and reified in response to the anxiety provoked by immigration. Yet LGM illustrates

63. Appadurai, *Fear of Small Numbers*, 4–5.

64. Bhabha, "DissemiNation," 293.

65. Teresa Watanabe and Hector Becerra, "How DJs Put 500,000 Marchers in Motion," *Los Angeles Times*, March 28, 2006, http://articles.latimes.com/2006/mar/28/local/me-march28

66. DeChaine, "Bordering," 49.

that the rhetorical process of bordering is a still more complex phenomenon. Though some have interpreted LGM through conventional bordering logics, viewing it as an "alien" discourse authorizing immigrant exclusion, others have understood it as a very "American" demand for inclusion. Both of these elements, I have argued, are evident in the LGM's rhetoric. The protest can be understood as a (re)bordering of its own, a performance of citizenship that blurred and expanded US citizenship and the US nation. Immigrant protestors in LGM appropriated conventional discourses of national identity in the service of constructing a hybrid US citizenship.

One conclusion I wish to advance concerns the sustained scholarly attention we pay to dominant logics of the border and immigration. If we take seriously a "dynamic conception of bordering practices," as DeChaine proposes, we cannot so easily conclude that alienization, in his words, "all but guarantees an irredeemable non-place for the racialized, alienized, border-crossing migrant in the United States today."[67] Certainly it is important to critique, in the tradition of critical rhetoric, the "domination" constructed by these discourses.[68] However, attention to LGM itself as bordering discourse evinces a civic imaginary that is multiform and confluent. As a vernacular rhetoric of citizenship, LGM demonstrates that even those who lack citizenship in the political, legal, or cultural sense can perform citizenship on a daily basis through rhetorical acts.

I echo the need for the "debunking of alienizing practices" in contemporary immigration discourse.[69] However, beyond the ways in which dominant discourses exclude immigrants or contribute to their assimilation, scholars need to consider how migrants and other minorities craft resistive rhetorics of citizenship. Drawing on a fundamental characteristic of immigrant identity—a doubleness that constitutes both a source of resistance and a source of anxiety—LGM constructed a hybrid enactment of US citizenship. Privileging questions concerning how Latina/os and migrants are represented in dominant society rather than the discourses of Latina/os and migrants themselves may contribute to the perception that these groups are apolitical and/or vulnerable. Equally necessary is further reflection on how migrants and Latina/os enact agency and identity through performances of citizenship and national belonging. LGM calls on scholars to attend not only to the bordering logics that exclude immigrants but also to the efforts of migrant groups and Latina/os to challenge these borders and redraw the nation in more inclusive ways.

As a case study in a discursive or performative perspective on citizenship, LGM provides a second group of insights for the study of citizenship more generally. LGM illustrates the intimate connection between notions of hybridity and the study of civic performance. As my analysis demonstrates, LGM enacted hybrid citizenship in at least three dimensions: hybrid rhetorical form, a confluence of rhetorical functions, and a fusion of traditions and identities. First, like earlier social protests, LGM consisted of a hybrid rhetorical form, or what others have called an intersectional rhetoric, which fused multiple modes of discourse—visual, verbal, and embodied; signs, chants, flags, and physi-

67. DeChaine, "Bordering," 59. Emphasis added.

68. Raymie E. McKerrow, "Critical Rhetoric: Theory and Praxis," *Communication Monographs* 56 (1989): 91–111.

69. DeChaine, "Bordering," 61.

cal presence—into a "a hybrid political space."[70] Second, LGM fused multiple functions and varied audiences, including a media spectacle of political agency, a moment of social movement solidarity, a public claim to American-ness, and an attempt to forge a Latina/o-immigrant people. Like earlier social protests, it enacted elements of political argument, cultural performance, ethnic solidarity, and civic ritual. Third, in its rhetorical "content" LGM appealed to a fusion of cultural traditions and identities that challenged bordering logics, whiteness, single nation-state identification, and cultural homogeneity. The link between hybridity and civic performance suggests a relationship that should be explored, and scholars interested in studying citizenship from a rhetorical dimension could pay particular attention to the hybrid form, function, and content of those enactments.

To this end, LGM provides a final conclusion I wish to advance concerning the possibilities of hybrid rhetoric in US citizenship and democracy. Considering its hybrid dimensions, LGM represents an example of what Enck-Wanzer has called a "radical democratic style."[71] This style is marked by the fusion of multiple forms of rhetoric and the synthesis of multiple citizenship discourses and conventions. Through their radical democratic performance, protestors challenged the conventional model of the disembodied "good citizen," who conventionally expresses "himself" as an informed, rational, and eloquent speaker.[72] This "ideal" model of democratic discourse works hand in hand with discourses of alienization to regularly exclude and silence immigrants and minorities based on their legal, racial, gender, and cultural difference, for the public sphere "proscribes conditions for citizenship enactment and the voices that are to be included in and excluded from deliberation."[73] Yet protestors' enactments of US citizenship—their attempts to create space and have a voice—radically contested these exclusionary logics.

As Eric King Watts argues, voice demands ethical and emotional acknowledgment by the dominant culture; it demands to be heard. In the case of LGM, the "voice" of the protestors was "not detachable" from their bodies but imbued with "ideology and identity."[74] Moreover, their protest contested the regulation of political space and momentarily democratized the public sphere. "*Aquí estamos, y no nos vamos, y si nos echan regresamos!*" [We are here, and we are not leaving, and if they kick us out, we'll return!], the protestors shouted, carving out a radical discursive space and a voice within American society. Therefore, the radical democratic style of LGM represents what Robert Ivie has called the "dirt work" of democracy; that is, LGM momentarily mucked up the works.[75] By contesting conventions of democratic discourse—in who could speak, what they could say, and how they could say it—LGM exemplifies the possibility of diverse forms of discourse to expand civic identity, invigorate deliberation, and further the ongoing struggle to enact democracy.

70. Enck-Wanzer, "Trashing the System," 191.

71. Darrel Enck-Wanzer, "A Radical Democratic Style? Tradition, Hybridity, and Intersectionality," *Rhetoric & Public Affairs* 11 (2008): 459–65.

72. Ronald Walter Greene, "John Dewey's Eloquent Citizen: Communication, Judgment, and Postmodern Capitalism," *Argumentation & Advocacy* 39 (2003): 189–200.

73. DeChaine, "Bordering," 60.

74. Eric King Watts, "'Voice' and 'Voicelessness' in Rhetorical Studies," *Quarterly Journal of Speech* 87 (2001): 192.

75. Robert L. Ivie, "Rhetorical Deliberation and Democratic Politics in the Here and Now," *Rhetoric & Public Affairs* 5 (2002): 279.

LEFT OUT BUT NOT SHUT DOWN

POLITICAL ACTIVISM AND THE UNDOCUMENTED STUDENT MOVEMENT

Roberto G. Gonzales

INTRODUCTION

Adorned in her cap and gown, Andrea Gómez[1] sat quietly as hundreds watched. In a few short months she would be entering a master's program in Applied Social Research at the California State University at Fullerton, but this day was one she had been looking forward to for over four years. All of the hours spent in preparation had paid off. There she sat with several others wearing their own caps and gowns, but there was something different about this day. This was no graduation ceremony, and Andrea and the others were not in line to receive their diplomas. Instead of wearing smiles and anxious expressions, these students were bound at their hands with tape covering their mouths. This spectacle was a planned action organized by high school, college, and university students throughout Orange County in an attempt to draw public attention to the ways in which current immigration laws restrict and silence some of the nation's brightest and most talented students.

These efforts were part of a larger series of actions that took place May 1, 2006, in Santa Ana, California, and in scores of cities across the country. At twenty-two years old, Andrea was not only one of the youngest of the day's organizers, but also one of the central leaders of the coalition of immigrant rights and advocacy groups that set the stage for the Orange County May Day protests. When reflecting back on that day, she proudly exclaims, "It was awesome! Even though many of the organizers involved had forgotten about students, we were able to become an important part of that day. We were able to truly represent students."[2]

Roberto G. Gonzales is assistant professor in the School of Social Service Administration at the University of Chicago.

Reprinted with special permission of the Northwestern University School of Law, *Northwestern Journal of Law and Social Policy*, from "Left Out but Not Shut Down: Political Activism and the Undocumented Student Movement," *Northwestern Journal of Law and Social Policy* 3 (2): 219–39 by Roberto G. Gonzales. Copyright © 2008 by Northwestern University School of Law, *Northwestern Journal of Law and Social Policy*.

1. To protect confidentiality, all names of individuals and organizations have been replaced with pseudonyms.

2. Interview with Andrea Gómez in Orange County, Cal. (Feb. 4, 2007).

YOUTH, AGENCY, AND THE MARCHES
IN AN ERA OF UNAUTHORIZED SETTLEMENT

This inclusion of youth as both subjects and active participants in political organizing is something that young people like Andrea have worked tirelessly at achieving. After spending days in strategy meetings with more than forty other student leaders, on May 1, 2006, Andrea and two hundred other students stood on stage making their concerns heard. While this day was an important one for Andrea and countless others, this was not her introduction to political participation. Long before this spring afternoon, the circumstances of Andrea's life shaped both her political and educational trajectories.

In the spring of 2006, cities across the United States witnessed unprecedented numbers of people taking to the streets in protest (see Cisneros, this volume). Sparked by the passage in the House of an anti-immigrant Congressional bill, supported by powerful allies, and alerted by effective communication networks, millions of people in big cities and small towns took to the streets and used their feet to express their disapproval.[3] From traditional immigrant metropolises like New York, Los Angeles, and Chicago, to newer immigrant destination cities like Milwaukee, Denver, and Atlanta, these political demonstrations grew into a national effort to mobilize against punitive immigration laws. In Los Angeles alone, more than 500,000 people crowded the streets and parks in peaceful protest on March 25, 2006.[4] Across the nation, hundreds of thousands of people, young and old, and along a wide spectrum of ethnic communities, walked out of school, gave up their wages for a day, and marched in the streets of U.S. cities. Until then quiet and largely out of public sight, these protestors loudly and visibly carried flags, banners, and placards to show their willingness to stand up for the rights of immigrant workers and students.

Among these demonstrators were large groups of young immigrants and children of immigrants who marched side-by-side with their parents and community members. The efforts of Andrea's group were matched by those of other youth groups across the country. About 700 high school students in El Paso, Texas, walked out of their schools in late March, while an estimated 70,000 walked out in San Diego County; 35,000 in Los Angeles County and about 3,500 students in Dallas demonstrated in the streets.[5] These are only a few examples of countless political actions by youth and adults alike that took place across the United States.

In the aftermath of these large demonstrations, scholars, politicians, and pundits have tried to make sense of how they happened and what they would mean for the future. Many asked if this was the beginning of a new civil rights movement, if it was a rebirth of the Chicano movement, and if these protests were a flash in the pan or part of a larger political agenda. While the first two questions are provocative, it is the final question that has perhaps the greatest relevance and importance to scholars, policymakers, and elected officials: would such participation translate into broader political participation by immigrant communities?

3. In particular, people responded to HR 4437, the bill sponsored by Representative James Sensenbrenner, Jr. (R-Wis.), which would criminalize entire immigrant communities and those who would aid them.

4. Teresa Watanabe & Hector Becerra, *500,000 Pack Streets to Protest Immigration Bills*, L.A. TIMES, Mar. 26, 2006, at A1.

5. Gary Younge, *Ignore Youth at Your Peril*, GUARDIAN WKLY., June 16–22, 2006, at 5.

Indeed, as they walked out of schools and marched in the streets, these young protestors participated in large numbers, and significant portions of them have continued to engage in civic and political action. Long after the marches, student groups continue to work tirelessly to educate community members and school officials, assist students, and organize for policy change.

Nevertheless, the legality of their situation remains salient. As undocumented *residents*, many of the young students are without full political rights, cannot naturalize, and cannot vote. This complex reality calls into question the political currency of an informal existence. However, unauthorized students are not without the ability to take willing and purposive action in the face of social restraints. Student involvement in the immigrant rights marches of the spring of 2006 brings to mind the relationship between structure and human agency that occupied the minds of social theorists more than twenty years ago.[6] In the face of an impending tightening of rights and a hostile populace, students like Andrea stood up to take independent action that would move them from the status of unwilling victims to active participants.

In part, Andrea's story is not unique. She is part of the growing number of "1.5"[7] and second-generation children born to unauthorized parents and raised in the United States. Along with the native-born and the immigrant children under the age of eighteen, they number five million.[8] Of these, approximately 1.8 million are unauthorized[9] with few chances to regularize their status. Each year, an estimated 65,000 unauthorized students graduate from high school without the benefits of full societal participation.[10] Another 15,000 (nearly one-fifth) fail to graduate.[11]

Since the changes brought about in the 1960s, there has been a transformation in the general landscape of the United States. In particular, stepped-up border enforcement and the passage of free-trade agreements have transformed once-circular migration patterns into permanent and unauthorized migrant settlement.[12] Although Mexican migration has constituted a steady stream, contemporary migration is characterized by greater numbers and a large unauthorized population with a larger presence in urban areas.[13] Over the last two decades, the number of unauthorized families has grown to 6.6 million as increased

6. *See generally* ANTHONY GIDDENS, THE CONSTITUTION OF SOCIETY: OUTLINE OF THE THEORY OF STRUCTURATION (1984).

7. Sociologist Rubén G. Rumbaut employed the concept of the 1.5 generation to distinguish immigrant children from first and second generations; immigrants who arrive in the United States in their late teens or as adults are generally designated as first generation, those who come as children are considered to be 1.5 generation, and those born in the United States to at least one immigrant parent are second-generation. *See generally* Rubén G. Rumbaut, *Ages, Life Stages, and Generational Cohorts: Decomposing the Immigrant First and Second Generations in the United States*, 38 INT'L MIGRATION REV. 1160 (2004).

8. Jeffrey S. Passel, *Size and Characteristics of the Unauthorized Migrant Population in the U.S.*, Pew Hispanic Center, Mar. 7, 2006, *available at* http://pewhispanic.org/reports/report.php?ReportID=61 (last visited Aug. 6, 2008).

9. *Id.*

10. Unauthorized immigrants by law cannot legally work, vote, serve on juries, or, in most states, drive.

11. Passel, *supra* note 8.

12. *See generally* DOUGLAS S. MASSEY, JORGE DURAND & NOLAN J. MALONE, BEYOND SMOKE AND MIRRORS: MEXICAN IMMIGRATION IN THE ERA OF ECONOMIC INTEGRATION (2002).

13. *See* ROGER D. WALDINGER, STRANGERS AT THE GATES: NEW IMMIGRANTS IN URBAN AMERICA (2001).

labor migration and a corresponding increase in settlement have dramatically altered the complexity of the Latino migrant family.[14] As a result, an increasing number of children are being raised in the United States without the protections and privileges of citizenship.

Once Andrea's family crossed the border into the United States, they began their new lives as unauthorized migrants ("illegal aliens" in the common pejorative), and as a result are confronted with major challenges. Today, an estimated 11.5 to 12 million unauthorized immigrants reside in the United States.[15] Living in the shadows, these adults and their children struggle to balance the contradictory and conflicting meanings inscribed by immigration laws and economic practices. Indeed, over the last one hundred years, a series of adjustments and transformations in immigration laws and labor recruitment have shaped the nature of communities and social and economic mobility for Mexican immigrants in the United States (see De Genova, this volume).

Meanwhile, local and national policies have oscillated to satisfy competing views, resulting in changing and arbitrary definitions of legality and mixed messages for migrants. Moreover, contradictions between the United States' economic and immigration policies have created a steady and growing number of largely Latino low-wage laborers to meet the needs of the economy, a large number of whom work without the protections and privileges of legal status. In addition, unauthorized migrant settlement has contributed to larger numbers of unauthorized children growing into adulthood, for which legal status, poor schools, and poverty conspire to make political, social, and economic incorporation extremely complicated.

UNAUTHORIZED STUDENTS AND UNCERTAIN FUTURES

The spring demonstrations provided the impetus for voter drives and grassroots immigrant rights activism throughout the country.[16] They also attracted workers and students who had never been involved in any type of political movement up until then.[17] However, the image of the "awakened giant" that has been used quite frequently since then[18] does little more than reify simplistic and misleading notions that immigrants and immigrant communities had been theretofore powerless and paralyzed. To be sure, the immigrant rights marches mobilized more people than any other time in the history of the United States.[19] However, to imagine that these actions were merely spontaneous eruptions of pent-up feelings without acknowledging underlying community organizing processes and the historic antecedents of previous community efforts misses the manner in which the mobilizations were organized. Moreover, such assumptions also obscure the ways in which political participation takes root in immigrant communities.

14. *Id.*

15. Passel, *supra* note 8.

16. Daniel González, *Migrant Rights Groups Seek 1 Million Voters*, ARIZ. REPUBLIC, Aug. 3, 2006, at A1, *available at* http://www.hispanic7.com/migrant_rights_groups_seek_1_million_voters.htm (last visited Aug. 6, 2008).

17. Michelle Mittlestadt, *Rousing a Sleeping Giant*, DALLAS MORNING NEWS, June 25, 2006, at A1.

18. Watanabe & Becerra, *supra* note 4.

19. *Id.*

The spring marches demonstrated that despite legal and social marginalization, immigrants activated alternate forms of participation as a common reaction to impending legislation and a shared experience. The growth of the unauthorized population over the last two decades coincided with the accumulative growth of 1.5 and second-generation children in large proportions. Because these children's fates are largely interlinked with the fates of their unauthorized parents, their stake in what happens in the larger immigration debates is indisputable.

While unauthorized children and adolescents are confronted with numerous barriers and exclusions, they are entitled by law to an education. In 1982, the Supreme Court of the United States ruled in *Plyler v. Doe* that undocumented children are "persons" under the Fourteenth Amendment of the Constitution and thus can assert claims under the Equal Protection Clause. The Court further held that children cannot be denied access to public elementary and secondary education on the basis of their legal status.[20]

This case has had profound implications for children, families, and school districts throughout the country for the last twenty-five years. The *Plyler* ruling also has important implications for school-based leadership and civic engagement opportunities. Thanks to *Plyler*, hundreds of thousands of children have gone on to receive their education. As a result of their participation in school, many of these youngsters develop ties to teachers, counselors, and peers. Through these networks, some of these students also join school-based clubs and organizations, where they begin to gain experience in community service and develop leadership skills.

Some states have granted unauthorized students in-state tuition to public colleges and universities,[21] enabling a small but significant minority of unauthorized students the opportunity to pursue post-secondary education.[22] It is not a coincidence that many groups, like Andrea's, are forming on college and university campuses. Encouraged by in-state tuition policies, like California's AB 540,[23] undocumented students now feel some measure of inclusion. Beyond the instrumental functions of the law, such policies also provide a less stigmatizing label that signals students' legal permission on one hand, and gives them a legitimized identity on the other. Undocumented students in California, for example, can call themselves AB 540 students, a name they can more safely use in public—as few people know the meaning—and one around which they can rally.

However, these state laws, which provide in-state tuition and allow more students educational and civic opportunities, are only applicable in the classroom and do not provide any means for changing one's immigration status. As a result, when finished with their

---

20. *Plyler*, 457 U.S. at 230.

21. Since 2001, ten states have passed laws permitting certain undocumented students who have attended and graduated from their primary and secondary schools to pay the same tuition as their in-state classmates at public institutions of higher education. The states are California, Illinois, Kansas, Nebraska, New Mexico, New York, Oklahoma, Texas, Utah, and Washington.

22. *See* Elizabeth Redden, *An In-State Tuition Debate*, INSIDE HIGHER EDUC., Feb. 28, 2007, http://www.insidehighered.com/news/2007/02/28/immigration (last visited Aug. 6, 2008).

23. California Assembly Bill 540 amended the California Education Code section 68130.5 to create a new exemption from payment of non-resident tuition. Students who have attended a California high school for three years *and* received a California high school diploma or its equivalent, such as a GED, are exempt from paying non-resident tuition.

post-secondary education, these highly educated student leaders have as few options as their parents. They are left with few choices other than to advocate for their rights to become full citizens.

What are the consequences of growing up "American," yet living with only partial access to the mechanisms that promote social mobility, and what, in particular, about living an informal existence provides the impetus for political participation? Unauthorized students have unique circumstances that set them apart from their immigrant parents and their native-born peers. Their lives are profoundly shaped by parallel processes of growing into adolescence and adulthood and acculturating to the norms and standards of U.S. culture. They find themselves between two worlds, betwixt and between their country of birth and the country they call home. In the words of many I have spoken to, they are *ni de aquí, ni de allá* (neither here, nor there). Most of them only know their birth country through their parents' stories. They may feel a nostalgic connection to their homeland, but do not have the ability to visit without having to make a clandestine crossing in order to return. At the same time, they feel the negative impact of racism in their own schools and communities. Yet with every year lived in the United States, they feel a growing distance between them and their parents as they become more acculturated. Ironically, though, each of these years also brings them closer to the consequences and limitations of their unauthorized status.

These children, born abroad yet brought at an early age to live in the United States by their parents, represent a relatively new but significant population. Their generation fits somewhere between the first and second generations, and therefore is commonly referred to as the 1.5 generation. They are not of the first generation because they did not choose to migrate, but they are not of the second generation either, as they were born and spent part of their childhood in their country of birth. While they have some association with their countries of origin, their primary identification is affected by experiences growing up American. They, at times, straddle two worlds and are often called upon to assist their parents in the acculturation and adaptation process. However, their dual frames of reference provide both advantage and difficulty.

Unlike their parents, most do not migrate with the understanding of toiling in low-wage jobs. To be sure, their fates are shaped by larger processes of labor demand and immigrant restriction. However, they have grown up in the United States and have aspirations and expectations similar to those of their native-born and legal immigrant peers.[24] Their immigration status, however, separates them from their peers, as their aspirations cannot be fully realized without significant changes to the laws governing their rights to full participation. As a result, unauthorized students are fighting for their place at the table, in the classroom, and in the workforce.

While unauthorized students find open, albeit limited, avenues to participation in school, they are often left out of broader political processes. United States immigration laws determine who is eligible to receive benefits and to participate in the country's labor market and political system. As such, the law is instrumental in determining how newcomers participate politically. In order to vote, serve on juries, and receive most health benefits, citizenship is

24. *See generally* Herbert Gans, *Second Generation Decline: Scenarios for the Economic and Ethnic Futures of the Post-1965 American Immigrants*, 15 ETHNIC & RACIAL STUDIES 173 (1992).

essential. Legal permanent residents, while not able to experience the full range of benefits citizenship offers, do have more opportunities than unauthorized migrants, such as the ability to work lawfully. However, unauthorized students do not have such opportunities, as their immigration status shuts them out of many forms of participation.

These students' lived realities provide strong evidence for the assertion that immigration policies hold strong salience in the lives of immigrants, as they have the power to designate statuses and determine who gets what. Social scientists have pointed out that such designations of "illegal alien," "green card holder," and "citizen" are arbitrary categories that separate people, endow status, and dictate who is in and who is out.[25]

Indeed, unauthorized settlement has legal and political implications, restricting unauthorized families' ability to participate in political activity as well as day-to-day life. As social scientists have noted, immigration policies affect personal decisions such as work, driving, and going to school.[26] Scholars have also demonstrated that these policies have a strong power over immigrants. Kitty Calavita, for example, argues that immigration laws, rather than controlling immigration, control and marginalize immigrants.[27] Susan Coutin concurs, asserting that these laws in effect criminalize migrant behavior.[28] Migrants understand the law and how it restricts them and behave accordingly. Does all of this mean, though, that these young women and men are completely disenfranchised? Coutin points out that migrants can and do exercise purposive action as they create what she calls legitimate spaces for work, political, and social life.[29]

A CASE STUDY

Over the course of more than a year, I spent time with the Orange County Immigrant Student Group (OCISG),[30] an organization of Latino college and university student volunteers, organized collectively to assist students, educate the community, and advocate for changes in legislation. Many of these students are *Plyler* beneficiaries, having gone through California public schools. Thanks to *Plyler*, many of them have enjoyed a full range of activities in school, including clubs and community service opportunities. However, upon graduation from high school, they face the limitations of their status.

My point of entrée into this group was an undergraduate student at my own university, Esperanza Rivas. Prior to this, I had known Esperanza for almost four years. We began our respective graduate and undergraduate studies at the same time and were both living in a city eight miles from campus, taking the bus to school. We had both come from Chicago

---

25. *See, e.g.*, Cecilia Menjívar, *Liminal Legality: Salvadoran and Guatemalan Immigrants' Lives in the United States*, 111 AM. J. SOC. 999 (2006).

26. Susan B. Coutin, *Questionable Transactions as Grounds for Legalization: Immigration, Illegality, and Law*, 37 CRIME LAW & SOCIAL CHANGE 19–36 (2002) [hereinafter *Questionable Transactions*].

27. KITTY CALAVITA, IMMIGRANTS AT THE MARGINS: LAW, RACE, AND EXCLUSION IN SOUTHERN EUROPE 10–13 (2005).

28. Susan B. Coutin, *Differences within Accounts of U.S. Immigration Law*, 19 POLAR: POL. & LEGAL ANTHROPOLOGY REV. 11, 11–19 (1996).

29. *Questionable Transactions, supra* note 26, at 21–41.

30. The name of the organization has been changed to ensure confidentiality.

and had many similar experiences. Over the years, we ran into each other occasionally, but it was not until the early spring of Esperanza's last year at the university that we had a conversation about her status and her involvement in OCISG. At the time, I was trying to identify young adults in the community who were actively engaged in civic and political activity. I soon started attending meetings and becoming acquainted with the individual members.

The young men and women of OCISG represent a broad range of legal statuses and each of the three tiers of California's post-secondary public education system: California Community Colleges, California State Universities, and Universities of California.[31] While the majority of the group is made up of students currently in school, many others have already graduated from four-year institutions and some even hold advanced degrees. Most of the members were born in another country and have lived most of their lives in an unauthorized existence. The following discussion is drawn from my observations and the self-narratives of these young adults.[32]

The March

It is a warm Friday evening in late April 2006. Andrea Gómez and more than twenty-five others sit around the table at a local community college. This is the weekly meeting of the OCISG. Students take turns expressing their opinions and voicing their concerns. There is a nervous excitement in the room, as Andrea and the group divvy up tasks for the weekend. May 1, 2006, the big day, is only three days away, and there is so much to do before then. At least a dozen different high schools, colleges, and universities have signed on to participate, and the coordination of those students alone is quickly becoming a logistical nightmare. The banner is not yet finished, and someone has to collect the caps and gowns. Andrea asks over the buzz in the room, "Is the press release ready?" As the meeting progresses, committees form and various students step up to take responsibility for the various tasks. Soon the plan starts to take shape, and some of the tension is eased. The excitement can be seen on the students' faces.

The inclusion of the OCISG in the larger march was not something that was automatically considered in the beginning of the planning discussions. In fact, many of the youth groups that were involved in the marches nationally had to assert themselves and fight for the inclusion; they joined existing immigrants' rights groups or participated in ad hoc demonstrations. Immigrant rights groups did not intentionally leave them out of the larger process, however, as much as student issues were not a prominent part of anyone's broader agenda. Andrea and others like her, however, felt it important that the student voice be a central part of the marches and demonstrations.

---

31. University of California schools have been designated as the state's primary academic research institutions, awarding doctoral and professional degrees, in addition to undergraduate degrees; California State University campuses provide undergraduate and graduate instruction through the master's degree and limited doctoral degrees; and the California Community Colleges provide academic and vocational education to high school graduates and returning adult students.

32. From January 2006 to August 2007, I spent time with this particular group as a participant observer. During this time, I took field notes of my time in meetings and other interactions with group members. I also conducted in-depth, semi-structured interviews with some of the group members as a part of a larger research project.

Because of these efforts, on May first, more than three hundred students came out to participate in the OCISG-planned action, showing the organizers and community members alike that students were not only concerned about the larger debate, they were also stepping up to be active participants in the quest for solutions. Moreover, it gave the students of OCISG a sense of achievement and showed them that they were part of the broader community struggle.

Political Socialization

While the 2006 marches saw the inclusion of college students and the student access issue, OCISG members like Andrea were no strangers to political activity and civic engagement. Many of the leadership skills and organizing experiences these young people possess were incubated on high school and university campuses. In fact, most of the members of OCISG were involved in numerous clubs and organizations as early as high school.

In high school, Andrea was noticed by her teacher for being a leader among her peers in class. Over the first weeks of school, Andrea's teacher paid close attention to her interactions with other students. Within a short time, she was asked to take part in an initiative spearheaded by the vice principal. For the next two years, Andrea served on an advisory council that gave recommendations to the administration about how to address racial and ethnic tensions at the school. This experience served as a catalyst for later leadership positions for Andrea in college and the community, and incited what she referred to as a "sense of ownership in [her] education and development."[33]

In fact, through participation in school-based extracurricular activities, many members of OCISG developed important organizational skills, and an awareness of community issues and their ability to be a part of the solution. Having gained early leadership skills and community experience in high school, many of these students went on to higher levels of participation in college. At the time of my study, several members of OCISG held leadership positions in campus clubs or other community groups.

Concurrently, as these students moved on to college, the limitations of their unauthorized status began to become increasingly more salient in their day-to-day lives. Having been raised and schooled in the United States, many unauthorized students have aspirations similar to their United States-born peers. Unable to secure financial aid for school and uncertain of their futures, many OCISG members turned to immigrant rights groups and activities as a way to do something for themselves and their families. A majority of the members had participated in voter drives, and had organized for driver's license bills and the broader legalization movement.

Involvement in these organizing campaigns prompted students across many campuses to turn inward and to take steps in organizing for themselves. Beginning in the mid-1980s, many college and university officials in counseling centers and admissions offices started to identify these students and bring them together.[34] Out of these efforts, coalitions like the

33. Interview with Andrea Gómez, *supra* note 2.

34. Hinda Seif, *"Wise Up!" Undocumented Latino Youth, Mexican-American Legislators, and the Struggle for Higher Education Access*, 2 LATINO STUD. 210, 210–30 (2004).

Leticia A Network in California began to push for policy change, in-state tuition policies were crafted, and campus support groups began to take shape.[35] Inspired by these efforts, students began to form campus support groups.[36] However, much of the early advocacy work was done by university officials on behalf of the students. Most adults in the community believed that it was better that U.S. citizen advocates fight it out in the trenches and save undocumented students from the potential dangers of speaking out publicly. As student groups became more organized, and individual students began to find comfort in knowing they were not alone, they sharpened their focus to issues of educational access. Equipped with the important skills of organizing and knowledge of the immigrants' rights movement, students began to stand up for themselves.

The Aftermath

In the aftermath of the marches, students quietly returned to their communities and campuses to regroup and develop strategies for continued work. In California, networks of student groups and advocates began to take shape, and the young people of OCISG went out into schools, churches, and community-based organizations to provide education to the broader community.

The seeds for activity after the marches were sown by organizing efforts as early as 2001.[37] Over the last few years, working to promote legislation such as the Development, Relief, and Education for Alien Minors Act (DREAM Act)[38] was the central activity for most immigrant student groups. In fact, DREAM Act advocacy work gave many unauthorized students a means to participate in the political process around a matter of direct relevance to them. Students became involved in activities on the ground: contacting legislators, mobilizing their various communities, and staging public actions. By the fall of 2004, momentum had built up to the extent that several Los Angeles-based organizations, including an immigrants' rights coalition and a Korean immigrant organization, along with students, participated in a two-week fast and vigil that led to national participation in a twenty-four hour hunger strike.[39]

As the movement grew and the policy process slowed, many of the leaders turned their attention toward the community. At the same time, many undocumented students had started to matriculate at colleges and universities thanks to in-state tuition laws. Having been the first wave to chart their paths to and through college, these students began organizing younger students. Taken together, these streams have produced a very active community agenda. Students have organized collectively in groups like OCISG to provide information to various sectors of the community—students, parents, teachers, and counselors. These

35. ALEJANDRA RINCON, UNDOCUMENTED IMMIGRANTS AND HIGHER EDUCATION: SI SE PUEDE! (2008).

36. Douglas McGray, *The Invisibles*, L.A. TIMES, Apr. 23, 2006, West Magazine, at 19.

37. *See generally* Seif, *supra* note 80, for a discussion of an organizing effort in 2001 around California Assembly Bill 540.

38. The Development, Relief, and Education for Alien Minors (DREAM) Act (S. 1545), was introduced on July 31, 2003, to provide a mechanism to obtain legal residency for certain undocumented students who are able to meet certain conditions.

39. *See, e.g.*, Jennifer Mena, *"DREAM Act" Offers Hope to Immigrant Students*, L.A. TIMES, Sept. 19, 2004, at B1.

young organizers realize that within the community there is a general lack of information among families and even school officials about the rights that undocumented students and families have to pursue higher education. Not only are many unaware of in-state tuitions laws, like California's Assembly Bill 540, but many do not even know whether undocumented students are allowed to go on to post-secondary education.

Many students have also noted a great deal of misinformation within community colleges and universities, as the front line staff in admissions offices, those with whom students are in direct contact, often do not know that undocumented students have the right to a college education, much less how to process students without social security numbers.

Such was the case with Karina Torres. When it came time to apply to college, Karina was without any assistance. None of her teachers ushered her through the process, and nobody within her peer network knew any other undocumented students in college. Unaware of her legal options, Karina did not know where to find the necessary information. Instead of going to a four-year college, she settled for a community college. She explained:

> I didn't know anything about AB 540 so [that's] the reason [why] I didn't go to university. Well first of all was because I was lacking the money so even if I were . . . well maybe if I knew the information I could have gotten a scholarship or something. But I didn't know anything. I didn't even know we had AB 540 so I thought I was going to pay like twenty thousand so I was like "no way I was going to pay that." And I didn't have a job, so I was like "even if I get a job I couldn't still be able to afford it." So that's why I didn't go. Nobody told me anything. I don't know if my counselors knew, but they never told me anything.[40]

Similarly, in a group meeting, Priscilla Hernández shared with other participants a harrowing experience she had when trying to apply to college:[41]

> I remember one time. That year I took off I went to apply for a job and the guy said your interview went fine. You're a great person. And I'm all, "so I'm gonna get the job?" and he said "yeah, come on Saturday, oh but wait, bring a California ID and bring your social security. Without that you can't get a job." That just put me down, and so I was just like "I'm not going to go to school, I don't care, I don't care. I'm just gonna not go to school and work my whole life." Then my mom and my sister were like, "no, no you have to go to school. You have to prove them wrong," and I was all proud, I'm really going to go forward in life, but then again something stopped me. When I applied on the computer, two weeks later they said there was a hold on my registration, and because of my resident status. When I went, some girl attended me and she said, "We'll take it off, we just have to prove that you have papers." She went to the back and she made me wait for a long time, and some other lady came and said, "What's the problem?" And I said, "I'm just trying to get my hold out so I can register for classes," and she just started being mean. She's like, "Are you legal?" And I said, "Yeah." And she's like, "Did you come here illegally?" And I just stared at her and I was like, "What kinds of questions are those?" And she asked me, "Do you have a border pass? Do you have a border ID? How did you get here? How much did you pay for the coyote to come

---

40. Interview with Karina Torres in Orange County, Cal. (Dec. 16, 2006).

41. Priscilla's testimony comes from a community workshop in Orange County, California, on November 20, 2006.

over here?" And I was just . . . I felt bad because I was gonna go to school and she was putting me down, and I came to school happy and I came out really sad. And the lady had told me the only way that you're going to come to this school is if you fill out these papers and you get your high school records. I wasn't going to let that stop me. I went to the high school and I got the records and when I went back I showed her my papers and she said, "Ok, well your hold is off. You may register for class." For me, I always thought I was born here because I came here when I was one, so I don't remember when I was in Mexico. I don't remember anything. I can't believe that some little numbers set me apart from everyone else.

Priscilla had the ambition not to be stopped, but her example is illustrative of the consequences of an ill-informed and anti-immigrant public with respect to undocumented students. That is, even college admissions counselors either did not know what to do about her situation or felt that they had the right to ask demeaning questions. The experiences of Karina and Priscilla are the day-to-day examples that are continually passed on by the members of OCISG to affirm the importance of their work.

The Contexts of Their Work and Lives

Because of their role in the Santa Ana march on May 1, 2006, OCISG members have become highly visible in the community. They are constantly being sought out by schools, civic organizations, and community members to give presentations, staff booths at conferences, and train staff members. They have also been honored by Orange County Human Relations and the League of United Latin American Citizens because of their ongoing work within the community. This community education component has become such a central activity that OCISG members meet weekly to discuss ongoing and current projects.

Community activity at such a high level by a group of young adults expected to be waiting in the shadows runs contrary to conventional wisdom and much of the scholarly literature regarding youth participation. The contexts of their lives, however, provide important clues about why these young people are engaged at such high levels. Indeed, at first glance there is much evidence to assume that their immigrant status would serve to keep them politically disenfranchised and away from civic activity. Most of these young adults are well aware of the anti-immigrant climate within California and the broader United States and the consequences of their organizing, including the threat of deportation. Moreover, their status puts them in close contact and conflict with the laws of the state and this significantly limits their options for participation.

At every turn, undocumented students are presented with constraints on their ability to civically participate. While certain avenues are closed, others are restricted. Because of such limitations, accomplishing the most simple of tasks often means taking risks. For example, buying a cell phone, obtaining a library card, or even renting a movie all involve difficulty and embarrassment. Even more prohibitive, undocumented students cannot work legally to cover the costs of their education. Thus, in order to pay for their schooling, they must take jobs within the informal economy, such as tutoring and cosmetics sales. At every turn, exposing themselves is tantamount to putting their lives on the line, as any of these pursuits can place them face-to-face with immigration authorities. Unauthorized students also have limited access to health care and social services. Increasingly more medical services are off-limits to the undocumented, and many community job training programs and activities require work permits, at a minimum.

Even traveling can prove to be a major problem. In most states, unauthorized migrants cannot obtain a driver's license.[42] Hence, they cannot purchase a car, buy insurance, or legally drive. In order to get to and from school and work, then, the unauthorized students/residents must rely on public transportation. In cities with good public transportation systems like New York and Chicago, this is a viable, though limited, option. In sprawling metropolises like Los Angeles, however, reliance on public transportation severely limits employment and school options.

Taken together, these numerous barriers severely limit the mobility of these young adults. Nevertheless, since the marches, as demonstrated by the proliferation of immigrant student groups, civic activity has been on the rise among undocumented youth on college campuses and in communities. The OCISG has become so busy, it has recently moved into its own office, even though no one in the organization receives a salary.

Students Organizing for Themselves

Despite the dangers involved in speaking out publicly, many students become frustrated by the limitations of their status and want to do something to remedy their situation. Moreover, students are finding strength and courage in numbers. One important consequence of the spring immigrant rights marches was the participation of thousands of high school and college students to show the nation as well as their peers that there are, indeed, hundreds of groups across the country in the same situation and willing to engage in the civic and political activity necessary for improving their circumstances.

Normally, many immigrant students live their outside lives in isolation, afraid to disclose their status and therefore not connecting with others who are similarly situated. After spending more than three years at her university, isolated and not knowing anyone else in her situation, Esperanza happened upon OCISG while doing a school project. On a few occasions, she tried to contact campus groups to get involved in DREAM Act work but could not find any student groups that wanted to work on it as a priority. During her senior year, she met César Meraz, the co-chair at the time, who introduced her to OCISG. Inspired by César's commitment to the issue, Esperanza ultimately joined the group. As she describes, "OCISG is a mix of people affected and not. I can actually help myself and others. I can change others' lives as well as my own."[43]

When I met Rosalba González, another OCISG member, she had all the education and credentials needed to be a teacher. The only thing that was missing was the right to work. Within her community of educators, she saw a great void. Her participation was driven by a desire to change those "who are in the position to change lives."[44] As she says, "I would like to raise awareness in the community because it's really missing among educators, in par-

42. Daniel C. Vock, *Tighter License Rules Hit Illegal Immigrants*, STATELINE, Aug. 24, 2007, http://www.stateline.org/live/details/story?contentId=234828 (last visited Aug. 6, 2008).

43. Interview with Esperaza Rivas in Orange County, Cal. (Jan. 16, 2007).

44. Rosalba González, Nimo Flores, and Eva Beltran's quotes are also taken from the November 20, 2006, Orange County workshop. *See supra* note 41.

ticular. So that's why I participate. I would like to donate my story and be able to help out." Rosalba has emerged as one of the state's leaders in the student movement and in OCISG. She is well known by the community at large and is often invited to speak in schools.

OCISG member Nimo Flores is younger than Rosalba, yet he shares the desire to educate the community. He recently transferred from a local community college to the California State University at Long Beach. He has been fortunate to have a financial sponsor who pays his tuition. Nimo is well aware of how his circumstances may differ from others, and consistently counts his fortunes. People are often surprised by his level of optimism, something he uses to educate and inspire others:

> I believe that since I'm in this situation . . . by using the arts as a way to teach other people, [I can] educate other people about the injustices that happen around the world. I think that it is a good way to change people's minds for the better and so that there is peace and justice in the world.

Eva Beltran, on the other hand is less optimistic. She has been out of school for a few years, and does not see a way to change her situation. She does, however, see the need to tell her story so that others can advocate for her:

> I'm still waiting for my papers. . . . I've been here since I was nine. I'm twenty-six years old. It's a big issue for me. It really affects my life 'cause I can't really pursue my career. I finished a credential program for a Special Ed teacher, like almost three years ago. And I can't work. So I'm working, but it's not what I really want to do. So that's why I'm here, 'cause I think everyone needs to hear our stories. And that we're really trying.

Other members, like Concepcion Arango, have been able to regularize their immigrant status, but continue to stay involved. And others, like Bobby Jackson and Lani Tañón, although personally unaffected, have dedicated their time and committed their efforts toward legalization efforts. Each of these young people has his or her own motivations for the work he or she does. The common contextual experience, however, is that of being an undocumented student.

Tensions Between Being Active and Risking Harm

Because of the current anti-immigrant climate and intensification in deportations (see Boehm, this volume; Coutin, this volume), the involvement of these students puts them in precarious positions. In September 2006, I was asked to invite Andrea to speak on a panel on immigrant youth at a conference at the University of Chicago. I had written a short piece about her and OCSIG, and the conference organizers felt she would be perfect for the panel they were planning. I gave the organizers Andrea's contact information and left it up to them to contact her. They soon followed up with a phone conversation. But upon learning of her undocumented status, they decided that it would be unethical to risk her deportation or any other potential legal complications by putting her on a plane to Chicago. Andrea urged them to reconsider their position because she felt that it was important for her to represent her own voice, rather than having someone else speak for her (I was invited to speak on the panel as her substitute).

The issue came up in conversation at an October OCISG meeting as the group was deciding about who should talk to members of the press and how they should identify themselves.[45] The conversation was initiated when a reporter came in and asked to interview some of the group members. The reporter informed them that he was doing a story about AB 540 students and wanted to conduct some interviews. The group felt a little uncomfortable with this and asked the reporter to wait outside for a few minutes while they decided how to approach the situation. Tezcatlipoca Villa, one of the group's more soft-spoken and thoughtful members, reminded the group of an article that he had brought in the previous week about a young activist whose family faced deportation charges because of her activism. Tezcatlipoca voiced concern and fear about the danger any sort of public outing posed to members of OCISG. This led to a broader philosophical question about public activism and the dangers of self-outing.

As they continued to debate about the issue, Ernesto Rodríguez, a longtime community leader, brought up an article that had appeared in one of the local newspapers that showed a picture of two of the group's leaders and listed their initials. Many of the members felt that the group should use more caution and discretion when dealing with the press and in public forums.

Andrea's position, however, evoked the current spirit of activism of many unauthorized students. She brought up the University of Chicago conference and voiced the need for undocumented students to be able to tell their own stories, unfiltered. She told the group that she felt strongly that while advocates were important to the movement, it was important for people to hear directly from unauthorized students their own narratives, circumstances, and struggles. She explained, "It's time for undocumented students to stand up for ourselves, and if we do not do it for ourselves, we will have lost everything we're fighting for."[46]

CONCLUSION

As students mobilized in the United States for immigrant rights in the spring of 2006, others across the globe have met frustration and dissatisfaction with protest. In Chile, more than 600,000 students missed classes to demand free public transportation, lower college entrance exam fees, and greater participation in government.[47] Meanwhile, in France, two separate occasions produced youth outrage and protest, as young minority and immigrant youth revolted against public officials and more than one million university students occupied, blockaded, and closed hundreds of schools.[48] While each of these actions was carried out separately, they signal a rebirth of civic engagement and activism among young people in the face of perceived injustice, which has important consequences for the future.

In the United States today, it is the sons and daughters of the most recent waves of disenfranchised immigrants who have reinvigorated the sprit of student political involvement. Young people like Andrea have taken up the mantle of mobilizing others like them, taking

---

45. OCISG Regular Meeting, in Orange County, California (Sept. 19, 2006).
46. Interview with Andrea Gómez, *supra* note 2.
47. Younge, *supra* note 5.
48. *Id.*

their concerns to the streets to assert their place in history and fight for their own position in society. The decision to migrate to the United States was not theirs; however, they do not know any other home. Thanks to *Plyler,* these young people do have the right to attend elementary and secondary school here. Those experiences have led some of them to develop leadership skills and an orientation toward community service. However, without the possibility of making that education and experience count toward legal and unrestricted access to the fundamental rights that citizens enjoy and to key social institutions within U.S. society, their options are extremely limited. With their backs against the wall and too much to lose, they push forward. Investments in education over the years made possible by *Plyler* and the support of their families, teachers, and community provide them with the impetus to make the most of those opportunities. Moreover, leadership experiences in school have provided the necessary skills to actualize their organizing and advocacy pursuits. However, the potential consequences are frightening. By elevating their visibility, they risk being identified by authorities and anti-immigrant groups and, as such, leave themselves vulnerable to deportation and hate crimes.

While scholars, analysts, and policy makers ponder questions about a rise in immigrant political participation, new generations of activists are being born out of the very struggle to "become American," and in the process they are rewriting their own stories.

15 | FROM BORDER CONTROL TO BORDER CARE

THE POLITICAL AND ETHICAL POTENTIAL OF SURVEILLANCE

James P. Walsh

INTRODUCTION

Although traditionally peripheral to surveillance studies, the regulation of international boundaries and mobility has received increasing scholarly attention. As political interfaces and putative markers of national sovereignty and identity, territorial borders constitute privileged sites of social closure and control. Since the late 19th century, states have "monopolized the legitimate means of movement" (Torpey 2000, 5) and transformed borders into institutionalized zones of regulation defined by a matrix of surveillance that includes border patrols, military checkpoints, medical inspections and quarantines, X-ray machines, integrated biometric databases, visas, passports, and other official forms of identification. Consequently, while it is spread throughout the social body, nowhere is the state's gaze more pervasive, exclusionary, and encroaching than at its territorial and jurisdictional boundaries. Additionally, practices of border control and surveillance are constitutive and profoundly political, as they bound, protect, and order society. In constructing and reproducing the categories of citizen and alien, "encaging" (Mann 1993, 61) social relations, and securing and extending sovereignty—both physically and symbolically—over territories and populations, boundary maintenance projects a sense of institutional coherence and renders perceptions of a unified social order axiomatic and uncontested.

Although existing research has illuminated the role of surveillance in monitoring and managing mobile populations, it has tended to overlook other important activities, including the strategic use of surveillance by activist groups. As a result, scholarship has generally interpreted watching, locating, and identifying as innately authoritative and disempowering practices directed toward gatekeeping and exclusion. But what happens when observational technologies and strategies are turned *against* the state's gatekeepers and surveillance sys-

James P. Walsh is visiting assistant professor in the Department of Sociology and Anthropology at the University of Richmond.

Reprinted with permission of the Surveillance Studies Network, from "From Border Control to Border Care: The Political and Ethical Potential of Surveillance," *Surveillance & Society* 8 (2): 113–130 by James P. Walsh. Copyright © 2010 the Surveillance Studies Network.

tems? How should such instances impact scholarly understandings of surveillance as a potential tool of resistance, empowerment, and democratization?

In addressing these questions, I assess two interventions employed to address the human
consequences of contemporary immigration control: (1) counter-surveillance and (2) strategic and symbolic acts of "de-bordering." While both share common interests in rendering
perceived injustice visible, they can be differentiated based on their tactics and overriding
objectives. The first refers to the use of surveillance to promote transparency and democratic accountability by "watching the watchers" and turning the gaze of authority against
itself (see Huey et al. 2006). "De-bordering," meanwhile, represents broader transformative
approaches that employ surveillance to humanize the border environment. While it also
seeks to alter existing arrangements, unlike counter-surveillance, such actions are more systemic or counter-hegemonic; rather than implementing a direct response or counter-gaze,
they pursue ethical and practical activities that assist migrants, recast the terms of official
discourse, and challenge existing institutional arrangements.

Three specific practices are of particular interest, the first of which is a form of counter-
surveillance and the other two constitute forms of "de-bordering." They include (1) the use
of digital photography and video recording equipment to monitor vigilante organizations;
(2) the coordination of citizen-organized foot patrols to locate and assist migrants in danger; and (3) the use of Geographic Information Systems (GIS) and other locational technologies to augment the placement of water stations in the desert and dissemination of
maps providing their locations. These three activities, advanced (respectively, although
there is some overlap between the groups' activities) by the ACLU, No More Deaths, and
Humane Borders, provide instrumental and expressive responses to border militarization
and securitization.

Many scholars have already noted how border control and surveillance exceed the exclusive purview of nation-states and are also carried out by emergent practitioners such
as supranational institutions, municipalities, private security firms, airlines, travel agents,
and vigilante patrols (Guiraudon 2001). While emphasizing the distributed and heterogeneous nature of surveillance, I also intend to reorient analysis by illuminating how private
citizens and civil-society actors have used observational technologies and practices as
mechanisms of *empowerment*—here defined as a demonstrable improvement in the economic, juridical, social, or symbolic status of marginalized groups. Paying attention to
such dynamics should result in a more nuanced understanding of border control as a
complex institutional field defined by negotiation and struggle among multiple actors,
both internal and external to the state, and help assess the activists' use of surveillance in
protecting migrants and in promoting a *moral geography* of recognition, responsibility,
and hospitality.

This chapter is divided as follows. First, with particular attention to the US-Mexico border, I summarize received scholarship on globalization, surveillance, and national boundaries. Second, I apply studies emphasizing surveillance's flexibility and ambiguity to the
institutional field of the border. Here I argue that, along with restricting entry and expelling
"undesirables," observational technologies and practices may also be applied to promoting
human security and challenging perceived injustice. Finally, before offering a brief sum-

mary and conclusion, I situate this argument empirically, analyzing the use and framing of surveillance by border activists. This third section also assesses each group's transformative potential and relations with state authorities and official border practitioners.

BORDER SURVEILLANCE AND THE RISE OF THE GATEKEEPER STATE: BOUNDARY MAINTENANCE IN AN AGE OF GLOBALIZATION

While an exhaustive discussion is beyond this chapter's scope, it is essential to note that globalization involves more than transnational mobilities, flows, and exchanges; it is equally defined by practices of gatekeeping, immobilization, and exclusion. For many individuals, rather than "flexible citizenship" (Ong 1999), the most striking trend of the last century has been the growth and increasingly preemptive, punitive, and technologically sophisticated nature of border control and surveillance.

Under such conditions, migrants encounter a highly stratified "mobility regime" (Shamir 2005) where all travelers are identified, sorted, and classified as desirable or undesirable, safe or risky, and, thus, admissible or inadmissible (see Heyman this volume). Consequently, access to the territories and societies of rich nations has emerged as a significant determinant of life-chances and a primary axis of global inequality (Bauman 1998). For tourists, professionals, and other affluent transients, borders are generally experienced as conduits or zones of transit where surveillance is "thin," momentary, and superficial (Torpey 2007). For undocumented workers, *sanspapiers*, and other "undesirables," borders are sites of intensive scrutiny, closure, and trauma where surveillance is "thick" (Torpey 2007) and functions as a "banopticon" (Bigo 2002) oriented towards exclusion rather than correction or discipline. Through regimes of surveillance and classification, states do not merely control movements but also enact rituals of "purification and prophylaxis" (Douglas 1966) that construct and codify moral distinctions between those worthy and unworthy of membership. Here those marked as undeserving and undesirable are constituted as "anti-citizens" whose presence is deemed hazardous and whose sociopolitical existence is rendered invisible and unauthorized (Inda 2006). Thus, more than just administrative techniques, border patrols, workplace raids, and related forms of surveillance provide normative performances that call into existence the very categories and divisions (legal/illegal, alien/citizen) they purport to represent and enforce.

Nowhere are these trends more visible than along the US-Mexico border. Despite America's perennial definition as a "nation of immigrants," politicians and the general public have recently displayed a deep ambivalence about this heritage, as demonstrated by rising restrictionary sentiments and the alignment of the migrant with multiple suspect categories and "folk devils," whether the pauper, recalcitrant minority, and diseased, or the criminal, terrorist, and subversive (see Chavez this volume). Additionally, for state officials many foreigners—given their precarious juridical status—constitute an inherent criminal element and "legal impossibility" (Ngai 2004, 4). Amidst these moral panics, since the early 1990s the US government has recalibrated enforcement efforts between ports of entry.

Officially termed "targeted enforcement" and "prevention through deterrence," these strategies have included: (1) the strengthening of the country's border architecture through new stadium lighting and reinforced steel fencing; (2) formal interfacing and intelligence sharing with the military; (3) high-profile enforcement efforts with names ranging from Operation Blockade to Gatekeeper; and (4) the use of sophisticated information technologies and surveillance systems ranging from unmanned aerial vehicles to seismic and infrared sensors (see Heyman this volume). The logic underlying this shift was that targeting highly trafficked urban corridors (like San Diego and El Paso) would redirect migrants into "hostile terrain" less "suited for crossing and more suited for enforcement" (U.S. Border Patrol 1994, 7). Additionally, in contrast to prior strategies that focused on locating and apprehending individuals already in the US, it was assumed that preemptive "forward deployment strategies," by increasing the physical, financial, and psychic costs associated with crossing through isolated rural areas, would dissuade potential migrants (U.S. Department of Justice 1998).

Following the terrorist attacks of September 11, 2001, securitization strategies have been further accelerated as media pundits and government officials have described the border as an ungoverned frontier prone to terrorist infiltration, thereby transforming the migrants into categorically suspect security risks. Additionally, with the establishment of the Department of Homeland Security (DHS) as the central policing agency, the Bush administration introduced a sweeping reinscription of national spatiality. These measures have included the deployment of the National Guard to strategic sectors; further funding for recruitment, hiring, and surveillance technologies; and the construction of 700 miles of new fencing, which, once completed, will make the US-Mexico divide the most heavily guarded border in the developed world (see Heyman this volume).

The government is not alone in its aggressive efforts, as vigilante organizations have emerged to provide additional surveillance and policing. Although existing in numerous forms over the past 150 years, border vigilantes, which now include the Minuteman Project, Minutemen Civil Defense Corps, American Border Patrol, Border Patrol Auxiliary, and Cyber-vigilantes, have recently proliferated (Walker 2007). Guided by insular nationalism and viewing undocumented migration as an affront to national sovereignty and security, vigilantes have engaged in civilian-led border watches and patrols, the use of unmanned surveillance drones, and the installation of their own high-tech fencing and surveillance cameras near the border (see Chavez this volume).

Heightened securitization efforts have had egregious human consequences. While failing to curb illicit entries, forward deployment strategies have instead forced migrants into the unforgiving desert and mountain terrain of Southern Arizona. As a result, the number of deaths due to dehydration, drowning, and exposure has drastically increased (see Doty this volume). Since 1994 over 5,000 migrants have perished in transit; this is likely a conservative estimate given that the vast desert landscape likely holds hundreds, if not thousands, of more bodies. Although often labeled "unintended consequences" (Cornelius 2001), given current policies' stated intent of escalating the risks, dangers, and physical costs associated with illicit entry, migrant fatalities are hardly unanticipated. Additionally, current enforcement efforts rest on an ugly paradox in which the insecurity of the other is justified to protect and foster the life of the social body (Burke 2007). In depriving migrants of adequate protections while willfully exposing them to undue environmental risks and dangers, current approaches have turned the border into a zone of abjection—a place where "immigrants are channeled into danger" and "immigrant life is . . . disavowed to the point of death" (Inda 2006, 26, 174).

THE INDETERMINACY OF THE GAZE:
RECONCEPTUALIZING SURVEILLANCE AS AN EMPOWERING PRACTICE

As indicated above, the use of surveillance in administering borders and disciplining mobility is already well documented. What has not been sufficiently recorded, however, is surveillance's ambiguity or double life and employment in undermining borders and their attendant consequences.

Treated as an elite-based phenomenon involving the conscious and coordinated monitoring of individuals and groups to govern their attributes and conduct, surveillance was indicted by much of the early scholarly literature as an innately disciplinary, hierarchical, and intrusive mechanism of social control and moral regulation (Burnham 1983; Dandeker 1990). While the field has yet to entirely jettison such assumptions, surveillance studies has made significant strides in challenging one-dimensional and overly pessimistic accounts. Without discounting the status of surveillance as a powerful form of social instrumentation, studies increasingly note that observational technologies and practices are flexible and "under-determined" (Monahan 2008) and can be "repurposed" toward empowering and democratic ends. Their use is inherently situational: "By themselves, they are unremarkable tools . . . as vital to the maintenance of our welfare and freedom as they are to . . . [despotic] designs" (Scott 1998, 4).

Applicable to all systems of authority, notions of a "dialectic of control" (Giddens 1987) are especially salient in the present. Through the mass production and dissemination of new technologies (such as camcorders, laptops, and cell phone cameras), surveillance has been "democratized," as anyone with the necessary purchasing power has access to mechanisms of social monitoring (Marx 2003). According to Haggerty (2006, 29), with the capacities of watching and monitoring now broadly distributed, "traditional hierarchies of visibility are being undermined, . . . reconfigured," and leveled in ways that may empower the watched and those mobilizing on their behalf. Thus, to truly understand surveillance in its various forms, we must approach the concept contextually, with an emphasis on the goals and intentions of its practitioners. Drawing on such insights, Lyon (2001) has argued that surveillance is most fruitfully viewed as an open and processual field defined by the logics of *care* and *control*, with the former term referring to humanitarian and protective impulses and the latter to technical and disciplinary ones. While this conceptualization should not be overemphasized as, in many instances, forms of surveillant "care" are hegemonic in nature and entrench prevailing power asymmetries by functioning as tools of legitimation, Lyon's distinction assists in underscoring the intrinsically protean quality of observational strategies.

Despite growing attention to the ambiguous and multivalent nature of surveillance, research on migration and mobility has continued to assume a framework of *border control* in which watching and monitoring are aligned with gatekeeping, regulating access, and excluding and expelling unwanted populations (see Inda 2006; Shamir 2005; Torpey 2000).

Consequently, when studying instances of resistance and empowerment, researchers treat surveillance as a target, rather than a tool, of resistance, and analysis centers on if and how it may be eliminated. While the impact of official practices of territorial and social boundary maintenance can hardly be overestimated, many of the techniques and tools implicated in the administration of political borders can also be appropriated by opposing actors. In the following discussion I draw on the work of three activist organizations to inform and add complexity to extant scholarship, shifting analysis to forms of *border care* neglected by scholars interested in surveillance, borders, and mobility.

WATCHING OUT FOR MIGRANTS: SURVEILLANCE AND BORDER ACTIVISM

Border securitization has received increased scrutiny and criticism from multiple religious and secular activist organizations. Viewing government policies as immoral, ineffective, and complicit in the inexorable rise of deaths in transit, several organizations have employed surveillance technologies and practices to protect and physically help migrants. Focusing on three of the most active and visible—Humane Borders, No More Deaths, and the ACLU—I discuss how each organization has used surveillance to challenge existing policy regimes and effectuate counter-geographies which transcend legal and moral categories of illegality. As the following indicates, in addition to challenging surveillance's use as a mechanism of control and exclusion, all three organizations are also engaged in a deeper counterhegemonic struggle over the nature of border care—what it is, how it is practiced, and whom it is directed towards.

Humane Borders

Founded in 2000 by Robin Hoover, a pastor from Tucson, Arizona, Humane Borders is a faith-based humanitarian organization dedicated to "taking death out of the immigration equation" and creating a "just and humane border environment" (Hoover 2008). As a coalition of human-rights groups, congregations, and legal advocacy organizations, the group draws on over 10,000 volunteers and, through grants from Pima County, Arizona, and private donations, has an annual budget of $200,000. The organization is best known for two practices that utilize geospatial surveillance systems: the strategic placement, installation, and maintenance of water stations throughout the Southwest, and the creation and distribution of maps providing their locations and other lifesaving information.

Humane Borders began its construction of water stations in 2001. As of 2009 the group maintains 102 stations across the Southwest, each one stocked with a 100-gallon water tank, food, clothing, and first-aid kits. Marked by a blue flag flown from a thirty-foot pole, each station is visible from a considerable distance. The flag displays the group's logo, a drinking gourd with water pouring from it—a direct allusion to the 19th-century antislavery Underground Railroad, as well as to the group's humanitarian mission (Hoover 2008).

To augment these activities, since 2002 Humane Borders has assembled maps to monitor, record, and analyze migratory routes and the rate and spatial distribution of fatalities. Initially these maps were constructed using portable GPS devices, Adobe Photoshop, and information from the Pima County morgue, Border Patrol, and Mexican Consulate in Tucson. Humane Borders used the information on the spatial coordinates of migrant fatalities to make informed operational judgments; upon identifying a cluster of deaths, the organization would place water stations a few miles south. However, given the ongoing game of "cat and mouse" between migrants and the Border Patrol, crossing routes required continuous monitoring and such practices became prohibitively inefficient and time-consuming (Humane Borders 2005).

In 2005 the Environmental Systems Research Institute, a leading commercial vendor of GIS software, donated a license for its ArcView 9.1 program. As electronically mediated forms of "dataveillance," GIS technologies do not simply capture, store, and represent locational data, but also allow clusters of geographic information to be quantitatively analyzed. With the assistance of geographers at the University of Georgia, Humane Borders has created a geodatabase of spatial data to uncover statistical correlations between deaths and environmental factors and "help . . . make strategic decisions . . . about water station placement and . . . show, in a graphic way, how [they] help mitigate the loss of life" (Humane Borders 2008). Mirroring practices of "risk-based" crime control, where spatial data is used to assess threats, discern the probability of future events, and minimize their occurrence, Humane Borders' practices also demarcate zones of danger and risk. For the organization, however, the monitoring and analysis of locational information is oriented to constructing more compassionate cartographies based on human security. Through their deployment of sophisticated technological infrastructures, the geography of the border has been reconstituted. Contra the Border Patrol and DHS, the surveillance systems installed by Humane Borders survey, register, and identify bodies and movements to create settings based on unrestricted access and the material and symbolic restoration of life and personhood.

GIS technologies have also been used to construct border maps distributed in communities across Mexico and Central America. Displaying a 60- by 50-mile stretch of the Arizona border, these maps provide: (1) details concerning terrain, cell phone coverage, and locations of border fencing; (2) color-coded symbols signifying the locations of water stations, Border Patrol rescue beacons, and recent fatalities; and (3) three black, concentric rings demonstrating the distance one can expect to cover on foot in one to three days. The maps also provide emergency contact numbers and encourage migrants to travel with someone they trust and bring adequate food and water, the phone numbers of relatives, personal identification, and comfortable shoes.

Citing ethical notions of informed consent, Hoover argues that the maps are necessary educational devices: "Many migrants don't have any information. [Smugglers] are lying to them. If we can give them information . . . they could make an informed decision whether to come or not" (Dellios 2006, 1A). For migrants who decide to come, the maps assist in minimizing risks and securing safe passage. Additionally, given the lack of public discourse concerning the human consequences of government policy, they render visible border securitization and surveillance, calling into question their modus operandi and outcomes.

Although several political officials and media pundits view Humane Border's actions as tantamount to facilitating illicit entry, the Border Patrol has largely embraced a stance of tacit acquiescence. Although the two entities' larger objectives of care and control are at odds, the organizations have, to a certain extent, entered a partnership or "handshake" agreement in which Border Patrol officers will not patrol near nor monitor water stations, while activists pledge to provide only water and emergency medical care and to contact the Border Patrol when injured migrants require transportation. Humane Borders says that "we are not in an adversarial relationship with the . . . Border Patrol. They don't want to pick up dead bodies any more than we do" (quoted in Cunningham 2002, 190). The organization even justifies its practices on the grounds that they are cost-effective solutions and augment governmental enforcement, claiming:

> Our water stations give agents . . . more time to achieve their objectives of deterrence and apprehension, instead of spending time on search and rescue missions. We provide an extra pair of eyes and ears and we frequently call the . . . Border Patrol to effect rescue missions. (Hoover 2003a, 1)

The group has also engaged in a series of "cooperative moves" in which "efforts to resist surveillance . . . involve collusion with surveillors" (Marx 2003, 383). Here, the organization not only obtains the support of government authorities but actively cooperates with them. Specifically, Humane Borders has negotiated the installation of public safety communications equipment on observational towers mandated by the Secure Border Initiative (see Doty, this volume). Attaching such equipment to the towers permits migrants to contact 911 emergency responders—but nobody else—on their cell phones. Overcoming initial reservations, the group's leadership noted that, while the government's strategy was costly and misguided, the vast majority of migrant deaths occurred outside cell phone coverage areas and more than half of all rescues were initiated by migrants using cell phones. Installing emergency response systems, the organization thus concluded, would help to "spread an electronic umbrella of safety" over the borderlands (Humane Borders 2008, 1).

Such alignments are open to critique on the grounds that linking humanitarian and state practices may create new avenues for cooptation by allowing the government to promote further securitization under the guise of humanitarian impulses. Humane Borders is fully conscious of such issues and has spent considerable time debating its relations with state actors. Ultimately, its leadership has decided that, given the institutional environment in which the group operates as well as the urgency of the situation, communications and alignments with governmental authorities are unavoidable in order to respond effectively to rising migrant fatalities.

No More Deaths

Founded in 2004 by several Tucson-based religious leaders, including Catholic Bishop Gerard Kincanas and Presbyterian pastor John Fife, No More Deaths is a diverse ensemble of religious activists and human rights groups dedicated to providing direct humanitarian relief to migrants. Claiming to take the "sanctuary of the church to the desert" (Hagan 2008, 108), the organization believes that "around-the-clock, non-violent, physical humanitarian presence . . . [is] the single most effective response to the tragic crisis" (No More Deaths 2008a, 6). These activities are conceived as a "civil initiative" in which the *nomos* of the state and its unjust consequences are challenged through non-violent protest and the "conviction that people of conscience must work openly and in community to uphold ... human rights" (No More Deaths 2008b).

No More Deaths began by undertaking Samaritan patrols through the Sonoran desert to locate migrants in need of medical and humanitarian assistance and, if necessary, to evacuate them to a medical facility or turn them over to the Border Patrol's search and rescue division. Patrol volunteers also leave bottles of water in the desert and distribute "know your rights" cards informing migrants of their legal rights when dealing with the Border Patrol and other authorities. In addition to first aid and basic medical training, the group's volunteers learn basic tracking techniques, as well as how to use GPS technologies to monitor migrant activity and map the dominant crossing trails (No More Deaths 2008b). Such patrols provide a foil to the Minutemen and Border Patrol. Although all three groups engage in direct observation to monitor migrants and render the border region visible or "legible" (Scott 1998), for No More Deaths, rather than disciplining the national landscape and foreign bodies, practices of surveying and tracking are subordinated to caring for the other.

The organization expanded its operations in 2004, establishing biblically inspired "Ark of the Covenant" camps as bases for coordinating search and rescue patrols. Although several exist, the central camp is in Arivaca, Arizona, within a few miles of the Mexican border. These moveable camps are intended to symbolize God's guiding presence during the Israelites' sojourn in Egypt and—in addition to providing humane assistance—also serve as sites of religious ceremonies to commemorate the thousands who have lost their lives (Hagan 2008).

Since 2006, volunteers have also begun working in migrant aid centers in Nogales, Agua Prieta, and Naco (three communities in the Mexican state of Sonora) to provide basic care and emotional support to migrants repatriated to Mexico. Such practices were expanded when it became apparent that migrants were frequently mistreated by Border Patrol officers and by guards at Immigration and Customs Enforcement (ICE) detention facilities. In response, trained volunteers and medical professionals have engaged in watchdog functions to systematically document abuse and mitigate inequality by revealing the inner workings of government institutions. After providing medical care, volunteers will ask migrants if they are willing to complete a voluntary survey detailing their treatment by government agents. Collected information is then classified by category of violation, date, and project site and transferred into a site-specific spreadsheet and encrypted online database. In 2008 this compilation was published through a formal report entitled "Crossing the Line," which documented 345 cases of abuse in the arrest, detention, and repatriation process. Abuses included denial of food, water, and medical care, along with instances of physical and verbal abuse (No More Deaths 2008c).

As demonstrated by its extensive scrutiny of state agents, No More Deaths' relationship with the Border Patrol is much more contentious than that of Humane Borders. This more adversarial stance derives in part from the organization's founding by former members of the 1980s sanctuary movement, which sought to provide aid and refuge to Central American migrants denied asylum status by the US government (Cunningham 2002). Although one of its leaders (John Fife) was criminally convicted on charges of harboring and conspiracy, since its creation No More Deaths has pledged to work openly and legally and not to attempt to evade state agents or directly encourage surreptitious entry. No More Deaths had one serious brush with the law in 2005, when two volunteers were indicted for alien smuggling after they were found transporting three severely dehydrated migrants to a local hospital. The charges, which threatened to criminalize humanitarian aid and legally equated the volunteers with human smugglers, were later dismissed on the grounds that, due to prior meetings with the Border Patrol, the organization reasonably believed its actions were officially sanctioned. However, the presiding US district judge noted that in future instances volunteers "could be arrested and charged, at the least, with reckless disregard of the law" (quoted in Fan 2008, 719). More recently, several members of the organization have been cited and prosecuted for littering after leaving bottled water in the Buenos Aires National Wildlife Refuge without explicit permission.

While the organization has not pursued these actions as intentional forms of civil disobedience, the resulting surveillance and prosecutions have created new political opportunities as they "enable the observed to shape the images scrutiny produces" (Coutin 1995, 565) and promulgate alternative legal and moral claims. Specifically, through hearings, trials, and the extensive press coverage they have garnered, No More Deaths' has publicized its message in the hopes of mobilizing others and contesting established regimes of "legal truth" (Coutin 1995). Accordingly, the organization argues that government policies have created a "public health emergency" while simultaneously prohibiting established rights of rescue and assistance by requiring individuals and humanitarian organizations to obtain government permission to save lives. In the words of the group's attorney, Margo Cowan: "We have a right to do what we are doing and a moral obligation. We are in the epicenter of a warzone" (Becker 2005, 3a).

The American Civil Liberties Union

The oldest and most famous of the groups in question, the ACLU is a nationwide, nonpartisan organization invested in "protecting the principles of freedom and equality set forth in the US constitution and civil rights laws" (ACLU 2008a). Founded, in part, to protect aliens during the Palmer raids of World War I, the group has, historically, been closely allied with the immigrant rights movement. Breaking from traditional technical challenges through "impact litigation," the organization has, since 2004, engaged in direct forms of legal observation along the southern border. Although the ACLU was troubled by claims of abuse by the Border Patrol and local law enforcement, its presence was motivated primarily by the Minuteman Project's decision to undertake civilian-led border watches in April 2005.

Led by Ray Ybarra, a graduate student at Stanford Law School, the ACLU trained more than 500 volunteers during 2004–2006 in the proper use of video surveillance equipment to monitor vigilante organizations across the Southwest. Known as the Legal Observers Project, this initiative, although targeting different agents and locales, was consciously modeled after Copwatch and other organizations where ordinary citizens "watch the watchers" by monitoring the actions of on-duty police officers (Ybarra 2007). Using observational and imaging technologies, including digital cameras, cell phones, and camcorders, legal observers monitor the nation's gatekeepers and vigilante groups to prevent or document misconduct and brutality. Envisioned as rational and unaffected subjects, participants are to serve as "neutral observers" who "should not become involved in crowd control, conflict resolution or speaking for the demonstrators" (Walker 2007, 172). Thus, the organization employs the objectifying and subjectifying gazes of witnessing and discipline to curb the coercive impulses of vigilantes. First, legal watch-dogging documents violence and abuse to provide potential witnesses and facilitate prosecution. Second, monitoring efforts are intended to prevent events from ever happening, thereby creating a deterrent effect. In the later instance, surveillance is not simply exercised over vigilantes but, in facilitating forms of self-control, is exercised *through* them. As Ybarra has stated: "By standing behind someone with a video camera . . . and [through] communication to others, [vigilantes are] less likely to enact their rage on a migrant" (Ybarra 2007, 409).

The ACLU has also engaged in traditional legal contestation, filing open records requests through the Freedom of Information Act to uncover patterns of migrant abuse (Ybarra 2007). These actions are similar to those of No More Deaths but work explicitly through formal legal channels and do not directly document migrant grievances, relying instead on institutional disclosure and compliance. The ACLU is especially concerned with recent spikes in fatalities at ICE holding facilities and notes that its actions should help challenge the institution's culture of secrecy by rendering the administrative process transparent. In particular it asserts that the "DHS must not be allowed to keep information about in-custody deaths secret," adding the department must "be held publicly accountable when it fails to provide . . . health care mandated by our constitution" (ACLU 2008b). According to reports issued by the group, migrants are routinely subjected to illegal searches, physical and psychological abuse, and deprived of food and medical attention; in extreme cases, they have allegedly been murdered.

REFRAMING THE GAZE:
SURVEILLANCE AND GRAMMARS OF RESISTANCE

In addition to instrumental objectives, each group's practices display expressive or interpretive dimensions. In linking surveillance to democratic accountability and humanitarian imperatives rather than technical or regulatory ones, the organizations studied seek to render power visible and transform dominant "fields of vision" on a deeper symbolic level. For social movements, the processes of claim-making and framing are central in legitimating their practices and mobilizing public bystanders. Frames are here defined as "action oriented sets of meanings and beliefs that inspire and legitimate the activities and campaigns" of social movements (Benford and Snow 2000, 614). More than facilitating collective action, framing is profoundly political and, by constituting and naming certain issues as public concerns, displays independent structure-forming effects. According to Coutin (2005, 22), recasting the terms of the immigration debate may help "redefine the space occupied by unauthorized migrants by contesting their state-defined status of criminality and . . . illegal presence." However, framing constrains as well as facilitates the dynamics of collective action. The cultural idioms and repertoires selected by movements place clear parameters upon their style of protest, and structure the perceived desirability of particular alternatives (Benford and Snow 2000). Below, I discuss the different frames employed by each organization and the degree to which they adequately address the needs of the undocumented. As subsequently elaborated, while some of the practices and outlooks in question display limitations, the group's strategies are most fruitfully viewed as complementary approaches that should be employed in concert to systemically address the border crisis.

Liberal Doctrines of Privacy and Civil Liberties

The ACLU embraces liberal political principles, including a minimalist theory of the state and perceptions of society as an aggregation of free, rights-bearing, rational individuals. The organization's central goal is to promote formal legal equality and remove illegitimate external constraints and intrusions that violate civil liberties. For migrants, the organization's values and practices are clearly significant. Given their illicit and outsider status, the undocumented are both uniquely vulnerable to abuse and the least likely to report it, or even display awareness of their legal rights and entitlements. Thus, the ACLU's practices of direct observation and legal contestation help to create a space of protection, visibility, and transparency in which migrants are shielded from discrimination and mistreatment by state authorities and other actors. Specifically, noting that the country's constitutional and legal doctrines extend basic civil rights (due process, equal protection etc.) to all persons—citizen or otherwise—the organization attempts to ensure that the intended parameters of the nation's juridical order and protections are upheld. In these regards, despite its attempts to ensure that rights and protections encapsulate more than formal members of the citizen-body, the ACLU fails to articulate a cosmopolitan theory of human rights as it remains wedded to national frameworks of domestic and constitutional law.

When employed uncritically or in isolation from broader public goals, the practices and principles of the ACLU display significant limitations. First, it is questionable whether methods of detached, objective, and impersonal observation targeting individual agents of surveillance can effectively challenge larger, less visible institutional arrangements. Lacking an alternative vision for the future, watching the watchers through existing legal channels is not only unlikely to result in substantive improvements, but may actually prove counterproductive. In particular, scholars have noted that, when subjected to greater scrutiny, institutions frequently implement counter-neutralization strategies (Marx 2009). Upon learning of the ACLU's plans, the Minutemen toned down their inflammatory rhetoric, implemented a "no contact, no engagement" policy, and conducted background checks for all volunteers. Thus, while reducing the likelihood of direct confrontations, the ACLU's actions have also inadvertently contributed to the Minutemen's "mainstreaming" and establishment as a voice in the immigration debate (see Chavez, this volume). More fundamentally, strategies of legal observation embrace an additive rather than transformative approach to surveillance, believing that oversight from responsible citizens and organizations will inhibit authoritarian impulses. On the contrary, it is entirely plausible that strategies of an "eye for an eye" will breed greater suspicion, secrecy, and covertness (Marx 2003, 2009).

Additionally, the group's agenda incompletely expresses the needs of migrants. Commenting on attempts to reduce questions of surveillance to matters of privacy and non-interference, many scholars argue that an uncritical deference to liberal individualism ignores the importance of substantive citizenship and active, public commitments to justice, egalitarianism, and respect. As observed in John Gilliom's (2001) study of welfare mothers, privacy advocates' attempts to establish an autonomous, inaccessible "protected [and] non-public zone around the individual" (120) risk endorsing "an uncaring world of neglect in which the most needy ... are cut off from the support ... of a broader community" (123). For the subjects of this study—poor migrants whose very existence is "unauthorized"— commitments to privacy and personal protections have little relevance to their experiences of marginalization and do little to bring about manifest improvements in their life chances. According to Williams (2007, 31), more than protection from government encroachments, immigrants "need a language with which to make a case for their entitlement to ... public life." In this context, to comprehensively address injustice, the frameworks of privacy, personal freedom, and other abstract legal principles must be dovetailed into a broader social approach grounded in positive freedoms and collective recognition and obligations (Lyon 2001). Absent such connections, merely upholding the freedom to be "left alone" risks further entrenching contemporary patterns of social atomization. As the following indicates, faith-based movements articulate a broader, more collective approach as they present spiritually grounded forms of cosmopolitanism rooted in human security and dignity.

Spiritually Based Cosmopolitanism

The strategy and outlook of Humane Borders and No More Deaths departs significantly from the secular conception of individual rights. These two organizations' faith-based approaches provide demonstrable instances of how surveillance practices can be reclaimed and redirected towards "re-embodying persons" and caring for and welcoming others (Lyon 2001). As previously noted, while the two organizations have adopted different approaches vis-à-vis the legal order, this is less a reflection of divergent moral convictions than of the idiosyncrasies of their interventions. Humane Borders' extensive dependence on information and authorization from government entities in order to operate effectively has necessitated the adoption of less adversarial approaches. In contrast, No More Deaths has exploited the ostensible illegality of some of its practices to directly challenge "legal truth" and to ensure that humanitarian interventions remain permissible. Nonetheless, religious teachings are central in legitimating and orienting both groups' actions and provide a moral repertoire for critiquing existing policy approaches. Thus, despite following different paths, both groups are guided by commitments to spiritual communality and cosmopolitanism in ways that challenge the state-imposed moral and socio-legal distinctions of citizen, alien, and illegality.

Demonstrating what has been labeled the "deprivatization" of the church (Casanova 1994), publicly engaged interpretations of scripture guide both groups' use of surveillance and definition of migration as a social justice issue. As Hoover of Humane Borders states, "Sometimes ... biblical texts have greater heuristic value than ... politics. Even though they are old ... they offer ... more contemporaneous analysis than otherwise imagined" (Hoover 2004, 1). Religion's increased role in connecting public and private morality can, of course, hardly be reduced to causes of social justice or liberation; reactionary groups including the Ku Klux Klan and the Moral Majority have also engaged Christian teachings and symbols. In particular, since the 1970s evangelical movements and the Christian right have advocated for the tightening of traditional cultural and civilization borders associated with, *inter alia*, marriage, sexuality, nationalism, and patriotism (Wilcox and Larson 2006). Thus, in addition to contesting political notions of sovereignty and security, Humane Borders and No More Deaths are also engaged in a struggle over symbolic boundaries as they seek to reclaim Christian values and principles in the service of progressive causes. Accordingly, the organizations embrace a "social theology" (Hoover 2004) and a "faith and moral imperative that transcends borders" (No More Deaths 2008a).

One central biblical teaching that has inspired both groups is Christ's identification with and emphasis on responsibility for marginalized groups. This conviction is stressed through frequent allusions to the Good Samaritan, or one who unconditionally cares for strangers and the Parable of the Last Judgment, which includes the following passage: "I was thirsty and you gave me drink; I was a stranger and you took me in" (Matthew 25:35). Additionally, biblical figures and events are viewed as allegories of present circumstances. Individuals from Abraham to Jesus are compared to undocumented migrants, and the exile and sojourn of the Israelites in Egypt provides a reminder of the centrality of displacement and migration in the Judeo-Christian tradition. No More Deaths' training manual begins with a quotation from the Torah: "Know the heart of the stranger for you too were strangers" (quoted in Hagan 2008, 108), and the Humane Borders website displays the following biblical passage: "They will neither hunger nor thirst, nor will the desert heat or sun beat upon them. He who has compassion on them will guide them and lead them beside springs of water" (Isaiah 49:10). In applying Christian teachings to emergent social dilemmas, both groups demonstrate that religion is capable of challenging accepted narratives and offering the potential of social change.

Furthermore, by employing surveillance in the service of care and protection, both groups embrace a moral geography of hospitality and recognition lacking amidst the growing suspicion, surveillance, and exclusion of strangers. According to Derrida (2000), how strangers are approached and treated defines a group's position within the world, the values it holds, and the nature and durability of rights, duties, membership, and belonging. In embracing a "transformative faith tradition" (Hoover 2003b, 6) where "justice and compassion cross all borders" (No More Deaths 2008a), both groups incorporate surveillance practices into global forms of grassroots activism that seek to construct alternative political spaces based on deterritorialized notions of respect, duty, aid, and mercy. Accordingly, both groups reject national borders as ontological givens that prefigure and circumscribe moral action. According to one No More Deaths volunteer:

> A reporter asked me . . . "Why as an American are you doing this?" That's always funny to me . . . it's a people thing. . . . There's this imaginary line drawn across the desert. That doesn't make any sense. For someone to become illegal as soon as they cross that line—they are just people. (Quoted in Cabrera 2008, 84–5)

Hoover similarly highlights the personhood of every individual, regardless of nationality: "When we look at the face of the migrant, far too often it is a dead migrant. It is not a person trying to cheat the system, not a person trying to cheat us. . . . When we look at what is going on, we need to see the people and our leaders need to see us looking" (Humane Borders 2006, 1).

Roxanne Doty has argued that such claims are consistent with a cosmopolitan sense of global community, solidarity, trust, and interdependence in which duty towards the other is unconditional, a primary condition of being human based on relations of moral proximity rather than physical distance, political loyalty, or identity (Doty 2006). On a deeper level, by fostering a durable sense of care for the foreign other, the vision of Humane Borders and No More Deaths militates against the underlying divisions and inequalities that perpetuate undocumented migration. As practical solutions, both group's actions may appear minor and ineffectual, however, in refusing to work within existing logics or systems they enable a transvaluation of surveillance and borders, opening a space for pursuing alternative and more hopeful arrangements. According to Lyon (2001, 153):

> To ask what might happen if surveillance were guided by an ontology of peace rather than . . . violence, an ethic of care rather than control . . . may appear as a weak alternative. But weak in what sense? Is the only conceivable action to counterpose dominative power with its equal? If not then, weak solutions might be worth a try.

CONCLUSION

By detailing and analyzing the use of often sophisticated observational practices by border activists, this article has highlighted interventions and actors left unexplored in extant work on surveillance, borders, and mobility. While the administration of territorial borders remains a significant instantiation of state authority central to the exercise and accumulation of political and symbolic power, treating the state as the exclusive agent of border surveillance or assuming that surveillance is inherently repressive endorses a narrow and undersocialized view of observational techniques and practices. Noting there is more to surveillance than initially meets the eye, this chapter has advanced a broader definition, recognizing that observing, locating, and classifying may be conducted in the interest of protecting rights, redressing injustices, enabling democratic participation, buttressing moral criticism, and advocating for alternative practices. Further, this chapter calls attention to the need to study surveillance as a dynamic and interactive process in which the boundaries between watcher and watched are often indeterminate and where, despite inequalities of power, subordinates are able to contest and challenge gatekeepers, order enforcers, and other formal authorities. Acknowledging this duality allows the researcher to venture beyond the empirically obvious, challenge excessively authoritarian accounts, and, most importantly, advance a publicly engaged brand of scholarship that explores surveillance's empowering potential.

Examining the collective actions and cultural framings of border activists provides a window into the uses of surveillance in constructing counter-geographies of hope, and promoting a more inclusive and egalitarian social order. Though I have noted various limitations in these groups' strategies—including Humane Borders' reluctant cooperation with the Border Patrol and DHS, and the ACLU's neutral monitoring of authority or ideational frameworks based on grammars of privacy and liberal individualism—I do not mean to imply that activists should dispense with their practices. Their efforts are best conceived as complementary approaches and components of a multi-pronged challenge to the emergent "homeland security state." Using surveillance to assist migrants and monitor authority is unlikely to bring a halt to the tragic border crisis but they are certainly steps in the right direction. In opposing the criminalization and securitization of migration, activists face daunting and seemingly insurmountable obstacles, but, as Weber (1946, 128) reminded us, "All historical experience confirms . . . that man [sic] would not have attained the possible unless time and again he had reached out for the impossible."

WORKS CITED

American Civil Liberties Union (ACLU). 2008a. About Us. http://www.aclu.org/about [accessed 12/15/2008].

———. 2008b. ACLU Sues Department of Homeland Security for Information on Deaths in Immigration Detention Centers. June 25. http://www.aclu.org/immigrants/detention/35784prs2008 0625.html [accessed 12/01/2008].

Bauman, Zygmunt. 1998. *Globalization: The Human Consequences.* Cambridge: Polity Press.

Becker, Andrew. 2005. Volunteers Reach Out to Save Migrants. *Dallas Morning News,* August 25, 3a.

Benford, Robert and David Snow. 2000. Framing Processes and Social Movements. *Annual Review of Sociology* 26: 611–639.

Bigo, Didier. 2002. Security and Immigration: Toward a Critique of the Governmentality of Unease. *Alternatives* 27(1): 1205–1234.

Burke, Anthony. 2007. *Beyond Security, Ethics and Violence.* London: Routledge.

Burnham, David. 1983. *The Rise of the Computer State.* New York: Vintage.

Cabrera, Luis. 2008. Global Citizenship as the Completion of Cosmopolitanism. *Journal of International Political Theory* 4(1): 84–104.

Casanova, Jose. 1994. *Public Religions in the Modern World.* Chicago: University of Chicago Press.

Cornelius, Wayne. 2001. Death at the Border: Efficacy and Unintended Consequences of US Immigration Control Policy. *Population and Development Review* 27(4): 661–685.

Coutin, Susan Bibler. 1995. Smugglers or Samaritans in Tucson, Arizona: Producing and Contesting Legal Truth. *American Ethnologist* 22(3): 549–571.

———. 2005. Contesting Criminality: Illegal Immigration and the Spatialization of Legality. *Theoretical Criminology* 9(1): 5–33.

Cunningham, Hilary. 2002. Transnational Social Movements and Sovereignties in Transition: Charting New Interfaces of Power at the U.S.-Mexico Border. *Anthropologica* 44(2): 185–196.

Dandeker, Christopher. 1990. *Surveillance, Power, and Modernity.* New York: St. Martin's Press.

Dellios, Hugh. 2006. Mexican Map Shows Perils of Crossing. *Chicago Tribune,* January 26, 1A.

Derrida, Jacques. 2000. *Of Hospitality.* Stanford: Stanford University Press.

Douglas, Mary. 1966. *Purity and Danger.* New York: Praeger.

Doty, Roxanne. 2006. Fronteras Compasivas and the Ethics of Unconditional Hospitality. *Millennium* 35(1): 53–74.

Fan, Mary. 2008. When Deterrence and Death Mitigation Fall Short. *Law and Society Review* 42(4): 701–735.

Giddens, Anthony. 1987. *The Nation-State and Violence.* Berkeley: University of California Press.

Gilliom, John. 2001. *Overseers of the Poor.* Chicago: University of Chicago Press.

Guiraudon, Virginie. 2001. De-nationalizing Control: Analyzing State Responses to Constraints on Migration Control. In *Controlling a New Migration World*, eds. Virginie Guiraudon and Christian Joppke, 31–64. London: Routledge.

Hagan, Jacqueline. 2008. *Migration Miracle*. Cambridge, MA: Harvard University Press.

Haggerty, Kevin. 2006. Tear Down the Walls: On Demolishing the Panopticon. In *Theorizing Surveillance*, ed. David Lyon, 23–45. London: Willan Publishing.

Hoover, Robin. 2003a. Subcommittee Testimony. Testimony provided at the House Government Reform Committee's Subcommittee on Criminal Justice, Drug Policy and Human Resources Investigative hearing entitled The Impact of the Drug Trade on Border Security and National Parks, March 10, in Sells, Arizona.

———. 2003b. On Vigilantism. CCIS Working Paper Number 82. La Jolla: University of California San Diego. http://www.ccis-ucsd.org/PUBLICATIONS/wrkg82.pdf

———. 2004. Oded's Indictment. Paper presented at the International Conference on Migration and Theology, Notre Dame University, September 18, South Bend, Indiana.

———. 2008. "The Story of Humane Borders." Originally published in *A Promised Land, A Perilous Journey: Theological Perspectives on Migration*, edited by Daniel G. Groody and Gioacchino Campese. Notre Dame, IN: University of Notre Dame Press. http://robinhoover.com/uploads/THE _STORY_OF_HUMANE_BORDERS_2008.pdf

Humane Borders. 2005. Desert Fountain Newsletter. Tucson: Humane Borders: February/March.

———. 2006. Call to Elected Officials and Candidates. http://robinhoover.com/uploads/CALL_TO _GOVERNOR_4-3-06.pdf [accessed 12/15/08].

———. 2008. Desert Fountain Newsletter. Tucson: Humane Borders: August.

Huey, Laura, Kevin Walby, and Aaron Doyle. 2006. Cop Watching in the Downtown Eastside. In *Surveillance and Security*, ed. Torin Monahan. 149–166. Rutgers: Rutgers University Press.

Inda, Jonathan. 2006. *Targeting Immigrants*. Malden, MA: Blackwell.

Lyon, David. 2001. *Surveillance Society*. London: Open University Press.

Mann, Michael. 1993. *The Sources of Social Power, Volume Two*. London: Cambridge University Press.

Marx, Gary. 2003. A Tack in the Shoe: Neutralizing and Resisting the New Surveillance. *Journal of Social Issues* 59(2): 369–390.

———. 2009. A Tack in the Shoe and Taking off the Shoe: Neutralization and Counter-neutralization Dynamics. *Surveillance & Society* 6(3): 101–111.

Monahan, Torin. 2008. Editorial: Surveillance and Inequality. *Surveillance & Society* 5(3): 217–226.

Ngai, Mae. 2004. *Impossible Subjects*. Princeton: Princeton University Press.

No More Deaths. 2008a. Faith Based Principles for Immigration Reform. http://www.nomoredeaths .org/Information/faithbased.html [accessed 12/01/08].

———. 2008b. History and Mission of No More Deaths. http://www.nomoredeaths.org/Information/ history-and-mission-of-no-more-deaths.html [accessed 11/18/08].

———. 2008c. *Crossing the Line: Human Rights Abuses of Migrants in Short-Term Custody on the Arizona/Sonora Border*. Tucson, AZ: No More Deaths. http://www.nomoredeaths.org/index.php/ Abuse-Report. http://www.nomoredeaths.org/View-document-details/9-Crossing-The-Line -Human-Rights-Abuses-of-Migrants-in-Short-term-Custody.html [accessed 11/12/10].

Ong, Aihwa. 1999. *Flexible Citizenship*. Durham: Duke University Press.

Scott, James. 1998. *Seeing Like a State*. New Haven: Yale University Press.

Shamir, Ronen. 2005. Without Borders? Notes on Globalization as a Mobility Regime. *Sociological Theory* 23(2): 197–217.

Torpey, John. 2000. *The Invention of the Passport.* Cambridge: Cambridge University Press.

———. 2007. Through Thick and Thin: Surveillance After 9/11. *Contemporary Sociology* 35(2): 116–119.

U.S. Border Patrol. 1994. *Border Patrol Strategic Plan: 1994 and Beyond.* Washington, DC: U.S. Border Patrol.

U.S. Department of Justice. 1998. *Operation Gatekeeper: New Resources, Enhanced Results.* Washington, DC: U.S. Department of Justice.

Walker, Christopher. 2007. Border Vigilantism and Comprehensive Immigration Reform. *Harvard Latino Law Review* 10: 135–174.

Weber, Max. 1946. *From Max Weber.* London: Oxford University Press.

Wilcox, Clyde and Carin Larson. 2006. *Onward Christian Soldiers?* Boulder: Westview.

Williams, Rhys. 2007. Liberalism, Religion, and the Dilemma of Immigrant Rights. In *Religion and Social Justice for Immigrants*, ed. Pierrette Hondagneu-Sotelo, 16–34. New Brunswick: Rutgers University Press.

Ybarra, Ray. 2007. Thinking and Acting Beyond Borders: An Evaluation of Diverse Strategies to Challenge Vigilante Violence. *Stanford Journal of Civil Rights and Civil Liberties* 3(2): 377–424.

INDEX

ABM, 152, 153, 158–159, 161

Absconder Apprehension Initiative, 63

Ackleson, Jason, 99, 108

Activism: by immigrant youth, 283–284; by unions, 159, 256, 262. *See also* Border activism; Public protests; Undocumented student movement

Agamben, G., 131, 132, 132n1, 138

Aggravated felonies: cancellation of removal unavailable for, 84; detention and deportation for committing, 66, 71, 83–84, 237; offenses classified as, 15, 62, 92, 185, 210, 237

Agriprocessors meatpacking plant (Postville, IA) worksite raid, 1–2, 17, 21, 25

Aguilar, David V., 212

Alien Friends Act of 1798, 79

Aliens: Arizona's SB 1070 on transporting, 170; DHS goal of deporting all removable, 11, 14; redefining border between citizens and, 253–254, 266–268; subversive, 82; U.S. immigration law's definition of, 82n17. *See also* Criminal aliens; Illegal aliens

American Apparel, 149–150, 152–153, 158, 159–160, 161

American Civil Liberties Union (ACLU): border activism efforts of, 294–295, 296–297; challenged Hazleton, PA's anti-immigration law, 190; and migrant deaths, 19, 139; obtained injunction on Social Security numbers regulation, 160

Amezcua, Jesus, 233–234

Anarchist Act of 1918, 82

Annerino, John, 139

Antigang policies, 234–235, 235n1

Antiterrorism and Effective Death Penalty Act (AEDPA): anti-immigration stipulations of, 52, 210; expanded definition of "aggravated felony," 15, 62, 83, 185, 237

Arango, Concepcion (pseud.), 282

Aretxaga, Begoña, 221

Arizona: anti-immigration propositions in, 170; became main immigrant entry point, 169; demographic trends in, 167–169; Legal Arizona Workers Act, 158, 165, 170, 171. *See also* Arizona SB 1070; Minuteman Project

Arizona SB 1070, 146, 165–177; blocking of portions of, 166, 169; declared unconstitutional, 14n20; demographic context for, 166–169; examples of impact on immigrants, 172–176; human rights infringed upon by, 170–172; impact beyond Arizona, 172–176; overview of, 14n20, 14, 165–166, 169–170, 176–177; related Arizona laws preceding, 170; states considering similar legislation, 172

Asen, Robert, 254, 257, 258, 259

Ashcroft, John, 87, 88, 89, 200

Asylum: antiterrorism legislation's impact on U.S. policy on, 86; detention of seekers of, 65, 66, 203, 208–209; granted to Salvadoran deportee, 245; unequal legal treatment for seekers of, 204

Attrition through enforcement, 23, 169

Baker, Lori, 140

Balderrama, Francisco E., 208

Balibar, E., 137, 139

Bare life, 96, 129–141; biopower and, 130, 131–137; defined, 131; as element of prevention through deterrence, 135–136; geographic space providing moral alibi for, 130, 137–139, 138n11; resistance to strategy creating, 26–27, 130, 140–141. *See also* Migrant deaths

Barletta, Lou, 188n2, 188–189, 190, 191

Barry, Tom, 163

Beasley, Vanessa, 258

Belcher, O., 131, 140

Beltran, Eva (pseud.), 282

Bender, Steven, 202, 208

Bennett, Bill, 121

Bhabha, Homi, 260

Bigo, D., 182, 183

Boeing Corporation, 135n8, 135

Bolton, Susan, 166

Orange County Immigrant Student Group (OCISG) (pseud.), case study of, 275–283, 276n32
Overhill Farms, 153, 158, 159, 159n67

Padilla, José, 201, 211
Palmer Raids, 82
Patel, Sunita, 16
PATRIOT Act, 63–64, 65, 86, 185
Paying the Price (Urban Institute), 20–21
Pennsylvania: Hazleton Illegal Immigration Relief Act (IIRA), 188n2, 188–191; variations of "Illegal Immigration Relief Act" in, 186
Personal Responsibility and Work Opportunity Reconciliation Act, 52–53
Pew Hispanic Center, on psychological state of U.S. Latinos, 22–23
Pineda, Richard, 257
Pinochet, Augusto, 263
Plyler v. Doe, 68, 273, 275, 284
Postville, IA worksite raid, 1–2, 17, 21, 25
Prevention through deterrence: bare life as element of, 135–136; border strategies expanded with, 134n7, 134–135; connection between local, national, and international politics illustrated by, 133–134, 184; detention and deportation as element of, 17–18; expansions of policy of, 8–10, 183–185; harsh geographic conditions as element of, 130, 132, 137–139, 138n11; migrant deaths as result of, 19–20, 129, 131, 135; resistance to, 26–27, 130, 140–141; strategies employed for, 287–288
Prisons: federal, 16–17; holding immigrant detainees, 16n24, 16–17, 17n26; noncitizen detentions as expanding segment of, 91–92, 237–238; for-profit, 16. *See also* Detention facilities
Proposition 187, California, 13n19, 133, 134, 137, 185
Protest marches. *See La Gran Marcha* (LGM)
Public opinion: of immigrant vs. criminal defendants, 67; of U.S.-Mexico border as dangerous war zone, 116–120
Public protests, 24–25, 270. *See also La Gran Marcha* (LGM)
Puetz, Nathalie, 217
Puwar, Nirmal, 125

Quota Law of 1921, 43

Race: as context for Latino immigrant detention, 210–212; as factor in Fourth Amendment stops, 66, 75; Foucault on, and border politics, 130, 132, 133, 136; and U.S. citizenship granted through "back door," 166
"Racial battle fatigue," 176
Racial profiling, 89–90, 134, 202
Racism, of border enforcement strategies, 134, 137, 139
Raids: as ICE practice for interior policing, 11–12, 145; "silent raids," 2n2, 145–146, 151–153. *See also* Worksite raids

Reagan, Ronald/Reagan administration, 118, 154, 184–185
REAL ID Act, 86
Reed, Mark, 163
Refugee Act of 1980, 50
Refugee detention, 208–209
Reimers, David, 47, 49
Removal: cancellation of, 84; of criminal aliens, 91, 237–238; defined, 15n21, 219; expedited, 9n15, 9–10, 15–16n23. *See also* Deportation
Resistance. *See* Border activism
Returns, 15n21, 219
Reyes, Silvester, 133
Rivas, Esperanza (pseud.), 275–276, 281
Rodriguez, Cruz, 25
Rodríguez, Ernesto (pseud.), 283
Rodriguez, Jose, 233
Rodríguez, Raymond, 208
Rojas, Ismael, 155–156
Rosaldo, Renato, 124, 201
Rose, N., 183
Rumbaut, Rubén, 202, 271n7
Rushing, Rocky, 242

Salvadoran deportees, 196, 233–246; alienation of, within El Salvador, 240–242; dangers in El Salvador for, 242–245; number of, 15, 238; transformative nature of deportation for, 239–240. *See also* Sanchez, Alex
Samaritans, 131
Sanchez, Alex: alienation within El Salvador, 241; arrest of, 233–234; childhood of, 235–236; on criminal justice policies fueling violence, 244–245; current status of, 246; dangers of return to El Salvador for, 242; deportation of, 239, 240; granted political asylum, 245; returned to U.S., 239
Saucedo, Renee, 155, 162
SB 1070. *See* Arizona SB 1070
Schuck, Peter, 203
Schwarzenegger, Arnold, 123
Secure Border Initiative (SBI), 8–9, 11, 134n6, 134–135; SBI*net*, 8–9, 135
Secure Border Strategic Plan (Department of Homeland Security), 11
Secure Communities program, 13, 29
Secure Fence Act, 9
Segura-Marcial, Ana Rosa, 138
Self-deportations, 23, 151, 169
Sensenbrenner, James Jr., 185, 270n3
Service Employees International Union, 159, 256
Service Processing Centers (SPCs), 16
Shifting Borders (Ono and Sloop), 256
Shim, Kyumin, 108
"Silent raids," 2n2, 145–146, 151–153
Silerio, Erlinda, 159
Simcox, Chris, 121, 122, 123
Simon, Jonathan, 2, 4, 237
Sloop, John, 256, 259